CW01508441

Date Due

S.		
JUN 29 1969 K P		
JUN 1 1971 M		
DEC 16 76 D		
DEC 9 80 JE 23		
MAY 12 80 D T		
JUL 14 1992		

RATIONALISM IN EUROPE.

VOL. I.

HISTORY

OF THE

RISE AND INFLUENCE

OF THE SPIRIT OF

RATIONALISM IN EUROPE.

BY

W. E H. LECKY, M.A.

REVISED EDITION.

IN TWO VOLUMES.

VOL. I.

NEW YORK:

D. APPLETON AND COMPANY,

1906.

G.S. 1369

INTRODUCTION.

DURING the fierce theological controversies that accompanied and followed the Reformation, while a judicial spirit
was as yet unknown, while each party imagined itself the
representative of absolute and necessary truth in opposition to absolute and fatal error, and while the fluctuations
of belief were usually attributed to direct miraculous agency,
it was natural that all the causes of theological changes
should have been sought exclusively within the circle of
theology. Each theologian imagined that the existence of
the opinions he denounced was fully accounted for by the exertions of certain evil-minded men, who had triumphed by
means of sophistical arguments, aided by a judicial blindness
that had been cast upon the deluded. His own opinions
on the other hand, had been sustained or revived by apostles raised for the purpose, illuminated by special inspiration, and triumphing by the force of theological argu
ments. As long as this point of view continued, the position of the theologian and of the ecclesiastical historian was
nearly the same. Each was confined to a single province,
and each, recognising a primitive faith as his ideal, had to
indicate the successive innovations upon its purity. But

when towards the close of the eighteenth century the decline of theological passions enabled men to discuss these matters in a calmer spirit, and when increased knowledge produced more comprehensive views, the historical standing-point was materially altered.   It was observed that every great change of belief had been preceded by a great change in the intellectual condition of Europe, that the success of any opinion depended much less upon the force of its arguments, or upon the ability of its advocates, than upon the predisposition of society to receive it, and that that predisposition resulted from the intellectual type of the age. As men advance from an imperfect to a higher civilisation, they gradually sublimate and refine their creed.   Their imaginations insensibly detach themselves from those grosser conceptions and doctrines that were formerly most powerful, and they sooner or later reduce all their opinions into conformity with the moral and intellectual standards which the new civilisation produces.   Thus, long before the Reformation, the tendencies of the Reformation were manifest.   The revival of Grecian learning, the development of art, the reaction against the schoolmen, had raised society to an elevation in which a more refined and less oppressive creed was absolutely essential to its well-being.   Luther and Calvin only represented the prevailing wants, and embodied them in a definite form.   The pressure of the general intellectual influences of the time determines the predispositions which ultimately regulate the details of belief; and though all men do not yield to that pressure with the same facility, all large bodies are at last controlled.   A change of speculative opinions does not imply an increase of the data upon which those opinions rest, but a change of the habits of thought and mind which they reflect. Definite arguments are the symptoms and pretexts, but seldom the causes of the change. Their chief merit is to accelerate the inevitable crisis. They derive their force and efficacy from their conformity with the mental habits of those to whom they are addressed. Reasoning which in one age would make no impression whatever, in the next age is received with enthusiastic applause. It is one thing to understand its nature, but quite another to appreciate its force.

And this standard of belief, this tone and habit of thought, which is the supreme arbiter of the opinions of successive periods, is created, not by the influences arising out of any one department of intellect, but by the combination of all the intellectual and even social tendencies of the age. Those who contribute most largely to its formation are, I believe, the philosophers. Men like Bacon, Descartes, and Locke have probably done more than any others to set the current of their age. They have formed a certain cast and tone of mind. They have introduced peculiar habits of thought, new modes of reasoning, new tendencies of enquiry. The impulse they have given to the higher literature, has been by that literature communicated to the more popular writers; and the impress of these master-minds is clearly visible in the writings of multitudes who are totally unacquainted with their works. But philosophical methods, great and unquestionable as is their power, form but one of the many influences that contribute to the mental habits of society. Thus the dis

coveries of physical science, entrenching upon the domain
of the anomalous and the incomprehensible, enlarging our
conceptions of the range of law, and revealing the connection of phenomena that had formerly appeared altogether
isolated, form a habit of mind which is carried far beyond
the limits of physics. Thus the astronomical discovery,
that our world is not the centre and axis of the material
universe, but is an inconsiderable planet occupying to all
appearance an altogether insignificant and subordinate position, and revolving with many others around a sun which
is itself but an infinitesimal point in creation, in as far as
it is realised by the imagination, has a vast and palpable
influence upon our theological conceptions. Thus the
commercial or municipal spirit exhibits certain habits of
thought, certain modes of reasoning, certain repugnances
and attractions, which make it invariably tend to one class
of opinions. To encourage the occupations that produce
this spirit, is to encourage the opinions that are most congenial to it. It is impossible to lay down a railway without creating an intellectual influence. It is probable that
Watt and Stephenson will eventually modify the opinions
of mankind almost as profoundly as Luther or Voltaire.

If these views be correct, they establish at once a broad
distinction between the province of the theologian and
that of the historian of opinions. The first confines his
attention to the question of the truth or falsehood of particular doctrines, which he ascertains by examining the
arguments upon which they rest ; the second should endeavour to trace the causes of the rise and fall of those
doctrines which are to be found in the general intellectual

condition of the age. The first is restricted to a single department of mental phenomena, and to those logical connections which determine the opinions of the severe reasoner; the second is obliged to take a wide survey of the intellectual influences of the period he is describing, and to trace that connection of congruity which has a much greater influence upon the sequence of opinions than logical arguments.

Although in the present work we are concerned only with the last of these two points of view, it will be necessary to consider briefly the possibility of their coexistence; for this question involves one of the most important problems in history—the position reserved for the individual will and the individual judgment in the great current of general causes.

It was a saying of Locke, that we should not ask whether our will is free, but whether WE are free; for our conception of freedom is the power of acting according to our will, or, in other words, the consciousness, when pursuing a certain course of action, that we might, if we had chosen, have pursued a different one. If, however, pushing our analysis still further, we ask what it is that determines our volition, I conceive that the highest principles of liberty we are capable of attaining are to be found in the two facts, that our will is a faculty distinct from our desires, and that it is not a mere passive thing, the direction and intensity of which are necessarily determined by the attraction and repulsion of pleasure and pain. We are conscious that we are capable of pursuing a course which is extremely distasteful, rather than another course which would be extremely agreeable; that in doing so we are making a continual and painful effort; that every relaxation of that effort produces the most lively pleasure; and that it is at least possible that the motive which induces us to pursue the path of self-abnegation, may be a sense of right altogether uninfluenced by prospects of future reward. We are also conscious that if our desires act powerfully upon our will, our will can in its turn act upon our desires. We can strengthen the natural powers of our will by steadily exerting it. We can diminish the intensity of our desires by habitually repressing them; we can alter, by a process of mental discipline, the whole symmetry of our passions, deliberately selecting one class for gratification and for development, and crushing and subduing the others. These considerations do not, of course, dispel the mystery which perhaps necessarily rests upon the subject of free-will. They do not solve the questions, whether the will can ever act without a motive, or what are its relations to its motives, or whether the desires may not sometimes be too strong for its most developed powers; but they form a theory of human liberty which I believe to be the highest we can attain. He who has realised, on the one hand, his power of acting according to his will, and, on the other hand, the power of his will to emancipate itself from the empire of pain and pleasure, and to modify and control the current of the emotions, has probably touched the limits of his freedom.

The struggle of the will for a right motive against the pressure of the desires, is one of the chief forms of virtue;

and the relative position of these two influences, one of the chief measures of the moral standing of each individual. Sometimes, in the conflict between the will and a particu lar desire, the former, either through its own natural strength, or through the natural weakness of its opponent, or through the process of mental discipline I have describ ed, has obtained a supreme ascendency which is seldom or never seriously disturbed. Sometimes, through causes that are innate, and perhaps more frequently through causes for which we are responsible, the two powers exhibit al most an equipoise, and each often succumbs to the other. Between these two positions there are numerous grada- tions; so that every cause that in any degree intensifies the desires, gives them in some cases a triumph over the will.

The application of these principles to those constantly-recurring figures which moral statistics present is not diffi- cult. The statistician, for example, shows that a certain condition of temperature increases the force of a passion— or, in other words, the temptation to a particular vice; and he then proceeds to argue, that the whole history of that vice is strictly regulated by atmospheric changes. The vice rises into prominence with the rising tempera- ture; it is sustained during its continuance, it declines with its decline. Year after year, the same figures and the same variations are nearly reproduced. Investigations in the most dissimilar nations only strengthen the proof; and the evidence is so ample, that it enables us, within certain limits, even to predict the future. The rivers that rise and fall with the winter torrents or the summer drought; the insect life that is called into being by the

genial spring, and destroyed by the returning frost; the
aspect of vegetation, which pursues its appointed changes
through the recurring seasons; these do not reflect more
faithfully or obey more implicitly external influences, than
do some great departments of the acts of man.

This is the fact which statistical tables prove, but what
is the inference to be deduced from them? Not, surely,
that there is no such thing as free-will, but, what we
should have regarded as antecedently probable, that the
degree of energy with which it is exerted is in different
periods nearly the same. As long as the resistance is
unaltered, the fluctuations of our desires determine the
fluctuations of our actions. In this there is nothing extraordinary. It would be strange indeed if it were otherwise
—strange if, the average of virtue remaining the same, or
nearly the same, an equal amount of solicitation did not
at different periods produce the same, or nearly the same,
amount of compliance. The fact, therefore, that there is
an order and sequence in the history of vice, and that
influences altogether independent of human control contribute largely to its course, in no degree destroys the freedom of will, and the conclusion of the historian is perfectly reconcilable with the principles of the moralist.
From this spectacle of regularity, we simply infer that the
changes in the moral condition of mankind are very slow;
that there are periods when, certain desires being strengthened by natural causes, the task of the will in opposing
them is peculiarly arduous; and that any attempt to write
a history of vice without taking into consideration external influences, would be miserably deficient.

Again, if we turn to a different class of phenomena, nothing can be more certain to an attentive observer, than that the great majority even of those who reason much about their opinions have arrived at their conclusions by a process quite distinct from reasoning. They may be perfectly unconscious of the fact, but the ascendency of old associations is upon them; and, in the overwhelming majority of cases, men of the most various creeds conclude their investigations by simply acquiescing in the opinions they have been taught. They insensibly judge all questions by a mental standard derived from education; they proportion their attention and sympathy to the degree in which the facts or arguments presented to them support their foregone conclusions; and they thus speedily convince themselves that the arguments in behalf of their hereditary opinions are irresistibly cogent, and the arguments against them exceedingly absurd. Nor are those who have diverged from the opinions they have been taught necessarily more independent of illegitimate influences. The love of singularity, the ambition to be thought intellectually superior to others, the bias of taste, the attraction of vice, the influence of friendship, the magnetism of genius,—these and countless other influences into which it is needless to enter, all determine conclusions. The number of persons who have a rational basis for their belief is probably infinitesimal; for illegitimate influences not only determine the convictions of those who do not examine, but usually give a dominating bias to the reasonings of those who do. But it would be manifestly absurd to conclude from this, that reason has no part or function in the formation of opinions. No mind, it is true, was ever al together free from distorting influences ; but in the struggle between the reason and the affection which leads to truth, as in the struggle between the will and the desires which leads to virtue, every effort is crowned with a measure of success, and innumerable gradations of progress are mani- fested. All that we can rightly infer is, that the process of reasoning is much more difficult than is commonly sup- posed ; and that to those who would investigate the causes of existing opinions, the study of predispositions is much more important than the study of arguments.

The doctrine, that the opinions of a given period are mainly determined by the intellectual condition of society, and that every great change of opinion is the consequence of general causes, simply implies that there exists a strong bias which acts upon all large masses of men, and eventu- ally triumphs over every obstacle. The inequalities of civilisation, the distorting influences arising out of special circumstances, the force of conservatism, and the efforts of individual genius, produce innumerable diversities ; but a careful examination shows that these are but the eddies of an advancing stream, that the various systems are being all gradually modified in a given direction, and that a certain class of tendencies appears with more and more prominence in all departments of intellect. Individuals may resist the stream; and this power supplies a firm and legitimate stand- ing-point to the theologian : but these efforts are too rare and feeble to have much influence upon the general course.

To this last proposition there is, however, an important exception to be made in favour of men of genius, who are commonly at once representative and creative. They embody and reflect the tendencies of their time, but they also frequently materially modify them, and their ideas become the subject or the basis of the succeeding developments. To trace in every great movement the part which belongs to the individual and the part which belongs to general causes, without exaggerating either side, is one of the most delicate tasks of the historian.

What I have written will, I trust, be sufficient to show the distinction between the sphere of the historian and the sphere of the theologian. It must, however, be acknowledged that they have some points of contact ; for it is impossible to reveal the causes that called an opinion into being without throwing some light upon its intrinsic value. It must be acknowledged, also, that there is a theory or method of research which would amalgamate the two spheres, or, to speak more correctly, would entirely subordinate the theologian to the historian. Those who have appreciated the extremely small influence of definite arguments in determining the opinions either of an individual or of a nation—who have perceived how invariably an increase of civilisation implies a modification of belief, and how completely the controversialists of successive ages are the puppets and the unconscious exponents of the deep under-current of their time, will feel an intense distrust of their unassisted reason, and will naturally look for some guide to direct their judgment. I think it must be admitted that the general and increasing tendency, in the present day, is to seek such a guide in the collective wisdom of mankind as it is displayed in the developments of history.

In other words, the way in which our leading thinkers, con sciously or unconsciously, form their opinions, is by endeav ouring to ascertain what are the laws that govern the succes- sive modifications of belief; in what directions, towards what conceptions, the intellect of man advances with the advance of civilisation ; what are the leading characteristics that mark the belief of civilised ages and nations as com- pared with barbarous ones, and of the most educated as compared with the most illiterate classes.   This mode of reasoning may be said to resolve itself into three problems. It is necessary, in the first place, to ascertain what are the general intellectual tendencies of civilisation ; it is then ne- cessary to ascertain how far those tendencies are connected, or, in other words, how far the existence of one depends upon and implies the existence of the others; and it is necessary, in the last place, to ascertain whether they have been accom- panied by an increase or diminution of happiness, of virtue, and of humanity.

My object in the present work has been, to trace the history of the spirit of Rationalism; by which I under- stand, not any class of definite doctrines or criticisms, but rather a certain cast of thought, or bias of reasoning, which has during the last three centuries gained a marked as- cendency in Europe.   The nature of this bias will be ex- hibited in detail in the ensuing pages, when we examine its influence upon the various forms of moral and intellec- tual development.   At present, it will be sufficient to say, that it leads men on all occasions to subordinate dogmatic theology to the dictates of reason and of conscience, and, as a necessary consequence, greatly to restrict its influence upon life. It predisposes men, in history, to attribute all kinds of phenomena to natural rather than miraculous causes; in theology, to esteem succeeding systems the expressions of the wants and aspirations of that religious sentiment which is planted in all men; and, in ethics, to regard as duties only those which conscience reveals to be such.

It is manifest that, in attempting to write the history of a mental tendency, some difficulties have to be encountered quite distinct from those which attend a simple relation of facts. No one can be truly said to understand any great system of belief, if he has not in some degree realised the point of view from which its arguments assume an appearance of plausibility and of cogency, the habit of thought which makes its various doctrines appear probable, harmonious, and consistent. Yet, even in the great controversies of the present day—even in the disputes between the Catholic and the Protestant, it is evident that very few controversialists ever succeed in arriving at this appreciation of the opinions they are combating. But the difficulty becomes far greater when our research extends over forms of belief of which there are no living representatives, and when we have not merely to estimate the different measures of probability subsisting in different societies, but have also to indicate their causes and their changes. To reconstruct the modes of thought which produced superstitions that have long since vanished from among us; to trace through the obscurity of the distant past that hidden bias of the imagination which—deeper than any strife of arguments, deeper than any change of creed—determines in each succeeding age the realised belief; to grasp the

2

principle of analogy or congruity according to which the conceptions of a given period were grouped and harmonised,
and then to show how the discoveries of science, or the
revolutions in philosophy, or the developments of industrial or political life, introduced new centres of attraction,
and made the force of analogy act in new directions; to
follow out the process till the period when conclusions the
reason had once naturally and almost instinctively adopted
seem incongruous and grotesque, and till the whole current
of intellectual tendencies is changed :—this is the task
which devolves upon every one who, not content with relating the fluctuations of opinions, seeks to throw some
light upon the laws that govern them.

Probably, the greatest difficulty of such a process of
investigation arises from the wide difference between professed and realised belief. When an opinion that is opposed to the age is incapable of modification and is an obstacle to progress, it will at last be openly repudiated; and
if it is identified with any existing interests, or associated
with some eternal truth, its rejection will be accompanied
by paroxysms of painful agitation. But much more frequently civilisation makes opinions that are opposed to it
simply obsolete. They perish by indifference, not by controversy. They are relegated to the dim twilight land
that surrounds every living faith; the land, not of death,
but of the shadow of death; the land of the unrealised and
the inoperative. Sometimes, too, we find the phraseology,
the ceremonies, the formularies, the external aspect of
some phase of belief that has long since perished, connected with a system that has been created by the wants and

is thrilling with the life of modern civilisation. They re-
semble those images of departed ancestors, which, it is said,
the ancient Ethiopians were accustomed to paint upon their
bodies, as if to preserve the pleasing illusion that those
could not be really dead whose lineaments were still visible among them, and were still associated with life. In
order to appreciate the change, we must translate these
opinions into action, must examine what would be their
effects if fully realised, and ascertain how far those effects
are actually produced. It is necessary, therefore, not
merely to examine successive creeds, but also to study the
types of character of successive ages.

It only remains for me, before drawing this introduction to a close, to describe the method I have employed in
tracing the influence of the rationalistic spirit upon opinions. In the first place, I have examined the history and
the causes of that decline of the sense of the miraculous,
which is so manifest a fruit of civilisation. But it soon
becomes evident that this movement cannot be considered
by itself; for the predisposition in favour of miracles grows
out of, and can only be adequately explained by, certain
conceptions of the nature of the Supreme Being, and of the
habitual government of the universe, which invariably accompany the earlier, or, as it may be termed, the anthropomorphic stage of intellectual development. Of the nature of this stage we have some important evidence in the
history of art, which is then probably the most accurate
expression of the religious realisations ; while the history of
the encroachments of physical science upon our first notions
of the system of the world, goes far to explain its decay

Together with the intellectual movement, we have to consider a moral movement that has accompanied it, which
has had the effect of diminishing the influence of fear as
the motive of duty, of destroying the overwhelming importance of dogmatic teaching, and of establishing the su-
premacy of conscience. This progress involves many important consequences; but the most remarkable of all is the
decay of persecution, which, I have endeavoured to show,
is indissolubly connected with a profound change in theological realisations. I have, in the last place, sought to
gather fresh evidence of the operations of the rationalistic
spirit in the great fields of politics and of industry. In the
first, I have shown how the movement of secularisation has
passed through every department of political life, how the
progress of democracy has influenced and been influenced
by theological tendencies, and how political pursuits contribute to the formation of habits of thought, which affect
the whole circle of our judgments. In the second, I have
traced the rise of the industrial spirit in Europe; its colli-
sions with the Church; the profound moral and intellectual changes it effected; and the tendency of the great
science of political economy, which is its expression.

I am deeply conscious that the present work can furnish at best but a meagre sketch of these subjects, and that
to treat them as they deserve would require an amount
both of learning and of ability to which I can make no pre-
tension. I shall be content if I have succeeded in detecting some forgotten link in the great chain of causes, or in
casting a ray of light on some of the obscurer pages of the
history of opinions.

CONTENTS

OF

THE FIRST VOLUME.

CHAPTER I.

THE DECLINING SENSE OF THE MIRACULOUS.

ON MAGIC AND WITCHCRAFT.

The Belief in Satanic Miracles, having been universal among Protestants and Roman Catholics, passed away by a silent and unreasoning process under the influence of Civilisation—Witchcraft arose from a vivid Realisation of Satanic Presence acting on the Imagination—and afterwards on the Reason—Its Existence and Importance among Savages—The Christians attributed to Magic the Pagan Miracles—Constantine and Constantius attempted to subvert Paganism by persecuting Magic—Magical Character soon attributed to Christian Rites—Miracle of St. Hilarion—Persecution suspended under Julian and Jovian, but afterwards renewed—Not entirely due to Ecclesiastical Influence—Compromise between Christianity and Paganism—Prohib-ited Pagan Rites continue to be practised as Magic—From the Sixth to the Twelfth Century, extreme Superstition with little Terrorism, and, consequently, little Sorcery —Effects of Eclipses, Comets, and Pestilence on the Superstition—The Cabalists—Psellus—The Revival of Literature in the Twelfth Century produced a Spirit of Re-bellion which was encountered by Terrorism—which, acting on the Popular Creed, produced a bias towards Witchcraft—The Black Death—Influence of the Reforma-tion in stimulating Witchcraft—Luther—The Inquisitors—The Theology of Witch-craft—First Evidence of a Rationalistic Spirit in Europe—Wier—answered by

CHAPTER II.

THE DECLINING SENSE OF THE MIRACULOUS.

THE MIRACLES OF THE CHURCH.

CHAPTER III. *

ÆSTHETIC, SCIENTIFIC, AND MORAL DEVELOPMENTS OF RATIONALISM

The Expectation of Miracles grows out of the Religious Conceptions of an early Stage of
Civilisation, and its Decline implies a general Modification of Religious Opinions—
Fetishism probably the First Stage of Religious Belief—Examples of Fetish Notions
in the Early Church—Patristic Opinions concerning the Cross and the Water of Baptism—Anthropomorphism the next Stage—Men then ascribe the Government of the
Universe to Beings like themselves; but, being unable to concentrate their Attention
on the Invisible, they fall into Idolatry—Idolatry a Sign sometimes of Progress, and
sometimes of Retrogression—During its continuance, Art is the most faithful Expression of Religious Realisation—Influence of the National Religions on the Art of Per-
sia, Egypt, India, and Greece—The Art of the Catacombs altogether removed from
Idolatry—Its Freedom from Terrorism—Its Symbolism—Progress of Anthropomorphism—Position of the First Person of the Trinity in Art—Growing Worship of the
Virgin—Strengthened by Gnosticism—by Dogmatic Definitions—by Painting, Celibacy, and the Crusades—Its Moral Consequences—Growth of Idolatrous Conceptions
—Stages of the Veneration of Relics—Tendency towards the Miraculous invests
Images with peculiar Sanctity—The Portrait of Edessa—The Image at Paneas—Conversion of the Barbarians makes Idolatry general—Decree of Illiberis—The Iconoclasts—The Second Council of Nice—St. Agobard—Mahometanism the sole Example
of a great Religion restraining Semi-barbarians from Idolatry—Three Causes of its
Success—Low Condition of Art during the Period of Mediæval Idolatry—Difference
between the Religious and Æsthetic Sentiment—Aversion to Innovation—Contrast
between the Pagan and Christian Estimate of the Body—Greek Idolatry faded into
Art—Its Four Stages—A corresponding Transition takes place in Christendom—Greek
Influence on Art—Iconoclasm—Tradition of the Deformity of Christ—The Byzantine
Style—Broken by a Study of Ancient Sculpture renewed by Nicolas of Pisa—Christian School of Giotto and Fra Angelico—Corresponded with the Intellectual Character of the Time—Influence of Dante—Apocalyptic Subjects—Progress of Terrorism
in Art—Increase of Scepticism—Religious Paintings regarded simply as Studies of the
Beautiful—Influence of Venetian Sensuality—Sensuality favourable to Art—Parallel
of Titian and Praxiteles—Influence of the Pagan Sculpture—History of Greek
Statues after the rise of Christianity—Reaction in favour of Spiritualism led by Savonarola—Complete Secularisation of Art by Michael Angelo—Cycle of Painting completed—A corresponding Transition took place in Architecture—Fluctuations in the
Estimate in which it has been held represent Fluctuations of Religious Sentiments—
Decline of Gothic Architecture—Brunelleschi—St. Peter's—Intellectual Importance
of the History of Art—The Euthanasia of Opinions—Continued Revolt against Anthropomorphism—Results from the Totality of the Influences of Civilisation, but especially from the Encroachments of Physical Science on the old Conceptions of the
Government of the Universe—In the Early Church, Science was subordinated to

CHAPTER IV.

ON PERSECUTION.

PART I.

THE ANTECEDENTS OF PERSECUTION.

Persecution is the result, not of the personal Character of the Persecutors, but of the Principles they profess—Foundations of all Religious Systems are the Sense of Virtue and the Sense of Sin—Political and Intellectual Circumstances determine in each

RATIONALISM IN EUROPE.

CHAPTER I.

ON THE DECLINING SENSE OF THE MIRACULOUS.

MAGIC AND WITCHCRAFT.

THERE is certainly no change in the history of the last 300 years more striking, or suggestive of more curious enquiries, than that which has taken place in the estimate of the miraculous. At present, nearly all educated men receive an account of a miracle taking place in their own day, with an absolute and even derisive incredulity which dispenses with all examination of the evidence. Although they may be entirely unable to give a satisfactory explanation of some phenomena that have taken place, they never on that account dream of ascribing them to supernatural agency, such an hypothesis being, as they believe, altogether beyond the range of reasonable discussion. Yet, a few centuries ago, there was no solution to which the mind of man turned more readily in every perplexity. A miraculous account was then universally accepted as perfectly credible, probable, and ordinary. There was scarcely a village or a church that had not, at some time, been the scene of supernatural interposi·

tion. The powers of light and the powers of darkness were
regarded as visibly struggling for the mastery. Saintly
miracles, supernatural cures, startling judgments, visions,
prophecies, and prodigies of every order, attested the activity of the one, while witchcraft and magic, with all their
attendant horrors, were the visible manifestations of the
other.

I propose in the present chapter to examine that vast
department of miracles, which is comprised under the several
names of witchcraft, magic, and sorcery. It is a subject
which has, I think, scarcely obtained the position it deserves
in the history of opinions, having been too generally treated
in the spirit of the antiquarian, as if it belonged entirely to
the past, and could have no voice or bearing upon the controversies of the present. Yet, for more than fifteen hundred
years, it was universally believed that the Bible established,
in the clearest manner, the reality of the crime, and that an
amount of evidence, so varied and so ample as to preclude
the very possibility of doubt, attested its continuance and its
prevalence. The clergy denounced it with all the emphasis
of authority. The legislators of almost every land enacted
.aws for its punishment. Acute judges, whose lives were
spent in sifting evidence, investigated the question on countless occasions, and condemned the accused. Tens of thousands of victims perished by the most agonising and pro-
tracted torments, without exciting the faintest compassion ;
and, as they were for the most part extremely ignorant and
extremely poor, sectarianism and avarice had but little
influence on the subject.[1] Nations that were completely

---

[1] The general truth of this statement can scarcely, I think, be questioned,
though there are, undoubtedly, a few remarkable exceptions. Thus the
Templars were accused of sorcery, when Philip the Beautiful wished to con-

separated by position, by interests, and by character, on this one question were united. In almost every province of Germany, but especially in those where clerical influence predominated, the persecution raged with a fearful intensity. Seven thousand victims are said to have been burned at Trèves, six hundred by a single bishop of Bamberg, and eight hundred in a single year in the bishopric of Würtzburg.[1] In France, decrees were passed on the subject by the Parliaments of Paris, Toulouse, Bordeaux, Rheims, Rouen, Dijon, and Rennes, and they were all followed by a harvest of blood. At Toulouse, the seat of the Inquisition, four hundred persons perished for sorcery at a single execution, and fifty at Douay in a single year. Remy, a judge of Nancy, boasted that he had put to death eight hundred witches in sixteen years. The executions that took place at

fiscate their property; and the heretical opinions of the Vaudois may possibly have had something to say to the trials at Arras, in 1459; and, indeed, the name Vauderie was at one time given to sorcery. There were, moreover, a few cases of obnoxious politicians and noblemen being destroyed on the accusation; and during the Commonwealth there were one or two professional witch-finders in England. We have also to take into account some cases of convent scandals, such as those of Gauffridi, Grandier, and La Cadière; but, when all these deductions have been made, the prosecutions for witchcraft will represent the action of undiluted superstition more faithfully than probably any others that could be named. The overwhelming majority of witches were extremely poor; they were condemned by the highest and purest tribunals (ecclesiastical and lay) of the time; and as heretics were then burnt without difficulty for their opinions, there was little temptation to accuse them of witchcraft, and besides all parties joined cordially in the persecution. Grillandus, an Italian inquisitor of the fifteenth century, says—'Isti sortilegi, magici, necromantici, et similes sunt cæteris Christi fidelibus pauperiores, sordidiores, viliores, et contemptibiliores, in hoc mundo Deo permittente calamitosam vitam communiter peragunt, Deum verum infelici morte perdunt et æterni ignis incendio cruciantur.' (*De Sortilegiis*, cap. iii.) We shall see hereafter that witchcraft and heresy represent the working of the same spirit on different classes, and, therefore, usually accompanied each other.

[1] Wright's *Sorcery*, vol. i. p. 186; Michelet, *La Sorcière*, p. 10.

Paris in a few months were, in the emphatic words of an old writer, 'almost infinite.'[1] The fugitives who escaped to Spain were there seized and burned by the Inquisition. In that country the persecution spread to the smallest towns, and the belief was so deeply rooted in the popular mind, that a sorcerer was burnt as late as 1780. Torquemada devoted himself to the extirpation of witchcraft as zealously as to the extirpation of heresy, and he wrote a book upon the enormity of the crime.[2] In Italy, a thousand persons were executed in

[1] On French witchcraft, see Thiers' *Traité des Superstitions*, tom. i. pp. 134–136; Madden's *History of Phantasmata*, vol. i. pp. 306–310; Garinet, *Histoire de la Magie en France, passim,* but especially the Remonstrance of the Parliament of Rouen, in 1670, against the pardon of witches, p. 337; Bodin's *Démonomanie des Sorciers.* The persecution raged with extreme violence all through the south of France. It was a brilliant suggestion of De Lancre, that the witchcraft about Bordeaux might be connected with the number of orchards—the Devil being well known to have an especial power over apples. (See the passage quoted in Garinet, p. 176.) We have a fearful illustration of the tenacity of the belief in the fact that the superstition still continues, and that blood has in consequence been shed during the present century in the provinces that border on the Pyrenees. In 1807, a beggar was seized, tortured, and burned alive for sorcery by the inhabitants of Mayenne. In 1850, the Civil Tribunal of Tarbes tried a man and woman named Soubervie, for having caused the death of a woman named Bedouret. They believed that she was a witch, and declared that the priest had told them that she was the cause of an illness under which the woman Soubervie was suffering. They accordingly drew Bedouret into a private room, held her down upon some burning straw, and placed a red-hot iron across her mouth. The unhappy woman soon died in extreme agony. The Soubervies confessed, and indeed exulted in their act. At their trials they obtained the highest possible characters. It was shown that they had been actuated solely by superstition, and it was urged that they only followed the highest ecclesiastical precedents. The jury recommended them to mercy; and they were only sentenced to pay twenty-five francs a year to the husband of the victim, and to be imprisoned for four months. (Cordier, *Légendes des Hautes-Pyrénées.* Lourdes, 1855, pp. 79–88) In the *Rituel Auscitain,* now used in the diocese of Tarbes, it is said—' On doit reconnaître que non seulement il peut y avoir, mais qu'il y a même quelquefois des personnes qui sont véritablement possédées des esprits malins.' (Ibid. p. 90.)

[2] Llorente, *History of the Inquisition* (English Translation), pp. 129–142.

a single year in the province of Como; and in other parts of
the country, the severity of the inquisitors at last created an
absolute rebellion.[1] The same scenes were enacted in the
wild valleys of Switzerland and of Savoy. In Geneva, which
was then ruled by a bishop, five hundred alleged witches
were executed in three months; forty-eight were burnt at
Constance or Ravensburg, and eighty in the little town of
Valery, in Savoy.[2] In 1670, seventy persons were condemned in Sweden,[3] and a large proportion of them were burnt.
And these are only a few of the more salient events in that
long series of persecutions which extended over almost every
country, and continued for centuries with unabated fury. The
Church of Rome proclaimed in every way that was in her
power the reality and the continued existence of the crime.

Amongst other cases, more than thirty women were burnt at Calahorra, in
1507. A Spanish monk, named Castanaga, seems to have ventured to question
the justice of the executions as early as 1529 (p. 131). See also Garinet, p.
176; Madden, vol. i. pp. 311–315. Toledo was supposed to be the head-
quarters of the magicians, probably because, in the twelfth and thirteenth
centuries, mathematics, which were constantly confounded with magic, flourished there more than in any other part of Europe. Naudé, *Apologie pour les
Grands Hommes soupçonnez de Magie* (Paris, 1625), pp. 81, 82. See also
Buckle's *History of Civilisation*, vol. i. p. 334, *note*, and Simancas, *De Catholicis Institutionibus*, pp. 463–468.

[1] Spina, *De Strigibus* (1522), cap. xii.; Thiers, vol. i. p. 138; Madden, vol.
i. p. 305. Peter the Martyr, whom Titian has immortalised, seems to have
been one of the most strenuous of the persecutors. Spina, *Apol.*, c. ix.

[2] Madden, vol. i. pp. 303, 304. Michelet, *La Sorcière*, p. 206. Sprenger
ascribes Tell's shot to the assistance of the devil. *Mall. Mal.*, pars ii. c. xvi.
Savoy has always been especially subject to those epidemics of madness which
were once ascribed to witches, and Boguet noticed that the principal wizards
he had burnt were from that country. An extremely curious account of a
recent epidemic of this kind in a little village called Morzines will be found in
Une Relation sur une Epidémie d'Hystéro-Démonopathie en 1861, par le Docteur
A. Constans (Paris, 1863). Two French writers, Alain Kardec and Mirville,
have maintained this epidemic to be supernatural.

[3] Compare Plancey, *Dict. Infernale*, art. *Blokula ;* Hutchinson on *Witch
craft*, p. 55; Madden, vol. i. p. 354.

She strained every nerve to stimulate the persecution. She taught by all her organs that to spare a witch was a direct insult to the Almighty, and to her ceaseless exertions is to be attributed by far the greater proportion of the blood that was shed. In 1484, Pope Innocent VIII. issued a bull which gave a fearful impetus to the persecution, and he it was who commissioned the Inquisitor Sprenger, whose book was long the recognised manual on the subject, and who is said to have condemned hundreds to death every year. Similar bulls were issued by Julius II. in 1504, and by Adrian VI. in 1523. A long series of Provincial Councils asserted the existence of sorcery, and anathematised those who resorted to it. 'The universal practice of the Church was to place magic and sorcery among the reserved cases, and at prônes to declare magicians and sorcerers excommunicated;'[1] and a form of exorcism was solemnly inserted in the ritual. Almost all the great works that were written in favour of the executions were written by ecclesiastics. Almost all the lay works on the same side were dedicated to and sanctioned by ecclesiastical dignitaries. Ecclesiastical tribunals condemned thousands to death, and countless bishops exerted all their influence to multiply the victims. In a word, for many centuries it was universally believed, that the continued existence of witchcraft formed an integral part of the teaching of the Church, and that the persecution that raged through Europe was supported by the whole stress of her infallibility.[2]

[1] Thiers, *Superst.*, vol. i. p. 142.

[2] For ample evidence of the teaching of Catholicism on the subject, see Madden's *History of Phant.*, vol. i. pp. 234–248 ; Des Mousseaux, *Pratiques des Démons* (Paris, 1854), pp. 174–177 ; Thiers' *Superst.*, tom. i. pp. 138–163. The two last-mentioned writers were ardent Catholics. Thiers, who wrote in 1678 (I have used the Paris edition of 1741), was a very learned and moderate

Such was the attitude of the Church of Rome with reference to this subject, but on this ground the Reformers had no conflict with their opponents. The credulity which Luther manifested on all matters connected with diabolical intervention, was amazing, even for his age; and, when speaking of witchcraft, his language was emphatic and unhesitating. 'I would have no compassion on these witches,' he exclaimed, 'I would burn them all!'[1] In England the establishment of the Reformation was the signal for an immediate outburst of the superstition; and there, as elsewhere, its decline was represented by the clergy as the direct consequence and the exact measure of the progress of religious scepticism. In Scotland, where the Reformed ministers exercised greater influence than in any other country, and where the witch trials fell almost entirely into their hands, the persecution was proportionately atrocious. Probably the ablest defender of the belief was Glanvil, a clergyman of the English Establishment; and one of the most influential was Baxter, the greatest of the Puritans. It spread, with Puritanism, into the New World; and the executions in Massachusetts form one of the darkest pages in the his-

theologian, and wrote under the approbation of 'the doctors in the faculty of Paris:' he says—'On ne sçauroit nier qu'il y ait des magiciens ou des sorciers (car ces deux mots se prennent ordinairement dans la même signification) sans contredire visiblement les saintes lettres, la tradition sacrée et profane, les lois canoniques et civiles et l'expérience de tous les siècles, et sans rejeter avec impudence l'autorité irréfragable et infaillible de l'Eglise qui lance si souvent les foudres de l'excommunication contr'eux dans ses Prônes' (p. 132). So also Garinet—'Tous les conciles, tous les synodes, qui se tinrent dans les seize premiers siècles de l'église s'élèvent contre les sorciers; tous les écrivains ecclésiastiques les condamnent avec plus ou moins de sévérité' (p. 26). The bull of Innocent VIII. is prefixed to the *Malleus Malificarum*.

Colloquia de Fascinationibus. For the notions of Melanchthon on these subjects, see Baxter's *World of Spirits*, pp. 126, 127. Calvin, also, when remodelling the laws of Geneva, left those on witchcraft intact.

tory of America. The greatest religious leader of the last
century[1] was among the latest of its supporters.

If we ask why it is that the world has rejected what was
once so universally and so intensely believed, why a narrative of an old woman who had been seen riding on a broomstick, or who was proved to have transformed herself into a
wolf, and to have devoured the flocks of her neighbours, is
deemed so entirely incredible, most persons would probably
be unable to give a very definite answer to the question. It
is not because we have examined the evidence and found it
insufficient, for the disbelief always precedes, when it does
not prevent, examination. It is rather because the idea of
absurdity is so strongly attached to such narratives, that it
is difficult even to consider them with gravity. Yet at one
time no such improbability was felt, and hundreds of persons have been burnt simply on the two grounds I have
mentioned.

When so complete a change takes place in public opinion,
it may be ascribed to one or other of two causes. It may
be the result of a controversy which has conclusively settled
the question, establishing to the satisfaction of all parties a
clear preponderance of argument or fact in favour of one
opinion, and making that opinion a truism which is accepted
by all enlightened men, even though they have not themselves examined the evidence on which it rests. Thus, if
any one in a company of ordinarily educated persons were
to deny the motion of the earth, or the circulation of the
blood, his statement would be received with derision, though
it is probable that some of his audience would be unable to
demonstrate the first truth, and that very few of them could
give sufficient reasons for the second. They may not them-

[1] Wesley

selves be able to defend their position; but they are aware
that, at certain known periods of history, controversies on
those subjects took place, and that known writers then
brought forward some definite arguments or experiments,
which were ultimately accepted by the whole learned world
as rigid and conclusive demonstrations. It is possible, also,
for as complete a change to be effected by what is called the
spirit of the age. The general intellectual tendencies pervading the literature of a century profoundly modify the
character of the public mind. They form a new tone and
habit of thought. They alter the measure of probability.
They create new attractions and new antipathies, and they
eventually cause as absolute a rejection of certain old opinions as could be produced by the most cogent and definite
arguments.

That the disbelief in witchcraft is to be attributed to
this second class of influences; that it is the result, not of
any series of definite arguments, or of new discoveries, but
of a gradual, insensible, yet profound modification of the
habits of thought prevailing in Europe; that it is, thus, a
direct consequence of the progress of civilisation, and of its
influence upon opinions; must be evident to any one who
impartially investigates the question. If we ask what new
arguments were discovered during the decadence of the belief, we must admit that they were quite inadequate to account for the change. All that we can say of the unsatis-
factory nature of confessions under torture, of the instances
of imposture that were occasionally discovered, of the malicious motives that may have actuated some of the accusers, might have been said during the darkest periods of
the middle ages. The multiplication of books and the increase of knowledge can have added nothing to these ob-

vious arguments. Those who lived when the evidences of witchcraft existed in profusion, and attracted the attention of all classes and of all grades of intellect, must surely have been as competent judges as ourselves, if the question was merely a question of evidence. The gradual cessation of the accusations was the consequence, and not the cause, of the scepticism. The progress of medical knowledge may have had considerable influence on the private opinions of some writers on the subject, but it was never influential upon the public mind, or made the battle-ground of the controversy. Indeed, the philosophy of madness is mainly due to Pinel, who wrote long after the superstition had vanished; and even if witchcraft had been treated as a disease, this would not have destroyed the belief that it was Satanic, in an age when all the more startling diseases were deemed supernatural, and when theologians maintained that Satan frequently acted by the employment of natural laws. One discovery, it is true, was made during the discussion, which attracted great attention, and was much insisted on by the opponents of the laws against sorcery. It was, that the word translated 'witch' in the Levitical condemnation may be translated 'poisoner.'[1] This discovery in itself is, however, obviously insufficient to account for the change. It does not affect the enormous mass of evidence of the workings of witchcraft, which was once supposed to have placed the belief above the possibility of doubt. It does not affect such passages as the history of the witch of Endor, or of the demoniacs in the New Testament, to which the believers in

---

[1] This was first, I believe, asserted by Wier. In England it was much maintained during the reign of Charles II. The other side of the question was supported on the Continent by Bodin, and in England by Glanvil, Mora Casaubon, &c.

witchcraft triumphantly appealed. Assuming the existence of witches—assuming that there were really certain persons who were constantly engaged in inflicting, by diabolical agency, every form of evil on their neighbours, and whose machinations destroyed countless lives—there can be no doubt that these persons should be punished with death, altogether irrespectively of any distinct command. The truth is, that the existence of witchcraft was disbelieved before the scriptural evidence of it was questioned. A disbelief in ghosts and witches was one of the most prominent characteristics of scepticism in the seventeenth century. At first it was nearly confined to men who were avowedly freethinkers, but gradually it spread over a wider circle, and included almost all the educated, with the exception of a large proportion of the clergy. This progress, however, was not effected by any active propagandism. It is not identified with any great book or with any famous writer. It was not the triumph of one series of arguments over another. On the contrary, no facts are more clearly established in the literature of witchcraft than that the movement was mainly silent, unargumentative, and insensible; that men came gradually to disbelieve in witchcraft, because they came gradually to look upon it as absurd; and that this new tone of thought appeared, first of all, in those who were least subject to theological influences, and soon spread through the educated laity, and last of all took possession of the clergy.

It may be stated, I believe, as an invariable truth, that, whenever a religion which rests in a great measure on a system of terrorism, and which paints in dark and forcible colours the misery of men and the power of evil spirits, is intensely realised, it will engender the belief in witchcraft or magic. The panic which its teachings will create, will overbalance the faculties of multitudes. The awful images of evil spirits of superhuman power, and of untiring malignity, will continually haunt the imagination. They will blend with the illusions of age or sorrow or sickness, and will appear with an especial vividness in the more alarming and unexplained phenomena of nature.

This consideration will account for the origin of the conception of magic in those ages when belief is almost exclusively the work of the imagination. At a much later period, the same vivid realisation of diabolical presence will operate powerfully on the conclusions of the reason. We have now passed so completely out of the modes of thought which predominated in the sixteenth and seventeenth centuries, and we are so firmly convinced of the unreality of witchcraft, that it is only by a strong effort of the imagination that we can realise the position of the defenders of the belief. Yet it is, I think, difficult to examine the subject with impartiality, without coming to the conclusion that the historical evidence establishing the reality of witchcraft is so vast and so varied, that it is impossible to disbelieve it without what, on other subjects, we should deem the most extraordinary rashness. The defenders of the belief, who were often men of great and distinguished talent, maintained that there was no fact in all history more fully attested, and that to reject it would be to strike at the root of all historical evidence of the miraculous. The belief implied the continual occurrence of acts of the most extraordinary and impressive character, and of such a nature as to fall strictly within human cognisance. The subject, as we have seen, was examined in tens of thousands of cases, in almost every country in Europe, by tribunals which included the acutest lawyers and ecclesiastics of the

age, on the scene and at the time when the alleged acts had
taken place, and with the assistance of innumerable sworn
witnesses. The judges had no motive whatever to desire the
condemnation of the accused; and, as conviction would be
followed by a fearful death, they had the strongest motives
to exercise their power with caution and deliberation. The
whole force of public opinion was directed constantly and
earnestly to the question for many centuries; and, although
there was some controversy concerning the details of witchcraft, the fact of its existence was long considered undoubted.
The evidence is essentially cumulative. Some cases may be
explained by monomania, others by imposture, others by
chance coincidences, and others by optical delusions; but,
when we consider the multitudes of strange statements that
were sworn and registered in legal documents, it is very difficult to frame a general rationalistic explanation which will
not involve an extreme improbability. In our own day, it
may be said with confidence, that it would be altogether
impossible for such an amount of evidence to accumulate
round a conception which had no substantial basis in fact.
The ages in which witchcraft flourished were, it is true,
grossly credulous; and to this fact we attribute the belief,
yet we do not reject their testimony on all matters of secular
history. If we considered witchcraft probable, a hundredth
part of the evidence we possess would have placed it beyond the region of doubt. If it were a natural but a very
improbable fact, our reluctance to believe it would have
been completely stifled by the multiplicity of the proofs.

Now, it is evident that the degree of improbability we
attach to histories of witches, will depend, in a great measure, upon our doctrine concerning evil spirits, and upon the
degree in which that doctrine is realised. If men believe

that invisible beings, of superhuman power, restless activity, and intense malignity, are perpetually haunting the world, and directing all their energies to the temptation and the persecution of mankind; if they believe that, in past ages, these spirits have actually governed the bodily functions of men, worked miracles, and foretold future events,—if all this is believed, not with the dull and languid assent of custom, but with an intensely realised, living, and operative assurance; if it presents itself to the mind and imagination as a vivid truth, exercising that influence over the reason, and occupying that prominence in the thoughts of men, which its importance would demand, the antecedent improbability of witchcraft would appear far less than if this doctrine was rejected or was unrealised. When, therefore, we find a growing disposition to reject every history which involves diabolical intervention as intrinsically absurd, independently of any examination of the evidence on which it rests, we may infer from this fact the declining realisation of the doctrine of evil spirits.

These two considerations will serve, I think, to explain the history of witchcraft, and also to show its great significance and importance as an index of the course of civilisation. To follow out the subject into details would require a far greater space than I can assign to it, but I hope to be able to show, sufficiently, what have been the leading phases through which the belief has passed.

In the ruder forms of savage life, we find the belief in witchcraft universal,[1] and accompanied, in most instances, by features of peculiar atrocity. The reason of this is obvious. Terror is everywhere the beginning of religion.

[1] On the universality of the belief, see Herder, *Philosophy of History,* b. viii. c. 2; Maury, *Histoire de Magie, passim.*

The phenomena which impress themselves most forcibly on the mind of the savage are not those which enter manifestly into the sequence of natural laws and which are productive of most beneficial effects, but those which are disastrous and apparently abnormal. Gratitude is less vivid than fear, and the smallest apparent infraction of a natural law produces a deeper impression than the most sublime of its ordinary operations. When, therefore, the more startling and terrible aspects of nature are presented to his mind, when the more deadly forms of disease or natural convulsion desolate his land, the savage derives from these things an intensely realised perception of diabolical presence. In the darkness of the night; amid the yawning chasms and the wild echoes of the mountain gorge; under the blaze of the comet, or the solemn gloom of the eclipse; when famine has blasted the land; when the earthquake and the pestilence have slaughtered their thousands; in every form of disease which refracts and distorts the reason; in all that is strange, portentous, and deadly, he feels and cowers before the supernatural. Completely exposed to all the influences of nature, and completely ignorant of the chain of sequence that unites its various parts, he lives in continual dread of what he deems the direct and isolated acts of evil spirits. Feeling them continually near him, he will naturally endeavour to enter into communion with them. He will strive to propitiate them with gifts. If some great calamity has fallen upon him, or if some vengeful passion has mastered his reason, he will attempt to invest himself with their authority; and nis excited imagination will soon persuade him that he has succeeded in his desire. If his abilities and his ambition place him above the common level, he will find in this belief the most ready path to power. By professing to hold com-

munion with and to control supernatural beings, he can ex
ercise an almost boundless influence over those about him
and, among men who are intensely predisposed to believe in
the supernatural, a very little dexterity or acquaintance with
natural laws will support his pretensions. By converting
the terror which some great calamity has produced into
anger against an alleged sorcerer, he can at the same time
take a signal vengeance upon those who have offended him,
and increase the sense of his own importance. Those whose
habits, or appearance, or knowledge, separate them from the
multitude, will be naturally suspected of communicating
with evil spirits; and this suspicion will soon become a certainty, if any mental disease should aggravate their peculiarities. In this manner the influences of ignorance, imagination, and imposture will blend and coöperate in creating a
belief in witchcraft, and in exciting a hatred against those
who are suspected of its practice, commensurate with the
terror they inspire.

In a more advanced stage of civilisation, the fear of
witches will naturally fade, as the habits of artificial life
remove men from those influences which act upon the imagination, and as increasing knowledge explains some of the
more alarming phenomena of nature. The belief, however,
that it is possible, by supernatural agency, to inflict evil
upon mankind, was general in ancient Greece and Rome;
and St. Augustine assures us that all the sects of philosophers admitted it, with the exception of the Epicureans,
who denied the existence of evil spirits. The Decemvirs
passed a law condemning magicians to death. A similar
law was early enacted in Greece; and, in the days of Demos-
thenes, a sorceress named Lemia was actually executed.[1]

[1] Garinet, pp. 13, 14.

The philosophy of Plato, by greatly aggrandising the sphere of the spiritual, did much to foster the belief; and we find that whenever, either before or after the Christian era, that philosophy has been in the ascendant, it has been accompanied by a tendency to magic. Besides this, the ancient civilisations were never directed earnestly to the investigation of natural phenomena; and the progress made in this respect was, in consequence, very small. On the whole however, the persecution seems to have been, in those coun tries, almost entirely free from religious fanaticism. The magician was punished because he injured man, and not because he offended God.

In one respect, during the later period of Pagan Rome, the laws against magic seem to have revived, and to have taken a somewhat different form, without, however, representing any phase of a religious movement, but simply a political requirement. Under the head of magic were comprised some astrological and other methods of foretelling the future; and it was found that these practices had a strong tendency to foster conspiracies against the emperors. The soothsayer often assured persons that they were destired to assume the purple, and in that way stimulated them to rebellion. By casting the horoscope of the reigning emperor, he had ascertained, according to the popular belief, the period in which the government might be assailed with most prospect of success; and had thus proved a constant cause of agitation. Some of the forms of magic had, also, been lately imported into the empire from Greece; and were therefore repugnant to the conservative spirit that was dominant. Several of the emperors, in consequence, passed edicts against the magicians, which were executed with considerable though somewhat spasmodic energy.' But although magicians were occasionally persecuted, it is not to be inferred from this that everything that was comprised under the name of magic was considered morally wrong. On the contrary, many of the systems of divination formed an integral part of religion. Some of the more public modes of foretelling the future, such as the oracles of the gods, were still retained and honoured; and a law, which made divination concerning the future of the emperor high treason, shows clearly the spirit in which the others were suppressed. The emperors desired to monopolise the knowledge of the future, and consequently drew many astrologers to their courts, while they banished them from other parts of the kingdom.' They were so far from attaching the idea of sacrilege to practices which enabled them to foretell coming events, that Marcus Aurelius and Julian, who were both passionately attached to their religion, and who were among the best men who have ever sat upon a throne, were among the most ardent of the patrons of the magicians.

Such was the somewhat anomalous position of the magicians in the last days of Pagan Rome, and it acquires a great interest from its bearing on the policy of the Christian emperors.

When the Christians were first scattered through the Roman empire, they naturally looked upon this question with a very different spirit from that of the heathen. Inspired by an intense religious enthusiasm, which they were nobly sealing with their blood, they thought much less of the civil

---

' This very obscure branch of the subject has been most admirably treated by Maury, *Histoire de la Magie* (Paris, 1860), pp. 78–85. An extremely learned and able work, from which I have derived great assistance.

' Maury, ch. iv.

than of the religious consequences of magic, and sacrilege
seemed much more terrible in their eyes than anarchy. Their
position, acting upon some of their distinctive doctrines, had
filled them with a sense of Satanic presence, which must have
shadowed every portion of their belief, and have predisposed
them to discover diabolical influence in every movement of
the pagan. The fearful conception of eternal punishment,
adopted in its most material form, had flashed with its full
intensity upon their minds. They believed that this was the
destiny of all who were beyond the narrow circle of their
Church, and that their persecutors were doomed to agonies
of especial poignancy. The whole world was divided between the kingdom of God and the kingdom of Satan. The
persecuted Church represented the first, the persecuting
world the second. In every scoff that was directed against
their creed, in every edict that menaced their persons, in
every interest that opposed their progress, they perceived
the direct and immediate action of the devil. They found a
great and ancient religion subsisting around them. Its gorgeous rites, its traditions, its priests, and its miracles had
preoccupied the public mind, and presented what seemed at
first an insuperable barrier to their mission. In this religion
they saw the especial workmanship of the devil, and their
strong predisposition to interpret every event by a miraculous standard, persuaded them that all its boasted prodigies
were real. Nor did they find any difficulty in explaining
them. The world they believed to be full of malignant
demons, who had in all ages persecuted and deluded mankind. From the magicians of Egypt to the demoniacs of the
New Testament, their power had been continually manifested.
In the chosen land they could only persecute and afflict; but

among the heathen, they possessed supreme power, and were universally worshipped as divine.

This doctrine, which was the natural consequence of the intellectual condition of the age, acting upon the belief in evil spirits, and upon the scriptural accounts of diabolical intervention, had been still further strengthened by those Platonic theories which, in their Alexandrian form, had so profoundly influenced the early teachings of the Church.[1] According to these theories, the immediate objects of the devotions of the pagan world were subsidiary spirits of finite power and imperfect morality—angels, or, as they were then called, demons—who acted the part of mediators; and who, by the permission of the supreme and inaccessible Deity, regulated the religious government of mankind. In this manner, a compromise was effected between monotheism and polytheism. The religion of the state was true and lawful, but it was not irreconcilable with pure theism. The Christians had adopted this conception of subsidiary spirits; but they maintained them to be not the willing agents, but the adversaries, of the Deity; and the word demon, which, among the pa-

---

[1] The Alexandrian or Neo-Platonic school probably owed a great part of its influence over early Christianity to its doctrine of a divine Trinity—the Unity, the Logos, and the energising Spirit—which was thought by some to harmonise with the Christian doctrine. Many persons have believed that Neo-Platonic modes both of thought and expression are reflected in St. John's Gospel. The influence which this school exercised over Christianity forms one of the most remarkable pages in ecclesiastical history. From it the orthodox derived a great part of their metaphysics; and, in a great measure, their doctrine concerning the worship of demons, to which St. Paul was long thought to have alluded. From it the Gnostics, the first important sect of Christian heretics, obtained their central doctrine of the Æons, which Julian endeavoured to con solidate into a rival system. On the doctrine of the demons, in its relation to heathen worship, see the chapter on Neo-Platonism in Maury, and the curious argument, based on the Platonic theory, which occupies the greater part of the eighth book of the *De Civitate Dei*.

gans, signified only a spirit below the level of a Divinity, among the Christians signified a devil.

This notion seems to have existed in the very earliest period of Christianity ; and, in the second century, we find it elaborated with most minute and detailed care. Tertullian, who wrote in that century, assures us that the world was full of these evil spirits, whose influence might be descried in every portion of the pagan creed. Some of them belonged to that band of rebels who had been precipitated with Satan into the abyss. Others were the angels who, in the antediluvian world, had become attached to the daughters of men ; and who, having taught them to dye wool, and to commit the still more fearful offence of painting their faces, had been justly doomed to eternal suffering.[1] These were now seeking in every way to thwart the purposes of the Almighty, and their especial delight was to attract to themselves the worship which was due to Him alone. Not only the more immoral deities of heathenism, not only such divinities as Venus, or Mars, or Mercury, or Pluto, but also those who appeared the most pure, were literally and undoubtedly diabolical. Minerva, the personification of wisdom, was a devil, and so was Diana, the type of chastity, and so was Jupiter, the heathen conception of the Most High. The spirits who were worshipped under the names of departed heroes, and who were supposed to have achieved so many

[1] *De Cultu Fœminarum*, lib. i c. 2. This curious notion is given on the authority of the prophecy of Enoch, which was thought by some—and Tertullian seems to have inclined to their opinion—to be authoritative Scripture. St. Augustine suggests, that the 'angels' who were attached to the antediluvians were possibly devils—incubi, as they were called—and that the word angel, in the writings attributed to Enoch, and in all parts of Scripture, signifying only messenger, may be applied to any spirit, good or bad. (*De Civ. Dei*, lib. xv. cap. 23.) This rule of interpretation had, as we shall see, an important influence on the later theology of witchcraft.

acts of splendid and philanthropic heroism, were all devils who had assumed the names· of the dead. The same condemnation was passed upon those bright creations of a poetic fancy, the progenitors of the mediæval fairies, the nymphs and dryads who peopled every grove and hallowed every stream.[1] The air was filled with unholy legions,[2] and the traditions of every land were replete with their exploits. The immortal lamp, which burnt with an unfading splendour in the temple of Venus; the household gods that were transported by invisible hands through the air; the miracles which clustered so thickly around the vestal virgins, the oracular shrines, and the centres of Roman power, were all attestations of their presence. Under the names of Sylvans and Fauns, and Dusii, they had not only frequently appeared among mankind, but had made innumerable women the objects of their passion. This fact was so amply attested, that it would be impudence to deny it.[3] Persons possessed

---

[1] Much the same notions were long after held about the fairies. A modern French writer states, that till near the middle of the eighteenth century, a mass was annually celebrated in the Abbey of Poissy, for the preservation of the nuns from their power. (Des Mousseaux, *Pratiques des Démons*, p. 81.)

[2] One sect of heretics of the fourth century—the Messalians—went so far as to make spitting a religious exercise, in hopes of thus casting out the devils they inhaled. (Maury, p. 317.)

[3] 'Hoc negare impudentiæ videatur' (St. Aug. *De Civ. Dei*, lib. xv. cap. 23). The Saint, however, proceeds to say, 'Non hic aliquid audeo temere definire.'— See also Justin Martyr, *Ap.* c. v. The same notion was perpetuated through the succeeding ages, and marriage with devils was long one of the most ordinary accusations in the witch trials. The devils who appeared in the female form were generally called succubi, those who appeared like men, incubi (though this distinction was not always preserved). The former were comparatively rare, but Bodin mentions a priest who had commerce with one for more than forty years, and another priest who found a faithful mistress in a devil for half a century: they were both burnt alive (*Démonomanie des Sorciers*, p. 107). Luther was a firm believer in this intercourse (*Ibid.*). The incubi were much more common; and hundreds, perhaps thousands, of women have been burnt on account of the belief in them. It was observed, that they had a

with devils were constantly liberated by the Christians, and tombs of the exorcists have been discovered in the catacombs.[1] If a Christian in any respect deviated from the path of duty, a visible manifestation of the devil sometimes appeared to terrify him. A Christian lady, in a fit of thoughtless dissipation, went to the theatre, and at the theatre she became possessed with a devil. The exorcist remonstrated with the evil spirit on the presumption of its act. The devil replied apologetically, that it had found the

peculiar attachment to women with beautiful hair; and it was an old Catholic belief, that St. Paul alluded to this in that somewhat curious passage, in which he exhorts women to cover their heads, because of the 'angels' (Sprenger, *Mall. Mal.*, Pars i. Quæst. 4; and Pars ii. Quæst. 2). The incubi generally had no children, but there were some exceptions to this rule, for Nider the inquisitor assures us, that the island of Cyprus was entirely peopled by their sons (*Mall. Malifi.*, p. 522). The ordinary phenomenon of nightmare, as the name imports, was associated with this belief (see a curious passage in Bodin, p. 109). The Dusii, whose exploits St. Augustine mentions, were Celtic spirits, and are the origin of our 'Deuce' (Maury, p. 189). For the much more cheerful views of the Cabalists, and other secret societies of the middle ages, concerning the intercourse of philosophers with sylphs, salamanders, &c., see that very curious and amusing book, *Le Comte de Gabalis, ou Entretiens sur les Sciences Secrètes* (Paris, 1671). Lilith, the first 'wife of Adam, concerning whom the Rabbinical traditions are so full, who was said to suck the blood of infants, and from whose name the word lullaby (Lili Abi) is supposed by some to have been derived, was long regarded as the queen of the succubi (Plancey, *Dict. Inf.*, art. *Lilith*). The Greeks believed that nightmare resulted from the presence of a demon named Ephialtes.

[1] There is one of these inscriptions in the Museum at the Lateran, and another in the catacomb of St. Callista. In the Church of Rome there is an order of exorcists, whose functions are confined to baptisms; and with these Mr. Spencer Northcote, in his book on the Catacombs, identifies the ancient inscriptions. I have not done so, because it is quite certain that, in primitive Christianity, the practice of exorcising possessed persons was general; and because Sprenger asserts, that the employment of exorcising at baptisms was not introduced till a later period (*Mall. Mal.*, Pars ii. Quæst. 2). Sprenger does not give his authority, but as he is usually well informed on matters of tradition, and as he treats the omission as a difficulty, I have adopted his view See also Neander's *Hist.*, vol. ii. p. 370.

4

woman in its house.[1] The rites of paganism had in some degree pervaded all departments of life, and all were therefore tainted with diabolical influence. In the theatre, in the circus, in the market-place, in all the public festivals, there was something which manifested their presence. A Christian soldier, on one occasion, refused even to wear a festal crown, because laurels had been originally dedicated to Bacchus and Venus; and endured severe punishment rather than comply with the custom. Much discussion was elicited by the transaction, but Tertullian wrote a treatise [2] maintaining that the martyr had only complied with his strict duty.

The terror which such a doctrine must have spread among the early Christians may be easily conceived. They seemed to breathe an atmosphere of miracles. Wherever they turned, they were surrounded and beleaguered by malicious spirits, who were perpetually manifesting their presence by supernatural acts. Watchful fiends stood beside every altar; they mingled with every avocation of life, and the Christians were the special objects of their hatred. All this was universally believed; and it was realised with an intensity which, in this secular age, we can scarcely conceive. It was realised as men realise religious doctrines, when they have devoted to them the undivided energies of their lives, and when their faith has been intensified in the furnace of persecution.

[1] Tertullian *De Spectaculis*, cap. xxvi. Another woman, this writer assures us, having gone to see an actor, dreamed all the following night of a winding sheet, and heard the actor's name ringing, with frightful reproaches, in her ears. To pass to a much later period, St. Gregory the Great, in the sixth century, mentions a nun who, when walking in a garden, began to eat without making the sign of the cross. She had a bitter cause to repent of her indecent haste, for she immediately swallowed a devil in a lettuce (*Dialogi*, lib. i. c. 4) The whole passage, which is rather long for quotation, is extremely curious.

[2] De Coronâ.

The bearing of this view upon the conception of magic is very obvious. Among the more civilised pagans, as we have seen, magic was mainly a civil, and in the last days of the empire, mainly a political crime. In periods of great political insecurity, it assumed considerable importance; at other periods it fell completely into the background. Its relation to the prevailing religion was exceedingly indeterminate, and it comprised many rites that were not regarded as in any degree immoral. In the early Church, on the other hand, it was esteemed the most horrible form of sacrilege, effected by the direct agency of evil spirits. It included the whole system of paganism, explained all its prodigies, and gave a fearful significance to all its legends. It assumed, in consequence, an extraordinary importance in the patristic teaching, and acted strongly and continually on the imaginations of the people.

When the Church obtained the direction of the civil power, she soon modified or abandoned the tolerant maxims she had formerly inculcated; and, in the course of a few years, restrictive laws were enacted, both against the Jews and against the heretics. It appears, however, that the multitude of pagans, in the time of Constantine, was still so great, and the zeal of the emperor so languid, that he at first shrank from directing his laws openly and avowedly against the old faith, and an ingenious expedient was devised for sapping it at its base, under the semblance of the ancient legislation. Magic, as I have said, among the Romans, included not only those appeals to evil spirits, and those modes of inflicting evil on others, which had always been denounced as sacrilegious, but also certain methods of foretelling the future, which were not regarded as morally wrong, but only as politically dangerous. This latter de-

partment formed an offshoot of the established religion, and
had never been separated from it with precision. The laws
had been devised for the purpose of preventing rebellions or
imposition, and they had been executed in that spirit. The
Christian emperors revived these laws, and enforced them
with extreme severity, but directed them against the religion
of the pagans.[1] At first, that secret magic which the decemvirs had prohibited, but which had afterwards come into
general use, was alone condemned; but, in the course of a
few reigns, the circle of legislation expanded, till it included
the whole system of paganism.

Almost immediately after his conversion, Constantine
enacted an extremely severe law against secret magic. He
decreed that any aruspex who entered into the house of a
citizen, for the purpose of celebrating his rites, should be
burnt alive, the property of his employers confiscated, and
the accuser rewarded.[2] Two years later, however, a procla-
mation was issued, which considerably attenuated the force
of this enactment, for it declared that it was not the intention of the emperor to prohibit magical rites which were
designed to discover remedies for diseases, or to protect the
harvests from hail, snow, or tempests.[3]

This partial tolerance continued till the death of Con
stantine, but completely passed away under his successor.
Constantius appears to have been governed by far stronger

---

[1] The history of this movement has been traced with masterly ability by
Maury, *Sur la Magie*, and also by Beugnot, *Destruction de Paganisme dans
l'Occident.*

[2] *Codex Theodosianus*, lib. ix. tit. xvi. c. 1, 2. The pagan historian Zosi-
mus observes, that when Constantine had abandoned his country's gods 'he
made this beginning of impiety, that he looked with contempt on the art of
foretelling' (lib. ii. c. 29); and Eusebius classifies his prohibition of prophecy
with the measures directed openly against paganism. (*Vita Const.*, lib. i. c. 16.)

[3] *Cod. Th.*, lib. ix. t. xvi. l. 3

convictions than his father. He had embraced the Arian heresy, and is said to have been much influenced by the Arian priests; and he directed his laws with a stern and almost passionate eagerness against the forms of magic which verged most closely upon the pagan worship. At the beginning of one of these laws, he complained that many had been producing tempests and destroying the lives of their enemies by the assistance of the demons, and he proceeded to prohibit in the sternest manner, and under pain of the severest penalties, every kind of magic. All who attempted to foretell the future—the augurs, as well as the more irregular diviners—were emphatically condemned. Magicians who were captured in Rome were to be thrown to the wild beasts; and those who were seized in the provinces to be put to excruciating torments, and at last crucified. If they persisted in denying their crime, their flesh was to be torn from their bones with hooks of iron.[1] These fearful penalties were directed against those who practised rites which had long been universal; and which, if they were not regarded as among the obligations, were, at least, among the highest privileges of paganism. It has been observed as a significant fact, that in this reign the title 'enemies of the human race,' which the old pagan laws had applied to the

---

[1] *Cod. Th.*, lib. ix. t. xvi. l. 4, 5, 6. The language is curious and very peremptory—thus, we read in law 4: 'Nemo haruspicem consulat, aut mathematicum, nemo hariolum. Augurum et vatum prava confessio conticescat. Chaldæi ac magi et ceteri quos maleficos ob facinorum magnitudinem vulgus appellat, nec ad hanc partem aliquid moliantur. Sileat omnibus perpetuo divinandi curiositas: etenim supplicium, capitis feret gladio ultore prostratus quicunque jussis obsequium denegaverit.' Another law (6) concludes: 'Si convictus ad proprium facinus detegentibus repugnaverit pernegando sit eculeo deditus, ungulisque sulcantibus latera perferat pœnas proprio dignas facinore.' On the nature of the punishments that were employed, compare the Commentary on the law, in Ritter's edition (Leipsic, 1738), and Beugnot, tom. i. p. 148.

Christians, and which proved so effectual in exasperating the popular mind, was transferred to the magicians.[1]

The task of the Christian emperors in combating magic was, in truth, one of the most difficult that can be conceived; and all the penalties that Roman barbarity could devise, were unable to destroy practices which were the natural consequence of the prevailing credulity. As long as men believed that they could easily ascertain the future, it was quite certain that curiosity would at length overpower fear. As long as they believed that a few simple rites could baffle their enemies, and enable them to achieve their most cherished desires, they would most unquestionably continue to practise them. Priests might fulminate their anathemas, and emperors multiply their penalties; but scepticism, and not terrorism, was the one corrective for the evil. This scepticism was nowhere to be found. The populace never questioned for a moment the efficacy of magic. The pagan philosophers were all infatuated by the dreams of Neo-Platonism, and were writing long books on the mysteries of Egypt, the hierarchy of spirits, and their intercourse with men. The Fathers, it is true, vehemently denounced magic, but they never seem to have had the faintest suspicion that it was a delusion. If Christianity had had nothing to oppose to the fascination of these forbidden rites, it would have been impossible to prevent the immense majority of the people from reverting to them; but, by a very natural process, a

---

[1] Beugnot, tom. i. p. 148. On these laws, M. Maury well says, 'De la sorte se trouvaient atteints les ministres du polythéisme les plus en crédit, les pratiques qui inspiraient à la superstition le plus de confiance. * * * Bien des gens ne se souciaient plus de rendre aux dieux le culte légal et consacré; mais les oracles, les augures, les présages, presque tous les païens y recouraient avec confiance, et leur en enlever la possibilité c'était leur dépouiller de ce qui faisait leur consolation et leur joie ' (pp. 117, 118).

series of conceptions were rapidly introduced into theology, which formed what may be termed a rival system of magic, in which the talismanic virtues of holy water, and of Christian ceremonies, became a kind of counterpoise to the virtue of unlawful charms. It is very remarkable, however, that, while these sacred talismans were indefinitely multiplied, the other great fascination of magic, the power of predicting the future, was never claimed by the Christian clergy. If the theory of the writers of the eighteenth century had been correct; if the superstitions that culminated in mediævalism had been simply the result of the knavery of the clergy; this would most certainly not have been the case. The Christian priests, like all other priests, would have pandered to the curiosity which was universal, and something analogous to the ancient oracles or auguries would have been incorporated into the Church. Nothing of this kind took place, because the change which passed over theology was the result, not of imposture, but of a normal development. No part of Christianity had a tendency to develop into an oracular system; and had such a system arisen, it would have been the result of deliberate fraud. On the other hand, there were many conceptions connected with the faith, especially concerning the efficacy of baptismal water, which, under the pressure of a materialising age, passed, by an easy and natural, if not legitimate transition, into a kind of fetishism, assimilating with the magical notions that were so universally diffused.

St. Jerome, in his life of St. Hilarion, relates a miracle of that saint which refers to a period a few years after the death of Constantius, and which shows clearly the position that Christian ceremonies began to occupy with reference to magic. It appears that a Christian, named Italicus, was ac-

customed to race horses against the pagan duumvir of Gaza,
and that this latter personage invariably gained the victory,
by means of magical rites, which stimulated his own horses,
and paralysed those of his opponent. The Christian, in despair, had recourse to St. Hilarion. The saint appears to
have been, at first, somewhat startled at the application, and
rather shrank from participating actively in horse-racing;
but Italicus at last persuaded him that the cause was worthy
of his intervention, and obtained a bowl of water which
Hilarion himself had consecrated, and which was, therefore,
endowed with a peculiar virtue. At length the day of the
races arrived. The chariots were placed side by side, and
the spectators thronged the circus. As the signal for the
start was given, Italicus sprinkled his horses with the holy
water. Immediately the chariot of the Christian flew with
a supernatural rapidity to the goal; while the horses of his
adversary faltered and staggered, as if they had been struck
by an invisible hand. The circus rang with wild cries of
wonder, of joy, or of anger. Some called for the death of
the Christian magician, but many others abandoned paganism in consequence of the miracle.[1]

The persecution which Constantius directed against the
magicians was of course suspended under Julian, whose
spirit of toleration, when we consider the age he lived in, the
provocations he endured, and the intense religious zeal he
manifested, is one of the most remarkable facts in history.
He was passionately devoted to those forms of magic which
the pagan religion admitted, and his palace was always

---

[1] *Vita Sancti Hilarionis.* This miracle is related by Beugnot. The whole
life of St. Hilarion is crowded with prodigies that illustrate the view taken in
the text. Besides curing about two hundred persons in a little more than a
month, driving away serpents, &c., we find the saint producing rain with the
same facility as the later witches.

.hronged with magicians. The consultation of the entrails, which Constantius had forbidden, was renewed at the coronation of Julian; and it was reported among the Christians, that they presented, on that occasion, the form of a cross, surmounted by a crown.[1] During the short reign of Jovian, the same tolerance seems to have continued; but Valentinian renewed the persecution, and made another law against 'impious prayers and midnight sacrifices,' which were still offered.[2] This law excited so much discontent in Greece, where it was directly opposed to the established religion, that Valentinian consented to its remaining inoperative in that province; but, in other portions of the empire, fearful scenes of suffering and persecution were everywhere witnessed.[3] In the East, Valens was persecuting, with impartial zeal, all who did not adopt the tenets of the Arian heresy. 'The very name of philosopher,' as it has been said, became 'a title of proscription;' and the most trivial offences were visited with death. One philosopher was executed, because, in a private letter, he had exhorted his wife not to forget to crown the portal of the door. An old woman perished, because she endeavoured to allay the paroxysms of a fever by magical songs. A young man, who imagined that he could cure an attack of diarrhœa by touching alternately a marble pillar and his body, while he repeated the vowels, expiated this not very alarming superstition by torture and by death.[4]

In reviewing these persecutions, which were directed by the orthodox and by the Arians against magicians, we

---

[1] St. Gregory Nazianzen (3rd oration against Julian).

[2] *Cod. Th.*, lib. ix. t. xvi. l. 7, &c.
Maury, pp. 118, 119.

[4] Ammianus Marcellinus, lib. xxix. c. 1, 2.

must carefully guard against some natural exaggerations. It would be very unfair to attribute directly to the leaders of the Church the edicts that produced them. It would be still more unfair to attribute to them the spirit in which those edicts were executed. Much allowance must be made for the personal barbarity of certain emperors and prefects; for the rapacity which made them seek for pretexts by which they might confiscate the property of the wealthy; and for the alarm that was created by every attempt to discover the successor to the throne. We have positive evidence that one or other of these three causes was connected with most of the worst outbursts of persecution; and we know, from earlier history, that persecutions for magic had taken place on political as well as on religious grounds, long before Christianity had triumphed. We must not, again, measure the severity of the persecution by the precise language of the laws. If we looked simply at the written enactments, we should conclude that a considerable portion of the pagan worship was, at an early period, absolutely and universally suppressed. In practice, however, the law was constantly broken. A general laxity of administration had pervaded all parts of the empire, to an extent which the weakest modern governments have seldom exhibited. Popular prejudice ran counter to many of the enactments; and the rulers frequently connived at their infraction. We find, therefore, that the application of the penalties that were decreed was irregular, fitful, and uncertain. Sometimes they were enforced with extreme severity. Sometimes the forbidden rites were practised without disguise. Very frequently, in one part of the empire persecution raged fiercely, while in another part it was unknown. When, however, all these qualifying circumstances have been admitted, it remains clear that a series of

laws were directed against rites which were entirely innocuous, and which had been long universally practised, as parts
of the pagan worship, for the purpose of sapping the religion
from which they sprang. It is also clear that the ecclesiastical leaders all believed in the reality of magic; and that they
had vastly increased the popular sense of its enormity, by
attributing to all the pagan rites a magical character. Under
Theodosius, this phase of the history of magic terminated.
In the beginning of his reign, that emperor contented himself with reiterating the proclamations of his predecessors;
but he soon cast off all disguise, and prohibited, under the
severest penalties, every portion of the pagan worship.

Such was the policy pursued by the early Church towards
the magicians. It exercised in some respects a very important influence upon later history. In the first place, a mass
of tradition was formed which, in later ages, placed the
reality of the crime above the possibility of doubt. In the
second place, the nucleus of fact, around which the fables of
the inquisitors were accumulated, was considerably enlarged.
By a curious, but very natural transition, a great portion of
the old pagan worship passed from the sphere of religion into
that of magic. The country people continued, in secrecy
and danger, to practise the rites of their forefathers. They
were told that, by those rites, they were appealing to powerful and malicious spirits; and, after several generations, they
came to believe what they were told, without, however,
abandoning the practices that were condemned. It is easier
for superstitious men, in a superstitious age, to change all the
notions that are associated with their rites, than to free their
minds from their influence. Religions never truly perish,
except by a natural decay. In the towns, paganism had
arrived at the last stage of decrepitude, when Christianity

arose ; and, therefore, in the towns, the victory of Christianity
was prompt and decisive ; but, in the country, paganism still
retained its vigour, and defied all the efforts of priests and
magistrates to eradicate it.   The invasion of the barbarians
still further strengthened the pagan element, and at last a
kind of compromise was effected.   Paganism, as a distinct
system, was annihilated, but its different elements continued
to exist in a transfigured form, and under new names.   Many
portions of the system were absorbed by the new faith.
They coalesced with the doctrines to which they bore most
resemblance, gave those doctrines an extraordinary prominence in the Christian system, and rendered them peculiarly acceptable and influential.   Antiquarians have long
since shown that, in almost every part of the Roman Catholic faith, the traces of this amalgamation may be detected.
Another portion of paganism became a kind of excrescence
upon recognised Christianity.   It assumed the form of innumerable superstitious rites, which occupied an equivocal
position, sometimes countenanced, and sometimes condemned, hovering upon the verge of the faith, associated and
intertwined with authorised religious practices, occasionally
censured by councils, and habitually encouraged by the more
ignorant ecclesiastics, and frequently attracting a more intense devotion than the regular ceremonies with which they
were allied.[1]   A third portion continued in the form of
magical rites, which were practised in defiance of persecution and anathemas, and which continued, after the nominal
suppression of paganism, for nearly eight centuries.[2]   These
rites, of course, only form *one* element, and perhaps not a

---

[1] Many hundreds of these superstitions are examined by Thiers.   A great
number also are given in Scott's *Discovery of Witchcraft.*

[2] Michelet, *La Sorcière,* p. 36, note.   See also Maury.

very prominent one, in the system of witchcraft; but any analysis which omitted to notice them would be imperfect. All those grotesque ceremonies which Shakspeare portrayed in *Macbeth* were taken from the old paganism. In numerous descriptions of the witches' sabbath, Diana and Herodias are mentioned together, as the two most prominent figures; and among the articles of accusation brought against witches, we find enumerated many of the old practices of the augurs.

In the sixth century, the victory of Christianity over paganism, considered as an external system, and the corruption of Christianity itself, were both complete; and what are justly termed the dark ages may be said to have begun. It seems, at first sight, a somewhat strange and anomalous fact that, during the period which elapsed between the sixth and thirteenth centuries, when superstitions were most numerous, and credulity most universal, the executions for sorcery should have been comparatively rare. There never had been a time, in which the minds of men were more completely imbued and moulded by supernatural conceptions; or in which the sense of Satanic power and Satanic presence was more profound and universal. Many thousands of cases of possession, exorcisms, miracles, and apparitions of the Evil One were recorded. They were accepted without the faintest doubt, and had become the habitual field upon which the imagination expatiated. There was scarcely a great saint who had not, on some occasion, encountered a visible manifestation of an evil spirit. Sometimes the devil appeared as a grotesque and hideous animal, sometimes as a black man, sometimes as a beautiful woman, sometimes as a priest haranguing in the pulpit, sometimes as an angel of

light, and sometimes in a still holier form.[1] Yet, strange as
it may now appear, these conceptions, though intensely
believed and intensely realised, did not create any great
degree of terrorism. The very multiplication of superstitions had proved their corrective. It was firmly believed
that the arch-fiend was for ever hovering about the Christian; but it was also believed that the sign of the cross, or a
few drops of holy water, or the name of Mary, could put him
to an immediate and ignominious flight. The lives of the
saints were crowded with his devices, but they represent
him as uniformly vanquished, humbled, and contemned.
Satan himself, at the command of Cyprian, had again and
again assailed an unarmed and ignorant maiden, who had
devoted herself to religion. He had exhausted all the powers
of sophistry in obscuring the virtue of virginity, and all the
resources of archangelic eloquence in favour of a young and
noble pagan who aspired to the maiden's hand; but the
simple sign of the cross exposed every sophism, quenched
every emotion of terrestrial love, and drove back the fiend,
baffled and dismayed, to the magician who had sent him.[2]
Legions of devils, drawn up in ghastly array, surrounded the
church towards which St. Maur was moving, and obstructed,
with menacing gestures, the progress of the saint; but a few
words of exorcism scattered them in a moment through the
air. A ponderous stone was long shown, in the Church of
St. Sabina at Rome, which the devil, in a moment of despair-

---

[1] On the appearances of the devil in the form of Christ, see the tract by
Gerson in the *Malleus Malef.*, vol. ii. p. 77 ; and also Ignatius Lupus, *in Edict.
S. Inquisitionis* (1603), p. 185.

[2] See this story very amusingly told, on the authority of Nicephorus, in
Binsfeldius *de Confessionibus Maleficorum* (Trèves, 1591), pp. 465–467. St.
Gregory Nazianzen mentions (Oration xviii.) that St. Cyprian had been a
magician.

ing passion, had flung at St. Dominick, vainly hoping to crush a head that was sheltered by the guardian angel. The Gospel of St. John suspended around the neck, a rosary, a relic of Christ or of a saint, any one of the thousand talismans that were distributed among the faithful, sufficed to baffle the utmost efforts of diabolical malice. The consequence of this teaching was a condition of thought, which is so far removed from that which exists in the present day, that it is only by a strong exertion of the imagination that we can conceive it. What may be called the intellectual basis of witchcraft, existed to the fullest extent. All those conceptions of diabolical presence, all that predisposition towards the miraculous, which acted so fearfully upon the imaginations of the fifteenth and sixteenth centuries, existed; but the implicit faith, the boundless and triumphant credulity with which the virtue of ecclesiastical rites was accepted, rendered them comparatively innocuous. If men had been a little less superstitious, the effects of their superstition would have been much more terrible. It was firmly believed that any one who deviated from the strict line of orthodoxy must soon succumb beneath the power of Satan ; but as there was no spirit of rebellion or of doubt, this persuasion did not produce any extraordinary terrorism.

Amid all this strange teaching, there ran, however, one vein of a darker character. The more terrible phenomena of nature were entirely unmoved by exorcisms and sprinklings, and they were invariably attributed to supernatural interposition. In every nation it has been believed, at an early period, that pestilences, famines, comets, rainbows, eclipses, and other rare and startling phenomena, were effected, not by the ordinary sequence of natural laws, but by the direct intervention of spirits. In this manner, the predisposition towards the miraculous, which is the characteristic of all semi-civilised nations, has been perpetuated, and the clergy have also frequently identified these phenomena with acts of rebellion against themselves. The old Catholic priests were consummate masters of these arts, and every rare natural event was, in the middle ages, an occasion for the most intense terrorism. Thus, in the eighth century, a fearful famine afflicted France, and was generally represented as a consequence of the repugnance which the French people manifested to the payment of tithes.[1] In the ninth century, a total eclipse of the sun struck terror through Europe, and is said to have been one of the causes of the death of a French king.[2] In the tenth century a similar phenomenon put to flight an entire army.[3] More than once, the apparition of a comet filled Europe with an almost maddening terror; and, whenever a noted person was struck down by sudden illness, the death was attributed to sorcery.

The natural result, I think, of such modes of thought would be, that the notion of sorcery should be very common, but that the fear of it should not pass into an absolute mania. Credulity was habitual and universal, but religious terrorism was fitful and transient. We need not, therefore, be surprised that sorcery, though very familiar to the minds of men, did not, at the period I am referring to, occupy that prominent position which it afterwards assumed. The idea of a formal compact with the devil had not yet been formed; but most of the crimes of witchcraft were recognised, anathematised, and punished. Thus, towards the end of the sixth century, a son of Fredegonda died after a short illness; and

---

[1] Garinet, p. 38. [2] Ibid. p. 42.
[3] Buckle's *Hist.* vol. i. p. 345 (note), where an immense amount of evidence on the subject is given.

numbers of women were put to the most prolonged and
excruciating torments, and at last burnt or broken on the
wheel, for having caused, by incantations, the death of the
prince.[1] In Germany, the *Codex de Mathematicis et Male-
ficiis*[2] long continued in force, as did the old Salic law on
the same subject in France. Charlemagne enacted new and
very stringent laws, condemning sorcerers to death, and
great numbers seem to have perished in his reign.[3] Hail
and thunderstorms were almost universally attributed to
their devices, though one great ecclesiastic of the ninth
century—Agobard, archbishop of Lyons—had the rare merit
of opposing the popular belief.[4]

There existed, too, all through the middle ages, and even
as late as the seventeenth century, the sect of the Cabalists,
who were especially persecuted as magicians. It is not easy
to obtain any very clear notion of their mystic doctrines,
which long exercised an extraordinary fascination over many
minds, and which captivated the powerful and daring intellects of Cardan, Agrippa, and Paracelsus. They seem to
have comprised many traditions that had been long current
among the Jews, mixed with much of the old Platonic
doctrine of demons, and with a large measure of pure naturalism. With a degree of credulity, which, in our age,
would be deemed barely compatible with sanity, but which
was then perfectly natural, was combined some singularly

[1] Garinet, pp. 14, 15.
[2] This was the title of the Roman code I have reviewed. Mathematicus
was the name given to astrologers: as a law of Diocletian put it, 'Artem geo-
metriæ disci atque exerceri publice interest. Ars autem mathematica damna-
b lis est et interdicta omnino.'
[3] Garinet, p. 39.
[4] Garinet, p. 45. He also saved the lives of some Cabalists. He was unfortunately one of the chief persecutors of the Jews in his time. Bedarride,
Hist. des Juifs, pp. 83, 87.

bold scepticism; and, probably, a greater amount was veiled under the form of allegories than was actually avowed. The Cabalists believed in the existence of spirits of nature, embodiments or representatives of the four elements, sylphs, salamanders, gnomes, and ondines, beings of far more than human excellence, but mortal, and not untinctured by human frailty. To rise to intercourse with these elemental spirits of nature was the highest aim of the philosopher. He who would do so, must sever himself from the common course of life. He must purify his soul by fasting and celibacy, by patient and unwearied study, by deep communion with nature and with nature's laws. He must learn, above all, to look down with contempt upon the angry quarrels of opposing creeds; to see in each religion an aspect of a continuous law, a new phase and manifestation of the action of the spirits of nature upon mankind.

It is not difficult to detect the conception which underlies this teaching. As, however, no religious doctrine can resist the conditions of the age, these simple notions were soon encrusted and defaced by so many of those grotesque and material details, which invariably resulted from mediæval habits of thought, that it is only by a careful examination that their outlines can be traced. It was believed that it was possible for philosophers to obtain these spirits in literal marriage; and that such a union was the most passionate desire of the spirit-world. It was not only highly gratifying for both parties in this world, but greatly improved their prospects for the next. The sylph, though she lived for many centuries, was mortal, and had in herself no hope of a future life; but her human husband imparted to her his own immortality, unless he was one of the reprobate, in which case he was saved from the pangs of hell by participating in the mortality of his bride. This general conception was elaborated in great detail, and was applied to the history of the Fall, and to the mythology of paganism, on both of which subjects the orthodox tenets were indignantly spurned. Scarcely any one seems to have doubted the reality of these spirits, or that they were accustomed to reveal themselves to mankind; and the coruscations of Aurora are said to have been attributed to the flashings of their wings.[1] The only question was, concerning their nature. According to the Cabalists, they were pure and virtuous. According to the orthodox, they were the incubi who were spoken of by St. Augustine; and all who had commerce with them were deservedly burnt.[2]

The history of the Cabalists furnishes, I think, a striking instance of the aberrations of a spirit of free-thinking in an age which was not yet ripe for its reception. When the very opponents of the Church were so completely carried away by the tide, and were engrossed with a mythological system as absurd as the wildest legends of the hagiology, it is not at all surprising that the philosophers who arose in the ranks of orthodoxy should have been extremely credulous, and that their conceptions should have been characterised by the

[1] Garinet, p. 35. This, however, is doubtful. Herder mentions that the Greenlanders believe the Aurora to be formed by spirits dancing and playing ball.

[2] On the Hebrew Cabala, see the learned work of M. Franck, and on the notions in the middle ages, and in the sixteenth and seventeenth centuries, *Le Comte de Gabalis*. Plancey, *Dict. Infernale*, art. *Cabale*. All the heathen gods were supposed to be sylphs or other aërial spirits. Vesta was the wife of Noah—Zoroaster, her son, otherwise called Japhet. The sin of Adam was deserting the sylph for his wife, and the story of the apple was allegorical, &c. This last notion appears to have been a relic of Manichæism, and was very common among the heretics of the tenth and eleventh centuries (Matter, *Hist. du Gnosticisme*, tom. iii. pp. 259, 260). Paracelsus was one of the principal asserters of the existence of the sylphs, &c.

coarsest materialism. Among the very few men who, in
some slight degree, cultivated profane literature during the
period I am referring to, a prominent place must be assigned
to Michael Psellus. This voluminous author, though he is
now, I imagine, very little read, still retains a certain position in literary history, as almost the only Byzantine writer
of reputation who appeared for some centuries. Towards
the close of the eleventh century he wrote his dialogue on
'The Operation of Demons;' which is, in a great measure,
an exposition of the old Neo-Platonic doctrine of the hierarchy of spirits, but which also throws considerable light on
the modes of thought prevailing in his time. He assures us
that the world was full of demons, who were very frequently
appearing among his countrymen, and who manifested their
presence in many different ways. He had himself never seen
one, but he was well acquainted with persons who had actual intercourse with them. His principal authority was a
Grecian, named Marcus, who had at one time disbelieved in
apparitions; but who, having adopted a perfectly solitary
life, had been surrounded by spirits whose habits and appearance he most minutely described. Having thus amassed
considerable information on the subject, Psellus proceeded
to digest it into a philosophical system, connecting it with
the teachings of the past, and unfolding the laws and operations of the spirit world. He lays it down as a fundamental
position that all demons have bodies. This, he says, is the
necessary inference from the orthodox doctrine that they endure the torment of fire.[1] Their bodies, however, are not,
like those of men and animals, cast into an unchangeable
mould. They are rather like the clouds, refined and subtle

---

[1] This was a very old notion. St. Basil seems to have maintained it very
strongly. Cudworth's *Int. System*, vol. ii. p. 648.

matter, capable of assuming any form, and penetrating into any orifice. The horrible tortures they endure in their place of punishment have rendered them extremely sensitive to suffering; and they continually seek a temperate and somewhat moist warmth in order to allay their pangs. It is for this reason that they so frequently enter into men and animals. Possession appears to have been quite frequent, and madness was generally regarded as one of its results. Psellus, however, mentions that some physicians formed an exception to the prevailing opinions, attributing to physical what was generally attributed to spiritual causes, an aberration which he could only account for by the materialism which was so general in their profession. He mentions incidentally the exploits of incubi as not unknown, and enters into a long disquisition about a devil who was said to be acquainted with Armenian.

We find then that, all through the middle ages, most of the crimes that were afterwards collected by the inquisitors in the treatises on witchcraft were known; and that many of them were not unfrequently punished. At the same time the executions, during six centuries, were probably not as numerous as those which often took place during a single decade of the fifteenth and sixteenth centuries. In the twelfth century, however, the subject passed into an entirely new phase. The conception of a witch, as we now conceive it—that is to say, of a woman who had entered into a deliberate compact with Satan, who was endowed with the power of working miracles whenever she pleased, and who was continually transported through the air to the Sabbath, where she paid her homage to the Evil One—first appeared.[1] The

---

[1] Maury, p. 185.

panic created by the belief advanced at first slowly, but after a time with a fearfully accelerated rapidity. Thousands of victims were sometimes burnt alive in a few years. Every country in Europe was stricken with the wildest panic. Hundreds of the ablest judges were selected for the extirpation of the crime. A vast literature was created on the subject, and it was not until a considerable portion of the eighteenth century had passed away, that the executions finally ceased.[1]

I shall now endeavour to trace the general causes which produced this outburst of superstition. We shall find, I think, that in this as in its earlier phases, sorcery was closely connected with the prevailing modes of thought on religious subjects; and that its history is one of the most faithful indications of the laws of religious belief in their relation to the progress of civilisation.

The more carefully the history of the centuries prior to the Reformation is studied, the more evident it becomes that the twelfth century forms the great turning point of the European intellect. Owing to many complicated causes, which it would be tedious and difficult to trace, a general revival of Latin literature had then taken place, which profoundly modified the intellectual condition of Europe, and which, therefore, implied and necessitated a modification of the popular belief. For the first time for many centuries, we find a feeble spirit of doubt combating the spirit of credulity; a curiosity for purely secular knowledge replacing, in some small degree, the passion for theology; and, as a consequence of these things, a diminution of the contemptuous

---

[1] The last judicial execution in Europe was, I believe, in Switzerland, in 1782 (Michelet's *Sorcière*, p. 415); the last law on the subject, the Irish Statute which was not repealed till 1821.

hatred with which all who were external to Christianity had been regarded. In every department of thought and of knowledge, there was manifested a vague disquietude, a spirit of restless and feverish anxiety, that contrasted strangely with the preceding torpor. The long slumber of untroubled orthodoxy was broken by many heresies, which, though often repressed, seemed in each succeeding century to acquire new force and consistency. Manichæism, which had for some time been smouldering in the Church, burst into a fierce flame among the Albigenses, and was only quenched by that fearful massacre in which tens of thousands were murdered at the instigation of the priests. Then it was that the standard of an impartial philosophy was first planted by Abelard in Europe, and the minds of the learned distracted by subtle and perplexing doubts concerning the leading doctrines of the faith. Then, too, the teachings of a stern and uncompromising infidelity flashed forth from Seville and from Cordova; and the form of Averroes began to assume those gigantic proportions, which, at a later period, overshadowed the whole intellect of Europe, and almost persuaded some of the ablest men that the reign of Antichrist had begun.[1] At the same time, the passion for astrology, and for the fatalism it implied, revived with the revival of

---

[1] For the history of this very remarkable movement, see the able essay of Renan on Averroes. Among the Mahometans the panic was so great, that the theologians pronounced logic and philosophy to be the two great enemies of their profession, and ordered all books on those dangerous subjects to be burnt. Among the Christians, St. Thomas Aquinas devoted his genius to the controversy; and, for two or three centuries, most of the great works in Christendom bore some marks of Averroes. M. Renan has collected some curious evidence from the Italian painters of the fourteenth century, of the prominence Averroes had assumed in the popular mind. The three principal figures in Orcagna's picture of Hell, in the Campo Santo at Pisa, are Mahomet, Antichrist, and Averroes.

pagan learning, and penetrated into the halls of nobles and the palaces of kings. Every doubt, every impulse of rebellion against ecclesiastical authority, above all, every heretical opinion, was regarded as the direct instigation of Satan, and their increase as the measure of his triumph. Yet these things were now gathering darkly all around. Europe was beginning to enter into that inexpressibly painful period in which men have learned to doubt, but have not yet learned to regard doubt as innocent; in which the new mental activity produces a variety of opinions, while the old credulity persuades them that all but one class of opinions are the suggestions of the devil. The spirit of rationalism was yet unborn; or if some faint traces of it may be discovered in the teachings of Abelard, it was at least far too weak to allay the panic. There was no independent enquiry; no confidence in an honest research; no disposition to rise above dogmatic systems or traditional teaching; no capacity for enduring the sufferings of a suspended judgment. The Church had cursed the human intellect by cursing the doubts that are the necessary consequence of its exercise. She had cursed even the moral faculty by asserting the guilt of honest error.

It is easy to perceive that, in such a state of thought, the conception of Satanic presence must have assumed a peculiar prominence, and have created a peculiar terror. Multitudes were distracted by doubts, which they sought in vain to re press, and which they firmly believed to be the suggestions of the devil. Their horror of pagans and Mahometans diminished more and more, as they acquired a relish for the philosophy of which the first, or the physical sciences of which the second were the repositories. Every step in knowledge increased their repugnance to the coarse material ism which was prevalent, and every generation rendered the general intellectual tendencies more manifestly hostile to the Chuich. On the other hand, that Church presented an aspect of the sternest inflexibility. Rebellion and doubt were, in her eyes, the greatest of all crimes; and her doctrine of evil spirits and of the future world supplied her with engines of terrorism which she was prepared to employ to the uttermost. Accordingly we find that, about the twelfth century, the popular teaching began to assume a sterner and more solemn cast, and the devotions of the people to be more deeply tinctured by fanaticism. The old confidence which had almost toyed with Satan, and in the very exuberance of an unfaltering faith had mocked at his devices, was exchanged for a harsh and gloomy asceticism. The aspect of Satan became more formidable, and the aspect of Christ became less engaging. Till the close of the tenth century, the central figure of Christian art had been usually represented as a very young man, with an expression of untroubled gentleness and calm resting on his countenance, and engaged in miracles of mercy. The parable of the Good Shepherd, which adorns almost every chapel in the Catacombs, was still the favourite subject of the painter; and the sterner representations of Christianity were comparatively rare. In the eleventh century, all this began to change. The Good Shepherd entirely disappeared, the miracles of mercy became less frequent, and were replaced by the details of the Passion and the terrors of the Last Judgment. The countenance of Christ became sterner, older, and more mournful. About the twelfth century, this change became almost universal. From this period, writes one of the most learned of modern archæologists, 'Christ appears more and more melancholy, and often truly terrible.

It is, indeed, the rex tremendæ majestatis of oui Dies Iræ. It is almost the God of the Jews making fear the beginning of wisdom.'[1] In the same age, we find the scourgings and the 'minutio monachi'—the practice of constant bleedings— rising into general use in the monasteries;[2] and, soon after, the Flagellants arose, whose stern discipline and passionate laments over prevailing iniquity directed the thoughts of multitudes to subjects that were well calculated to inflame their imaginations. Almost at the same time, religious persecution, which had been for many centuries almost unknown, amid the calm of orthodoxy, was revived and stimulated. In the beginning of the thirteenth century, Innocent III. instituted the Inquisition, and issued the first appeal to princes to employ their power for the suppression of heresy; and, in the course of the following century, the new tribunal was introduced; or, at least, executions for heresy had taken place in several great countries in Europe.

The terrorism which was thus created by the conflict between an immutable Church and an age in which there was some slight progress, and a real, though faint spirit of rebellion, gradually filtered down to those who were far too ignorant to become heretics. The priest in the pulpit or in the confessional; the monk in his intercourse with the

[1] Didron, *Iconographie Chrétienne, Histoire de Dieu* (Paris, 1843), p. 262. See, however, for the whole history of this very remarkable transition, pp. 255-273. To this I may add, that about the thirteenth century, the representations of Satan underwent a corresponding change, and became both more terrible and more grotesque (Maury, *Légendes Pieuses*, p. 136). The more the subject is examined, the more evident it becomes that, before the invention of printing, painting was the most faithful mirror of the popular mind; and that there was scarcely an intellectual movement that it did not reflect. On the general terrorism of this period, see Michelet, *Histoire de France*, tom. vii. pp. 140, 141.

[2] Madden, vol. i. pp. 359-395· Cabanis, *Rapports Physiques et Morais* tom. ii. pp. 77-79.

peasant; the Flagellant, by his mournful hymns, and by the spectacle of his macerations; above all, the inquisitor, by his judgments, communicated to the lower classes a sense of Satanic presence and triumph, which they naturally applied to the order of ideas with which they were most conversant. Ir an age which was still grossly ignorant and credulous, the popular faith was necessarily full of grotesque superstitions, which faithfully reflected the general tone and colouring of religious teaching, though they often went far beyond its limits. These superstitions had once consisted, for the most part, in wild legends of fairies, mermaids, giants, and dragons; of miracles of saints, conflicts in which the devil took a prominent part, but was invariably defeated, or illustrations of the boundless efficacy of some charm or relic. About the twelfth century they began to assume a darker hue, and the imaginations of the people revelled in the details of the witches' Sabbath, and in the awful power of the ministers of Satan. The inquisitors traversed Europe, proclaiming that the devil was operating actively on all sides; and among their very first victims were persons who were accused of sorcery, and who were, of course, condemned.[1] Such condemnations could not make the belief in the reality of the crime more unhesitating than it had been, but they had a direct tendency to multiply the accusations. The imaginations of the people were riveted upon the subject. A contagious terror was engendered. Some, whose minds were thoroughly diseased, persuaded themselves that they were in communion with Satan; all had an increasing predispositior t: see Satanic agency around them.

To these things should be added a long series of social and political events, into wh'ch it is needless to enter, for

[1] Garinet, p. 75.

they have very lately been painted with matchless vividness by one of the greatest of living writers.[1] A sense of insecurity and wretchedness, often rising to absolute despair, had been diffused among the people, and had engendered the dark imaginations, and the wild and rebellious passions, which, in a superstitious age, are their necessary concomitants. It has always been observed by the inquisitors that a large proportion of those who were condemned to the flames were women, whose lives had been clouded by some great sorrow; and that music, which soothes the passions, and allays the bitterness of regret, had an extraordinary power over the possessed.[2]

Under the influences which I have attempted to trace, the notion of witchcraft was reduced to a more definite form, and acquired an increasing prominence in the twelfth and thirteenth centuries. Most of the causes that produced it advanced by their very nature with an accelerating force, and the popular imagination became more and more fascinated by the subject. In the fourteenth century, an event occurred which was well calculated to give a fearful impulse to the terrorism; and which may, indeed, be justly regarded as one of the most appalling in the history of humanity. I allude, of course, to the black death. A great German physician has lately investigated, with much skill and learning, the history of that time; and he has recorded his opinion that, putting aside all exaggerated accounts, the number of those who died of the pestilence during the six years of its continuance, may be estimated, by a very moderate computation, at twenty-five millions, or a fourth part of the inhabitants of Europe.[3] Many great towns lost far more than half

<hr>

[1] Michelet, *La Sorcière.*   [2] Binsfeldius, p. 155.

[3] Hecker's *Epidemics of the Middle Ages*, p. 29. Boccaccio witnessed and described this pestilence.

their population; many country districts were almost de-populated.

It would be scarcely possible to conceive an event fitted to act with a more terrific force upon the imaginations of men. Even in our own day, we know how great a degree of religious terror is inspired by a pestilence; but, in an age when the supernatural character of disease was universally believed, an affliction of such unexampled magnitude produced a consternation which almost amounted to madness. One of its first effects was an enormous increase of the wealth of the clergy by the legacies of the terror-stricken victims. The sect of the Flagellants, which had been for a century unknown, reappeared in tenfold numbers, and almost every part of Europe resounded with their hymns. Then, too, arose the dancing mania of Flanders and Germany, when thousands assembled with strange cries and gestures, overawing by their multitudes all authority, and proclaiming, amid their wild dances and with shrieks of terror, the power and the triumph of Satan.[1] It has been observed that this form of madness raged with an especial violence in the dioceses of Cologne and Trèves, in which witchcraft was afterwards most prevalent.[2] In Switzerland and in some parts of Germany the plague was ascribed to the poison of the Jews; and though the Pope made a noble effort to dispel the illusion, immense numbers of that unhappy race were put to death. Some thousands are said to have perished in Mayence alone More generally, it was regarded as a divine chastisement, or as an evidence of Satanic power; and the most grotesque

---

[1] Hecker, p. 82. The dancers often imagined themselves to be immersed in a stream of blood. They were habitually exorcised.

[2] There is still an annual festival near Trèves in commemoration of the epidemic. Madden, vol. i. p. 420.

explanations were hazarded.   Boots with pointed toes had
been lately introduced, and were supposed by many to have
been peculiarly offensive to the Almighty.[1]   What, however,
we have especially to observe is, that the trials for witchcraft
multiplied with a fearful rapidity.[2]

In the fifteenth and sixteenth centuries they may be said
to have reached their climax.   The aspect which Europe
then presented was that of universal anarchy and universal
terrorism.   The intellectual influences which had been long
corroding the pillars of the Church had done their work,
and a fearful moral retrogression, aggravated by the newly-
acquired ecclesiastical wealth, accompanied the intellectual
advance.   Yet, over all this chaos, there was one great conception dominating unchanged.   It was the sense of sin and
Satan; of the absolute necessity of a correct dogmatic system to save men from the agonies of hell.   The Church,
which had long been all in all to Christendom, was heaving
in what seemed the last throes of dissolution.   The bounda-
ries of religious thought were all obscured.   Conflicting
tendencies and passions were raging with a tempestuous violence, among men who were absolutely incapable of enduring
an intellectual suspense, and each of the opposing sects proclaimed its distinctive doctrines essential to salvation.
Doubt was almost universally regarded as criminal, and

---

[1] Hecker, p. 82.

[2] Ennemoser, *Hist. of Magic*, vol. ii. p. 150.

I may here notice, by way of illustration, two facts in the history of art.
The first is, that those ghastly pictures of the dance of death, which were afterwards so popular, and which represented an imaginative bias of such a wild
and morbid power, began in the fourteenth century (*Peignot sur les Danses des
Morts*, pp. 26–31).   The second is, that in this same century the bas-reliefs on
cathedrals frequently represent men kneeling down before the devil, and
devoting themselves to him as his servants (Martonne, *Piété du Moyen Age*,
p. 137).

error as damnable; yet the first was the necessary condition, and the second the probable consequence, of enquiry. To tally unaccustomed to independent reasoning, bewildered by the vast and undefined fields of thought from which the opposing arguments were drawn; with a profound sense of the absolute necessity of a correct creed, and of the constant action of Satan upon the fluctuations of the will and of the judgment; distracted and convulsed by colliding sentiments, which an unenlightened psychology attributed to spiritual inspiration, and, above all, parched with a burning longing for certainty; the minds of men drifted to and fro under the influence of the wildest terror. None could escape the movement. It filled all Europe with alarm, permeated with its influence all forms of thought and action, absorbed every element of national life into its ever-widening vortex.

There certainly never has been a movement which, in its ultimate results, has contributed so largely to the emancipation of the human mind from all superstitious terrors as the Reformation. It formed a multitude of churches, in which the spirit of qualified and partial scepticism that had long been a source of anarchy, might expatiate with freedom, and be allied with the spirit of order. It rejected an immense proportion of the dogmatic and ritualistic conceptions that had almost covered the whole field of religion, and rendered possible that steady movement by which theology has since then been gravitating towards the moral faculty. It, above all, diminished the prominence of the clergy, and thus prepared the way for that general secularisation of the European intellect, which is such a marked characteristic of modern civilisation. Yet, inappreciably great as are these blessings, it would be idle to deny that, for a time, the Reformation aggravated the very evils it was intended to correct. It was, for a time, merely an exchange of masters. The Protestant asserted the necessity and the certainty of his distinctive doctrines, as dogmatically and authoritatively as the Catholic. He believed in his own infallibility quite as firmly as his opponent believed in the infallibility of the Pope. It is only by a very slow process that the human mind can emerge from a system of error; and the virtue of dogmas had been so ingrained in all religious thought, by the teaching of more than twelve centuries, that it required a long and painful discipline to weaken what is not yet destroyed. The nature of truth, the limits of human faculties, the laws of probabilities, and the conditions that are essential for an impartial research, were subjects with which even the most advanced minds were then entirely unfamiliar. There was, indeed, much cultivation of logic, considered in its most narrow sense; but there was no such thing as a comprehensive view of the whole field of mental science, of the laws and limits of the reason. There was also no conviction that the reason should be applied to every department of theology, with the same unflinching severity as to any other form of speculation. Faith always presented to the mind the idea of an abnormal intellectual condition, of the subversion or suspension of the critical faculties. It sometimes comprised more than this, but it always included this. It was the opposite of doubt and of the spirit of doubt. What irreverent men called credulity, reverent men called faith; and although one word was more respectful than the other, yet the two words were with most men strictly synonymous. Some of the Protestants added other and moral ideas to the word, but they firmly retained the intellectual idea. As long as such a conception existed, a period of religious convulsion was necessarily a period of extreme suffering and terror; and there can be little doubt that the Reformation was, in consequence, the most painful of all the transitions through which the human intellect has passed.

If the reader has seized the spirit of the foregoing re marks, he will already have perceived their application to the history of witchcraft. In order that men should believe n witches, their intellects must have been familiarised with the conceptions of Satanic power and Satanic presence, and they must regard these things with an unfaltering belief. In order that witchcraft should be prominent, the imaginations of men must have been so forcibly directed to these articles of belief, as to tinge and govern the habitual current of their thoughts, and to produce a strong disposition to see Satanic agency around them. A long train of circumstances, which culminated in the Reformation, had diffused through Christendom a religious terror which gradually overcast the horizon of thought, creating a general uneasiness as to the future of the Church, and an intense and vivid sense of Satanic presence. These influences were, it is true, primarily connected with abstruse points of speculative belief, but they acted in a twofold manner upon the grosser superstitions of the people. Although the illiterate cannot follow the more intricate speculations of their teachers, they can, as I have said, catch the general tone and character of thought which these speculations produce, and they readily apply them to their own sphere of thought. Besides this, the upper classes, being filled with a sense of Satanic presence, will be disposed to believe in the reality of any history of witchcraft. They will, therefore, prosecute the witches, and, as a necessary consequence, stimulate the delusion. When the belief is confined to the lower class, its existence will be languishing and unprogressive. But when legislators denounce it in

6

their laws, and popes in their bulls; when priests inveigh
against it in their pulpits, and inquisitors burn thousands at
the stake, the imaginations of men will be inflamed, the terror will prove contagious, and the consequent delusions be
multiplied. Now, popes and legislators, priests and inquisi
tors, will do these things just in proportion to the firmness
of their belief in the conceptions I have noticed, and to the
intensity with which their imaginations have been directed
to those conceptions by religious terrorism.

We have a striking illustration of the influence upon
witchcraft of the modes of thought which the Reformation
for a time sustained in the life of Luther. No single feature
was more clearly marked in his character than an intense and
passionate sense of sin. He himself often described, in the
most graphic language, how, in the seclusion of his monastery
at Wittenberg, he had passed under the very shadow of
death, how the gates of hell seemed to open beneath his feet,
and the sense of hopeless wretchedness to make life itself a
burden. While oppressed by the keenest sense of moral un-
worthiness, he was distracted by intellectual doubt. He only
arrived at the doctrines of Protestantism after a long and difficult enquiry, struggling slowly through successive phases
of belief, uncheered for many years by one word of sympathy, and oscillating painfully between opposing conclusions. Like all men of vivid imagination who are so circum-
stanced, a theological atmosphere was formed about his
mind, and became the medium through which every event
was contemplated. He was subject to numerous strange
hallucinations and vibrations of judgment, which he invariably attributed to the direct action of Satan. Satan became, in consequence, the dominating conception of his life.
In every critical event, in every mental perturbation, he re

cognised Satanic power.   In the monastery of Wittenberg,
he constantly heard the Devil making a noise in the cloisters;
and became at last so accustomed to the fact, that he related
that, on one occasion, having been awakened by the sound,
he perceived that it was *only* the Devil, and accordingly
went to sleep again.   The black stain in the castle of Wart-
burg still marks the place where he flung an ink-bottle at
the Devil.   In the midst of his long and painful hesitation on
the subject of transubstantiation, the Devil appeared to him,
and suggested a new argument.   In such a state of mind, he
naturally accepted, with implicit faith, every anecdote of
Satanic miracles.   He told how an aged minister had been
interrupted, in the midst of his devotions, by a devil who
was grunting behind him like a pig.   At Torgau, the Devil
broke pots and basins, and flung them at the minister's head,
and at last drove the minister's wife and servants half crazy
out of the house.   On another occasion, the Devil appeared
in the law courts, in the character of a leading barrister,
whose place he is said to have filled with the utmost propriety.   Fools, deformed persons, the blind and the dumb,
were possessed by devils.   Physicians, indeed, attempted to
explain these infirmities by natural causes; but those physicians were ignorant men; they did not know all the power
of Satan.   Every form of disease might be produced by
Satan, or by his agents, the witches; and none of the infirmities to which Luther was liable were natural, but his ear-ache
was peculiarly diabolical.   Hail, thunder, and plagues are all
the direct consequences of the intervention of spirits.   Many
of those persons who were supposed to have committed sui-
cide, had in reality been seized by the Devil and strangled by
him, as the traveller is strangled by the robber.   The Devil
could transport men at his will through the air.   He could be-

get children, and Luther had himself come in contact with one
of them. An intense love of children was one of the most
amiable characteristics of the great Reformer; but, on this
occasion, he most earnestly recommended the reputed rela-
tives to throw the child into a river, in order to free their
house from the presence of a devil. As a natural consequence of these modes of thought, witchcraft did not present
the slightest improbability to his mind. In strict accordance
with the spirit of his age, he continually asserted the existence
and frequency of the crime, and emphatically proclaimed the
duty of burning the witches.

I know, indeed, few stranger, and at the same time more
terrible pictures, than are furnished by the history of witchcraft during the century that preceded and the century that
followed the Reformation. Wherever the conflict of opinions
was raging among the educated, witchcraft, like an attendant
shadow, pursued its course among the ignorant;[1] and Protestants and Catholics vied with each other in the zeal with
which they prosecuted it. Never was the power of imagination—that strange faculty which casts the shadow of its
images over the whole creation, and combines all the phenomena of life according to its own archetypes—more strikingly evinced. Superstitious and terror-stricken, the minds of
men were impelled irresistibly towards the miraculous and
the Satanic, and they found them upon every side. The
elements of imposture blended so curiously with the elements
of delusion, that it is now impossible to separate them.
Sometimes an ambitious woman, braving the dangers of her

---

[1] *Colloquia Mensalia.* Erasmus was an equally firm believer in witchcraft.
(Stewart's *Dissertation*, p 57.)

[2] This coexistence has been noticed by many writers; and Naudé (*Apologie*
pp. 110, 111) observes, that nearly all the heresies previous to the Reformation
had been also accompanied by an outburst of sorcery.

act, boldly claimed supernatural power, and the haughtiest and the most courageous cowered humbly at her presence. Sometimes a husband attempted, in the witch courts, to cut the tie which his church had pronounced indissoluble; and numbers of wives have, in consequence, perished at the stake. Sometimes a dexterous criminal availed himself of the panic; and, directing a charge of witchcraft against his accuser, escaped himself with impunity. Sometimes, too, a personal grudge was avenged by the accusation, or a real crime was attributed to sorcery; or a hail-storm, or a strange disease, suggested the presence of a witch. But, for the most part, the trials represent pure and unmingled delusions. The defenders of the belief were able to maintain that multitudes had voluntarily confessed themselves guilty of commerce with the Evil One, and had persisted in their confessions till death. Madness is always peculiarly frequent during great religious or political revolutions;[1] and, in the sixteenth century, all its forms were absorbed in the system of witchcraft, and caught the colour of the prevailing predisposition.[2] Occasionally, too, we find old and half-doting women, at first convinced of their innocence, but soon faltering before the majesty of justice, asking timidly whether it is possible to be in connection with the Devil without being conscious of the fact, and at last almost persuading themselves that they had done what was alleged. Very often, the terror of the trial, the prospect of the most agonising of deaths, and the frightful tortures that were applied to the weak frame of an old and feeble woman,[3] overpowered her understanding;

[1] Buckle's *Hist.*, vol. i. p. 424, *note.*   [2] Calmeil.

[3] For a frightful catalogue of the tortures that were employed in these cases, see Scott's *Discovery of Witchcraft* (London, 1665), pp. 11, 12. All the old treatises are full of the subject. Sprenger recommends the tortures to be continued two or three days, till the prisoner was, as he expresses it, ' decenter

her brain reeled beneath the accumulated suffering, the con sciousness of innocence disappeared, and the wretched victim went raving to the flames, convinced that she was about to sink for ever into perdition. The zeal of the ecclesiastics in stimulating the persecution was unflagging. It was displayed alike in Germany, France, Spain, Italy, Flanders, Sweden, England, Scotland, and Ireland. An old writer who cordialʹy approved of the rigour tells us that, in the province of Como alone, eight or ten inquisitors were constantly employed; and he adds that, in one year, the number of persons they condemned amounted to a thousand; and that during several of the succeeding years, the victims seldom fell below one hundred.[1]

It was natural that a body of learned men like the inquisitors, whose habits of thought were eminently retrospective, should have formed some general theories connecting the phenomena of sorcery with past events, and reducing them to a systematic form. We accordingly find that, in the course of about three centuries, a vast literature was formed upon the subject. The different forms of witchcraft were all carefully classified and associated with particular doctrines; the whole philosophy of the Satanic was minutely investigated, and the prevailing mode of thought embodied in countless treatises, which were once regarded as masterpieces of orthodox theology.

It is very difficult for us in the present day to do justice to these works, or to realise the points of view from which they were written. A profound scepticism on all subjects

---

quæstionatus' (Pars iii. Quæst. 14, 15). The tortures were all the more horrible, because it was generally believed that the witches had charms to deaden their effect.

[1] Spina, cap. xii.

connected with the Devil underlies the opinions of almost
every educated man, and renders it difficult even to conceive
a condition of thought in which that spirit was the object of
an intense and realised belief. An anecdote which involves
the personal intervention of Satan is now regarded as quite
as intrinsically absurd, and unworthy of serious attention,
as an anecdote of a fairy or of a sylph. When, therefore, a
modern reader turns over the pages of an old treatise on
witchcraft, and finds hundreds of such anecdotes related with
the gravest assurance, he is often inclined to depreciate very
unduly the intellect of an author who represents a condition
of thought so unlike his own. The cold indifference to
human suffering which these writers display gives an additional bias to his reason; while their extraordinary pedantry,
their execrable Latin, and their gross scientific blunders, furnish ample materials for his ridicule. Besides this, Sprenger,
who is at once the most celebrated, and, perhaps, the most
credulous member of his class, unfortunately for his reputation, made some ambitious excursions into another field, and
immortalised himself by a series of etymological blunders,
which have been the delight of all succeeding scholars.[1]

But when all these qualifications have been made—and,
with the exception of the last, they would all apply to any
other writings of the same period—it is, I think, impossible

---

[1] 'Fœmina,' he assures us, is derived from Fe and minus, because women
have less faith than men (p. 65). Maleficiendo is from male de fides entiendo.
For diabolus we have a choice of most instructive derivations. It comes ' a
dia quod est duo, et bolus quod est morsellus, quia duo occidit, scilicet corpus
et animam. Et secundum etymologiam, licet Græce, interpretetur diabolus
clausus ergastulo: et hoc sibi convenit cum non permittitur sibi nocere quan-
tum veilet. Vel diabolus quasi defluens, quia defluxit, id est corruit, et spe-
cialiter et localiter' (p. 41). If the reader is curious in these matters, he will
find another astounding instance of verbal criticism, which I do not venture to
quote, in Bodin, *Dem.* p. 40.

to deny that the books in defence of the belief are not only far more numerous than the later works against it, but that they also represent far more learning, dialectic skill, and even general ability. For many centuries, the ablest men were not merely unwilling to repudiate the superstition; they often pressed forward earnestly, and with the most intense conviction, to defend it. Indeed, during the period when witchcraft was most prevalent, there were few writers of real eminence who did not, on some occasion, take especial pains to throw the weight of their authority into the scale. Thomas Aquinas was probably the ablest writer of the thirteenth century, and he assures us that diseases and tempests are the direct acts of the Devil; that the Devil can transport men at his pleasure through the air; and that he can transform them into any shape. Gerson, the Chancellor of the University of Paris, and, as many think, the author of 'The Imitation,' is justly regarded as one of the master-intellects of his age; and he, too, wrote in defence of the belief. Bodin was unquestionably the most original political philosopher who had arisen since Macchiavelli, and he devoted all his learning and acuteness to crushing the rising scepticism on the subject of witches. The truth is, that, in those ages, ability was no guarantee against error; because the single employment of the reason was to develop and expand premises that were furnished by the Church. There was no such thing as an uncompromising and unreserved criticism of the first principles of teaching; there was no such thing as a revolt of the reason against conclusions that were strictly drawn from the premises of authority. In our age, and in every other age of half belief, principles are often adopted without being fully developed. If a conclusion is drawn from them, men enquire, not merely whether the deduction

.s correct, but also whether its result seems intrinsically probable; and if it does not appear so, they will reject the conclusion, without absolutely rejecting the premise. In the ages of witchcraft, an inexorable logic prevailed. Men were so firmly convinced of the truth of the doctrines they were taught, that those doctrines became to them the measure of probability, and no event that seemed to harmonise with them presented the slightest difficulty to the mind. They governed the imagination, while they subdued the reason, and secular considerations never intervened to damp their assurance. The ablest men were not unfrequently the most credulous; because their ability was chiefly employed in discovering analogies between every startling narrative and the principles of their faith, and their success was a measure of their ingenuity.

It is these considerations that give the writings of the period I am referring to so great an importance in the history of opinions, and which also make it so difficult for us to appreciate their force. I shall endeavour to lay before the reader, in as concise a form as I am able, some of the leading principles they embodied; which, acting on the imagina tion, contributed to produce the phenomena of witchcraft and, acting on the reason, persuaded men that the narratives of witches were antecedently probable.[1]

It was universally taught that innumerable evil spirits were ranging over the world, seeking the present unhappiness and the future ruin of mankind; that these spirits were

[1] The principal authority on these matters is a large collection of Latin works (in great part written by inquisitors), extending over about two cen turies, and published under the title of *Malleus Maleficarum* (the title of Sprenger's book). It comprises the works of Sprenger, Nider, Basin, Molitor, Gerson, Murner, Spina, Laurentius, Bernardus, Vignitus, Grillandus, &c. I have noticed a great many other works in their places, and the reader may find reviews of many others in Madden and Plancy.

fallen angels, who had retained many, if not all, the angelic capacities; and that they, at all events, possessed a power and wisdom far transcending the limits of human faculties. From these conceptions, many important consequences were evolved. If these spirits are for ever hovering around us, it was said, it is surely not improbable that we should meet some signs of their presence. If they delight in the smallest misfortune that can befall mankind, and possess far more than human capacities for inflicting suffering, it is not surprising that they should direct against men the energies of superhuman malice. If their highest object is to secure the ultimate ruin of man, we need not wonder that they should offer their services to those who would bribe them by the surrender of their hopes. That such a compact can be made—that it is possible for men to direct the energies of evil spirits—was established by the clearest authority. 'Thou shalt not suffer a witch to live,' was the solemn injunction which had been more than once repeated in the Levitical code; and the history of the witch of Endor furnishes a detailed description of the circumstances of the crime. The Fathers had denounced magic with a unanimous and unvarying voice, and the writings of every nation bear traces of the universality of the belief. In an age which was essentially retrospective, it was impossible to name a tenet which could seem more probable, for there was none which was more closely connected with antiquity, both ecclesiastical and profane.

The popular belief, however, not only asserted the possibility and continued existence of witchcraft, it also entered into many of what we should now deem the most extravagant and grotesque details. In the first place, one of the most ordinary operations of the witch, or of the Devil acting at her command, was to cause tempests, which it was said frequently desolated the fields of a single person, leaving the rest of the country entirely untouched. If any one ventured to deny that Satan possessed, or was likely to exercise this power, he was speedily silenced by a scriptural precedent We read in the Old Testament that the Devil, by the Divine permission, afflicted Job; and that among the means which he employed was a tempest which destroyed the house in which the sons of the patriarch were eating. The description, in the book of Revelation, of the four angels who held the four winds, and to whom it was given to afflict the earth, was also generally associated with this belief; for, as St. Augustine tells us, the word angel is equally applicable to good or bad spirits. Besides this, the Devil was always spoken of as the prince of the air. His immense knowledge and his immense power would place the immediate causes of atmospheric disturbances at his disposal; and the sudden tempest would, therefore, be no violation of natural laws, but simply an instance of their application by superhuman power. These considerations were, it was thought, sufficient to remove all sense of the antecedent improbability of the facts which were alleged; but every uncertainty was dispelled by the uniform teaching of the Church. At all times, the Fathers and the mediæval saints had taught, like the teachers of every other religion in the same early stage of civilisation, that all the more remarkable atmospheric changes resulted from the direct intervention of spirits.[1] Rain seems to have been commonly associated, as it still is in the Church of England, with the intervention of the Deity; but wind and hail were invariably identified with the Devil. If the

---

[1] On the universality of this belief, in an early stage of civilisation, see Buckle's *History*, vol. i. p. 346.

Devil could originate a tempest, it followed, as a necessary consequence, that witches who had entered into compact with him had the same power.

The same principles of argument applied to disease. The Devil had afflicted Job with horrible diseases, and might therefore afflict others. Great pestilences were constantly described in the Old Testament as the acts of the angels; and the Devil, by the permission of the Deity and by virtue of his angelic capacities, might therefore easily produce them. The history of the demoniacs proves that devils could master and derange the bodily functions; and, therefore, to deny that they could produce disease, would be to impugn the veracity of these narratives; and the later ecclesiastical testimony on the subject, if not unanimous, was, at least, extremely strong. As, therefore, the more striking atmospheric disturbances were ascribed generally to the Devil, and, when the injury was spread over a small area, to witches; so, the pestilences which desolated nations were deemed supernatural, and every strange and unaccountable disease that fell upon an individual, a result of the malice of a sorcerer. If the witch could produce disease by her incantations, there was no difficulty in believing that she could also remove it.[1]

---

[1] There can be little doubt that a considerable amount of poisoning was mixed up with the witch cases. In ages when medical knowledge was scanty, and post mortem examinations unknown, this crime was peculiarly dreaded and appeared peculiarly mysterious. On the other hand, it is equally certain that the witches constantly employed their knowledge of the property of herbs for the purpose of curing disease, and that they attained, in this respect, a skill which was hardly equalled by the regular practitioners. To the evidence which Michelet has collected on this matter, I may add a striking passage from Grillandus. ' Quandoque vero provenit febris, tussis, dementia, phthisis, nydropsis, aut aliqua tumefactio carnis in corpore, sive apostema extrinsecus apparens: quandoque vero intrinsece apud intestina aliquod apostema sit adeo terribile et incurabile quod nulla pars medicorum id sanare et removere potest,

These propositions were unanimously and•firmly believed. They were illustrated by anecdotes, the countless numbers of which can only be appreciated by those who have studied the literature at its source. They were indelibly graven on the minds of men by hundreds of trials and of executions, and they were admitted by almost all the ablest men in Christendom.

There were other details, however, which excited consid-erable discussion. One of the most striking of these was the transportation of witches through the air. That an old woman could be carried some hundreds of miles in a few minutes on a broomstick or a goat, or in any other way the Devil might select, would, in the present day, be regarded as so essentially and grotesquely absurd, that it is probable that no conceivable amount of testimony would convince men of its reality. At the period of which I am writing, this rationalistic spirit did undoubtedly exist in a few minds; for it is noticed, though with extreme contempt, by some of the writers on the subject, who treated it as a manifest mental aberration; but it had not yet assumed any importance. The measure of probability was still essentially theological; and the only question that was asked was, how far the narratives conformed with the theological conception of a spirit. On this point there seemed, at first sight, much difficulty, and considerable ingenuity was applied to eluci-dating it. Satan, it was remembered, had borne Christ through the air, and placed him on a pinnacle of the temple· and therefore, said St. Thomas Aquinas, if he could do

nisi accedat alius maleficus, sive sortilegus, qui contrariis medelis et remediis ægritudinem ipsam meleficam tollat, quam facile et brevi tempore removere po-test, cæteri vero medici qui artem ipsius medicinæ profitentur nihil valent et no-sciunt afferre remedium.' (*Mall. Mal.*, vol. ii. pp. 393, 394.)

this to one body he could do it to all. The prophet Habak-kuk had been transported by a spirit from Judea to Babylon, and Philip the Evangelist had been the object of a similar miracle. St. Paul had likewise been carried, perhaps in the body, into the third heaven.

This evidence was ample and conclusive; but other per plexing difficulties arose. Nothing in the witch trials was more minutely described than the witches' Sabbath, and many hundreds of women had been burnt alive for attending it. Occasionally, however, it happened that, when a woman had been condemned on this charge by her own confession, or by the evidence of other witches, her husband came forth and swore that his wife had not left his side during the night in question. The testimony of so near a relative might, per-haps, be explained by perjury; but other evidence was ad-duced which it was more difficult to evade. It was stated that women were often found lying in a state of trance, in-sensible to pain, and without the smallest sign of life; that, after a time, their consciousness returned, and that they then confessed that they had been at the witches' Sabbath. These statements soon attracted the attention of theologians, who were much divided in their judgments. Some were of opin-ion that the witch was laboring under a delusion of the Devil; but they often added that, as the delusion originated in a compact, she should, notwithstanding, be burned. Others suggested a bolder and very startling explanation. That the same portion of matter cannot be in two places at once, is a proposition which rests entirely on the laws of nature; but those laws have no existence for the miraculous; and the miracle of transubstantiation seems to destroy all the improb-ability of the pluri-presence of a human body. At all events, the Devil might furnish, for the occasion, a duplicate body,

In order to baffle the ministers of justice. This latter opinion became extremely popular among theologians; and two famous Catholic miracles were triumphantly quoted in its support. St. Ambrose was, on one occasion, celebrating mass in a church at Milan, when he suddenly paused in the midst of the service. His head sank upon the altar, and he remained motionless, as in a trance, for the space of three hours. The congregation waited silently for the benediction. At last the consciousness of the saint returned, and he assured his hearers that he had been officiating at Tours at the burial of St. Martin, a statement which was, of course, in a few days verified. A similar miracle was related of St. Clement. This early saint, in the midst of a mass at Rome, was called away to consecrate a church at Pisa. His body, or an angel who had assumed its form, remained at Rome; but the saint was at the same time present at Pisa, where he left some drops of blood upon the marble for a memorial of the miracle.[1] On the whole, the most general opinion seems to have been, that the witches were sometimes transported to the Sabbath in body, and sometimes in spirit; and that devils occasionally assumed their forms in order to baffle the sagacity of the judges.[2]

Another important and much discussed department, was the connection between evil spirits and animals. That the Devil could assume the form of any animal[3] he pleased,

---

[1] Spina, *De Strigibus* (1522), cap. xi.

[2] All the phenomena of somnambulism were mixed up with the question. See, e. g., Spina, cap. x. and xi., where it is fully discussed. Many curious notions were held about somnambulism. One opinion was, that the somnambulists had never been baptised, or had been baptised by a drunken priest.

This belief was probably sustained by the great use made of animals in Christian symbolism as representatives of moral qualities. In different districts different animals were supposed to be in especial connection with spirits. Delrio mentions that the ancient Irish had such a veneration for wolves that they were accustomed to pray for their salvation, and to choose them as god

seems to have been generally admitted; and it presented no difficulty to those who remembered that the first appearance of that personage on earth was as a serpent, and that on one occasion a legion of devils had entered into a herd of swine. St. Jerome also assures us that, in the desert, St. Antony had met a centaur and a faun—a little man with horns growing from his forehead—who were possibly devils;[1] and, at all events, at a later period, the lives of the saints represent evil spirits in the form of animals as not unfrequent. Lycanthrepy, however, or the transformation of witches into wolves, presented more difficulty. The history of Nebuchadnezzar, and the conversion of Lot's wife, were, it is true, eagerly alleged in support of its possibility; but it was impossible to forget that St. Augustine appeared to regard lycanthropy as a fable, and that a canon of the council of Ancyra had emphatically condemned the belief. On the other hand, there was no opinion more universally held among the ancients. It had

---

fathers for their children (Thiers' *Superst.*, vol. ii. p. 198). Beelzebub, as is well known, was god of flies. 'Par ce qu'il n'y avoit pas une mouche en son temple, comme on dict qu'au Palais de Venise il n'y a pas une seule mouche et au Palais de Tolède qu'il n'y en a qu'une, qui n'est pas chose estrange ou nouvelle, car nous lisons que les Cyrénaïques, après avoir sacrifié au dieu Acaron, dieu des mouches, et les Grecs à Jupiter, surnommé Myiodes, c'est à dire mouchard, toutes les mouches s'envolaient en une nuée, comme nous lisons en Pausanias *In Arcadicis* et en Pline au livre xxix. cap. 6.' (Bodin, *Démon.*, p. 15.) Dancing bears and other intelligent animals seem to have been also connected with the Devil; and an old council anathematised at once magicians who have abandoned their Creator, fortune-tellers, and those 'qui ursas aut similes bestias ad ludum et perniciem simpliciorum circumferunt'—'for what fellowship can there be between Christ and Belial?' (Wier, *De Præst. Dæm.*, p. 557.) The ascription of intelligence to animals was general through the middle ages, but it was most prominent in the Celtic race. See a curious chapter on mystic animals in Dalyell's *Superstitions in Scotland*, and also the essay of Renan on *Celtic Poetry.* Muratori (*Antiq. Ital.*, Diss. xxix.) quotes an amusing passage from a writer of the eleventh century, concerning a dog which in that century was 'moved by the spirit of Pytho.'

[1] *Vita S. Pauli.*

been accepted by many of the greatest and most orthodox theologians, by the inquisitors who were commissioned by the popes, and by the law courts of most countries. The evidence on which it rested was very curious and definite. If the witch was wounded in the form of an animal, she retained that wound in her human form, and hundreds of such cases were alleged before the tribunals. Sometimes the hunter, having severed the paw of his assailant, retained it as a trophy; but when he opened his bag, he discovered in it only a bleeding hand, which he recognised as the hand of his wife.[1]

---

[1] 'L'existence des loups-garous est attestée par Virgile, Solin, Strabon, Pomponius Méla, Dionysius Afer, Varron, et par tous les jurisconsultes et démonomanes des derniers siècles. A peine commençait-on à en douter sous Louis XIV.' (Plancy, *Dict. Infernale*, *Lycanthropie*.) Bodin, in his chapter on Lycanthropy, and in our own day Madden (vol. i. pp. 334-358), have collected immense numbers of additional authorities. St. Augustine notices the subject with considerable hesitation, but on the whole inclines, as I have said, towards incredulity (*Civ. Dei*, lib. xviii. c. 17, 18). He also tells us that in his time there were some innkeepers, who were said to give their guests drugs in cheese, and thus to turn them into animals. (*Ibid.*) In the Salic laws of the fifth century there is a curious enactment ' that any sorceress who has devoured a man should on conviction be fined 200 sous ' (Garinet, p. 6). To come down to a later period, we find St. Thomas Aquinas asserting that 'Omnes angeli boni et mali, ex virtute naturali, habent potestatem transmutandi corpora nostra;' and, according to Bodin, Paracelsus and Fernel, the chief physician of Henry IV., held a similar belief. There is probably no country in Europe— perhaps no country in the world—in which some form of this superstition has not existed. It raged however especially where wolves abounded—among the Jura, in Norway, Russia, Ireland (where the inhabitants of Ossory, according to Camden, were said to become wolves once every seven years), in the Pyrenees and Greece. The Italian women usually became cats. In the East (as the ' Arabian Nights' show) many forms were assumed. A French judge named Boguet, at the end of the sixteenth century, devoted himself especially to the subject, burnt multitudes of lycanthropes, wrote a book about them, and drew up a code in which he permitted ordinary witches to be strangled before they were burnt, but excepted lycanthropes, who were to be burnt alive (Garinet, pp. 298-302). In the controversy about the reality of the transformation, Bodin supported the affirmative, and Binsfeldius the negative side. There is a form of

7

The last class of anecdotes I shall notice is that which appears to have grown out of the Catholic conception of celibacy. I mean the accounts of the influence of witchcraft upon the passions.

It is not difficult to conceive the order of ideas that produced that passionate horror of the fair sex which is such a striking characteristic of old Catholic theology. Celibacy was universally regarded as the highest form of virtue, and in order to make it acceptable, theologians exhausted all the resources of their eloquence in describing the iniquity of those whose charms had rendered it so rare. Hence, the long and fiery disquisitions on the unparalleled malignity, the inconceivable subtlety, the frivolity, the unfaithfulness, the unconquerably evil propensities of women, which were the terror of one age, and which became the amusement of the next. It is not very easy to read these diatribes with perfect gravity; but they acquire a certain melancholy significance from the fact, that the teaching they represent had probably a considerable influence in predisposing men to believe in witches, and also in producing the extreme callousness with which the sufferings of the victims were contemplated. The question why the immense majority of those who were accused of sorcery should be women, early attracted attention; and it was generally answered, not by the sensibility of their nervous constitution, and by their consequent liability to religous monomania and epidemics, but by the inherent wickedness of the sex. There was no subject on which

monomania under which men believe themselves to be animals, which is doubt-
'ess the nucleus around which the system was formed—a striking instance of
the development of the miraculous. See also Bourquelot, *La Lycanthropie.*
Among the many mad notions of the Abyssinians, perhaps the maddest is their
belief that blacksmiths and potters can change themselves into hyænas, and
ought therefore to be excluded from the sacrament (Hecker, *Epid.*, p. 120).

the old writers expatiated with more indignant eloquence, or with more copious illustration.[1] Cato, they said, had declared that 'if the world were only free from women, men would not be without the converse of the gods.' Cicero had said, that ' many motives will urge men to one crime, but that one passion will impel women to all crimes.' Solomon, whose means of observation had in this respect been exceedingly extensive, had summed up his experience in a long series of the most crushing apophthegms. Chrysostom only interpreted the general sentiment of the Fathers, when he pronounced woman to be 'a necessary evil, a natural temptation, a desirable calamity, a domestic peril, a deadly fascination, and a painted ill.' Doctor after doctor echoed the same lugubrious strain, ransacked the pages of history for illustrations of the enormities of the sex, and marshalled the ecclesiastical testimonies on the subject with the most imperturbable earnestness and solemnity. Men who had most seriously formed this estimate of the great majority of women; who esteemed celibacy the highest of virtues, and every temptation to abandon it the direct consequence of Satanic presence; came, by a very natural process, to regard all the 'phenomena of love' as most especially under the influence of the Devil. Hence, those wild gleams of strange and grotesque romance which, from time to time, light up the literature of witchcraft. Incubi and succubi were for ever wandering among mankind, alluring by more than human charms the unwary to their destruction, and laying plots which were but too often successful against the virtue of the saints. Sometimes, the witches kindled in the monastic breast a more terrestrial fire; and men told, with bated breath, how, under the spell of a vindictive woman, four successive abbots in a German monastery

---

[1] See especially the long strange chapter on the subject in Sprenger.

had been wasted away by an unholy flame.[1] Occasionally, with a still more refined malice, the Evil One assumed the appearance of some noted divine, in order to bring discredit upon his character; and an astonished maiden saw, prostrate at her feet, the form of one whom she knew to be a bishop, and whom she believed to be a saint![2] Nor was it only among those who were bound to celibacy that the deadly influences were exercised. The witches were continually disturbing, by their machinations, the joys of wedlock; and none can tell how many hundreds have died in agonies for afflicting with barrenness the marriage bed.[3]

---

[1] Sprenger, Pars I. Quæst. vii. At the request of St. Serenus and St. Equitius, the angels performed on those saints a counteracting surgical operation. (Nider, *Formic. de Mal.*, c. v.)

[2] See the curious story of St. Sylvanus, Bishop of Nazareth, in Sprenger Pars II. Quæst. i. cap. xi.). The Devil not only assumed the appearance of this holy man, in order to pay his addresses to a lady, but when discovered, crept under a bed, suffered himself to be dragged out, and declared that he was the veritable bishop. Happily, after a time, a miracle was wrought which cleared the reputation of the caluminated prelate.

[3] As few people realise the degree in which these superstitions were encouraged by the Church which claims infallibility, I may mention that the reality of this particular crime was implied, and its perpetrators anathematised, by the provincial councils or synods of Troyes, Lyons, Milan, Tours, Bourges, Narbonne, Ferrara, St. Malo, Mont Cassin, Orleans, and Grenoble; by the rituals of Autun, Chartres, Périgueux, Atun, Evreux, Paris, Angers, Arras, Châlons, Bologna, Troyes, Bourges, Alet, Beauvais, Meaux, Rheims, &c.; and by the degrees of a long series of bishops (Thiers, *Sup. Pop.*, tom. iv. ch. vii.). It was held, as far as I know, without a single exception, by all the inquisitors who presided at the witch-courts, and Sprenger gives a long account of the methods which were generally employed in convicting those who were accused of the crime. Montaigne appears to have been the first who openly denied it, ascribing to the imagination what the orthodox ascribed to the Devil; and this opinion seems soon to have become a characteristic of free-thinkers in France; for Thiers (who wrote in 1678) complains that 'Les esprits forts et les libertins qui donnent tout à la nature, et qui ne jugent des choses que par la raison, ne veulent pas se persuader que de nouveaux-mariés puissent par l'artifice et la malice du démon estre empêchés de se rendre le devoir conjugal (p 567)—a very wicked incredulity—' puisque l'Église, que est conduite par le Saint-Esprit, et qui par consé

I make no apology for having dwelt so long on a series of doctrines and arguments which the reader will probably deem very puerile, because their importance depends, not on their intrinsic value, but upon their relation to the history of opinions. The follies of the past, when they were adopted by the wisest men, are well worthy of study; and, in the case before us, they furnish, I think, an invaluable clue to the laws of intellectual development. It is often and truly said, that past ages were pre-eminently credulous, as compared with our own; yet the difference is not so much in the amount of the credulity, as in the direction which it takes. Men are always prepared to accept, on very slight evidence, what they believe to be exceedingly probable. Their measure of probability ultimately determines the details of their creed, and it is itself perpetually changing under the influence of civilisation. In the middle ages, and in the sixteenth and the beginning of the seventeenth century, the measure of probability was essentially theological. Men seemed to breathe an atmosphere that was entirely unsecular. Their intellectual and imaginative conceptions were all coloured by theological associations; and they accepted with cheerful alacrity any anecdote which harmonised with their habitual meditations. The predisposition to believe in the miraculous was so great, that it constructed, out of a small germ of reality, this vast and complicated system of witchcraft; accummulated around it an immense mass of the most varied and circumstantial evidence; persuaded all the ablest men for many centuries that it was incontestably true; conducted it unshaken through the scrutiny of the

quent ne peut errer, reconnoît qu'il se fait par l'opération du démon ' (p. 573). The same writer shows that the belief existed in the Church in the time of Theodousus (p. 568). The last sorcerer who was burnt in France perished on this charge (Garinet, p. 256).

law courts of every European nation; and consigned tens
of thousands of victims to a fearful and unlamented death.
There was not the smallest desire to explain away or soften
down miraculous accounts, in order to make them harmonise
with experience, because the minds of men were completely
imbued with an order of ideas that had no connection with
experience. If we could perceive evil spirits, untrammelled
by the laws of matter, actually hovering around us; if we
could observe them watching every action with a deadly
malignity, seeking with all the energies of superhuman
power the misery of mankind, and darkening with their
awful aspect every sphere in which we move; if we could
see the angel of destruction brandishing the sword of death
over the Assyrian hosts, or over the streets of Jerusalem;
and could behold Satan transporting Christ through the air,
or the demoniacs foaming in agony beneath his grasp, we
should probably reason on these matters in much the same
spirit as the theologians of the fifteenth and sixteenth centuries. Our minds would be so pervaded by these awful
images, that they would form a measure of probability entirely different from that which is formed by the experience
of life; a nervous consciousness of the continual presence of
evil spirits would accompany us for ever, and would for
ever predispose us to discover manifestations of their power.

The foregoing pages will, I trust, be sufficient to eluci-
date the leading causes upon which witchcraft depended.
They will show that it resulted, not from accidental circumstances, individual eccentricities, or even scientific ignorance,
but from a general predisposition to see Satanic agency in
life. It grew from, and it reflected, the prevailing modes
of religious thought; and it declined only when those modes
were weakened or destroyed. In almost every period of the

middle ages, there had been a few men who• in some degree dissented from the common superstitions ; but their opinions were deemed entirely incomprehensible, and they exercised no appreciable influence upon their contemporaries. Indeed, their doctrines, being generally veiled in a mystical form, were so perverted and materialised, that they not unfrequently increased the prevailing gloom. As long as the general credulity continued, as long as the minds of men were directed towards the miraculous and the Satanic, no efforts could eradicate the superstition. In such a condition of thought, men would always be more inclined to accept than to reject the evidence. They would refuse to scrutinise it with jealous suspicion ; and, though they might admit the existence of some imposture, they would never question the substantial justice of the belief. Not until the predisposition was changed ; not until men began to recoil from these narratives, as palpably and grossly improbable ; not until the sense of their improbability so overpowered the reverence for authority, as to make them seek in every way to evade the evidence, and to make them disbelieve it even when they were unable to disprove it, could this deadly superstition be rolled away. Its decline marks the rise, and its destruction the first triumph, of the spirit of rationalism in Europe.

We frequently find, in the writings of the inquisitors, language which implies that a certain amount of scepticism was, even in their time, smouldering in some minds. It was not, indeed, sufficient to make any deep impression on public opinion. It is identified with no great name,[1] and produced

---

[1] I should, perhaps, make one exception to this statement—Peter of Apono, a very famous physician and philosopher of Padua, who died in 1305. He appears to have entirely denied the existence of demons and of miracles ; and to have attempted, by the assistance of astrology, to construct a general philosophy of religion, casting the horoscope of each faith, and ascribing its rise

no great book; but it was yet sufficiently evident to elicit the anxiety of some theologians. 'Those men,' wrote Gerson, 'should be treated with scorn, and indeed sternly corrected, who ridicule theologians whenever they speak of demons, or attribute to demons any effects, as if these things were entirely fabulous. This error has arisen among some learned men, partly through want of faith, and partly through weakness and imperfection of intellect . . . . for, as Plato says, to refer everything to the senses, and to be incapable of turning away from them, is the greatest impediment to truth.'[1] Sprenger also, in a long chapter, instructed theologians how to meet a spirit of vague scepticism which had arisen among certain laymen; 'who had, indeed, no fixed method of reasoning, but were blindly groping in the dark, touching now on one point, and now on another.' An assembly of doctors of the University of Cologne,[2] which was held in 1487, lamented, and severely and authoritatively condemned, a still more startling instance of rebellion, arising from a quarter in which it was least to be expected. When the panic was raging most fiercely in the diocese of Cologne, some priests had attempted to allay the alarm by questioning the reality of the crime. About thirty years later, Spina mentions[*] that, in some places, the innumerable executions had aroused a spirit of most acrimonious opposition. Indeed,

---

and destiny to the influence of the stars. He was a disciple of Averroes—perhaps the founder of Averroism in Italy—and seems to have formed a school at Padua. When he was about eighty, he was accused of magic. It was said that he had acquired the knowledge of the seven liberal arts by seven familiar spirits whom he kept confined in a crystal; but he died before the trial was concluded, so the inquisitors were obliged to content themselves by burning his image. He was regarded as one of the greatest of magicians Compare Naudé, *Apol.*, pp. 380–391; Renan, *Averroes*, pp. 258, 259.

[1] *Mall. Mal.*, vol. ii. p. 253.   [2] *Mall. Mal.*, vol. i. pp. 460–468.
    Vol. ii. pp. 191, 299, 300.

in the north of Italy, a positive rebellion had broken out, accompanied by a tone of incredulity which that theologian piteously laments. 'Most imprudent, most undevout, and most unfaithful men will not believe the things they ought to believe; and what is still more lamentable, they exert all their influence to obstruct those who are destroying the enemies of Christ.' Such a conduct, Spina justly observes, was full of danger for those who were guilty of it, as they might themselves be justly punished for conniving at the crime; and it was a distinct reflection upon the Church which was represented by the inquisitors and upon the Pope by whom the inquisitors were commissioned. We find, too, the clergy claiming, in a very peremptory tone, the supreme jurisdiction of these cases, and occasionally alleging the misconduct of lay judges who had suffered witches to depart unharmed. All this scepticism, however, appears to have been latent and undefined; and it was not till 1563 that it was thrown into a systematic form by John Wier, in his treatise ' De Præstigiis Dæmonum.'

Wier was a learned and able physician of Clèves. He was convinced as a doctor that many of the victims were simply lunatics, and, being a very humane man, was greatly shocked at the sufferings they endured. He was a Protestant, and therefore, perhaps, not quite as much trammelled by tradition as some of his contemporaries; though in the present day his reverence for authority would be regarded as an absolute infatuation. He had not the slightest wish to revolt against any of the first principles of the popular teaching, or even to free himself from the prevailing modes of thought. He was quite convinced that the world was peopled by crowds of demons, who were constantly working miracles among mankind; and his only object was to recon-

cile his sense of their ubiquity, with his persuasion that
some of the phenomena that were deemed supernatural
arose from disease. He was of opinion that all the witches
were labouring under the delusions of the Devil. They did
not make an unholy compact, or ride through the air, or
arouse tempests, or produce disease, or become the concu-
bines of Satan; but the Devil had entered into them, and
persuaded them that they had done these things. The idea
of possession was thus so enlarged as to absorb the idea of
witchcraft. The bewitched person was truly afflicted by
the Devil, but the Devil had done this directly, and not by
the intervention of a witch, and had then thrown suspicion
upon some old woman, in order that the greatest possible
amount of suffering might be produced. Persons, he said,
were especially liable to diabolical possession, when their
faculties were impaired by disease, and their tempers acidu-
lated by suffering. In an eloquent and learned chapter on
' the credulity and fragility of the female sex,' he showed,
by the authority of the Fathers and the Greek philosophers,
that women were peculiarly subject to evil influences. He
also showed that the witches, in mental and moral infirmities,
were pre-eminent among their sex. He argued that the word
translated witch, in the Levitical law, may be translated
poisoner; and that the patristic notion of the intercourse
between angels and the antediluvian women, was inadmissi-
ble. The gross improbabilities of some parts of the popular
belief were clearly exhibited, and illustrated with much
unnecessary learning; and the treatise was prefaced by an
earnest appeal to the princes of Europe to arrest the effusion
of innocent blood.

The scepticism of this work cannot be regarded as audacious. In fact, Wier stands alone in the history of witch

craft, and differs essentially from all the later writers on the subject. He forms a link connecting two periods; he was as fully pervaded by the sense of the miraculous as his opponents, and he never dreamed of restricting the sphere of the supernatural. Such as it was, however, this book was the first attack of any importance on the received opinions, and excited among learned men considerable attention. Three editions were published, in a few years, at Basle and Amsterdam, which were then the centres of independent thought. It was translated into French in 1569. It was supplemented by a treatise 'De Lamiis,' and by a very curious catalogue of the leaders, and description of the organization, of hell.[1] Shortly after the publication of these last works, a book appeared in reply, from the pen of Bodin, the famous author of the 'Republic,' and one of the most distinguished philosophers in Europe.

Bodin was esteemed, by many of his contemporaries, the ablest man who had then arisen in France; and the verdict has been but little qualified by later writers.[2] Amid all the

---

[1] 'Pseudomonarchia Dæmonum'—one of the principal sources of information about this subject. He gives the names of seventy-two princes, and estimates their subjects at 7,405,926 devils. It is not quite clear how much he believed on the subject.

[2] A very old critic and opponent of his views on witchcraft quaintly speaks of him as 'Ce premier homme de la France, Jean Bodin, qui après avoir par une merveilleuse vivacité d'esprit accompagnée d'un jugement solide traicté toutes les choses divines, naturelles et civiles, se fust peut estre mescogneu pour homme, et eust esté pris infailliblement de nous pour quelque intelligence s'il n'eust laissé des marques et vestiges de son humanité dans cette démonomanie.' (Naudé, *Apol.*, 127 (1625). Bayle (*Dict. Phil.*) pronounced Bodin to have been 'one of the chief advocates of liberty of conscience of his time.' In our own day, Buckle (vol. i. p. 299) has placed him as an historian above Comines, and on a level with Macchiavelli; and Hallam, speaking of the 'Republic,' says, 'Bodin possessed a highly philosophical mind, united with the most ample stores of history and jurisprudence. No former writer on political philosophy had been either so comprehensive in his scheme, or so copious in his knowledge;

distractions of a dissipated and an intriguing court, and all
the labours of a judicial position, he had amassed an amount
of learning so vast and so various, as to place him in the very
first rank of the scholars of his nation. He has also the far
higher merit of being one of the chief founders of political
philosophy and political history, and of having anticipated
on these subjects many of the conclusions of our own day
In his judicial capacity he had presided at some trials of
witchcraft. He had brought all the resources of his scholar-
ship to bear upon the subject; and he had written a great
part of his 'Démonomanie des Sorciers' before the appearance of the last work of Wier.

The 'Démonomanie des Sorciers' is chiefly an appeal to
authority, which the author deemed on this subject so unanimous and so conclusive, that it was scarcely possible for
any sane man to resist it. He appealed to the popular belief
in all countries, in all ages, and in all religions. He cited
the opinions of an immense multitude of the greatest writers
of pagan antiquity, and of the most illustrious of the Fathers.
He showed how the laws of all nations recognised the existence of witchcraft; and he collected hundreds of cases which
had been investigated before the tribunals of his own or of
other countries. He relates with the most minute and circumstantial detail, and with the most unfaltering confidence,
all the proceedings at the witches' Sabbath, the methods
which the witches employed in transporting themselves
through the air, their transformations, their carnal intercourse with the Devil, their various means of injuring their

---

none, perhaps, more original, more independent and fearless in his inquiries
Two men alone, indeed, could be compared with him—Aristotle and Machiavel.
(*Hist. of Lit.*, vol. ii. p. 68.) Dugald Stewart is equally encomiastic (*Disserta
tion*, pp. 52–54).

enemies, the signs that lead to their detection, their confes
sions when condemned, and their demeanour at the stake.
As for the treatise of Wier, he could scarcely find words to
express the astonishment and the indignation with which he
had perused it. That a puny doctor should have dared to
oppose himself to the authority of all ages; that he should
have such a boundless confidence in his own opinions, and
such a supreme contempt for the wisest of mankind, as to
carp and cavil in a sceptical spirit at the evidence of one of
the most notorious of existing facts; this was, in truth, the
very climax of human arrogance, the very acme of human
absurdity. But, extreme as was the audacity thus displayed,
the impiety was still greater. Wier 'had armed himself
against God.' His book was a tissue of 'horrible blasphemies.' 'No one who is ever so little touched with the honour
of God, could read such blasphemies without a righteous
anger.' Not only had he dared to impugn the sentences of
so many upright judges; not only had he attempted to save
those whom Scripture and the voice of the Church had
branded as the worst of criminals; he had even ventured to
publish to the world the spells and incantations he had learned from a notorious sorcerer.[1] Who could reflect without

---

[1] Cornelius Agrippa, who had been the master of Wier. He was advocate-
general at Metz, and had distinguished himself by his efforts to prevent prosecu
tions for witchcraft, and by saving the life of a peasant woman whom Savin the
inquisitor wished to burn. He was, consequently, generally thought to be in
league with the Devil; and it is related that, on his death-bed, he drew off from
his neck a black dog, which was a demon, exclaiming that it was the cause of
his perdition (Garinet, pp. 121, 122). In his early days he had studied magic,
and had apparently come to the conclusion that it rested either on imposture or
on a superior knowledge of the laws of nature—a conclusion which he tried to
enforce in a book on the vanity of science. He was imprisoned for a year at
Brussels on the charge of magic, and ceaselessly calumniated after his death.
Before Wier, probably no one had done so much to combat the persecution,
and his reputation was sacrificed in the cause. See Plancy's *Dict. Infern.*, art.

consternation on the future of Christendom after such fearful disclosures? Who could question that the knowledge thus disseminated would multiply to an incalculable extent the number of witches, would vastly increase the power of Satan, and would be productive of countless sufferings to the innocent? Under these circumstances, so far from relaxing the prosecutions for witchcraft and sorcery, it was necessary to continue them with a redoubled energy; and surely, no one could be the object of a more just suspicion than a man who had written so impious a book, and who had shown such acquaintance with the secrets of so impious a profession. To pardon those whom the law of God condemned to death, was indeed beyond the province of princes. Those who were guilty of such an act had outraged the majesty of Heaven. They had virtually repudiated the Divine law, and pestilence and famine would inevitably desolate their dominions.[1] One fatal example there had been of a king tampering with his duty in this respect. Charles IX. had spared the life of the famous sorcerer Trois Echelles, on the condition of his informing against his colleagues; and it is to this grievous sin that the early death of the king is most probably to be ascribed: 'For the word of God is very certain, that he who suffers a man worthy of death to escape, draws the punishment upon himself, as the prophet said to king Ahab, that he should die for having pardoned a man worthy of death. For no one had ever heard of pardon being accorded to sorcerers.'[2]

Agrippa, and Thiers' *Superst.*, vol. i. pp. 142, 143. Naudé has also devoted a long chapter to Agrippa. Agrippa had not the good fortune to please any class of theologians. Among the Catholics he was regarded with extreme horror; and Calvin, in his work *De Scandalis*, treats him as one of the chief contemners of the Gospel.

[1] Pp. 217, 228.   P. 152.

Such were the opinions which were promulgated, towards
the close of the sixteenth century, by one of the most advanced intellects of one of the leading nations of Europe ;
promulgated, too, with a tone of confidence and of triumph,
that shows how fully the writer could count upon the sympathies of his readers. The 'Démonomanie des Sorciers' appeared in 1581. Only seven years afterwards, Montaigne
published the first great sceptical work in the French language ; and, among the many subjects on which his scepticism was turned, witchcraft occupied a prominent place. It
would be scarcely possible to conceive a more striking contrast, than his treatment of it presents to the works of Bodin
and of Wier. The vast mass of authority which those writers loved to array, and by which they shaped the whole
course of their reasoning, is calmly and unhesitatingly discarded. The passion for the miraculous, the absorbing
sense of diabolical capacities, have all vanished like a dream.
The old theological measure of probability has completely
disappeared, and is replaced by a shrewd secular common
sense. The statements of the witches were pronounced intrinsically incredible. The dreams of a disordered imagination, or the terrors of the rack, would account for many of
them ; but even when it is impossible to explain away the
evidence, it is quite unnecessary to believe it. 'There are,'
he said, 'proofs and arguments that are founded on expe
rience and facts. I do not pretend to unravel them. I often
cut them, as Alexander did the knot. After all, it is setting
a high value upon our opinions, to roast men alive on account of them.' We may not be able to discover an adequate solution of some statements on the subject, but we
should consider—and he here anticipated a mode of argument which was destined long afterwards to assume a most

prominent place in theological controversy—that it is far more probable that our senses should deceive us, than that an old woman should be carried up a chimney on a broom stick; and that it is far less astonishing that witnesses should lie, than that witches should perform the acts that were alleged.[1]

It has been justly remarked by Malebranche, that Montaigne is an example of a writer who had no pretensions to be a great reasoner, but who nevertheless exercised a most profound and general influence upon the opinions of mankind. It is not, I think, difficult to discover the explanation of the fact. In an age which was still spell-bound by the fascinations of the past, he applied to every question a judgment entirely unclouded by the imaginations of theologians, and unshackled by the dictates of authority. His originality consists, not so much in his definite opinions or in his arguments, as in the general tone and character of his mind. He was the first French author who had entirely emancipated himself from the retrospective habits of thought that had so long been universal; who ventured to judge all questions by a secular standard, by the light of common sense, by the measure of probability which is furnished by daily experience. He was, no doubt, perfectly aware that 'the laws of Plato, of the twelve tables, of the consuls, of the emperors, and of all nations and legislators—Persian, Hebrew, Greek, Latin, German, French, Italian, Spanish, English—had decreed capital penalties against sorcerers;' he knew that ' prophets, theologians, doctors, judges, and magistrates, had elucidated the reality of the crime by many thousand violent presumptions, accusations, testimonies, convictions,

[1] Liv. iii. c. 11.

repentances and voluntary confessions, persisted in to death;'[1] but he was also sensible of the extreme fallibility of the human judgment; of the facility with which the mind discovers, in the phenomena of history, a reflection of its preconceived notions; and of the rapidity with which systems of fiction are formed in a credulous and undiscriminating age. While Catholics, Protestants, and Deists were vying with each other in their adoration of the past; while the ambition of every scholar and of every theologian was to form around his mind an atmosphere of thought that bore no relation to the world that was about him; while knowledge was made the bond-slave of credulity, and those whose intellects were most shackled by prejudice were regarded as the wisest of mankind, it was the merit of Montaigne to rise, by the force of his masculine genius, into the clear world of reality; to judge the opinions of his age with an intellect that was invigorated but not enslaved by knowledge; and to contemplate the systems of the past, without being dazzled by the reverence that had surrounded them. He looked down upon the broad field of history, upon its clashing enthusiasms, its discordant systems, the ebb and flow of its ever-changing belief, and he drew from the contemplation a lesson widely different from his contemporaries. He did not, it is true, fully recognise those moral principles which shine with an unchanging splendour above the fluctuations of speculative opinions; he did not discover the great laws of eternal development which preside over and direct the progress of belief, infuse order into the seeming chaos, and reveal in every apparent aberration the traces of a superintending Providence; but he, at least, obtained an intense and real-

Bodin, p. 252.

:sed perception of the fallibility of the human intellect; a keen sense of the absurdity of an absolute deference to the past, and of the danger of punishing men with death on account of opinions concerning which we can have so little assurance. These things led him to suspect that witchcraft might be a delusion. The bent and character of his mind led him to believe that witchcraft was grossly improbable. He was the first great representative of the modern secular and rationalistic spirit. By extricating his mind from the trammels of the past, he had learned to judge the narratives of diabolical intervention by a standard and with a spirit that had been long unknown. The predisposition of the old theologians had been to believe that the phenomena of witchcraft were all produced by the Devil; and, when some manifest signs of madness or of imposture were exhibited, they attempted to accommodate them to their supernatural theory. The strong predisposition of Montaigne was to regard witchcraft as the result of natural causes; and, therefore, though he did not attempt to explain all the statements which he had heard, he was convinced that no conceivable improbability could be as great as that which would be involved in their reception. This was not the happy guess of ignorance. It was the direct result of a mode of thought which he applied to all theological questions. Fifty years earlier, a book embodying such conceptions would have appeared entirely incomprehensible, and its author would perhaps have been burnt. At the close of the sixteenth century, the minds of men were prepared for its reception, and it flashed like a revelation upon France. From the publication of the essays of Montaigne, we may date the influence of that gifted and ever enlarging rationalistic school, who gradually effected the destruction of the belief in witchcraft, not by refuting or explaining its evidence, but simply by making men more and more sensible of its intrinsic absurdity.

Thirteen years after Montaigne, Charron wrote his famous treatise on ' Wisdom.' In this work he systematised many of the opinions of Montaigne; but exhibited far less genius and originality than his predecessor. Like Montaigne, he looked with aversion on the miraculous; but, like Montaigne, his scepticism arose, not from any formal examination of evidence, but from a deep sense of the antecedent improbability. That which Montaigne had thrown into the form of strong doubt, Charron almost threw into the form of a denial. All through the seventeenth century, the same modes of thought continued, slowly but steadily sapping the old belief; but, though the industry of modern antiquarians has exhumed two or three obscure works that were published on the subject,[1] those works never seem to have attracted any serious attention, or to have had any appreciable influence in accelerating the movement. It presents a spectacle, not of argument or of conflict, but of a silent evanescence and decay. The priests continued to exorcise the possessed, to prosecute witches, and to anathematise as infidels all who questioned the crime. Many of the lawyers, reverting to the innumerable enactments in the law books, and to the countless occasions on

[1] Maury, pp. 221, 222. The principal of those writers was Naudé, whose *Apologie pour les Grands Hommes soupçonnez de Magie* contains much curious historical information in an extremely tiresome form. Naudé also wrote an exposure of the Rosicrucians, and a political work on *Coups d'État*, embodying the principles of Macchiavelli. He was the first librarian of the Mazarin library, in the foundation of which he had a considerable part. Bayle (*Pensées Diverses*, § ccxli.) calls him ' L'homme de France qui avoit le plus de lecture.' He is said to have reconstructed some of the dances of the ancients, and to have executed them in person before Queen Christina, in Sweden (Magnin, *Origines du Théâtre*, tom. i. p. 113). The *Apologie* was answered by a Capuchin named D'Autun, in a ponderous work called *L'Incrédulité Sçavante.*

which the subject had been investigated by the tribunals,
maintained the belief with equal pertinacity; but outside
these retrospective classes, the sense of the improbability of
witchcraft became continually stronger, till any anecdote
which involved the intervention of the Devil was on that account generally ridiculed. This spirit was exhibited especially among those whose habits of thought were most secular,
and whose minds were least governed by authority.[1] Some
great scholars and writers, who were fully sensible of the improbability of the belief, yet regarded the evidence as irresistible, and looked upon the subject with a perplexed and
timid suspension of judgment. La Bruyère said that the principles on which magic rests seem vague, uncertain, and vision-
ary; but that many embarrassing facts had been attested by
credible eye-witnesses; that it appeared equally difficult to
admit or to deny them; and that it was better to take a central position between the credulous who admitted all, and the
free-thinkers who rejected all.[2] Even Bayle seems to have
looked upon it in a similar spirit.[3] Descartes, though he did
not, as far as I am aware, ever refer directly to the subject,
probably exercised a considerable influence upon it, for the
tendency of his teaching was to emancipate the mind from
the power of tradition, to secularise philosophy, and to destroy the material notions that had long been associated with
spirits. Malebranche mentions that in his time some of the

---

[1] 'Ce furent les esprits forts du commencement du dix-septième siècle qui
s'efforcèrent les premiers de combattre le préjugé régnant de défendre de
malheureux fous ou d'indiscrets chercheurs contre les tribunaux. Il fallait
pour cela du courage, car on risquait, en cherchant à sauver la tête du pré-
venu, de passer soi-même pour un affidé du diable, ou ce que ne valait pas
mieux, pour un incrédule. Les libres penseurs, les libertins comme on les
appelait alors, n'avaient que peu de crédit.' (Maury, p. 221.)

[2] See the passage in Maury, p. 219.   [3] Ibid., p. 220.

parliaments had ceased to burn witches, and that within their jurisdiction the number of witches had declined. He inferred from this that the contagious power of imagination had created many of the phenomena. He analysed, with much acuteness, the process of thought which produced ly-canthropy; but, being a priest, he found it necessary to add, that real sorcerers should undoubtedly be put to death.[1] Voltaire treated the whole subject with a scornful ridicule; observed that, since there had been philosophers in France, witches had become proportionately rare; and summed up the ecclesiastical authorities for the belief as emphatically as Sprenger or Spina, but with a very different object.[2]

In the first half of the seventeenth century, the civil power uniformly exerted its energies for the destruction of witches. It was between the publication of the works of Montaigne and of Charron, that Boguet was presiding at the tribunal of St. Claude, where he is said to have burnt 600 persons, chiefly for lycanthropy. A few years later, the fifty executions at Douay, which I have already mentioned, took place; and, in 1642, Cardinal Mazarin wrote a letter to the bishop of Evreux, congratulating him warmly on the successful zeal he had manifested on the subject.[3] Towards the middle of the century, however, the growing incredulity had reached those in power; the prosecutions for witchcraft became more rare and languid; and, in 1672, Colbert direct

[1] *Recherche de la Vérité*, liv. ii. p. 3, c. 6.

[2] He said: 'Tous les pères de l'Église sans exception crurent au pouvoir de la magie. L'Église condamna toujours la magie, mais elle y crut toujours. Elle n'excommunia point les sorciers comme des fous qui étaient trompés, mais comme des hommes qui étaient réellement en commerce avec les diables.' (*Dict. Phil.*, art. *Superstition*.) This I believe to be quite true, but it was a striking sign of the times, that an opponent of magic could say so without ruining his cause.

[3] Garinet, p. 328.

ed the magistrates to receive no accusations of sorcery, and commuted in many cases the capital punishment for the crime into a sentence of banishment. It was when some of these commutations had been made, that the Parliament of Rouen drew up an extremely remarkable address to the king, protesting in a strain of high religious fervour, against the indulgence as directly contrary to the Word of God, to all the precedents of French law, and to all the traditions of the Christian religion.[1] After this time but few trials for sorcery took place—that of the Marshal of Luxembourg, in 1681, was, perhaps, the most remarkable—for the scepticism on the subject had already become very marked; and in the last twenty years of the seventeenth century, only seven sorcerers seem to have been burnt in France. Still later, in 1718, the Parliament of Bordeaux burnt a man upon this charge. After this period there were, indeed, one or two trials, but the prisoners were acquitted; the star of Voltaire had risen above the horizon, and the unsparing ridicule which his followers cast upon every anecdote of witches, intimidated those who did not share in the incredulity. The formularies for exorcism still continued, as they continue to the present day, in Roman Catholic rituals, and they were frequently employed all through the eighteenth century; but the more educated members of the clergy for the most part allowed the subject to fall into neglect, and discouraged the attempts of some of the order to revive it. Those who still clung to the traditions of the past must have found much difficulty in accounting for the progress of the movement. That Satan should occupy such an extremely small place in the minds of men was very lamentable, but that the miracu

lous signs of his presence should have so completely disappeared, was exceedingly perplexing. At the beginning of
the present century, the Abbé Fiard published a work designed to explain the difficulty. He showed that the philosophers and revolutionists of the last century were the representatives of the old sorcerers, that they acted under the
direct inspiration of Satan, and that their success was entirely due to Satanic power. Lest, however, it should be
said that this represented rather the moral than the miraculous influence of the Evil One, he added that many great and
startling miracles had accompanied the philosophic movement, and that these miracles had not even yet ceased. The
cures of Mesmer and the prophecies of Cagliostro should
both be ascribed to supernatural agency; but the most
startling of all the signs of diabolical presence was the ever-
increasing popularity of ventriloquism. On this last subject,
we are happily not left to our own unassisted conjectures,
for some learned divines of the fourteenth century had solemnly determined that man was designed to speak by his mouth;
and that, whenever he spoke in any other way, he did so by
the assistance of the Devil.[1]

The history of witchcraft in Protestant countries differs
so little from its history in Catholic ones, that it is not necessary to dwell upon it at much length. In both cases, a tendency towards the miraculous was the cause of the belief;
and the degree of religious terrorism regulated the intensity
of the persecution. In both cases, too, the rise and progress
of a rationalistic spirit were the origin and the measure of
its decline. In England, there was no regular enactment
against sorcery till 1541, when the nation was convulsed by

[1] Garinet, p. 280.

the first paroxysms of the Reformation. The crime had indeed been known at an earlier period, and a few executions
had taken place, but they were very rare; and, in producing
them, other motives seem to have been generally mixed
with superstition. Joan of Arc, the noblest of all the victims
of the belief, perished by English hands, though on French
soil, and under the sentence of a French bishop. Some years
after, the Duchess of Gloucester, having been accused by the
Cardinal of Beaufort of attempting the king's life by sorcery,
was compelled to do penance, while two of her servants were
executed. A few other cases have come down to us; but,
although the extreme imperfection of the old criminal registers
renders it very probable that there were others which are
forgotten, there can be little doubt that the superstition was
much less prominent in England than on the Continent.[1]
Owing partly to its insular position, and partly to the intense
political life that from the earliest period animated the
people, there was formed in England a fearless and self
reliant type of character essentially distinct from that which
was common in Europe, eminently free from morbid and
superstitious terrors, and averse to the more depressing aspects

[1] The most complete authority on this subject is the chronological table of
facts in Hutchinson's *Essay on Witchcraft* (1718). Hutchinson, who was a
very scrupulous writer, restricted himself for the most part to cases of which
he had learned precise particulars, and he carefully gives his authorities. The
number of executions he recounts as having taken place in 250 years, amounts
to many thousands. Of these only about 140 were in England. This, of
course, excludes those who were drowned or mobbed to death during the trial,
and those who were sentenced to other than capital punishments. All the
other writers I have seen place the English executions far higher; and it
seems, I think, certain that some executions escaped the notice of Hutchinson,
whose estimate is, however, probably much nearer the truth than those of most
writers. See also Wright's *Sorcery ;* and an article from the *Foreign Review*
on 'A Collection of Curious Tracts on Witchcraft,' reprinted in 1838. It is
quite impossible to arrive at anything like precision on this subject.

of religion. It was natural, however, that amid the conflicts of the Reformation, some of the darker superstitions should arise; and we accordingly find Cranmer, in one of his articles of visitation, directing his clergy to seek for 'any that use charms, sorcery, enchantments, witchcraft, soothsaying, or any like craft invented by the Devil.' We find also a very few executions under Henry VIII.; but in the following reign the law on the subject was repealed, and was not renewed till the accession of Elizabeth.[1] New laws were then made, which were executed with severity; and Jewell, when preaching before the queen, adverting to the increase of witches, expressed a hope that the penalties might be still more rigidly enforced. 'May it please your grace,' he added, 'to understand that witches and sorcerers within these few years are marvellously increased within your grace's realm. Your grace's subjects pine away even unto the death; their colour fadeth, their flesh rotteth, their speech is benumbed, their senses are bereft. . . . I pray God they never practise further than upon the subject.'[2] On the whole, however, these laws were far milder than those on the Continent. For the first conviction, witches who were not shown to have destroyed others by their incantations were only punished by the pillory and by imprisonment, while those who were condemned to death perished by the gallows instead of the stake. Besides this, torture, which had done

---

[1] The repeal was probably owing to the fact that witchcraft and pulling down crosses were combined together; and the law had, therefore, a Popish appearance.

[2] Sermons (Parker Society), p. 1028. Strype ascribes to this sermon the law which was passed the following year (*Annals of the Ref.*, vol. i. p. 11). The multitude of witches at the beginning of the reign of Elizabeth (which Strype notices) was the obvious consequence of the terrorism of the preceding reign, and of the religious changes acting in the way I have already described.

so much to multiply the evidence, had always been illegal in
England, and the witch-finders were compelled to content
themselves with pricking their victims all over in hopes of
discovering the insensible spot,[1] with throwing them into the
water to ascertain whether they would sink or swim, and
with keeping them during several successive nights without
sleep, in order to compel them to confess. These three
methods were habitually employed with signal success;
many women were in consequence condemned, and a considerable proportion of them were hung. But such scenes
did not take place without one noble protest. A layman
named Reginald Scott published, in 1584, his 'Discovery of
Witchcraft,' in which he unmasked the imposture and the
delusion of the system with a boldness that no previous
writer had approached, and with an ability which few subsequent writers have equalled. Keenly, eloquently, and un
flinchingly, he exposed the atrocious torments by which confessions were extorted, the laxity and injustice of the manner
in which evidence was collected, the egregious absurdities
that filled the writings of the inquisitors, the juggling tricks
that were ascribed to the Devil, and the childish folly of the
magical charms. He also availed himself in a very dexterous
manner of the strong Protestant feeling, in order to discredit
statements that emanated from the Inquisition. If the question was to be determined by argument, if it depended simply
or mainly upon the ability or learning of the controversialists,

---

[1] It is worthy of notice that anæsthesia is a recognised symptom of some
of the epidemic forms of madness. Speaking of that of Morzines, Dr. Constans says: 'L'anesthésie ne fait jamais défaut. J'ai pu pincer, piquer avec
une épingle les malades, enfoncer cette épingle sous les ongles ou de toute sa
longueur dans les bras, les jambes ou sur toute autre partie, sans provoquer l'ap-
parence d'une sensation douleureuse.' (*Épidémie d'Hystéro-Démonopathie en*
1861, p. 63.)

the treatise of Scott would have had a powerful effect; for it was by far the ablest attack on the prevailing superstition that had ever appeared, and it was written in the most popular style. As a matter of fact it exercised no appreciable influence. Witchcraft depended upon general causes, and represented the prevailing modes of religious thought. It was therefore entirely unaffected by the attempted refutation, and when James I. mounted the throne, he found the nation perfectly prepared to second him in his zeal against the witches.

James, although he hated the puritans, had caught in Scotland much of the tone of thought concerning Satanic power which the Puritans had always encouraged, and which was exhibited to the highest perfection in the Scottish mind. He was continually haunted by the subject. He had himself written a dialogue upon it; he had confidently ascribed his stormy passage on his return from Denmark to the machinations of the witches,[1] and he boasted that the Devil regarded him as the most formidable of opponents. Soon after his accession to the throne of England, a law was enacted which

[1] This storm was the origin of one of the most horrible of the many horrible Scotch trials on record. One Dr. Fian was suspected of having aroused the wind, and a confession was wrung from him by torture, which, however, he almost immediately afterwards retracted. Every form of torture was in vain employed to vanquish his obduracy. The bones of his legs were broken into small pieces in the boot. All the torments that Scottish law knew of were successively applied. At last, the king (who personally presided over the tortures) suggested a new and more horrible device. The prisoner, who had been removed during the deliberation, was brought in, and (I quote the contemporary narrative) 'his nailes upon all his fingers were riven and pulled off with an instrument, called in Scottish a turkas, which in England wee call a payre of pincers, and under everie nayle there was thrust in two needels over, even up to the heads.' However, notwithstanding all this, 'so deeply had the devil entered into his heart, that hee utterly denied all that which he before avouched,' and he was burnt unconfessed. (See a rare black-letter tract, reprinted in Pitcairn's *Criminal Trials of Scotland*, vol. i. part ii. pp. 213, 223.)

subjected witches to death on the first conviction, even though they should have inflicted no injury upon their neigh bours. This law was passed when Coke was Attorney-General, and Bacon a member of Parliament; and twelve bishops sat upon the Commission to which it was referred.[1] The prosecutions were rapidly multiplied throughout the country, but especially in Lancashire; and at the same time the general tone of literature was strongly tinged with the superstition. Sir Thomas Browne declared that those who denied the existence of witchcraft were not only infidels, but also, by implication, atheists.[2] Shakspeare, like most of the other dramatists of his time, again and again referred to the belief; and we owe to it that melancholy picture of Joan of Arc, which is, perhaps, the darkest blot upon his genius.[3] Bacon continually inveighed against the follies shown by magicians in their researches into nature; yet in one of his most important works he pronounced the three 'declinations

[1] Madden's *Phant.*, vol. i. p. 447.

[2] 'I have ever believed, and do now know, that there are witches; they that doubt them do not only deny them but spirits, and are obliquely and upon consequence a sort, not of infidels, but of atheists.' (*Religio Medici*, p. 24, ed. 1672.) Sir T. Browne did not, however, believe in incubi, or in lycanthropy.

[3] On the extent to which the belief was reflected in the dramatic literature of Elizabeth and James I., see Wright's *Sorcery*, vol. i. pp. 286, 296. It was afterwards the custom of Voltaire, when decrying the genius of Shakspeare, to dwell constantly on such characters as the witches in Macbeth. But such scenes, though in modern times they may have an unreal and grotesque appearance, did not present the slightest improbability at the time they were written. It is probable that Shakspeare, it is certain that the immense majority even of his most highly educated and gifted contemporaries, believed with an unfaltering faith in the reality of witchcraft. Shakspeare was, therefore, perfectly justified in introducing into his plays personages who were, of all others, most fitted to enhance the grandeur and the solemnity of tragedy, when they faithfully reflected the belief of the audience.

from religion' to be 'heresies, idolatry, and witchcraft.'[1] Selden took up a somewhat peculiar and characteristic position. He maintained that the law condemning women to death for witchcraft was perfectly just, but that it was quite unnecessary to ascertain whether witchcraft was a possibility. A woman might not be able to destroy the life of her neighbour by her incantations; but if she intended to do so, it was right that she should be hung.[2]

But, great as were the exertions made by James to extirpate witchcraft, they completely sink into insignificance before those which were made during the Commonwealth. As soon as Puritanism gained an ascendency in the country, as soon as its ministers succeeded in imparting their gloomy tenets to the governing classes, the superstition assumed a gigantic magnitude. During the few years of the Commonwealth, there is reason to believe that more alleged witches perished in England than in the whole period before and after.[3] Nor is this to be ascribed entirely to the judges or the legislators, for the judges in former reigns never shrank from condemning witches, and Cromwell was in most respects far superior to his predecessors. It was simply the natural result of Puritanical teaching acting on the mind, predisposing men to see Satanic influence in life, and consequently eliciting the phenomena of witchcraft. A panic on the subject spread through the country; and anecdotes of Satanic power soon crowded in from every side. The county of Suffolk was especially agitated, and the famous witchfinder, Matthew Hopkins, pronounced it to be infested with witches. A commission was accordingly issued, and

---

[1] *Advancement of Learning*, xxv. 22. It is true that this book was dedicated to the king, whose writings on the subject were commended.

[2] *Table-Talk.*   [3] Hutchinson, p. 68.

two distinguished Presbyterian divines were selected by the Parliament to accompany it. It would have been impossible to take any measure more calculated to stimulate the prosecution, and we accordingly find that in Suffolk sixty persons were hung for witchcraft in a single year.[1] Among others, an Anglican clergyman, named Lowes, who was now verging on eighty, and who for fifty years had been an irreproachable minister of his church, fell under the suspicion. The unhappy old man was kept awake for several successive nights, and persecuted 'till he was weary of his life, and was scarcely sensible of what he said or did.' He was then thrown into the water, condemned, and hung. According to the story which circulated among the members of the Established Church, he maintained his innocence manfully to the end. If we believe the Puritanical account, it would appear that his brain gave way under the trial, and that his accusers extorted from him a wild romance, which was afterwards, with many others, reproduced by Baxter 'for the conversion of the Sadducee and the infidel.'[2]

We have seen that the conception of witchcraft, which

This is alluded to in Hudibras:—

> 'Hath not this present Parliament
> A ledger to the devil sent
> Fully empowered to treat about
> Finding revolted witches out ?
> And has not he within a year
> Hanged threescore of them in one shire,' &c.

Second part, Canto iii.

[2] Baxter relates the whole story with evident pleasure. He says : 'Among the rest, an *old reading parson* named Lowis, not far from Framlingham, was one that was hanged, who confessed that he had two imps, and that one of them was always putting him on doing mischief, and (being near the sea) as he saw a ship under sail, it moved him to send him to sink the ship, and he consented, and saw the ship sink before him.' (*World of Spirits*, p. 53.) For the other view of the case, see Hutchinson, pp. 88–90.

had existed in England from the earliest period, assumed for the first time a certain prominence amid the religious terrorism of the Reformation; that its importance gradually increased as the trials and executions directed public attention to the subject; and that it, at last, reached its climax under the gloomy theology of the Puritans. It now only remains for me to trace the history of its decline.

In pursuing this task, I must repeat that it is impossible to follow the general intellectual tendencies of a nation with the degree of precision with which we may review the events or the arguments they produced. We have ample evidence that, at a certain period of English history, there was manifested in some classes a strong disposition to regard witch stories as absurd; but we cannot say precisely when the idea of grotesqueness was first attached to the belief, nor can we map out with exactness the stages of its progress. Speaking generally, however, there can be no doubt that it first became prominent in that great sceptical movement which followed the Restoration. The reaction against the austere rigidity of the last Government, had produced among the gayer classes a sudden outburst of the most derisive incredulity. From mocking the solemn gait, the nasal twang, and the affected phraseology of the Puritans, they naturally proceeded to ridicule their doctrines; and having soon discovered in witchcraft abundant materials for their satire, they made disbelief in it one of the tests of fashion. At the same time the higher intellectual influences were tending strongly to produce a similar movement among the learned. Hobbes, who was the most distinguished of living philosophers, had directed all the energies of his scepticism against incorporeal substances, had treated with unsparing ridicule the conceptions of demons and of apparitions, and had created in his disciples a predisposition to regard them as below contempt.[1] A similar predisposition was formed by the philosophy of Bacon, which had then acquired an immense popularity. The Royal Society[2] had been just established; a passion for natural philosophy, very similar to that which preceded the French Revolution, had become general; and the whole force of the English intellect was directed to the study of natural phenomena, and to the discovery of natural laws. In this manner there was formed a general disposition to attribute to every event a natural cause, which was soon followed by a conviction of the absurdity of explaining phenomena by a supernatural hypothesis, and which rapidly discredited the anecdotes of witches. There does not appear to have been any very careful scrutiny of their details, yet there was a growing indisposition to believe them, as they were discordant with the modes of thought which the experimental philosophy had produced.

By the combination of these three influences, a profound change was soon effected in the manner in which witchcraft was regarded. The sense of its improbability became for the first time general among educated laymen, and the number of the trials speedily diminished. In 1664, however, two women were hung in Suffolk, under a sentence of Sir Matthew Hale, who took the opportunity of declaring that the reality of witchcraft was unquestionable; 'for first, the Scriptures had affirmed so much; and secondly, the wisdom of all nations had provided laws against such persons, which is an argument of their confidence of such a crime.'

[1] On the opinions of Hobbes on this subject, and on his great influence in discrediting these superstitions, see Cudworth's *Intellectual System*, vol. i. p. 1.6.

[2] The (indirect) influence of the Royal Society on this subject is noticed by Hutchinson, and indeed most of the writers on witchcraft. See Casaubon on *Credulity*, p. 191.

Sir Thomas Browne, who was a great physician, as well as
a great writer, was called as a witness, and swore 'that he
was clearly of opinion that the persons were bewitched.'[1]

Seventeen years later, the defence of the dying belief was
taken up by Joseph Glanvil, a divine, who in his own day
was very famous, and who, I venture to think, has been surpassed in genius by few of his successors. Among his contemporaries he was especially praised as an able scholar and
dialectician, and as a writer whose style, though not untinctured by the pedantry of his age, often furnishes the noblest
examples of that glorious eloquence, so rich in varied and
majestic harmonies, of which Milton and the early Anglican
divines were the greatest masters. To us, however, who
look upon his career from the vantage ground of experience,
it assumes a far higher interest, for it occupies a most important position in the history of that experimental philosophy
which has become the great guiding influence of the English
mind. As the works of Glanvil are far less known than they
should be, and as his defence of witchcraft was intimately
connected with his earlier literary enterprises, I shall make
no apology for giving a general outline of his opinions.

To those who only know him as the defender of witchcraft, it may appear a somewhat startling paradox to say,
that the predominating characteristic of the mind of Glanvil
was an intense scepticism. He has even been termed by a
modern critic 'the first English writer who had thrown
scepticism into a definite form;'[2] and if we regard this expression as simply implying a profound distrust of human

[1] The report of this trial is reprinted in *A Collection of Rare and Curious Tracts relating to Witchcraft* (London, 1838).

[2] *Biographie Universelle*—an article which is also in the *Encyclopædia
Britannica*.

9

faculties, and not at all the rejection of any distinct dogmatic system, the judgment can hardly be disputed. And certain-ly, it would be difficult to find a work displaying less of the credulity and superstition that are commonly attributed to the believers in witchcraft than the treatise on 'The Vanity of Dogmatising, or Confidence of Opinions,'[1] in which Glan-vil expounded his philosophical views. Developing a few scattered hints of Bacon, he undertook to make a comprehen-sive survey of the human faculties, to analyse the distorting influences that corrode or pervert our judgments, to reveal the weakness and fallibility of the most powerful intellect, and to estimate the infinity of darkness that encircles our scanty knowledge. Not only did he trace, with the most vivid and unfaltering pen, the proneness to error that accom-panies the human intellect in the moments of its greatest con-fidence; not only did he paint in the darkest colours the tenacity and the inveteracy of prejudice; he even accepted to the fullest extent the consequence of his doctrine, and, with Descartes, enjoined a total abnegation of the opinions that have been received by education as the first condition of enquiry. He showed himself perfectly acquainted with the diversities of intellectual tone, or as he very happily termed them, the 'climates of opinion,' that belong to differ-

---

[1] There is a good review of this book in Hallam's *Hist. of Lit.*, vol. iii. pp. 358–362. It is, I think, by far the best thing Glanvil wrote, and he evidently took extraordinary pains in bringing it to perfection. It first appeared as a short essay; it was then expanded into a regular treatise; and still later, recast and published anew under the title of '*Scepsis Scientifica.*' This last edition is extremely rare, the greater part of the impression having, it is said (I do not know on what authority), been destroyed in the fire of London. It was answered by Thomas White, a once famous Roman Catholic controversialist I cannot but think that Paley was acquainted with the works of Glanvil, for their mode of treating many subjects is strikingly similar. Paley's watch simile is fully developed by Glanvil, in chap. v.

ent ages; and he devoted an entire chapter¹ to the decep-
tions of the imagination, a faculty which he treated with as
much severity as Butler.

On the publication of this treatise Glanvil had been
elected a fellow of the Royal Society, and became one of the
most distinguished of the small but able minority of the
clergy who cordially embraced the inductive philosophy.
To combat the strong antipathy with which this philosophy
was regarded in the Church, and to bring theology into harmony with its principles, was the task to which he devoted
the remainder of his life. Spratt, and in a less degree one
or two other divines, were employed in the same noble cause;
but the manner in which Glanvil conducted his enterprise
separates him, I think, clearly from his fellow-labourers.
For, while his contemporaries seem to have expected as the
extreme consequences of the philosophy, on the one hand a
period of passing disturbance, arising from the discovery of
apparent discrepancies between science and the Bible, and
on the other hand increased evidence of the faith, arising
from the solution of those difficulties and from the increased
perception of superintending wisdom exhibited in 'the wheel-
work of creation,' Glanvil perceived very clearly that a far
deeper and more general modification was at hand. He
saw that the theological system existing in a nation, is
intimately connected with the prevailing modes of thought
or intellectual condition; that the new philosophy was about
to change that condition; and that the Church must either
adapt herself to the altered tone, or lose her influence over
the English mind. He saw that a theology which rested
ultimately on authority, which branded doubt as criminal,
and which discouraged in the strongest manner every impar

¹ Chapter xi.

tial investigation, could not long co-exist with a philosophy
that encouraged the opposite habits of thought as the very beginning of wisdom. He saw that while men maintained every
strange phenomenon to be miraculous as long as it was unexplained, each advance of physical science must necessarily be
hostile to theology; and that the passionate adoration of
Aristotle; the blind pedantic reverence, which accounted the
simplest assertions of dead men decisive authorities; the retrospective habits of thought the universities steadily laboured
to encourage, were all incompatible with the new tendencies
which Bacon represented.[1] In an essay on 'Anti-fanatical
Religion and Free Philosophy,' which was designed to be a
continuation of the New Atlantis of Bacon, he drew a noble
sketch of an ideal church constructed to meet the wants of
an intellectual and a critical age. Its creed was to be framed
on the most latitudinarian principles, because the doctrines
that could be defended with legitimate assurance were but
few and simple. Its ministers were to be much less anxious
to accumulate the traditions of the past than to acquire 'the
felicity of clear and distinct thinking,' and 'a large compass
in their thoughts.' They were to regard faith, not as the
opposite of reason, but as one of its manifestations. Penetrated by the sense of human weakness, they were to rebuke

[1] He compares the leading scholars of his day to the mariner who returned
laden with common pebbles from the Indies, imagining that that must necessarily be rare that came from afar; and he accused them of asserting, on the
authority of Beza, that women have no beards, and on that of St. Augustine
that peace is a blessing. He pronounced university education in general, and
that of Oxford in particular, to be almost worthless. The indignation such
sentiments created at Oxford is very amusingly shown in Wood's *Athenæ*, arts.
Glanvil and *Crosse*. Crosse was a Fellow of Oxford (a D.D.), who at first
vehemently assailed Glanvil in prose, but at last changed his mode of attack,
and wrote comic ballads, which Wood assures us 'made Glanvil and his
Society ridiculous.'

the spirit of dogmatic confidence and assertion, and were to
teach men that, so far from doubt being criminal, it was the
duty of every man 'to suspend his full and resolved assent
to the doctrines he had been taught, till he had impartially
considered and examined them for himself.'

A religious system which is thus divested of the support
of authority, may be upheld upon two grounds. It may
be defended on the rationalistic ground, as according with
conscience, representing and reflecting the light that is in
mankind, and being thus its own justification; or it may be
defended as a distinct dogmatic system by a train of evidential reasoning. The character of his own mind, and the very
low ebb to which moral feeling had sunk in his age, induced
Glanvil to prefer the logical to the moral proof, and he believed that the field on which the battle must first be fought
was witchcraft.'

The 'Sadducismus Triumphatus,' which is probably the
ablest book ever published in defence of the superstition,
opens with a striking picture of the rapid progress of the scepticism in England.' Everywhere, a disbelief in witchcraft was

' He thought the fact of the miracles of witchcraft being contemporary,
would make it peculiarly easy to test them : 'for things remote or long past
are either not believed or forgotten; whereas, these being fresh and new, and
attended with all the circumstances of credibility, it may be expected they
should have most success upon the obstinacy of unbelievers.' (*Preface to the
Sadducismus.*)

' 'Atheism is begun in Sadducism, and those that dare not bluntly say
there is no God, content themselves (for a fair step and introduction) to deny
there are spirits or witches, which sort of infidels, though they are not ordinary among the mere vulgar, yet are they numerous in a little higher rank of
understandings.   And those that know anything of the world, know that most
of the looser gentry, and the small pretenders to philosophy and wit, are generally deriders of the belief of witches and apparitions.'   I need hardly say
that the word Atheism was, in the time of Glanvil, used in the very loosest
sense ; indeed, Dugald Stewart shows, that at one time the disbelievers in
apostolical succession were commonly denounced as Atheists. (*Dissert.*, p. 378.)

becoming fashionable in the upper classes; but it was a disbelief that arose entirely from a strong sense of its antecedent improbability. All who were opposed to the orthodox faith united in discrediting witchcraft. They laughed at it, as palpably absurd, as involving the most grotesque and ludicrous conceptions, as so essentially incredible that it would be a waste of time to examine it. This spirit had arisen since the Restoration, although the laws were still in force, and although little or no direct reasoning had been brought to bear upon the subject. In order to combat it, Glanvil proceeded to examine the general question of the credibility of the miraculous. He saw that the reason why witchcraft was ridiculed was, because it was a phase of the miraculous and the work of the devil; that the scepticism was chiefly due to those who disbelieved in miracles and the devil; and that the instances of witchcraft or possession in the Bible, were invariably placed on a level with those that were tried in the law courts of England. That the evidence of the belief was overwhelming, he firmly believed;[1] and this, indeed, was

---

[1] See a striking passage, pp. 3, 4:—' I must premise that this, being matter of fact, is only capable of the evidence of authority and of sense, and by both these the being of witches and diabolical contracts is most abundantly confirmed. All histories are full of the exploits of those instruments of darkness, and the testimony of all ages, not only of the rude and barbarous, but of the most civilised and polished world, brings tidings of their strange performances. We have the attestation of thousands of eye and ear witnesses, and those not of the easily deceivable vulgar only, but of wise and grave discerners, and that when no interest could oblige them to agree together in a common lie; I say we have the light of all these circumstances to confirm us 'n the belief of things done by persons of despicable power and knowledge, beyond the reach of art and ordinary nature. Standing public records have been kept of these well-attested relations, and epochas made of these unwonted events. Laws, in many nations, have been enacted against those vile practices; those among the Jews and our own are notorious. Such cases have been often determined with us, by wise and revered judges, upon clear and constructive evidence; and thousands in our own nation have suffered death for

scarcely disputed; but, until the sense of *à priori* improbability was removed, no possible accumulation of facts would
cause men to believe it. To that task he accordingly addressed himself. Anticipating the idea and almost the words of
modern controversialists, he urged that there was such a thing
as a credulity of unbelief; and that those who believed so
strange a concurrence of delusions as was necessary on the
supposition of the unreality of witchcraft, were far more credulous than those who accepted the belief.[1] He made his very
scepticism his principal weapon; and, analysing with much
acuteness the *à priori* objections, he showed that they rested
upon an unwarrantable confidence in our knowledge of the
laws of the spirit world; that they implied the existence of
some strict analogy between the faculties of men and of
spirits; and that, as such analogy most probably did not
exist, no reasoning based on the supposition could dispense
men from examining the evidence. He concluded with a
large collection of cases, the evidence of which was, as he
thought, incontestable.

The 'Sadducismus Triumphatus' had an extraordinary
success. Numerous editions were issued, and several very

their vile compact with apostate spirits. All this I might largely prove in
their particular instances, but that it is not needful; since those that deny the
being of witches do it, not out of ignorance of those heads of argument
which, probably, they have heard a thousand times, but from an apprehen-
sion that such a belief is absurd, and the things impossible.'

[1] 'I think those that can believe all histories are romances; that all the
wise could have agreed to juggle mankind into a common belief of ungrounded
fables; that the sound senses of multitudes together may deceive them, and
laws are built upon chimeras; that the gravest and wisest judges have been
murderers, and the sagest persons fools or designing impostors; I say those
that can believe this heap of absurdities, are either more credulous than those
whose credulity they reprehend, or else have some extraordinary evidence of
their persuasion, viz., that it is absurd or impossible there should be a witch
or apparition.' (P. 4.)

able men came forward to support its views. Henry More, the famous philosopher, wrote a warm eulogium to Glanvil, and drew up a long argument in the same spirit, in which he related several additional witch cases, and pronounced the opponents of the belief to be mere 'buffoons, puffed up with nothing but ignorance, vanity, and stupid infidelity.'[1] Casaubon, the learned dean of Canterbury, wrote to the same effect, but in more moderate language.[2] Cudworth, perhaps the most profound of all the great scholars who have adorned the English church, pronounced the scepticism on the subject of witches to be chiefly a consequence of the influence of Hobbes; and he added, that those who partook of that scepticism might be justly suspected of Atheism.[3] Several other divines pressed forward in the same spirit; and they made witchcraft, for a time, one of the chief subjects of controversy in England. On the other side, the discussion was extremely languid. No writer, comparable in ability or influence to Glanvil, More, Cudworth, or even Casaubon, appeared to challenge the belief; nor did any of the writings on that side obtain any success at all equal to that of the Sadducismus. The principal writer was a surgeon named Webster, whose work is remarkable as one of the earliest instances of the systematic application of a rationalistic interpretation to the magical miracles in the Bible. Accord

---

[1] His letters on the subject are prefixed to the *Sadducismus*.

[2] *On Credulity and Incredulity.* This Casaubon was son of the great Greek scholar.

[3] 'As for wizards and magicians, persons who associate and confederate themselves with these evil spirits for the gratification of their own revenge, .ust, ambition, and other passions; besides the Scriptures, there hath been so full an attestation given to them by persons unconcerned in all ages, that those our so confident exploders of them in this present age can hardly escape the suspicion of having some hankering towards atheism.' (*Int. Syst.*, vol. ii. p 650. See also vol. i. p. 1¦6.)

ing to him, the magicians in Egypt were ordinary jugglers, the witch of Endor had dressed up an accomplice to personate Samuel, the word witch in Leviticus only signified poisoner, the demoniacs were chiefly lunatics, and the Magdalene had been freed from seven vices.[1] An unknown scholar named Wagstaafe, at Oxford, also wrote two short works on the subject;[2] and one or two others appeared anonymously. The scepticism steadily increased.

A few years afterwards, a new and strenuous attempt was made to arrest it by accounts of fresh cases of witchcraft in America. The pilgrim fathers had brought to that country the seeds of the superstition; and, at the same time when it was rapidly fading in England, it flourished with fearful vigour in Massachusetts. Two Puritan ministers, named Cotton Mather and Parris, proclaimed the frequency of the crime; and, being warmly supported by their brother divines, they succeeded in creating a panic through the whole country. A commission was issued. A judge named Stoughton, who appears to have been a perfect creature of the clergy, conducted the trials. Scourgings and tortures were added to the terrorism of the pulpit, and many confessions were obtained. The few who ventured to oppose the prosecutions were denounced as Sadducees and infidels. Multitudes were thrown into prison, others fled from the country abandoning their property, and twenty-seven persons were executed. An old man of eighty was pressed to death—a

[1] Webster *on Witches.* The identification of the Scripture demoniacs with maniacs had been made by Hobbes also.

[2] Wagstaafe was a deformed, dwarfish scholar at Oxford, and was the special butt of the Oxonian wit (which in the seventeenth century does not appear to have been extremely brilliant). Poor Wagstaafe consoled himself by drinking whiskey punch; and having drunk too much, he died. (Wood's *Athenæ.*)

horrible sentence, which was never afterwards executed in
America. The ministers of Boston and Charlestown drew up
an address, warmly thanking the commissioners for their
zeal, and expressing their hope that it would never be
relaxed.[1]

In the first year of this persecution, Cotton Mather wrote
a history of the earliest of the trials. This history was introduced to the English public by Richard Baxter, who declared
in his preface that 'that man must be a very obdurate Sadducee who would not believe it.' Not content with having
thus given the weight of his great name to the superstition,
Baxter in the following year published his treatise on ' The
Certainty of the World of Spirits;' in which he collected,
with great industry, an immense number of witch cases; re-
verted in extremely laudatory terms to Cotton Mather and
his crusade; and denounced, in unmeasured language, all
who were sceptical upon the subject. This work appeared
in 1691, when the panic in America had not yet reached its
height; and being widely circulated beyond the Atlantic, is
said to have contributed much to stimulate the prosecutions.[2]
In England it produced little effect. The scepticism that was
already pervading all classes was steadily and silently increasing, under the influence of an intellectual movement that
was too general and too powerful for any individual genius
to arrest. At the time of the Restoration the belief had been
common among the most educated. In 1718, when Hutchinson wrote, it scarcely existed, except among the ignorant
and in a small section of the clergy.[3] Yet, in the interval,

---

[1] Bancroft, *History of the United States*, ch. xix. Hutchinson, pp. 95–119.

[2] Hutchinson, pp. 95–119.

[3] Mr. Buckle places the scepticism a little earlier. He says: 'This important revolution in our opinion was effected, so far as the educated classes are
concerned, between the Restoration and Revolution; that is to say, in 1660,

the vast preponderance of controversial literature had un questionably been on the conservative side. During that period no less than twenty-five works [1] are known to have appeared in England in defence of the belief; and among their authors we have seen some of the ablest men in England. The work of Baxter, notwithstanding the weight of his great name, and the very definite character of his statements, appears to have remained entirely unanswered till it was reviewed by Hutchinson twenty-six years after its publication. Yet it could do no more to arrest, than the work of Scott had done to produce, the scepticism. Three witches had been executed in 1682; and others, it is said, endured the same fate in 1712; but these were the last who perished judicially in England.[2] The last trial, at least of any notoriety, was that of Jane Wenham, who was prosecuted in 1712, by some Hertfordshire clergymen. The judge entirely disbelieved in witches, and accordingly charged the jury strongly in favour of the accused, and even treated with great disrespect the rector of the parish, who declared 'on his faith as a clergyman' that he believed the woman to be a witch. The jury, being ignorant and obstinate, convicted the prisoner; but the judge had no difficulty in obtaining a remission of her sentence. A long war of pamphlets ensued, and the clergy who had been engaged in the prosecution, drew up a document strongly asserting their belief in the guilt of the accused animadverting severely upon the conduct of the

the majority of educated men still believed in witchcraft; and in 1688, the majority disbelieved it.' (Vol. i. p. 333.) By 1718, however, the minority had become insignificant.

[1] Some of them, of course, were mere pamphlets, but a large proportion elaborate works. The catalogue is given by Hutchinson.

[2] Compare Hutchinson, p. 57, and Buckle, vol. i. p. 334. I say *judicially*, for in the *Times* of Sept. 24th, 1863, there is an account of an old man who was mobbed to death in the county of Essex as a wizard.

judge, and concluding with the solemn words, 'Liberavimus animas nostras.'[1]

It is probable that this was an instance of somewhat ex ceptional fanaticism; and that Hutchinson, who was himself a clergyman, represented the opinions of most of the more educated of his profession, when a few years later he de- scribed witchcraft as a delusion. In 1736, the laws on the subject were repealed, without difficulty or agitation; and there are very few instances of educated men regretting them. In 1768, however, John Wesley prefaced an account of an ap- parition that had been related by a girl named Elizabeth Hob- son, by some extremely remarkable sentences on the subject. 'It is true, likewise,' he wrote, 'that the English in general, and indeed most of the men of learning in Europe, have given up all accounts of witches and apparitions as mere old wives' fables. I am sorry for it, and I willingly take this opportunity of entering my solemn protest against this violent compliment which so many that believe the Bible pay to those who do not believe it. I owe them no such service. I take knowledge that these are at the bottom of the outcry which has been raised, and with such insolence spread through the land, in direct opposition, not only to the Bible, but to the suffrage of the wisest and best of men in all ages and nations. They well know (whether Christians know it or not) that the giving up witchcraft is in effect giving up the Bible.'[2]

In reviewing the history of witchcraft in England, it is impossible to avoid observing the singularly favourable con- trast which the Anglican Church presents, both to continen- tal Catholicism and to Puritanism. It is indeed true that

[1] Hutchinson, pp. 163–171. Some noble and liberal remarks.
[2] Journal, 1768.

ner bishops contributed much to the enactment of the laws
against witchcraft, that the immense majority of the clergy
firmly believed in the reality of the crime, and that they continued to assert and to defend it when the great bulk of educated laymen had abandoned it.   It is also true that the
scepticism on the subject of witches arose among those who
were least governed by the Church, advanced with the decline of the influence of the clergy, and was commonly
branded as a phase and manifestation of infidelity.   Yet, on
the other hand, it is impossible to deny that the general mod·
cration of the higher clergy was beyond all praise, and that
even those who were most credulous were singularly free from
that thirst of blood which was elsewhere so common.   On the
Continent, every attempt to substitute a lighter punishment
for death was fiercely denounced as a direct violation of the
Divine law.   Indeed, some persons went so far as to question
the lawfulness of strangling the witch before she was burnt.
Her crime, they said, was treason against the Almighty, and
therefore to punish it by any but the most agonizing deaths
was an act of disrespect to Him.   Besides, the penalty in the
Levitical code was stoning, and stoning had been pronounced
by the Jewish theologians to be a still more painful death
than the stake.[1]   Nothing of this kind was found in England.
There is, as far as I am aware, not a single instance of the
English clergy complaining of the leniency of the laws upon
the subject, or attempting to introduce torture into the trials.
Their zeal in stimulating the persecution by exorcisms and
fanatical preaching, was also comparatively languid.   As
early as the reign of James I., the Convocation made a canon
prohibiting any clergyman from exorcising a possessed person,
without a license from his bishop, and such licenses were

Bodin, p. 217.

scarcely ever granted.[1] Dr. Morton, a bishop of Lichfield, in
1620, employed himself with great, and at last successful,
zeal in detecting a case of imposture in a witch story which
was believed by a Catholic priest,[2] and he succeeded in saving
the life of the accused.   At a still earlier period, Dr. Harsnet, who was afterwards Archbishop of York, in an attack
upon 'Popish impostures,' boldly enumerated among them
most of the forms of witchcraft,[3] and appears to have been
entirely incredulous on the subject.   He was undoubtedly
wrong in ascribing witchcraft to Catholicism, for it flourished at least as vigorously under the shadow of Puritanism; yet
the expression of so bold an opinion is well worthy of notice,
and was, I believe, at the time it was written, a unique phenomenon among the English clergy.[4]   Hutchinson himself
wrote his history before the belief was entirely extinct.

   But that which shows most strikingly the moderation of
the Anglican clergy, is the comparatively small amount of
delusion which the history of English witchcraft presents.
On the Continent, there was undoubtedly much imposition ·
but, for the most part, the subject presents rather the aspect
of an epidemic or a mania.   The religious terrorism acted on
diseased imaginations, coloured every form of madness, and
predisposed the minds of men to solve every difficulty by a
supernatural hypothesis.   In England, on the other hand,
imposture appears the general characteristic.   The books on

---

[1] Hutchinson, Dedication.   [2] Ibid.   [3] Ibid.

[4] I, at least, have not been able to find any other case; but Sir Kenelm
Digby, in his annotation to the passage from Sir Thomas Browne, which I have
before quoted, says of the belief: 'There are divines of great note, and far
from any suspicion of being irreligious, that do not oppose it.' The book of
Dr. Harsnet is, I believe, rare. I only know it by the copious extracts
in Hutchinson. There is a notice of its author in Neal's *Hist. of the Puritans.*

the subject are full of cases of jugglers' tricks;[1] and, with the exception of the period when the Puritans were in the ascendant, it never seems to have assumed the appearance of a great and general panic. Indeed, in most of its worst man-ifestations, the fanaticism of Puritanism was manifested.[2]

In England, that fanaticism was bridled and repressed. There was one country, however, in which it obtained an absolute ascendancy. There was one country in which the Puritan ministers succeeded in moulding alike the character and the habits of the nation, and in disseminating their harsh and gloomy tenets through every section of society. While England was breaking loose from her most ancient superstitions, and advancing with gigantic strides along the paths of knowledge, Scotland still cowered in helpless sub-jection before her clergy. Never was a mental servitude more complete, and never was a tyranny maintained with more inexorable barbarity. Supported by public opinion, the Scottish ministers succeeded in overawing all opposition, in prohibiting the faintest expression of adverse opinions, in prying into and controlling the most private concerns of do-mestic life; in compelling every one to conform absolutely to all the ecclesiastical regulations they enjoined; and in, at last, directing the whole scope and current of legislation. They maintained their ascendancy over the popular mind by a sys-tem of religious terrorism, which we can now barely conceive. The misery of man, the anger of the Almighty, the fearful

[1] See Scott's *Discovery, passim.*

[2] Sir W. Scott has well noticed this influence of Puritanism on English witchcraft; and, in comparing the different sections of the Church, he says, 'On the whole, the Calvinists, generally speaking, were, of all the contending sects, the most suspicious of sorcery, the most undoubting believers in its ex-istence, and the most eager to follow it up with what they conceived to be the due punishment of the most fearful of crimes.' (*Demonology and Witchcraft,* Letter 8.)

power and continual presence of Satan, the agonies of hell, were the constant subjects of their preaching. All the most ghastly forms of human suffering were accumulated as faint images of the eternal doom of the immense majority of mankind. Countless miracles were represented as taking place within the land, but they were almost all of them miracles of terror. Disease, storm, famine, every awful calamity that fell upon mankind, or blasted the produce of the soil, was attributed to the direct intervention of spirits; and Satan himself was represented as constantly appearing in a visible form upon the earth.[1] Such teaching produced its natural effects. In a land where credulity was universal, in a land where the intellect was numbed and palsied by these awful contemplations, where almost every form of amusement was suppressed, and where the thoughts of men were concentrated with an undivided energy on theological conceptions, such teaching necessarily created the superstition of witchcraft. Witchcraft was but one form of the panic it produced; it was but the reflection by a diseased imagination of the popular theology. We accordingly find that it assumed the most frightful proportions and the darkest character. In other lands, the superstition was at least mixed with much of imposture; in Scotland it appears to have been entirely undiluted.[2] It was produced by the teaching of the clergy, and it was everywhere fostered by their persecution. Eagerly, passionately, with a thirst for blood that knew no mercy, with a zeal that never tired, did they accomplish their task.

[1] I need hardly refer to the noble description of the Scotch Kirk in Buckle's History—a description the substantial justice of which will be questioned by no one who is acquainted with the history of Scotch witchcraft. On the multitude of miracles and apparitions of Satan that were believed, see pp. 349–369

[2] The very remarkable fact, that no cases of imposture have been detected in Scotch witch-trials, is noted by Buckle, vol. ii. pp. 189, 190.

Assembled in solemn synod, the college of Áberdeen, in 1603, enjoined every minister to take two of the elders of his parish to make 'a subtle and privy inquisition,' and to question all the parishioners upon oath as to their knowledge of witches.[1] Boxes were placed in the churches for the express purpose of receiving the accusations.[2] When a woman had fallen under suspicion, the minister from the pulpit denounced her by name, exhorted his parishioners to give evidence against her, and prohibited any one from sheltering her.[3] In the same spirit, he exerted the power which was given him by a parochial organisation, elaborated perhaps more skilfully than any other in Europe. Under these circumstances, the witch-cases seem to have fallen almost entirely into the hands of the clergy. They were the leading commissioners. Before them the confessions were taken. They were the acquiescing witnesses or the directors of the tortures by which those confessions were elicited.[4]

And when we read the nature of these tortures, which were worthy of an oriental imagination ; when we remember that they were inflicted, for the most part, on old and feeble and half-doting women, it is difficult to repress a feeling of the deepest abhorrence for those men who caused and who encouraged them. If the witch was obdurate, the first, and it was said the most effectual, method of obtaining confession was by what was termed ' waking her.' An iron bridle or hoop was

Dalyell, *Darker Superstitions of Scotland*, p. 624.

[2] Ibid. p. 623.   [3] Ibid. p. 624, &c.

[4] See on this subject Pitcairn's *Criminal Trials of Scotland*, a vast repository of original documents on the subject. Pitcairn gives numbers of these confessions. He adds, 'The confessions were commonly taken before presbyteries, or certain special commissioners, who usually ranked among their number the leading clergy of those districts where their hapless victims resided.' (Vol. iii. p. 598.)

bound across her face with four prongs, which were thrust into her mouth. It was fastened behind to the wall by a chain, in such a manner that the victim was unable to lie down; and in this position she was sometimes kept for several days, while men were constantly with her to prevent her from closing her eyes for a moment in sleep.[1] Partly in order to effect this object, and partly to discover the insensible mark which was the sure sign of a witch, long pins were thrust into her body.[2] At the same time, as it was a saying in Scotland that a witch would never confess while she could drink, excessive thirst was often added to her tortures.[3] Some prisoners have been waked for five nights; one, it is said, even for nine.[4]

The physical and mental suffering of such a process was sufficient to overcome the resolution of many, and to distract

[1] 'One of the most powerful incentives to confession was systematically to deprive the suspected witch of the refreshment of her natural sleep. . . . Iron collars, or witches' bridles, are still preserved in various parts of Scotland, which had been used for such iniquitous purposes. These instruments were so constructed that, by means of a hoop which passed over the head, a piece of iron having four points or prongs was forcibly thrust into the mouth, two of these being directed to the tongue and palate, the others pointing outwards to each cheek. This infernal machine was secured by a padlock. At the back of the collar was fixed a ring, by which to attach the witch to a staple in the wall of her cell. Thus equipped, and night and day waked and watched by some skilful person appointed by her inquisitors, the unhappy creature, after a few days of such discipline, maddened by the misery of her forlorn and helpless state, would be rendered fit for confessing anything, in order to be rid of the dregs of her wretched life. At intervals fresh examinations took place, and these were repeated from time to time until her "contumacy," as it was termed, was subdued. The clergy and kirk sessions appear to have been the unwearied instruments of "purging the land of witchcraft;" and *to them, in the first instance, all the complaints and informations were made.*' (Pitcairn, vol. i. part 2, p. 50.)

[2] Dalyell, p. 645. The 'prickers' formed a regular profession in Scotland Burt's *Letters from the North of Scotland*, vol. i. pp. 227-234.

[4] Dalyell, p. 645.

the understanding of not a few. But *other and perhaps worse tortures were in reserve. The three principal that were habitually applied, were the pennywinkis, the boots, and the caschielawis. The first was a kind of thumb-screw; the second was a frame in which the leg was inserted, and in which it was broken by wedges, driven in by a hammer; the third was also an iron frame for the leg, which was from time to time heated over a brazier.[1] Fire-matches were some-times applied to the body of the victim.[2] We read, in a con-temporary legal register, of one man who was kept for forty-eight hours in 'vehement tortour' in the caschielawis; and of another who remained in the same frightful machine for eleven days and eleven nights, whose legs were broken daily for fourteen days in the boots, and who was so scourged that the whole skin was torn from his body.[3] This was, it is true, censured as an extreme case, but it was only an excessive application of the common torture.

How many confessions were extorted, and how many victims perished by these means, it is now impossible to say. A vast number of depositions and confessions are preserved, but they were only taken before a single court, and many others took cognisance of the crime. We know that in 1662, more than 150 persons were accused of witchcraft;[4] and that in the preceding year no less than fourteen commissions had been issued for the trials.[5] After these facts, it is scarcely necessary to notice how one traveller casually mentions having seen nine women burning together at Leith in 1664, or how, in 1678, nine others were condemned in a single

---

[1] Pitcairn.   [2] Dalyell, p. 657.
[3] Pitcairn, vol. i. part ii. p. 376. The two cases were in the same trial in 1596.
[4] Dalyell, p. 669   [5] Pitcairn, vol. iii. p. 597.

day.[1] The charges were, indeed, of the most comprehensive order, and the wildest fancies of Sprenger and Nider were defended by the Presbyterian divines.[2] In most Catholic countries, it was a grievance of the clergy that the civil power refused to execute those who only employed their power in curing disease.   In Scotland such persons were unscrupulously put to death.[3]   The witches were commonly strangled before they were burnt, but this merciful provision was very frequently omitted.   An Earl of Mar (who appears to have been the only person sensible of the inhumanity of the proceedings) tells how, with a piercing yell, some women once broke half-burnt from the slow fire that consumed them, struggled for a few moments with despairing energy among the spectators, but soon with shrieks of blasphemy and wild protestations of innocence sank writhing in agony amid the flames.[4]

The contemplation of such scenes as these is one of the most painful duties that can devolve upon the historian; but

---

[1] Dalyell, pp. 669, 670.

[2] For a curious instance of this, see that strange book, ' *The Secret Commonwealth*,' published in 1691, by Robert Kirk, minister of Aberfoil. He represents evil spirits in human form as habitually living among the Highlanders. Succubi, or, as the Scotch called them, Leannain Sith, seem to have been especially common; and Mr. Kirk (who identifies them with the ' *familiar spirits* ' of Deuteronomy) complains very sadly of the affection of many young Scotchmen for the ' fair ladies of this aërial order ' (p. 35). Capt. Burt relates a long discussion he had with a minister on the subject of old women turning themselves into cats. The minister said that one man succeeded in cutting off the leg of a cat who attacked him, that the leg immediately turned into that of an old woman, and that four ministers signed a certificate attesting the fact (vol. i. pp. 271–277). One of the principal Scotch writers on these matters was Sinclair, who was Professor of Moral Philosophy at Glasgow.

[3] Wright's *Sorcery*, vol. i. pp. 165, 166. Even to consult with witches was made capital.

[4] Pitcairn, vol. iii. p. 598. Another Earl of Mar had been himself bled to death for having, as was alleged, consulted with witches how to shorten the life of James III. (Scott's *Demonology*, let. ix.)

it is one from which he must not shrink, if he would form a just estimate of the past. There are opinions that may be traced from age to age by footsteps of blood; and the intensity of the suffering they caused is a measure of the intensity with which they were realised. Scotch witchcraft was but the result of Scotch Puritanism, and it faithfully reflected the character of its parent. It is true that, before the Reformation, the people had been grossly ignorant and superstitious; but it is also true, that witchcraft in its darker forms was so rare that no law was made on the subject till 1563; that the law was not carried to its full severity till 1590; that the delusion invariably accompanied the religious terrorism which the Scotch clergy so zealously maintained; and that those clergy, all over Scotland, applauded and stimulated the persecution.[1] The ascendancy they had obtained was boundless, and in this respect their power was entirely undisputed. One word from them might have arrested the tortures, but that word was never spoken. Their conduct implies, not merely a mental aberration, but also a callousness of feeling which has rarely been attained in a long career of vice. Yet these were men who had often shown, in the most trying circumstances, the highest and the most heroic virtues. They were men whose courage had never flinched when persecution was raging around; men who had never paltered with their consciences to attain the favours of a king; men

[1] Sir Walter Scott seems to think that the first great outburst of persecution began when James VI. went to Denmark to fetch his bride. Before his departure, he exhorted the clergy to assist the magistrates, which they did, and most especially in matters of witchcraft. The king was himself perfectly infatuated with the subject, and had this one bond of union with the ministers; and, as Sir W. S. says, 'during the halcyon period of union between kirk and king, their hearty agreement on the subject of witchcraft failed not to heat the fires against all persons suspected of such iniquity.' (*Demonology*, letter ix.) See also Linton's *Witch Stories*, p. 5.

whose self-devotion and zeal in their sacred calling had seldom been surpassed; men who in all the private relations of life were doubtless amiable and affectionate. It is not on them that our blame should fall; it is on the system that made them what they were. They were but illustrations of the great truth, that when men have come to regard a certain class of their fellow-creatures as doomed by the Almighty to eternal and excruciating agonies, and when their theology directs their minds with intense and realising earnestness to the contemplation of such agonies, the result will be an indifference to the suffering of those whom they deem the enemies of their God, as absolute as it is perhaps possible for human nature to attain.

In Scotland the character of theology was even more hard and unpitying than in other countries where Puritanism existed, on account of a special circumstance which in some respects reflects great credit on its teachers. The Scotch kirk was the result of a democratic movement, and for some time, almost alone in Europe, it was the unflinching champion of political liberty. It was a Scotchman, Buchanan, who first brought liberal principles into clear relief. It was the Scotch clergy who upheld them with a courage that can hardly be overrated. Their circumstances made them liberals, and they naturally sought to clothe their liberalism in a theological garb. They soon discovered precedents for their rebellions in the history of the judges and captains of the Jews; and accordingly the union of an intense theological, and an intense liberal feeling, made them revert to the scenes of the Old Testament, to the sufferings and also the conquests of the Jews, with an affection that seems now almost inconceivable. Their whole theology took an Old Testament cast. Their modes of thought, their very phraseology, were de rired from that source ; and the constant contemplation of the massacres of Canaan, and of the provisions of the Levitical code, produced its natural effect upon their minds.[1]

It is scarcely possible to write a history of the decline of witchcraft in Scotland, for the change of opinions was almost entirely unmarked by incidents on which we can dwell. At one period we find every one predisposed to believe in witches. At a later period we find that this predisposition has silently passed away.[2] Two things only can, I think, be asserted on the subject with confidence—that the sceptical movement advanced much more slowly in Scotland than in England, and that the ministers were among the latest to yield to it. Until the close of the seventeenth century, the trials were sufficiently common, but after this time they became rare. It is generally said that the last execution was in 1722; but Captain Burt, who visited the country in 1730, speaks of a woman who was burnt as late as 1727.[3] The same very keen observer was greatly struck by the extent to which the belief still continued in Scotland, at a time when it was quite abandoned by the educated classes in England ; and he found its most ardent supporters among the Presbyterian ministers. As late as 1773, ' the divines of the Associated Presbytery ' passed a resolution declaring their belief in witchcraft, and deploring the scepticism that was general.[4]

---

[1] It is rather remarkable that Bodin had also formed his theology almost exclusively from the Old Testament, his reverence for which was so great that some (Grotius and Hallam among others) have questioned whether he believed the New.

[2] The silent unreasoning character of the decline of Scotch witchcraft has been noticed by Dugald Stewart, *Dissert.* p. 508.

[3] Burt's *Letters from the North of Scotland*, vol. i. pp. 227–234, and 271–277. I suspect Burt has misdated the execution that took place in 1722, placing it in 1727.

[4] Macaulay, *Hist.*, vol. iii. p. 706.

I have now completed my review of the history of witch-craft, in its relation to the theologies of Rome, of England, and of Geneva. I have shown that its causes are to be sought, not within the narrow circle of doctrines and phe-nomena that are comprised under the name, but in the gen-eral intellectual and religious condition of the ages in which it flourished. I have shown, in other words, that witchcraft resulted, not from isolated circumstances, but from modes of thought; that it grew out of a certain intellectual tempera-ture acting on certain theological tenets, and reflected with almost startling vividness each great intellectual change. Arising amid the ignorance of an early civilisation, it was quickened into an intenser life by a theological struggle which allied terrorism with credulity, and it declined under the influence of that great rationalistic movement which, since the seventeenth century, has been on all sides encroach-ing on theology. I have dwelt upon the decadence of the superstition at considerable length; for it was at once one of the earliest and one of the most important conquests of the spirit of rationalism. There are very few examples of a change of belief that was so strictly normal, so little accele-rated by sectarian passions or individual genius, and there-fore so well suited to illustrate the laws of intellectual de-velopment. Besides this, the fact that the belief when real-ised was always followed by persecution, enables us to trace its successive stages with more than common accuracy, while the period that has elapsed since its destruction has, in a great measure, removed the subject from the turbid at-mosphere of controversy.

It is impossible to leave the history of witchcraft with-out reflecting how vast an amount of suffering has, in at least this respect, been removed by the progress of a rationalistic civilisation. I know that when we remember the frightful calamities that have from time to time flowed from theological divisions; when we consider the countless martyrs who have perished in the dungeon or at the stake, the millions who have fallen in the religious wars, the elements of almost undying dissension that have been planted in so many noble nations, and have paralysed so many glorious enterprises, the fate of a few thousand innocent persons who were burnt alive seems to sink into comparative insignificance. Yet it is probable that no class of victims endured sufferings so unalloyed and so intense. Not for them the wild fanaticism that nerves the soul against danger, and al most steels the body against torments. Not for them the assurance of a glorious eternity, that has made the martyr look with exultation on the rising flame as on the Elijah's chariot that is to bear his soul to heaven. Not for them the solace of lamenting friends, or the consciousness that their memories would be cherished and honoured by posterity. They died alone, hated and unpitied. They were deemed by all mankind the worst of criminals. Their very kinsmen shrank from them as tainted and accursed. The superstitions they had imbibed in childhood, blending with the illusions of age, and with the horrors of their position, persuaded them in many cases that they were indeed the bond-slaves of Satan, and were about to exchange their torments upon earth for an agony that was as excruciating, and was eternal. And, besides all this, we have to consider the terrors which the belief must have spread through the people at large; we have to picture the anguish of the mother, as she imagined that it was in the power of one whom she had offended to blast in a moment every object of her affection, we have to corceive, above all, the awful shadow that the

dread of accusation must have thrown on the enfeebled
faculties of age, and the bitterness it must have added to
desertion and to solitude. All these sufferings were the result of a single superstition, which the spirit of rationalism
has destroyed.

CHAPTER II.

ON THE DECLINING SENSE OF THE MIRACULOUS.

THE MIRACLES OF THE CHURCH.

THE same habits of mind which induced men at first to recoil from the belief in witchcraft with an instinctive and involuntary repugnance as intrinsically incredible, and afterwards openly to repudiate it, have operated in a very similar manner, and with very similar effects, upon the belief in modern miracles. The triumph, however, has not been in this case so complete, for the Church of Rome still maintains the continuance of miraculous powers; nor has the decay been so strictly normal, for the fact that most of the Roman Catholic miracles are associated with distinctively Roman Catholic doctrines has introduced much miscellaneous controversy into the question. But, notwithstanding these considerations, the general outlines of the movement are clearly visible, and they are well deserving of a brief notice.

If we would realise the modes of thought on this subject prior to the Reformation, we must quite dismiss from our minds the ordinary Protestant notion that miracles were very rare and exceptional phenomena, the primary object of which was always to accredit the teacher of some divine truth that

could not otherwise be established. In the writings of the
Fathers, and especially of those of the fourth and fifth centuries, we find them not only spoken of as existing in profusion, but as being directed to the most various ends. They
were a kind of celestial charity, alleviating the sorrows,
healing the diseases, and supplying the wants of the faithful.
They were frequent incitements to piety, stimulating the devotions of the languid, and rewarding the patience of the
fervent. They were the signs of great and saintly virtue,
securing universal respect for those who had attained a high
degree of sanctity, or assisting them in the performance of
their more austere devotions. Thus, one saint having retired
into the desert to lead a life of mortification, the birds daily
brought him a supply of food, which was just sufficient for
his wants; and when a kindred spirit visited him in his re-
tirement, they doubled the supply; and when he died, two
lions issued from the desert to dig his grave, uttered a long
howl of mourning over his body, and knelt down to beg a
blessing from the survivor.[1] Thus, another saint, who was
of opinion that a monk should never see himself naked, and
who had, therefore, scrupulously abstained from washing
since his conversion, stood one day in despair upon the banks
of a bridgeless stream, when an angel descended to assist
him, and transported him in safety across the dreaded element.[2] Besides this, the power of magic was, as we have
seen, fully recognised, both by Christians and Pagans, and
each admitted the reality of the miracles of the other
though ascribing them to the agency of demons.[3]

---

[1] Paul the Hermit. See his Life by St. Jerome. The visitor of Paul was
St. Anthony, the first of the hermits.

[2] Ammon (Socrates, lib. iv. c. 23).

[3] See some admirable remarks on this subject in Maury, *Légendes Pieuses*,

If we pass from the Fathers into the middle ages, we find ourselves in an atmosphere that was dense and charged with the supernatural. The demand for miracles was almost boundless, and the supply was equal to the demand. Men of extraordinary sanctity seemed naturally and habitually to obtain the power of performing them, and their lives are crowded with their achievements, which were attested by the highest sanction of the Church. Nothing could be more common than for a holy man to be lifted up from the floor in the midst of his devotions, or to be visited by the Virgin or by an angel. There was scarcely a town that could not show some relic that had cured the sick, or some image that had opened and shut its eyes, or bowed its head to an earnest worshipper. It was somewhat more extraordinary, but not in the least incredible, that the fish should have thronged to the shore to hear St. Anthony preach, or that it should be necessary to cut the hair of the crucifix at Burgos once a month, or that the Virgin of the Pillar, at Saragossa, should, at the prayer of one of her worshippers, have restored a leg that had been amputated.[1] Men who were afflicted with apparently hopeless disease, started in a moment into perfect health when brought into contact with a relic of Christ or of the Virgin. The virtue of such relics radiated in blessings

pp. 240–244. Also Farmer, on *Demoniacs*. There were exorcists, both among the Christians, Pagans, and Jews; and though they were not regularly formed into an order till the middle of the third century, they seem to have practised from almost the beginning. For much curious evidence on the subject, see Middleton, *Free Enquiry*, pp. 85–87; Bingham, *Antiquities of the Christian Church*, book iii. c. 4.

[1] There is a picture of the transaction in the cathedral of Saragossa, opposite the image. A group of extremely pretty angels are represented as fitting on a leg (ready made), while the patient is calmly sleeping. I believe, however, that the more approved story is, that the leg gradually grew. This is a miracle about which a vast amount has been written, and which the Spanish theologians are said to regard as peculiarly well established.

all around them. Glorious visions heralded their discovery, and angels have transported them through the air. If a missionary went abroad among the heathen, supernatural signs confounded his opponents, and made the powers of darkness fly before his steps. If a Christian prince unsheathed his sword in an ecclesiastical cause, apostles had been known to combat with his army, and avenging miracles to scatter his enemies. If an unjust suspicion attached to an innocent man, he had immediately recourse to an ordeal which cleared his character and condemned his accusers. All this was going on habitually in every part of Europe without exciting the smallest astonishment or scepticism. Those who know how thoroughly the supernatural element pervades the old lives of the saints, may form some notion of the multitude of miracles that were related and generally believed, from the fact that M. Guizot has estimated the number of these lives, accumulated in the Bollandist Collection, at about 25,000.[1] Yet this was but one department of miracles. It does not include the thousands of miraculous images and pictures that were operating throughout Christendom, and the countless apparitions and miscellaneous prodigies that were taking place in every country, and on all occasions. Whenever a saint was canonised, it was necessary to prove that he had worked miracles; but except on those occasions miraculous accounts seem never to have been questioned. The most

[1] *Hist. de Civilisation*, Leçon XVII. The Bollandist Collection was begun at Antwerp by a Jesuit named Bolland, in 1643, was stopped for a time by the French Revolution, but renewed under the patronage of the Belgian Chambers. It was intended to contain a complete collection of all the original documents on the subject. The saints are placed according to the calendar. Fifty-five large folio volumes have been published, but they only extend to the end of October. See a very beautiful essay on the subject by Renan, *Études Religieuses*. M. Renan says: 'Il me semble que pour un vrai philosophe un prison cellulaire avec ces cinquante-cinq volumes in-folio, serait un vrai paradis

educated, as well as the most ignorant, habitually resorted to the supernatural as the simplest explanation of every difficulty.

All this has now passed away. It has passed away, not only in lands where Protestantism is triumphant, but also in those where the Roman Catholic faith is still acknowledged, and where the mediæval saints are still venerated. St. Januarius, it is true, continues to liquefy at Naples, and the pastorals of French bishops occasionally relate apparitions of the Virgin among very ignorant and superstitious peasants; but the implicit, undiscriminating acquiescence with which such narratives were once received, has long since been replaced by a derisive incredulity. Those who know the tone that is habitually adopted on these subjects by the educated in Roman Catholic countries, will admit that, so far from being a subject for triumphant exultation, the very few modern miracles which are related are everywhere regarded as a scandal, a stumbling-block, and a difficulty. Most educated persons speak of them with undisguised scorn and incredulity; some attempt to evade or explain them away by a natural hypothesis; a very few faintly and apologetically defend them. Nor can it be said that what is manifested is merely a desire for a more minute and accurate examination of the evidence by which they are supported. On the contrary, it will, I think, be admitted that these alleged miracles are commonly rejected with an assurance that is as peremptory and unreasoning as that with which they would have been once received. Nothing can be more rare than a serious examination, by those who disbelieve them, of the testimony on which they rest. They are repudiated, not because they are unsupported, but because they are miraculous. Men are prepared to admit almost any conceivable concurrence of natural improbabilities rather than resort to the hypothesis of supernatural interference; and this spirit is exhibited, not merely by open sceptics, but by men who are sincere, though, perhaps, not very fervent believers in their Church. It is the prevailing characteristic of that vast body of educated persons, whose lives are chiefly spent in secular pursuits, and who, while they receive with unenquiring faith the great doctrines of Catholicism, and duly perform its leading duties, derive their mental tone and colouring from the general spirit of their age. If you speak to them on the subject, they will reply with a shrug and with a smile; they will tell you that it is indeed melancholy that such narratives should be put forth in the middle of the nineteenth century; they will treat them as palpable anachronisms, as obviously and intrinsically incredible; but they will add that it is not necessary for all Roman Catholics to believe them, and that it is unfair to judge the enlightened members of the Church by the measure of the superstitions of the ignorant.

That this is the general tone adopted by the great majority of educated Roman Catholics, both in their writings and in their conversation, will scarcely be a matter of dispute. It is also very manifest that it is the direct product and measure of civilisation. The districts where an account of a modern miracle is received with least derision, are precisely those which are most torpid and most isolated. The classes whose habits of thought are least shocked by such an account, are those which are least educated and least influenced by the broad current of civilisation. If we put aside the clergy and those who are most immediately under their influence, we find that this habit of mind is the invariable concomitant of education, and is the especial characteristic of those persons whose intellectual sympathies are most extended, and who, therefore, represent most faithfully the various intellectual influences of their time. If you connect a nation which has long been insulated and superstitious with the general movement of European civilisation by means of railways or a free press or the removal of protecting laws, you will most infallibly inoculate it with this spirit.

It is further evident that this habit of thought is not a merely ephemeral movement, produced by some exceptional event, or by some transient literary fashion peculiar to our own century. All history shows that, in exact proportion as nations advance in civilisation, the accounts of miracles taking place among them become rarer and rarer, until at last they entirely cease.[1] In this fact we have a clear indication of the decline of the old habits of thought; for those who regard these miracles as real ascribe their disappearance to the progress of incredulity, while those who disbelieve them maintain that they were the results of a particular direction given to the imagination, and of a particular form of imposition created and suggested by the mediæval habits of thought. In other words, the old spirit, according to one class, is the condition, and according to the other class, the cause of the miracles; and, therefore, the cessation of miraculous narratives, when unaccompanied by an avowed change of creed, implies the decay of that spirit.

If these propositions be true—and I scarcely think that any candid person who seriously examines the subject can

---

[1] This has been noticed in an extremely ingenious fashion by Bishop Spratt:—'God never yet left himself without a witness in the world; and it is observable that He has commonly chosen the dark and ignorant ages wherein to work miracles, but seldom or never the times when natural knowledge prevailed: for He knew there was not so much need to make use of extraordinary signs when men were diligent in the works of His hands and attentive to the impressions of His footsteps in His creatures.' (*Hist. of Royal Society,* p. 350.)

question them—they lead irresistibly to a very important general conclusion. They show that the repugnance of men to believe miraculous narratives is in direct proportion to the progress of civilisation and the diffusion of knowledge. It is not simply that science explains some things which were formerly deemed supernatural, such as comets or eclipses. We find the same incredulity manifested in Roman Catholic countries towards alleged miracles by saints, or relics, or images, on which science can throw no direct light, and which contain no element of improbability, except that they are miraculous. It is not simply that civilisation strengthens Protestantism at the expense of the Church of Rome. We find this spirit displayed by Roman Catholics themselves, though the uniform tendency of their theology is to destroy all notion of the antecedent improbability of modern miracles; and though the fact that these miracles are only alleged in their own Church should invest them with a peculiar attraction. It is not even that there is an increasing repugnance to an unscrutinising and blindfold faith. Alleged miracles are rejected with immediate unreasoning incredulity by the members of a Church which has done everything in its power to prepare the mind for their reception. The plain fact is, that the progress of civilisation produces invariably a certain tone and habit of thought, which makes men recoil from miraculous narratives with an instinctive and immediate repugnance, as though they were essentially incredible, independently of any definite arguments, and in spite of dogmatic teaching. Whether this habit of mind is good or evil, I do not now discuss. That it exists wherever civilisation advances, is, I conceive, incontestable.

We may observe, however, that it acts with much greater force against contemporary than against historical miracles

Roman Catholics who will reject with immediate ridicule an account of a miracle taking place in their own day, will speak with considerable respect of a precisely similar miracle that is attributed to a mediæval saint. Nor is it at all difficult to discover the reason of this distinction. Events that took place in a distant past, are not realised with the same intense vividness as those which take place among ourselves. They do not press upon us with the same keen reality, and are not judged by the same measure. They come down to us invested with a legendary garb, obscured by the haze of years, and surrounded by circumstances that are so unlike our own that they refract the imagination, and cloud and distort its pictures. Besides this, many of these narratives are entwined with the earliest associations of the Roman Catholic child; the belief in them is infused into his yet undeveloped mind, and they are thus at no period brought in contact with a matured and unbiassed judgment. We find, therefore, that although these general habits of thought do, undoubtedly, exercise a retrospective influence, that is not their first or their most powerful effect.

In Protestant countries there has not been as complete a change as that which we have been considering, for Protestantism was only called into existence when the old habits of thought had greatly declined. The Reformation was created and pervaded by the modern spirit; and its leaders were compelled, by the exigencies of their position, to repudiate the miraculous accounts of their time. They could not with any consistency admit that the Almighty had selected as the peculiar channels of His grace, and had glorified by countless miracles, devotions which they stigmatised as blasphemous, idolatrous, and superstitious. We find, accordingly, that from the very beginning, Protestantism looked upon

modern miracles (except those which were comprised under
the head of witchcraft) with an aversion and distrust that
contrasts remarkably with the unhesitating credulity of its
opponents. The history of its sects exhibits, indeed, some
alleged miracles, which were, apparently, the result of ignorance or enthusiasm, and a very few which were obvious
impositions. Such, for example, was the famous voice from
the wall in the reign of Queen Mary, which proclaimed the
mass to be idolatrous; just as the crucifix in Christ's Church,
at Dublin, shed tears of blood in the following reign, because the Protestant service was introduced into Ireland.
On the whole, however, the new faith proved remarkably
free from these forms of deception; and its leaders generally
concurred in the belief, that miracles had ceased when Christianity had gained a definite ascendancy in the world. The
Patristic writings are full of miraculous accounts; and most
of the reformers, and especially those in England, treated
Patristic authority with great respect; so that the line of demarcation between the miraculous and the non-miraculous
age, was generally drawn at about the period when the most
eminent of the Fathers had passed away. As this was not
very long after Christianity had obtained a complete command of the civil power, many plausible arguments could
be urged in support of the view, which appears, in England
at least, to have been universal.

When Locke was writing his famous 'Letters on Toleration,' he was led to a consideration of the Patristic miracles
by an argument which seems then to have been deemed very
forcible, but which, as it belongs to a different 'climate of
opinion' from our own, would now be regarded as both fu-
tile and irreverent. It was absolutely necessary, it was contended, under ordinary circumstances, for the well-being of

Christianity, that it should be supported by persecution; that is to say, that the civil power should suppress its opponents. When Christianity was still unrecognised by government, it existed in an abnormal condition; the laws of nature were suspended in its favour, and continual miracles ensured its triumph. When, however, the conversion of Constantine placed the civil power at its disposal, the era of the supernatural was closed. The power of persecuting was obtained; and, therefore, the power of working miracles was withdrawn. The alliance between Church and State being instituted, Christianity had arrived at its normal and final position, and exceptional assistance had become unnecessary.' This argument, the work of the theologians of Oxford, was not likely to stagger Locke; but the historical question which it opened was well calculated to arrest that keen and fearless intellect, so little accustomed to bow before unsupported authority, and at that very time engaged in the defence of toleration against the entire weight of ecclesiastical tradition. He appears to have consulted Sir Isaac Newton; for, in one of Newton's letters, we find a somewhat hesitating passage upon the subject. 'Miracles,' Newton wrote, ' of good credit continued in the Church for about two or three hundred years. Gregorius Thaumaturgus had his name from thence, and was one of the latest who was eminent for that gift; but of their number and frequency I am not able to give you a just account. The history of those

---

This argument, in a modified form, has been reproduced by Muzarelli (a Roman theologian of some note) in his *Treatise on the Inquisition.* He cites the destruction of Ananias and Sapphira, and of Simon Magus. This class of miracles, he says, has ceased; and the Inquisition is, in consequence, required. I know this very remarkable treatise by a translation in the fifth volume of Henrion, *Histoire de l'Eglise.*

ages is very imperfect.'[1] Locke does not appear to have
adopted this view. In reply to the Oxford argument, he
wrote a very remarkable passage, which did not, apparently,
attract at the time the attention it deserved; but which,
long afterwards, obtained an extremely conspicuous place in
the discussion. 'This, I think,' he said, 'is evident, that he
who will build his faith or reasonings upon miracles deliv-
ered by Church historians, will find cause to go no further
than the Apostles' time, or else not to stop at Constantine's,
since the writers after that period, whose word we readily
take as unquestionable in other things, speak of miracles in
their time, with no less assurance than the Fathers before
the fourth century; and a great part of the miracles of the
second and third centuries stand upon the credit of the writers of the fourth.'[2]

After this time, the subject of the miracles of the Fathers
seems to have slept until public attention was called to it by
the well-known work of Middleton. That the 'Free Inquiry'
was a book of extraordinary merit, that it displayed great
eloquence, great boldness, and great controversial dexterity,
and met with no opposition at all equal to its abilities, will
scarcely be denied. But, in order to appreciate its success,
we should consider, besides these things, the general character of the age in which it appeared. During the half century
that elapsed between Locke and Middleton, many influences
that it would be tedious to examine, but to which Locke
himself by his philosophy most largely contributed, had profoundly modified the theology of England. The charm and

---

[1] Brewster's *Life of Newton*, p. 275. There is another letter from Newton
to Locke on the subject, in King's *Life of Locke*, vol. i. p. 415; but it is little
more than a catalogue of authorities.

[2] Third Letter on *Toleration*, p. 269.

fascination which the early Fathers exercised upon the divines of the previous century had quite passed away. The Patristic works fell rapidly into neglect, and the very few who continued to study them were but little imbued with their spirit. Nothing, indeed, could be more unlike the tone of the Fathers, than the cold, passionless, and prudential theology of the eighteenth century; a theology which re-garded Christianity as an admirable auxiliary to the police force, and a principle of decorum and of cohesion in society, but which carefully banished from it all enthusiasm, veiled or attenuated all its mysteries, and virtually reduced it to an authoritative system of moral philosophy. There never had been a time when divines had such a keen dread of anything that appeared absurd or grotesque. The spirit that, in the previous century, had destroyed the belief in witchcraft, passed in its full intensity into their works. Common sense was the dominating characteristic of all they wrote. Gene-rous sentiments, disinterested virtue, reverential faith, sub-lime speculations, had passed away. Every preacher was employed in showing that Christianity was in all respects perfectly in accordance with human reason, in eliminating or obscuring whatever could shock the feelings or offend the judgment, in representing religion as intended to refine and harmonise society, to embellish all the relations of life, to give a higher sanction to the dictates of human prudence, and to extend the horizon of that prudence beyond the grave. As a consequence of this state of mind, there was an increas-ing indisposition to accept miracles like those of the Fathers, which were not included in the evidences of Christianity, and a decreasing reverence for the writers on whose testi-mony they rest.

It was in the midst of this movement of thought, that

Middleton published his great attack upon the Patristic
miracles, and brought into clear relief both the difficulties
and the importance of the subject. The writings of the
Fathers contain numerous accounts of miracles which they
alleged to have taken place in their own day and under
their own notice, and which are of such a nature, and are
related in such a manner, that it seems scarcely possible to
avoid the conclusion that they had really taken place, or else
that the Fathers deliberately palmed them off upon the credulity of their readers. The works of the first century that
have come down to us are extremely scanty, and consist
almost entirely of short epistles written without any historical or controversial purpose, for the encouragement or edification of believers ; but even in this century, the martyrdom
of St. Polycarp supplies an account which is clearly miraculous. Justin Martyr, who wrote very early in the second
century, and it is said not more than fifty years after the
death of St. John, distinctly asserts the continuance of
miracles in his time, and from this date the evidence is ample
and unbroken. The Protestant theory is, that miracles became gradually fewer and fewer, till they at last entirely
disappeared. The historical fact is, that, generation after
generation, the miraculous accounts became more numerous,
more universal, and more extraordinary. 'As far as the
church historians can illustrate or throw light upon anything,
there is not a single point in all history so constantly, explicitly, and unanimously confirmed by them all, as the continual succession of those powers through all ages, from the
earliest father who first mentions them down to the time of
the Reformation.'[1] If, then, we gave even a general cre-
dence to the historical evidence upon the subject, we should

[1] Preface to the *Free Inquiry.*

be carried down, without pause or chasm, into the depths
of the middle ages; and we should be compelled to admit,
that what Protestants regard as the worst superstitions of
the Church of Rome, were for centuries the habitual and
special channels of supernatural favour. If again, in defiance
of all the ordinary rules of historical criticism, we believed
the assertions of the writers of the fourth century, but
refused to credit the equally positive testimony of the writers
of the ninth century, we should still be met by the same
difficulty, though in a modified form. It may be contended,
that the Fathers of the fourth century were not Roman Catholics; but it is quite certain that they were not, in the ordinary sense of the word, Protestants. It is quite certain that
there existed among them many practices, forms of devotion,
and doctrinal tendencies, which may not have been actually
Roman Catholic, but which, at least, hung upon the extreme
verge of Catholicism, which inevitably gravitated to it, and
which were the germs and the embryos of mediæval theology.
Now, it is precisely in connection with this department of
their theology that the miraculous accounts are most numerous.

Such was the great difficulty of the question, regarded
from the Protestant point of view. Middleton met it by an
attack upon the veracity of the Fathers, which was so
eloquent, so uncompromising, and so admirably directed,
that all England soon rang with the controversy. He contended that the religious leaders of the fourth century had
admitted, eulogised, and habitually acted upon principles
that were diametrically opposed, not simply to the aspirations
of a transcendent sanctity, but to the dictates of the most
common honesty. He showed that they had applauded
falsehood, that they had practised the most wholesale for-

gery, that they had habitually and grossly falsified history, that they had adopted to the fullest extent the system of pious frauds, and that they continually employed them to stimulate the devotion of the people. These were the charges which he brought against men, around whose brows the saintly aureole had sparkled for centuries with an unfading splendour; against those great Fathers who had formed the theological systems of Europe; who had been the arbitrators of so many controversies, and the objects of the homage of so many creeds. The evidence he adduced was pointed directly at the writers of the fourth century; but he carried his argument back to a still earlier period. 'When we reflect,' he says, 'on that surprising confidence and security with which the principal Fathers of this fourth century have affirmed as true what they themselves had either forged, or what they knew at least to be forged, it is natural to suspect that so bold a defiance of sacred truth could not be acquired or become general at once, but must have been carried gradually to that height by custom and the example of former times, and a long experience of what the credulity and superstition of the multitude would bear.'[1]

It is manifest that an attack of this kind opened out questions of the gravest and widest character. It shook the estimate of the Fathers which had been general, not only in the Church of Rome, but in a great degree among the ablest of the Reformers. In the Church of England especially, the Patristic writings had been virtually regarded as almost equal in authority to those of the inspired writers. The first great theological work of the English Reformation was 'The Apology,' in which Jewel justified the Reformers, by pointing out the deviations of the Church of Rome from the

[1] Introductory Chapter.

Patristic sentiments. It had ever been the pride of the great divines of the seventeenth century that they were the most profound students of the Patristic writings, the most faithful representatives of their spirit, and the most loyal respecters of their authority. The unsupported assertion of a Father had always been regarded as a most weighty, if not a decisive, argument in controversy. But surely this tone was idle and worse than idle, if the estimate of Middleton was correct. If the Fathers were in truth men of the most unbounded credulity and of the laxest veracity; if the sense of the importance of dogmas had, in their minds, completely superseded the sense of rectitude, it was absurd to invest them with this extraordinary veneration. They might still be reverenced as men of undoubted sincerity, and of the noblest heroism; they might still be cited as witnesses to the belief of their time, and as representing the tendencies of its intellect; but their pre-eminent authority had passed away. The landmarks of English theology were removed. The traditions on which it rested were disturbed. It had entered into new conditions, and must be defended by new arguments. But beyond all this, there were other, and, perhaps, graver questions suggested. Under what circumstances was it permitted to reject the unanimous and explicit testimony of all ecclesiastical historians? What was the measure of their credulity and of their veracity? What again was the degree of the antecedent improbability of miracles, the criteria separating the true from the false, and the amount of testimony required to substantiate them?

These were the great questions which were evoked in 1748, by this Doctor of Divinity, and they were sufficient for many years to attract the attention of the ablest enquirers in England. Among the laity, the work of Middleton

seems to have met with great acceptance. Among the clergy its impetuous, uncompromising, and sceptical tone naturally excited much alarm, and the University of Oxford
signalised itself in opposition; but it is a remarkable sign of
the times that the Fathers found no abler defenders than
Church and Dodwell. Gibbon, who was then a very young
man, and already entangled in the arguments of Bossuet,
lost his remaining faith in Protestantism during the discussion.
He could not, he said, bring himself at that time to adopt the
conclusions of Middleton, and he could not resist the evidence that miracles of good credit had continued in the
Church after the leading doctrines of Catholicism had been
introduced. He accordingly embraced those doctrines, and
left the University without taking his degree. Hume investigated the subject from a philosophical point of view; he
endeavoured to frame a general doctrine, determining the
relation between miraculous narratives and historical testimony, the comparative improbability of the reality of miracles and of the unveracity of historians; and the result was
his 'Essay on Miracles.'[1] Farmer, reproducing an old notion
of Lightfoot, Webster, and Semler, and anticipating in this
respect the current of German rationalism, attempted to ex-

---

[1] Hume's *Essay* was avowedly an application (right or wrong) of Tillotson's
famous argument against transubstantiation. It is not so generally known
that his method of reasoning had been also anticipated by Locke, who, in a
very remarkable passage in his common-place book, contends that men should
not believe any proposition that is contrary to reason, on the authority either
of inspiration or of miracle, for the reality of the inspiration or of the miracle
can only be established by reason. 'It is harder,' he says, 'to believe that
God should alter or put out of its ordinary course some phenomenon of the
great world for once, and make things act contrary to their ordinary rule pur-
posely, that the mind of men might do so always after, than that this is some
fallacy or natural effect of which he knows not the cause, let it look ever so
strange' (King, *Life of Locke*, vol. i. pp. 230, 231). See, too, the chapter on
Reason and Faith, in the *Essay on the Human Understanding.*

plain the diabolical possessions of Scripture by the ordinary phenomena of epilepsy.[1] Warburton and Douglas, with probably most of the ablest of the clergy, abandoning the Patristic miracles, proceeded to establish the peculiar character and evidence of the miracles recorded by the Evangelists; and the general adoption of this tone may be said to have ushered in a new phase in the history of miracles.

It has often been remarked as a singular fact, that almost every great step which has been made by the English intellect in connection with theology, has been made in spite of the earnest and persistent opposition of the University of Oxford. The attitude which that university preserved during the Middletonian controversy, was precisely the same as that which it had exhibited towards the two great questions of the previous century. The advocates of the theory of civil liberty in opposition to the theory of passive obedience, and the advocates of toleration as opposed to persecution, had found at Oxford their most unflinching and most able adversaries. In our own century, when the secularisation of politics was forced upon the public mind by the discussions on the Test Act and on Catholic Emancipation, and when it had become evident to all attentive observers that this question was destined to be the battle-field of the contest between modern civilisation and tradition, the University of Oxford showed clearly that its old spirit had lost none of its intensity, though it had lost much of its influence. Still later, in 1833, a great reactionary movement emanated from the same quarter, and was directed avowedly against the habits of religious

---

[1] Farmer, who was a dissenting minister, desired to destroy the difficulty arising from the fact that miracles were generally represented as attesting both truth and error, He attempted to show that there were no such things as diabolical miracles of any kind.

thought which modern civilisation had everywhere produced.
Its supporters denounced these habits as essentially and fun·
damentally false.   They described the history of English theology for a century and a half as a history of uninterrupted
decadence.   They believed, in the emphatic words of their
great leader, that 'the nation was on its way to give up revealed truth.' [1]   After a time, the movement tended to Catholicism with a force and rapidity that it was impossible to
mistake.   It produced a defection which was quite unparalleled in magnitude since that which had taken place under
the Stuarts; and which, unlike the former movement, was
altogether uninfluenced by sordid considerations.   The point
which I desire to notice in connection with this defection, as
illustrating the tendency I am tracing in the present chapter,
is the extremely small place which the subject of Roman
Catholic miracles occupied in the controversy.

If we ask what are the grounds on which the cessation
of miracles is commonly maintained, they may, I suppose,
be summed up much as follows :—

Miracles, it is said, are the divine credentials of an inspired messenger announcing doctrines which could not otherwise be established.   They prove that he is neither an
impostor nor an enthusiast ; that his teaching is neither the
work of a designing intellect nor of an over-heated imagination.   From the nature of the case, this could not be proved
in any other way.   If the Almighty designed to reveal to
mankind a system of religion distinct from that which is reflected in the works of nature, and written on the consciences of men, He must do so by the instrumentality of an
inspired messenger.   If a teacher claims to be the special
organ of a Divine communication revealing supernatural

Newman's *Anglican Difficulties*, p. 54.

truths, he may be justly expected to authenticate his mission in the only way in which it can be authenticated, by the performance of supernatural acts. Miracles are, therefore, no more improbable than a revelation; for a revelation would be ineffectual without miracles. But, while this consideration destroys the common objections to the Gospel miracles, it separates them clearly from those of the Church of Rome. The former were avowedly exceptional; they were absolutely necessary; they were designed to introduce a new religion, and to establish a supernatural message. The latter were simply means of edification; they were directed to no object that could not otherwise be attained; and they were represented as taking place in a dispensation that was intended to be not of sight but of faith. Besides this, miracles should be regarded as the most awful and impressive manifestations of Divine power. To make them habitual and commonplace would be to degrade if not to destroy their character, which would be still further abased if we admitted those which appeared trivial and puerile. The miracles of the New Testament were always characterised by dignity and solemnity; they always conveyed some spiritual lesson, and conferred some actual benefit, besides attesting the character of the worker. The mediæval miracles, on the contrary, were frequently trivial, purposeless, and unimpressive; constantly verging on the grotesque, and not unfrequently passing the border.

Such is, I think, a fair epitome of the common arguments in favour of the cessation of miracles; and they are undoubtedly very plausible and very cogent; but, after all, what do they prove? Not that miracles have ceased; but that, supposing them to have ceased, there is nothing surprising or alarming in the fact. A man who has convinced himself of the

falseness of the ecclesiasticial miracles, may very fairly ad-
duce these considerations to prove that his conclusion does not
impugn the Biblical narratives, or introduce confusion or
incoherence into the system of Providence; but this is the full
extent to which they can be legitimately carried. As an *à
priori* proof, they are far too weak to withstand the smallest
amount of positive testimony. Miracles, it is said, are intended
exclusively to accredit an inspired messenger. But, after
all, what proof is there of this? It is simply an hypothesis,
plausible and consistent it may be, but entirely unsupported
by positive testimony. Indeed, we may go further, and say
that it is distinctly opposed to your own facts. You may repudiate the unanimous belief of the early Christians, that
miracles were ordinary and commonplace events among all
nations; you may resist the strong arguments that may be
drawn from the unsurprised reception of the Christian miracles, and from the existence of the demoniacs and of the exorcists; but at least you must admit, that the Old Testament
relates many miracles which will not fall under your canon.
The creation was a miracle, and so was the deluge, and so
was the destruction of the cities of the plain. The Old
Testament miracles are, in many respects, unlike those of the
New Testament: is it impossible that there should be another class different from either? But the ecclesiastial mira
cles, it is said, are often grotesque; they appear *primâ facie*
absurd, and excite an irresistible repugnance. A sufficiently
dangerous test in an age in which men find it more and more
difficult to believe any miracles whatever. A sufficiently dangerous test for those who know the tone that has been long
adopted, over an immense part of Europe, towards such narratives as the deluge, or the exploits of Samson, the speaking ass, or the possessed pigs! Besides this, a great pro

portion of the ecclesiastical miracles •are simply repro-
ductions of those which are recorded in the Bible; and
if there are mingled with them some that appear manifest impostures, this may be a very good reason for treating
these narratives with a more jealous scrutiny, but is certainly no reason for maintaining that they are all below contempt.   The Bible neither asserts nor implies the revocation
of supernatural gifts; and if the general promise that these
gifts should be conferred may have been intended to apply
only to the Apostles, it is at least as susceptible of a different
interpretation.   If these miracles were actually continued, it
is surely not difficult to discover the beneficial purpose that
they would fulfil.   They would stimulate a languid piety;
they would prove invaluable auxiliaries to missionaries labouring among barbarous and unreasoning savages, who,
from their circumstances and habits of mind, are utterly incapable of forming any just estimate of the evidences of the
religion they are expected to embrace.   Even in Europe, the
results of the controversies of the last 300 years have not
been so entirely satisfactory as to leave no room for some
more decisive proofs than the ambiguous utterances of a remote antiquity.   To say that these miracles are false because
they are Roman Catholic, is to assume the very question at
issue.   The controversy between Protestantism and Catholicism comprises an immense mass of complicated and hetero-
geneous arguments.   Thousands of minds have traversed
these arguments, and have found at each step their faith in
Protestantism confirmed.   Thousands of minds have pursued
the same course with results that were diametrically opposite.   The question is, whether an examination of the alleged
miracles of Catholicism would not furnish a decisive crite-
rion, or at least one of the most powerful arguments, for
12

determining the controversy. What evidence of the truth
of Catholicism could be stronger than that its distinctive
doctrines had been crowned by tens of thousands of miracles, that a supernatural halo had encircled it wherever it appeared, and had cast a glory upon all its triumphs ? [1]   What
proof of the falsehood of Catholicism could be more decisive
than that it was unable to establish any of the immense
mass of miracles which it had asserted; that all these were
resolved and dissipated before a searching criticism; that
saints had been canonised, forms of worship established,
countless bulls and pastorals issued, innumerable rejoicings,
pageantries, processions, and pilgrimages authoritatively instituted, public opinion all through Christendom violently and
continuously agitated, on account of alleged events which had
either no existence, or which were altogether misunderstood ?
Making every allowance for the errors of the most extreme
fallibility, the history of Catholicism would on this hypothesis represent an amount of imposture probably unequalled
in the annals of the human race. If, again, you say that

---

[1] E. g., one of the questions of dispute is the veneration of relics. Now
St. Augustine, the ablest and most clear-headed of all the Fathers, and a man
of undoubted piety, solemnly asserts that in his own diocese of Hippo, in the
space of two years, no less than seventy miracles had been wrought by the
body of St. Stephen, and that in the neighbouring province of Calama, where
the relic had previously been, the number was incomparably greater. He gives
a catalogue of what he deems undoubted miracles, which he says he had
selected from a multitude so great, that volumes would be required to relate
them all. *In that catalogue we find no less than five cases of restoration of
life to the dead. (De Civ. Dei*, lib. xxii. c. 8.) This statement is well known to
readers of Gibbon and Middleton; but, as far as I know, the only High
Churchman who has referred to it is Mr. Ward (*Ideal of a Christian Church*,
pp. 138–140), who notices it merely to lament the very different tone with
which we now speak of the miraculous. This aspect of the Patristic writings
has been very clearly and honestly brought out in Isaac Taylor's *Ancient
Christianity.*

you have formed a definite and unhesitating opinion on the
subject from other arguments, I reply that, putting aside all
other considerations this answer might suggest, it does not
apply to the Tractarian movement we are considering.   The
transition from the Church of England to the Church of
Rome, which was made by so many in consequence of that
movement, was not abrupt or unwavering.   It was, on the
contrary, slow, painful, hesitating, and dubious.   Some of
those who made it have described themselves as trembling
for months, and even years, between the opposing creeds,
their minds vibrating and oscillating to and fro; countless
difficulties, colliding principles, modes of reasoning the most
various, blending and neutralising sentiments of every hue,
torturing their minds with doubt, and sometimes almost
destroying by their conflict the very faculty of judgment.
Surely one might have imagined that men in such a position
would have gladly exchanged those shifting speculations
that so constantly elude the grasp and bewilder the mind,
and catch their colour from each changing mode of thought,
for the comparatively firm and definite ground of historical
criticism!   The men were admirably fitted for such criticism.
They were pre-eminently scholars and antiquarians, and in
its intellectual aspect the movement was essentially a resus-
citation of the past.   Nor did the age seem at first sight less
suited for the enterprise.   In the time of the Reformers the
study of evidences, and indeed all searching investigation
into the facts of the past, were unknown.   When, however,
Tractarianism arose, the laws of historical criticism were developed to great perfection, and they were attracting an
immense proportion of the talent of Europe.   In English
theology, especially, they had become supreme.   The attacks
which Woolston and his followers had made upon the scrip-

tural miracles had been repelled by Lardner and Paley with such unexpected vigour, with such undoubted ability, and, as it was long thought, with such unanswerable success, that all theological reasoning had been directed to this channel. Yet in the Tractarian movement the subject of modern miracles can scarcely be said to have exercised a perceptible influence. Gibbon, as we have seen, had gone over to Rome chiefly through a persuasion of their reality. Chillingworth still earlier had declared that the same reason had been one of those which had induced him to take the same step. Pascal had based his defence of Jansenism in a great measure upon the miracle of the Holy Thorn. But at Oxford these narratives hardly excited a serious attention. What little influence they had was chiefly an influence of repulsion; what little was written in their favor was written for the most part in the tone of an apology, as if to attenuate a difficulty rather than to establish a creed.[1]

This was surely a very remarkable characteristic of the Tractarian movement, when we remember the circumstances and attainments of its leaders, and the great prominence which miraculous evidence had long occupied in England. It was especially remarkable when we recollect that one of the great complaints which the Tractarian party were making against modern theology was, that the conception of the supernatural had become faint and dim, and that its manifestations were either explained away or confined to a distant past. It would seem as if those who were most conscious of the character of their age were unable, in the very midst of their opposition, to free themselves from its tendencies.

[1] Dr. Newman's very able essay (prefixed to Fleury's *History*) is essentially an *apology* for the ecclesiastical miracles; and the miracles of the English saints, about which we have lately heard so much, never seem to have been regarded as evidential.

If we look beyond the Tractarian movement, we find a still more startling illustration of the prevailing feeling in the extraordinary strides which professed and systematised Rationalism has made in most Protestant countries. The extent to which Continental Protestantism has gravitated towards it has been recognised on all sides, and has excited the greatest hopes in some and the greatest alarm in others. It is worthy too of remark, that the movement has been most manifest in those countries where the leading Churches are not connected with very elaborate creeds or with liturgical services, and where the reason, being least shackled by tradition, is most free to follow the natural sequence of its developments. It is true that the word Rationalism is somewhat vague, and comprises many different modifications of belief. This consideration has constantly been urged by those who are termed orthodox Protestants in a tone of the most contemptuous scorn, but with a complete forgetfulness of the fact that for 300 years Protestantism itself was invariably assailed by the very same objection, and was invariably defended on the twofold ground that variations of belief form the necessary consequence of honest enquiry, and that amid its innumerable diversities of detail there were certain radical conceptions which gave a substantial unity to the discordant sects. Much the same general unity may be found among the various modifications of Protestant Rationalism. Its central conception is the elevation of conscience into a position of supreme authority as the religious organ, a verifying faculty discriminating between truth and error. It regards Christianity as designed to preside over the moral development of mankind, as a conception which was to become more and more sublimated and spiritualised as the human mind passed into new phases, and was able to bear the splendour of a more unclouded light. Religion it be lieves to be no exception to the general law of progress, but rather the highest form of its manifestation, and its earlier systems but the necessary steps of an imperfect development. In its eyes the moral element of Christianity is as the sun in heaven, and dogmatic systems are as the clouds that intercept and temper the exceeding brightness of its ray. The insect whose existence is but for a moment might well imagine that these were indeed eternal, that their majestic columns could never fail, and that their luminous folds were the very source and centre of light. And yet they shift and vary with each changing breeze; they blend and separate; they assume new forms and exhibit new dimensions; as the sun that is above them waxes more glorious in its power, they are permeated and at last absorbed by its increasing splendour; they recede, and wither, and disappear, and the eye ranges far beyond the sphere they had occupied into the infinity of glory that is above them.

This is not the place to enter into a critical examination of the faults and merits of Rationalism. A system which would unite in one sublime synthesis all the past forms of human belief, which accepts with triumphant alacrity each new development of science, having no stereotyped standard to defend, and which represents the human mind as pursuing on the highest subjects a path of continual progress towards the fullest and most transcendent knowledge of the Deity, can never fail to exercise a powerful intellectual attraction. A system which makes the moral faculty of man the measure and arbiter of faith, must always act powerfully on those in whom that faculty is most developed. This idea of continued and uninterrupted development is one that seems absolutely to override our age. It is scarcely possible to open any really able book on any subject without encountering it in some form. It is stirring all science to its very depths; it is revolutionising all historical literature. Its prominence in theology is so great that there is scarcely any school that is altogether exempt from its influence. We have seen in our own day the Church of Rome itself defended in 'An Essay on Development,' and by a strange application of the laws of progress.

These elements of attraction do much to explain the extraordinary rapidity with which Rationalism has advanced in the present century, in spite of the vagueness and obscurity it often exhibits and the many parodoxes it has engendered. But it is well worthy of notice that the very first direction which these speculations invariably take—the very sign and characteristic of their action—is an attempt to explain away the miracles of Scripture. This is so emphatically the distinctive mark of Rationalism, that with most persons it is the only conception the word conveys. Wherever it appears it represents and interprets the prevailing disinclination to accept miraculous narratives,¹ and will resort to every artifice of interpretation in order to evade their force. Its preva· lence, therefore, clearly indicates the extent to which this aversion to the miraculous exists in Protestant countries, and the rapidity with which it has of late years increased.

Every one who has paid any attention to these subjects has a natural inclination to attribute the conclusions he has arrived at to the efforts of his own reason, acting under the

¹ A large section of German theologians, as is well known, even regard the impossibility, or at all events the unreality, of miraculous accounts as axiomatic. Thus Strauss calmly remarks: 'We may summarily reject all miracles, prophecies, narratives of angels and demons, and the like, as simply impossible and irreconcilable with the known and universal laws which govern the course of events.'—Introduction to the *Life of Jesus.*

influen.e of an unbiassed will, rather than to a general pre-disposition arising out of the character of his age. It is probable, therefore, that the members of the rationalistic school would very generally deny being influenced by any other considerations than those which they allege in their defence, and would point to that system of minute and critical Biblical investigation which Germany has produced as the true source of their opinions. I cannot but think that it is much less the cause than the result, and that we have a clear indication of this in the fact that a precisely similar tendency of opinions is shown in another quarter where this criticism has never been pursued. I allude to the freethinkers, who are scattered in such profusion through Roman Catholic countries. Anyone who has attentively examined that great school, which exercises so vast an influence over the literature and policy of our age, must have perceived that it is in many respects widely removed from the old Voltairian spirit. It is no longer exclusively negative and destructive, but is, on the contrary, intensely positive, and in its moral aspect intensely Christian. It clusters around a series of essentially Christian conceptions—equality, fraternity, the suppression of war, the elevation of the poor, the love of truth, and the diffusion of liberty. It revolves around the ideal of Christianity, and represents its spirit without its dogmatic system and its supernatural narratives. From both of these it unhesitatingly recoils, while deriving all its strength and nourishment from Christian ethics.

Such are, I conceive, the general outlines of this movement, which bears an obvious relationship to Protestant Rationalism, and which has been advancing through Europe with still more rapid and triumphant strides. He must indeed be wilfully blind to the course of history who does not perceive that during the last hundred years these schools have completely superseded the dogmatic forms of Protestantism as the efficient antagonists of the Church of Rome, as the centres towards which those who are repelled from Catholicism are naturally attracted. In the sixteenth and to a certain degree in the seventeenth century, Protestantism exercised a commanding and controlling influence over the affairs of Europe. Almost all the great questions that agitated the minds of men were more or less connected with its progress. It exhibited, indeed, many unseemly dissensions and many grotesque extravagances; but each of its sects had a rigid and definite dogmatic system, and exercised a powerful influence on those who were around it. Whoever was dissatisfied with the teaching of the Church of Rome was almost immediately attracted and absorbed by one of these systems, and threw himself into the new dogmatism with as much zeal as he had exhibited in the old one. During the last century all this has changed. Of the many hundreds of great thinkers and writers, in every department, who have separated from the teachings and practices of Catholicism, it would be difficult to name three men of real eminence and unquestionable sincerity who have attached themselves permanently to any of the more conservative forms of Protestantism. Amid all those great semi-religious revolutions which have unhinged the faith of thousands, and have so profoundly altered the relations of Catholicism and society, Protestant Churches have made no advance and have exercised no perceptible influence. It has long been a mere truism to say that we are passing through a state of chaos, of anarchy, and of transition. During the past century the elements of dissolution have been multiplying all around us. Scarcely ever before has so large a proportion of the literature of Europe exhibited an open hostility or a contemptuous indifference towards Catholicism. Entire nations have defied its censures and confiscated its property, and wrested every department of politics from its control. But while Catholicism has been thus convulsed and agitated to its very basis; while the signs of its disintegration are crowding upon us on every side; while the languor and feebleness it exhibits furnish a ready theme for every moralist and a problem for every philosopher, the Protestant sects have gained nothing by the decay of their ancient rival. They have still retained their ecclesiastical organisations and their ancient formularies, but the magnetism they once possessed has wholly vanished. Of all the innumerable forms into which the spirit of dogmatism crystallised after the Reformation, not one seems to have retained the power of attracting those beyond its border. Whatever is lost by Catholicism is gained by Rationalism; [1] wherever the spirit of Rationalism recedes, the spirit of Catholicism advances. Towards the close of the last century France threw off her allegiance to Christianity, endeavoured to efface all the traditions of her past, and proclaimed a new era in the religious history of mankind. She soon repented of her temerity, and retired from a position which she had found untenable. Half the nation became ultramontane Roman Catholics; the other half became indifferent or Rationalist. [2] The great majority of Continental writers have repudiated the doctrines of Ca-

[1] Italy since the late political changes, and as a consequence of the direction given to the national sympathies by those changes, furnishes, perhaps, a slight exception; but even there the conquests of Protestantism are insignificant as compared with those of Freethinking, and it is said that among Protestants the Plymouth Brethren, who are among the least dogmatic, have also been among the most successful.

[2] I need hardly remind the reader how forcibly and eloquently this point has been brought out by Macaulay, in his Essay on *Ranke's History*.

tholicism, and pursue their speculations without paying the smallest deference to its authority. In the sixteenth century all such persons would have attached themselves to some definite form of Protestantism; they now assume a position which was then entirely unexampled, and would have appeared entirely inexplicable. The age of heresiarchs has passed.[1] Among very ignorant people new dogmatic systems, as Mormonism has shown, may still be successful; but among the educated classes they seem to have lost all their attraction and power. The immense missionary organisations of England succeed indeed in occasionally attracting a few isolated individuals in Roman Catholic countries to Protestantism; but we look in vain for the natural flow and current of thought which in former times impelled vast portions of society to its communion, and imparted an influence to all the great questions in Europe. The only movements which in the faintest degree reproduce the fascination of the sects of the sixteenth century are philanthropic and democratic efforts, like those of St. Simon or Mazzini. All the great intellectual problems that convulse Europe are connected with the rights of nationalities, the progress of democracy, or the dignity of labour. These have now taken the place of those dogmatic questions which in the sixteenth century formed the mainsprings of the policy of Christendom, and which in the nineteenth century have become entirely uninfluential.

[1] M. de Montalembert, in his *Life of Lacordaire*, has observed of Lamennais, that there is probably no instance in history of a man possessing so eminently the gifts of a great heresiarch making so little impression by his defection from the Church, and failing so completely to become the nucleus of a sect. After all, however, this was quite natural. The course which Lamennais pursued stimulated a great intellectual movement; but it was not, and was never intended to be, in the direction of a sect.

This is, undoubtedly, an extremely remarkable and an extremely significant contrast. Honest men will hardly deny its existence. Wise men will not shut their eyes to the fact or refuse to look steadily at its consequences. Coupled with the rationalistic movement that has taken place within Protestantism, it has inclined very many writers to conclude that the earlier forms of Protestantism were merely transitional; that their continued existence depends not on any life that is in them, but on the force of habit and of tradition; that perpetual progress in the domain of belief is the natural destiny and the inevitable law of Protestantism; and that the fate of Lot's wife is reserved for those Churches which look back on the city of dogmatism from which they fled. To assume, however, that religious life has been extirpated in Protestant Churches, because they appear to have lost the power of influencing those who are around them, is to look for it in only one form. It is to ignore the intense and practical fervour, the moralising influences, the spirit of bold and earnest enquiry, that are so abundantly found within their borders. To infer from this general movement that dogmatic Protestantism is an imperfect development, which intellects unshackled by its traditions will never embrace, and which the current of civilisation must ultimately transform or overthrow, is undoubtedly far more plausible; yet, as an argument against the truth of Protestantism, it is based entirely upon the assumption that the general tendency of civilisation is necessarily towards truth rather than error. One conclusion, however, we may most certainly and most safely draw from the movement we are considering. It is, that the general current and bias of the intellect of the age is in the direction of Rationalism; in other words, that there is a strong predisposition to value the spirit and moral element of

Christianity, but to reject dogmatic systems and more especially miraculous narratives.

We have seen that this tendency was not uninfluential in
Tractarianism itself, although that system was organized as
a protest and a bulwark against the tendencies of the age.
Among those who are usually called orthodox Protestants, it
has been clearly shown in the rapid decline of the evidential
school. The pre-eminence that school obtained in England
during the last century is certainly not to be attributed to
any general tendency towards the miraculous. Lardner and
Paley and their followers acted strictly on the defensive, and
were therefore compelled to meet their assailants on the
ground which those assailants had selected. The spirit of
scepticism, which at the Reformation extended only to the
authority of particular Churches or to the justice of par
ticular interpretations of Scripture, had gradually expanded
till it included the whole domain of theology, and had pro·
duced a series of violent attacks upon the miracles. It was
to repel these attacks that the evidential school arose, and
the aunals of religious controversy narrate few more complete victories than they achieved. Of all the English deisti-
cal works of the eighteenth century, the influence of two
and only two survived the controversy. Hume's Essay on
Miracles, though certainly not unquestioned and unassailed,
cannot be looked upon as obsolete or uninfluential. Gibbon
remains the almost undisputed master of his own field, but
his great work does not directly involve, though it undoubt
edly trenches on, the subject of Christian evidences. But if
we except these two, it would be difficult to conceive a more
complete eclipse than the English deists have undergone.
Woolston and Tindal, Collins and Chubb, have long since
passed into the region of shadows, and their works have

mouldered in the obscurity of forgetfulness. Bolingbroke is now little more than a brilliant name, and all the beauties of his matchless style have been unable to preserve his philosophy from oblivion. Shaftesbury retains a certain place as one of the few disciples of idealism who resisted the influence of Locke; but his importance is purely historical. His cold and monotonous though exquisitely polished dissertations have fallen into general neglect, and find few readers and exercise no influence. The shadow of the tomb rests upon them all; a deep unbroken silence, the chill of death, surrounds them. They have long ceased to wake any interest, or to suggest any enquiries, or to impart any impulse to the intellect of England. This was the result of the English controversies of the eighteenth century, which on the conservative side consisted mainly of a discussion of miraculous evidence. It is undoubtedly very remarkable in itself, but much more so when we contrast it with what was taking place in Roman Catholic countries. Voltaire and Rousseau not only succeeded in holding their ground, but they met with no opponent whom the wildest enthusiasm could place upon their level. Their works elicited not a single refutation, I might almost say not a single argument or criticism, that has come down with any authority to our own day. Diderot, Raynal, and several other members of the party have taken a place in French literature which is probably permanent, and which is certainly far higher than was obtained by any of their opponents.

One might have supposed from this contrast that the evidential school, which had been crowned with such marked success, would have enjoyed a great and permanent popularity; but this expectation has not been realised. In Germany, Kant from the beginning pronounced this mode of reasoning to be unphilosophical; ' in England, Colefidge succeeded in bringing it into complete disrepute; and every year the disinclination to stake the truth of Christianity on the proof of miracles becomes more manifest. A small body of theologians continue, indeed, to persevere in the old plan, and no one will speak of their labours with disrespect; yet they are themselves witnesses to the generality of the movement, for they complain bitterly that they are labouring in a wilderness, and that the old method has been on all sides abandoned and neglected.² We find, everywhere, that the prevailing feeling is to look upon the defence of Christianity as a matter not external to but part of religion. Belief is regarded not as the result of an historical puzzle, the solution of an extremely complicated intellectual problem which presents fewest difficulties and contradictions, but as the recognition by conscience of moral truth. In other words, religion in its proofs as in its essence is deemed a thing belonging rather to the moral than the intellectual portion of human nature. Faith and not reason is its basis; and this faith is a species of moral perception. Each dogma is the embodiment and inadequate expression of a moral truth, and is worthless except as it is vivified by that truth. The progress of criticism may shift and vary the circumstances of an historical faith, the advent of new modes of thought may make ancient creeds lifeless and inoperative, but the spirit that underlies them is eternal. The ideal and type of character will acquire new fascination when detached from the material conceptions of an early civilisation. The idolatry of dogmas will pass away; Christianity, being rescued from the sectarianism and

---

¹ On Kant's influence on German Rationalism see Rose, *On Protestantism in Germany*, pp. 183–190.

² See, for example, the first and second Essays in *Aids to Faith*.

intolerance that have defaced it, will shine by its own moral
splendour, and, sublimated above all the sphere of controversy, will assume its rightful position as an ideal and not a
system, as a person and not a creed.

We find also, even among the supporters of the evidential
school, a strong tendency to meet the Rationalists, as it were,
halfway—to maintain that miracles are valid proofs, but that
they do not necessarily imply the notion of a violation of
natural law with which they had been so long associated.
They are, it is said, performed simply by the application of
natural means guided by supernatural knowledge.   The idea
of interference can present no difficulty to anyone who admits
human liberty;[1] for those who acknowledge that liberty
must hold that man has a certain power of guiding and con
trolling the laws of matter, that he can of his own free will
produce effects which would not have been produced without
his intervention, and that in proportion as his knowledge of
the laws of nature advances his power of adapting them to
his purposes is increased.   That mind can influence matter
is itself one of the laws of nature.   To adapt and modify
general laws to special purposes is the occupation and the
characteristic of every intelligence, and to deny this power
to Divine intelligence seems but little removed from atheism.
It is to make the Deity the only torpid mind in the universe.
There is therefore, it is said, nothing improbable in the belief
that Omniscience, by the selection of natural laws of which
we are ignorant, could accomplish all those acts which we
call miraculous.[2]   According to this notion, a miracle would

[1] See Mansel's 'Essay on Miracles' in the *Aids to Faith.*

[2] For an exposition of this view I cannot do better than refer to an article
on 'The Supernatural' in the *Edinburgh Review* for October, 1862, and to the
works there referred to.   I select a few sentences from the article which contain the substance of the argument: 'The reign of law in nature is indeed, as

not differ, generically, from a human act, though it would still be strictly available for evidential purposes. Miracles would thus be separated from a conception with which almost all the controversialists of the last century had identified them, and which is peculiarly repugnant to the tendencies of our age.

We have now taken a sufficiently extensive survey of the history of miracles to enable us to arrive at a general conclusion. We have seen that ever since that revival of learning which preceded the Reformation, and dispelled the torpor and ignorance in which Europe had been for centuries immersed, the human mind has been pursuing on this subject a uniform and an unvarying course. The degrees in which different nations and churches have participated in the movement have been very various, but there is no part of Europe which has been uninfluenced by its progress. Reactionary parties have themselves reflected its character, and have at last been swept away by the advancing stream. All the

far as we can observe, universal. But the common idea of the supernatural is that which is at variance with natural law, above it or in violation of it. . . . . Hence it would appear to follow that, to a man thoroughly possessed of the idea of natural law as universal, nothing ever could be admitted as supernatural. . . . But then we must understand nature as including every agency which we see entering, or can conceive from analogy capable of entering, into the causation of the world. . . . The power of men in respect of physical laws extends only, first, to their discovery and ascertainment, and then to their use. . . . A complete knowledge of all natural laws would give, if not complete power, at least degrees of power immensely greater than those which we now possess. . . . The relation in which God stands to those rules of His government which are called laws is, of course, an inscrutable mystery; but those who believe that His will does govern the world must believe that, ordinarily at least, He does govern it by the choice and use of means; nor have we any certain reason to believe that He ever acts otherwise. Signs and wonders may be wrought, for aught we know, by similar instrumentality—by the selection and use of laws of which men knew nothing.' That miracles were performed simply by the employment of unknown natural laws was maintained long since by Malebranche, and also, I think, by Butler.

13

weight of tradition and of learning, all the energies of conservatism of every kind, have been opposed to its progress, and all have been opposed in vain. Generation after generation the province of the miraculous has contracted, and the circle of scepticism has expanded. Of the two great divisions of these events, one has completely perished. Witchcraft and diabolical possession and diabolical disease have long since passed into the region of fables. To disbelieve them was at first the eccentricity of a few isolated thinkers; it was then the distinction of the educated classes in the most advanced nations; it is now the common sentiment of all classes in all countries in Europe. The countless miracles that were once associated with every holy relic and with every village shrine have rapidly and silently disappeared. Year by year the incredulity became more manifest even where the theological profession was unchanged. Their numbers continually lessened until they at last almost ceased; and any attempt to revive them has been treated with a general and undisguised contempt. The miracles of the Fathers are passed over with an incredulous scorn, or with a significant silence. The rationalistic spirit has even attempted to explain away those which are recorded in Scripture, and it has materially altered their position in the systems of theology. In all countries, in all churches, in all parties, among men of every variety of character and opinion, we have found the tendency existing. In each nation its development has been a measure of intellectual activity, and has passed in regular course through the different strata of society. During the last century it has advanced with a vastly accelerated rapidity; the old lines of demarcation have been everywhere obscured, and the spirit of Rationalism has become the great centre to which the intellect of

Europe is manifestly tending. If we trace the progress of the movement from its origin to the present day, we find that it has completely altered the whole aspect and complexion of religion. When it began, Christianity was regarded as a system entirely beyond the range and scope of human reason : it was impious to question ; it was impious to examine ; it was impious to discriminate. On the other hand, it was visibly instinct with the supernatural. Miracles of every order and degree of magnitude were flashing forth incessantly from all its parts. They excited no scepticism and no surprise. The miraculous element pervaded all literature, explained all difficulties, consecrated all doctrines. Every unusual phenomenon was immediately referred to a supernatural agency, not because there was a passion for the improbable, but because such an explanation seemed far more simple and easy of belief than the obscure theories of science. In the present day Christianity is regarded as a system which courts the strictest investigation, and which, among many other functions, was designed to vivify and stimulate all the energies of man. The idea of the miraculous, which a superficial observer might have once deemed its most prominent characteristic, has been driven from almost all its entrenchments, and now quivers faintly and feebly through the mists of eighteen hundred years.[1]

[1] When men first grasped the truth that the tendency of the human mind was from polytheism to monotheism, there were some who at once rushed on to atheism, considering that to be a continuation of the same movement. The disbelief in ghosts led many to materialism, and the discovery that man was not the centre of all the contrivances of nature made not a few deny final causes. Just so, Science having shown that the phenomena of nature do not result (as everyone once supposed) from direct and isolated acts of intervention, multitudes have passed by the impetus of the movement to the denial of the possibility of miracles. To say that Omnipotence cannot reverse the laws of His appointment is a contradiction in terms. To say that an Infinite mind

Such has been the result of the general intellectual movement we have been reviewing. To those who believe that
the highest measure of truth we possess is furnished by an
examination of the successive developments and tendencies
manifested by the collective wisdom of mankind, it will be
invaluable as displaying one of the most unquestionably general movements that history records. To those, on the other
hand, who separate themselves from the spirit of their age,
and look forward to the future as to a period of predicted
apostasy, it will furnish an example of one of the most subtle
and powerful distorting influences by which the human mind
is ensnared. Such persons will do well to observe that, with
the exception of supernatural disease and other physical phenomena, none of these changes have been effected by the
action of direct arguments, but rather by a predisposition
arising out of the prevailing habits of thought. Scientific
explanations have, indeed, been given of some alleged mira-

---

never modifies those laws for special purposes, and in a manner that exceeds
both human capacities and human comprehension, is to make an assertion that
is unproved and contrary to analogy. To say that the metaphysical conception
of Infinity precludes the notion of miracles is useless, because (as Mansel and
others have shown) the creation of the world is equally irreconcilable with
that conception, and because the existence of evil throws all such reasoning
into hopeless confusion. To say, in fine, that there was no use in miracles ac-
companying a revelation in an early stage of society, is completely to ignore
the passion for the wonderful and the dim perception of the moral which are
the characteristics of such a society. All these propositions flow naturally, but
not legitimately, out of the reaction against the 'Government by Miracle,' in
which Europe once believed. The *logical* consequences of the movement are,
I think, twofold. 1. The difficulty of proving miracles satisfactorily is incal-
culably increased, because it is shown that, in a certain phase of civilisation,
the belief in miracles necessarily arises, and that many thousands, which are
now universally rejected, were then universally believed, supported by a vast
amount of evidence, and entirely unconnected with imposition. 2. The essentially moral character which theology progressively acquires renders miraculous
evidence (except for a particular class of minds) useless.

cles, b1t it is an historical fact that those explanations were
preceded and elicited by a deep-seated incredulity on the subject, an instinctive and unreasoning repugnance to the old
belief which had long been manifest in literature. They
will observe, too, that if this repugnance be due in a great
measure to the increasing sense of law which physical sci
ences produce, it has been at least as closely connected with
the declining influence and realisation of dogmatic theology.
When theology occupies an exceedingly prominent place in
the affairs of life, and is the subject towards which the
thoughts of men are naturally and violently directed, the
mind will at last take a theological cast, and will judge all
secular matters by a theological standard. In a period,
therefore, when theology is almost coextensive with intellectual exertion, when the whole scope and tendency of literature, policy, and art is to subserve theological interests, and
when the imaginations of men are habitually inflamed by the
subject of their continual meditations, it is not at all surprising that belief in existing miracles should be universal. Such
miracles are perfectly congenial with the mental tone and
atmosphere that is general. The imagination is constantly
directed towards miraculous events, and readily forces its
conceptions upon the reason. When, however, the terrestrial
has been aggrandised at the expense of the theological; when,
in the progress of civilisation, art and literature and govern
ment become in a great measure secularised; when the mind
is withdrawn by ten thousand intellectual influences from
dogmatic considerations, and when the traces of these considerations become confused and unrealised, a new habit of
thought is gradually acquired. A secular atmosphere is
formed about the mind. The measure of probability is
altered. Men formerly expected in every event of life some

thing analogous to the theological notions on which they were continually meditating; they now judge everything by a secular standard. Formerly their natural impulse was to explain all phenomena by miracle; it is now to explain them by science. This is simply the result of a general law of the human mind, which is exemplified on countless occasions in the intercourse of society. The soldier, the lawyer, and the scholar will each obtain from his special pursuit a certain cast and character of thought, which he will display on all subjects, even those most remote from his immediate province. Just so, an age that is immersed in theology will judge everything by a theological, that is to say a miraculous standard; and an age that is essentially secular will judge everything by a secular, that is to say a rationalistic standard. It is therefore, I conceive, no chance coincidence that the decline of the sense of the miraculous has everywhere accompanied that movement of thought which has banished dogmatic influence from so many departments of life, and so greatly restricted it in others. In the present day this tendency has become so powerful that its influence extends to every earnest thinker, even though he does not as an individual participate in the indifference to dogma from which it sprang. Whoever succeeds in emancipating himself from the special influences of education and associations by which his opinions are in the first instance determined, will find the general course and current of contemporary literature the most powerful attraction to his mind. There are, it is true, a few exceptions to this rule. There are some intellects of such a repellent character, that the simple fact that one class of opinions or tendencies is dominant in their neighbourhood will be sufficient to induce them to adopt the opposite. These, however, are the exceptions

With most persons who really endeavour to form their opinions by independent thought, contemporary literature exercises an attracting and controlling influence which is extremely powerful if it is not irresistible. Owing to circumstances which I shall not pause to examine, it flashes upon them with a force and directness which is not possessed by the literature of any earlier period. The general tone of thought pervading it colours all their reasonings, influences and, if they are unconscious of its action, determines all their conclusions. In the present day this influence is essentially rationalistic.

There is one other subject of great importance which is naturally suggested by the movement we have been considering. We have seen how profoundly it has altered the character of Christian Churches. It has changed not only the outward form and manifestations, but the habits of thought, the religious atmosphere which was the medium through which all events were contemplated, and by which all reasonings were refracted. No one can doubt that if the modes of thought now prevailing on these subjects, even in Roman Catholic countries, could have been presented to the mind of a Christian of the twelfth century, he would have said that so complete an alteration would involve the absolute destruction of Christianity. As a matter of fact, most of these modifications were forced upon the reluctant Church by the pressure from without, and were specially resisted and denounced by the bulk of the clergy. They were represented as subversive of Christianity. The doctrine that religion could be destined to pass through successive phases of development was pronounced to be emphatically unchristian. The ideal church was always in the past; and immutability, if not retrogression, was deemed the condition of life. We can now judge this resistance by the clear light of experience. Dogmatic systems have, it is true, been materially weakened; they no longer exercise a controlling influence over the current of affairs. Persecution, religious wars, absorbing controversies, sacred art, and theological literature, which once indicated a passionate interest in dogmatic questions, have passed away or become comparatively uninfluential. Ecclesiastical power throughout Europe has been everywhere weakened, and weakened in each nation in proportion to its intellectual progress. If we were to judge the present position of Christianity by the tests of ecclesiastical history, if we were to measure it by the orthodox zeal of the great doctors of the past, we might well look upon its prospects with the deepest despondency and alarm. The spirit of the Fathers has incontestably faded. The days of Athanasius and Augustine have passed away never to return. The whole course and tendency of thought is flowing in another direction. The controversies of bygone centuries ring with a strange hollowness on the ear. But if, turning from ecclesiastical historians, we apply the exclusively moral tests which the New Testament so invariably and so emphatically enforces, if we ask whether Christianity has ceased to produce the living fruits of love and charity and zeal for truth, the conclusion we should arrive at would be very different. If it be true Christianity to dive with a passionate charity into the darkest recesses of misery and of vice, to irrigate every quarter of the earth with the fertilising stream of an almost boundless benevolence, and to include all the sections of humanity in the circle of an intense and efficacious sympathy; if it be true Christianity to destroy or weaken the barriers which had separated class from class and nation from nation, to free war from its harshest elements, and to make a consciousness of essential equality and of a genuine fraternity dominate over all accidental differences; if it be, above all, true Christianity to cultivate a love of truth for its own sake, a spirit of candour and of tolerance towards those with whom we differ—if these be the marks of a true and healthy Christianity, then never since the days of the Apostles has it been so vigorous as at present, and the decline of dogmatic systems and of clerical influence has been a measure if not a cause of its advance.

CHAPTER III.

ÆSTHETIC, SCIENTIFIC, AND MORAL DEVELOPMENTS OF RATIONALISM.

THE preceding chapters will, I trust, have sufficiently shown that during the last three centuries the sense of the miraculous has been steadily declining in Europe, that the movement has been so universal that no church or class of miracles has altogether escaped its influence, and that its causes are to be sought much less in special arguments bearing directly upon the question than in the general intellectual condition of society. In this, as in all other great historical developments, we have two classes of influences to consider. There are certain tendencies or predispositions resulting from causes that are deeply imbedded in the civilisation of the age which create the movement, direct the stream of opinions with irresistible force in a given direction, and, if we consider only great bodies of men and long periods of time, exercise an almost absolute authority. There is also the action of special circumstances and individual genius upon this general progress, retarding or accelerating its advance, giving it in different countries and in different spheres of society a peculiar character, and for a time associating it with movements with which it has no natural connection. I have endeavoured to show, that while numerous circumstances growing out of the complications of society have more or less influenced the history of the decline of the miraculous, there are two causes which dominate over all others, and are themselves very closely connected. One of these is the increasing sense of law, produced by physical sciences, which predisposes men more and more to attribute all the phenomena that meet them in actual life or in history to normal rather than to abnormal agencies; the other is the diminution of the influence of theology, partly from causes that lie within itself, and partly from the great increase of other subjects, which inclines men to judge all matters by a secular rather than by a theological standard.

But, as we have already in some degree perceived, and as we shall hereafter see more clearly, this history of the miraculous is but a single part or aspect of a much wider movement, which in its modern phases is usually designated by the name of Rationalism. The process of thought, that makes men recoil from the miraculous, makes them modify their views on many other questions. The expectation of miracles grows out of a certain conception of the habitual government of the world, of the nature of the Supreme Being, and of the manifestations of His power, which are all more or less changed by advancing civilisation. Sometimes this change is displayed by an open rejection of old beliefs. Sometimes it appears only in a change of interpretation or of realisation; that is to say, men gradually annex new ideas to old words, or they permit old opinions to become virtually obsolete. Each different phase of civilisation has its peculiar and congenial views of the system and government of the universe, to which the men of that time will gravitate; and although a revelation or a great effort of human genius

may for a time emancipate some of them from the conditions
of the age, the pressure of surrounding influences will soon
reassert its sway, and the truths that are unsuited to the
time will remain inoperative till their appropriate civilisation
has dawned.

I shall endeavour in the present chapter to trace the different phases of this development—to show how the conceptions both of the nature of the Deity and of the government of the universe are steadily modified before advancing
knowledge, and to analyse the causes upon which those
modifications depend.

It has been said, by a very high authority, that fetishism is the religion which men who are altogether uncivilised would naturally embrace; and, certainly, there can be
no question that the general characteristic of the earlier
stages of religious belief is to concentrate reverence upon
matter, and to attribute to it an intrinsic efficacy. This fetishism, which in its rudest form consists of the worship of a
certain portion of matter as matter, is shown also, though in
a modified and less revolting manner, in the supposition that
certain sacred talismans or signs possess an inherent efficacy
altogether irrespective of the dispositions of men. Of this
nature was the system of pagan magic, which attributed a
supernatural power to particular herbs, or ceremonies, or
words, and also the many rival but corresponding superstitions that were speedily introduced into Christianity. The
sign of the cross was perhaps the earliest of these. It was
adopted not simply as a form of recognition or as a holy
recollection, or even as a mark of reverence, but as a weapon
of miraculous power; and the writings of the Fathers are
crowded with the prodigies it performed, and also with the
many types and images that adumbrated its glory. Thus

we are reminded by a writer in the beginning of the second century, that the sea could not be traversed without a mast, which is in the form of a cross. The earth becomes fertile only when it has been dug by a spade, which is a cross. The body of man is itself in the same holy form. So also is his face, for the eyes and nose together form a cross; a fact to which Jeremiah probably alluded when he said, ' The breath of our nostrils is the anointed of the Lord.' [1]

Speculations no less strange and far-fetched were directed to the baptismal water. The efficacy of infant baptism, which had been introduced, if not in the Apostolic age, at least immediately after, was regarded as quite independent of any moral virtues either in the recipient or those about him; and in the opinion of some a spiritual change was effected by the water itself, without any immediate coöperation of the Deity, by a power that had been conferred upon the element at the period of the creation.[2] The incomparable grandeur of its position in the universe was a theme of the most rapturous eloquence. When the earth was still buried in the night of chaos, before the lights of heaven had been

---

[1] Justyn Martyr, *Apol.* i. Augustine thought the wooden ark floating on the Deluge a type of the cross consecrating the baptismal waters ; and Bede found a similar type in the rod of Moses stretched over the Red Sea. Another wise commentator suggested that Isaac had been saved from death, because, when ascending the mountain, he bore the ' wood of sacrifice' on his shoulder. The cross, however, seldom or never appears in art before the vision of Constantine. At first it was frequently represented richly ornamented with gems or flowers. As St. Fortunatus writes :—

> ' Arbor decora et fulgida
> Ornata regis purpura,
> Electa digno stipite
> Tam sancta membra tangere.'

The letter Tau, as representing the cross, was specially reverenced as opposed to Theta, the unlucky letter—the initial of θάνατος.

[2] See the curious argument in Tertullian, *De Bapt.* c. 5, 6, 7, 8.

called into being, or any living creature had tenanted the eternal solitude, water existed in all the plenitude of its perfection, veiling the unshapen earth, and glorified and sanctified for ever as the chosen throne of the Deity. By water God separated the heavens from the earth. Water became instinct with life when the earth was still barren and uninhabited. In the creation of man it might appear at first sight as if its position was ignored, but even here a more matured reflection dispelled the difficulty. For in order that the Almighty should mould the earth into the human form, it was obviously necessary that it should have retained something of its former moisture; in other words, that it should have been mixed with water.[1]

Such was the direction in which the human mind drifted, with an ever-increasing rapidity, as the ignorance and intellectual torpor became more general. The same habit of thought was soon displayed in every department of theology, and countless charms and amulets came into use, the simple

---

[1] 'Non enim ipsius quoque hominis figurandi opus sociantibus aquis absolutum est; de terra materia convenit, non tamen habilis nisi humecta et succida, quam scilicet ante quartum diem segregatæ aquæ in stationem suam superstite humore, limo temperant.' (Tertullian, *De Baptismo*, c. iii.) From this notion of the sanctity of water grew the custom of swimming witches—for it was believed that everything tainted with diabolical presence was repelled by it and unable to sink into its depths (Binsfeldius, *De Confess. Mal.* p. 315)—and also probably the many legends of transformed men restored to their natural condition by crossing a stream. Among the ancient philosophers, Thales had esteemed water the origin of all things, which more than one Father regarded as a kind of inspiration. Thus Minucius Felix: 'Milesius Thales rerum initium aquam dixit: Deum autem eam mentem quæ ex aqua cuncta formaverit. Vides philosophi principalis nobiscum penitus opinionem consonare.' (*Octavius*, c. xix.) The belief in the expiatory power of water was forcibly rebuked by Ovid:—

> 'Ah! nimiùm faciles, qui tristia crimina cædis
> Flumineâ tolli posse putatis aquâ!'

Fast. lib. ii.)

possession of which was supposed to guarantee the owner against all evils, both spiritual and temporal. Indeed, it may be questioned whether this form of fetishism was ever more prominent in paganism than in mediæval Christianity.

When men pass from a state of pure fetishism, the next conception they form of the Divine nature is anthropomorphism, which is in some respects very closely connected with the preceding, and which, like it, is diffused in a more or less modified form over the belief of almost all uncivilised nations. Those who have ceased to attribute power and virtue to inert matter, regard the universe as the sphere of the operations of spiritual beings of a nature strictly analogous to their own. They consider every unusual phenomenon the direct and isolated act of an unseen agent, pointed to some isolated object and resulting from some passing emotion. The thunder, the famine, or the pestilence is the result of an ebullition of spiritual anger; great and rapid prosperity is the sign of spiritual satisfaction. But at the same time the feebleness of imagination which in this stage makes men unable to picture the Deity other than as an unseen man, makes it also impossible for them to concentrate their thoughts and emotions upon that conception without a visible representation. For while it is a matter of controversy whether or not the innate faculties of the civilised man transcend those of the savage, it is at least certain that the intellectual atmosphere of each period tells so soon and so powerfully upon all men, that long before matured age the two classes are almost as different in their capacities as in their acquirements. The civilised man not only knows more than the savage, he possesses an intellectual strength, a power of sustained and patient thought, of concentrating his mind steadily upon the unseen, of disengaging his conceptions from the images of the senses, which the other is unable even to imagine. Present to the savage the conception of an unseen Being, to be adored without the assistance of any representation, and he will be unable to grasp it. It will have no force or palpable reality to his mind, and can therefore exercise no influence over his life. Idolatry is the common religion of the savage, simply because it is the only one of which his intellectual condition will admit, and, in one form or another, it must continue until that condition has been changed.

Idolatry may be of two kinds. It is sometimes a sign of progress. When men are beginning to emerge from the pure fetishism which is probably their first stage, they carve matter into the form of an intelligent being ; and it is only when it is endowed with that form, that they attribute to it a divine character. They are still worshipping matter, but their fetishism is fading into anthropomorphism. Sometimes, again, men who have once risen to a conception of a pure and spiritual Being, sink, in consequence of some convulsion of society, into a lower level of civilisation. They will then endeavour to assist their imaginations by representations of the object of their worship, and they will very soon attribute to those representations an intrinsic efficacy.

It will appear from the foregoing principles that, in the early anthropomorphic stages of society, visible images form the channels of religious devotions ; and, therefore, as long as those stages continue, the true history of theology, or at least of the emotional and realising parts of theology, is to be found in the history of art. Even outside the pale of Christianity, there is scarcely any instance in which the national religion has not exercised a great and dominating influence over the national art. Thus, for example, the two ancient nations in which the æsthetic development failed most remarkably to keep pace with the general civilisation were the Persians and the Egyptians. The fire that was worshipped by the first formed a fetish, at once so simple and so sublime, that it rendered useless the productions of the chisel; while the artistic genius of Egypt was paralysed by a religion which branded all innovation as a crime, made the profession of an artist compulsory and hereditary, rendered the knowledge of anatomy impossible by its prohibition of dissection, and taught men by its elaborate symbolism to look at every natural object, not for its own sake, but as the representative of something else. Thus, again, among the nations that were especially distinguished for their keen sense of the beautiful, India and Greece are preëminent; but there is this important difference between them. The Indian religion ever soared to the terrible, the unnatural, and the prodigious; and consequently Indian art was so completely turned away from nature, that all faculty of accurately copying it seems to have vanished, and the simplest subject was interwoven with grotesque and fanciful inventions. The Greek religion, on the other hand, was an almost pure naturalism, and therefore Greek art was simply nature idealised, and as such has become the universal model.[1]

But it is with Christian art that we are now especially concerned, and it is also Christian art which most faithfully reflects the different stages of religious development, ena-

[1] See Winckelmann, *Hist. of Art ;* Raoul-Rochette, *Cours d'Archéologie ;* and the lectures of Barry and Fuseli. This particular characteristic of Indian art has been forcibly noticed by Mr. Ruskin in one of his Edinburgh lectures. Lessing ascribes the imperfections of Persian art to its almost exclusive employment for military subjects; but this was itself a consequence of the small encouragement religion gave to art. On the great difference of the ideal of beauty in different nations, which has also exercised a great influence on the development of art, see some curious evidence collected by Ch. Comte, *Traité de Législation,* liv. iii. ch. 4.

14

bling us to trace, not merely successive phases of belief, but what is much more important for my present purpose, successive phases of religious realisation.

The constant fall of the early Jews into idolatry, in spite of the most repeated commands and the most awful punishments, while it shows clearly how irresistible is this tendency in an early stage of society, furnished a warning which was at first not altogether lost upon the Christian Church. It is indeed true that art had so long been associated with paganism—its subjects, its symbolism, and its very tone of beauty, were so derived from the old mythology—that the Christian artists, who had probably in many cases been formerly pagan artists, introduced a considerable number of the ancient conceptions into their new sphere. But, although this fact is perfectly incontestable, and although the readiness with which pagan imagery was admitted into the symbolism of the Church forms an extremely curious and instructive contrast to the tone which most of the Fathers adopted towards the pagan deities, nearly all these instances of appropriation were singularly judicious, and the general desire to avoid anything that might lead to idolatrous worship was very manifest.

The most important and the most beneficial effect of pagan traditions upon Christian art was displayed in its general character. It had always been a strict rule among the Greeks and Romans to exclude from sepulchral decorations every image of sadness. The funerals of the ancients were, indeed, accompanied by great displays of exaggerated and artificial lamentation; but once the ashes were laid in the tomb, it was the business of the artist to employ all his skill in depriving death of its terror. Wreaths of flowers, Bacchic dances, hunts, or battles, all the exuberance of the most buoyant life, all the images of passion or 6f revelry, were sculptured around the tomb; while the genii of the seasons indicated the inevitable march of time, and the masks that adorned the corners showed that life was but a player's part, to be borne for a few years with honour, and cast aside without regret.

The influence of this tradition was shown in a very remarkable way in Christianity. At first all Christian art was sepulchral art. The places that were decorated were the Catacombs; the chapels were all surrounded by the dead; the altar upon which the sacred mysteries were celebrated was the tomb of a martyr.[1] According to mediæval or even to modern ideas, we should have imagined that an art growing up under such circumstances would have assumed a singularly sombre and severe tone, and this expectation would be greatly heightened if we remembered the violence of the persecution. The very altar-tomb around which the Christian painter scattered his ornaments with most profusion was often associated with the memory of sufferings of the most horrible and varied character, and at the same time with displays of heroic constancy that might well have invited the talents of the artist. Passions, too, were roused to the highest point, and it would seem but natural that the great and terrible scenes of Christian vengeance should be depicted. Yet nothing of this kind appears in the Catacombs. With two doubtful exceptions, one at least being of the very latest period of art, there are no representations

---

[1] This is the origin of the custom in the Catholic Church of placing relics of the martyrs beneath the altars of the churches. It was also connected with the passage in the Revelations about the souls that were beneath the altar of God. In most early churches there was a subterranean chapel below the high altar, as a memorial of the Catacombs. A decree of the Second Council of Nice (A.D. 787) forbade the consecration of any church without relics.

of martyrdoms.¹ Daniel unharmed amid the lions, the unaccomplished sacrifice of Isaac, the three children unscathed amid the flames, or St. Peter led to prison, are the only images that reveal the horrible persecution that was raging. There was no disposition to perpetuate forms of suffering, no ebullition of bitterness or complaint, no thirsting for vengeance. Neither the Crucifixion, nor any of the scenes of the Passion, were ever represented; nor was the day of judgment, nor were the sufferings of the lost. The wreaths of flowers in which paganism delighted, and even some of the most joyous images of the pagan mythology, were still retained, and were mingled with all the most beautiful emblems of Christian hopes, and with representations of many of the miracles of mercy.

This systematic exclusion of all images of sorrow, suffering, and vengeance, at a time that seemed beyond all others most calculated to produce them, reveals the early Church in an aspect that is singularly touching, and it may, I think, be added, singularly sublime. The fact is also one of extreme importance in ecclesiastical history. For, as we shall hereafter have occasion to see, there existed among some of the theologians of the early Church a tendency that was diametrically opposite to this; a tendency to dilate upon such subjects as the torments of hell, the vengeance of the day of judgment, and, in a word, all the sterner portions of Christianity, which at last became dominant in the Church,

---

M. Raoul-Rochette thinks that there is but one direct and positive representation of a martyrdom—that of the Virgin Salome, and this is of a very late period of decadence (*Tableau des Catacombes*, p. 187). The same writer has collected (pp. 191, 192) a few instances from the Fathers in which representations of martyrdoms in the early basilicas are mentioned; but they are very few, and there can be no doubt whatever of the broad contrast early Christian art in this respect bears to that of the tenth and following centuries.

and which exercised an extremely injurious influence over
the affections of men.   But whatever might have been the
case with educated theologians, it was quite impossible for
this tendency to be very general as long as art, which was
then the expression of popular realisations, took a different
direction.   The change in art was not fully shown till late in
the tenth century.   I have already had occasion to notice
the popularity which representations of the Passion and of
the day of judgment then for the first time assumed; and it
may be added that, from this period, one of the main objects
of the artists was the invention of new and horrible tortures,
which were presented to the constant contemplation of the
faithful in countless pictures of the sufferings of the martyrs
on earth, or of the lost in hell.[1]

The next point which especially strikes us in the art of
the Catacombs is the great love of symbolism it evinced.
There are, it is true, a few isolated pictures of Christ and of
the Virgin, most of them of a late period; but by far the
greater number of representations were obviously symbolical,
and were designed exclusively as a means of instruction.
Of these symbols many were taken without hesitation from
paganism.   Thus, one of the most common is the peacock,
which in the Church, as among the heathen, was selected as
the emblem of immortality.   Partly, perhaps, on account of
its surpassing beauty, and partly from a belief that its flesh
never decayed,[2] it had been adopted by the ancients as the
nearest realisation of the conception of the phœnix, and at the
funeral of an empress the bird was sometimes let loose from

See Raoul-Rochette, *Tableau des Catacombes*, pp. 192-195; Didron,
Iconographie Chrétienne.
   [2] Which St Augustine said he had ascertained by experiment to be a fact,
and which he seemed to regard as a miracle. (*De Civ. Dei*, lib. xxxi., c. 4.)

among the ashes of the deceased.¹ Orpheus drawing all
men to him by his music, symbolised the attractive power of
Christianity.² The masks of paganism, and especially the
masks of the sun and moon, which the pagans adopted as
emblems of the lapse of life, continued to adorn the Christian
sarcophagi, the last being probably regarded as emblems ef
the resurrection.   The same thing may be said of the genii
of the seasons.³ Nor was this by any means the only form
under which the genii were represented. The ancients regarded them as presiding over every department of nature,

¹ See Ciampini, *Vetera Monumenta*, pars i. p. 115; and Maitland, *On the
Catacombs.* Raoul-Rochette, however, seems to regard the peacock rather as
the symbol, first of all of the apotheosis of an empress, and then generally of
apotheosis, the peacock having been the bird of Juno, the empress of heaven.

² Orpheus is spoken of by Eusebius as in this respect symbolising Christ.
The reverence that attached to him probably resulted in a great measure from
the fact that among the many apocryphal prophecies of Christ that circulated
in the Church, some of the most conspicuous were ascribed to Orpheus. See
on this symbol, Maitland, *On the Catacombs*, p. 110 ; Raoul-Rochette, *Tab. des
Cat.* p. 138; and, for a full examination of the subject, the great work of
Boldetti, *Osservazioni sopra i Cimiteri de' Santi Martyri* (Romæ, 1720), tom.
i. pp. 27–29. M. Rio (*Art Chrétien*, introd. p. 36), I think rather fancifully,
connects it with the descent of Orpheus to hell to save a soul. As other examples of the introduction of pagan gods into Christian art, I may mention
that there is an obscure picture in the catacomb of St. Calixtus, which R.
Rochette supposes to represent Mercury leading the souls of the dead to judgment (*Tab. des Cat.* pp. 148–151); and also that Hercules, though never, I
believe, represented in the Catacombs, appears more than once in the old
churches, St. Augustine having identified him with Samson. (See on this representation, and generally on the connection between pagan and Christian art,
that very curious and learned work, Marangoni, *Delle Cose Gentilesche e Profane Transportate ad uso delle Chiese* (Romæ, 1744), pp. 50, 51.) The sphinx
also was believed by some of the early Christians (e. g. Clement of Alexandria)
to be in some degree connected with their faith ; for they supposed it to be
copied from the Jewish image of the Cherubim, but they never reproduced it.
Some later antiquarians have attributed this curious combination of the Virgin
and the Lion to the advantages Egypt derives from these signs, through which
the sun passes at the period of the inundation of the Nile (Caylus, *Recueil
d'Antiquités*, t. i. p. 45).

³ Marangoni, *Delle Cose Gentilesche*, p. 45.

and many thought that a separate genius watched over the
destiny of each man. This conception very naturally coalesced with that of guardian angels,[1] and the pagan representation of the genii as young winged boys, naked, and
with gentle and joyous countenances, became very common
in early Christian art, and passed from it into the art of
later days. Even now, from the summit of the baldacchino
of St. Peter's, the genii of paganism look down on the
proudest ceremonies of Catholicism. Once or twice on the
Christian sarcophagi Christ is represented in triumph with
the sky, or perhaps more correctly 'the waters above the
firmament,' beneath his feet, in the form of a man extending
a veil above his head, the habitual pagan representation of
an aquatic deity.[2]

In addition to these symbols, which were manifestly taken
from paganism, there were others mainly or exclusively produced by the Church itself. Thus, the fish was the usual emblem of Christ, chosen because the Greek word forms the
initials of His name and titles,[3] and also because Christians
are born by baptism in water.[4] Sometimes, but much more
rarely, the stag is employed for the same purpose, because it
bears the cross on its forehead, and from an old notion that it
was the irreconcilable enemy of serpents, which it was supposed to hunt out and destroy.[5] Several subjects from the

[1] All this is fully discussed in Marangoni.

[2] *Ibid.* p. 45 ; Raoul-Rochette, *Tab. des Cat.*

[3] 'Ιχθύς. 'Ιησοῦς Χριστὸς Θεοῦ υἱὸς Σωτήρ. The initial letters of the
prophetic verses of the Sibyl of Erythra (St. Aug. *De Civ. Dei*, lib. xviii. cap.
23). The dolphin was especially selected because of its tenderness to its
young.

[4] 'Nos pisciculi secundum 'Ιχθύν nostrum Jesum Christum in aquâ nasci-
mur.' (Tertullian, *De Baptismo*, c. i.)

[5] Maury, *Légendes Pieuses*, pp. 173–178. This notion was, I imagine,
pagan. There is a bas-relief in the Vatican which seems to represent a stag

Bible of a symbolical character were constantly repeated.
Such were Noah in the attitude of prayer receiving the dove
into his breast, Jonah rescued from the fish's mouth, Moses
striking the rock, St. Peter with the wand of power, the three
children, Daniel in the lions' den, the Good Shepherd, the
dove of peace, the anchor of hope, the crown of martyrdom,
the palm of victory, the ship struggling through the waves
to a distant haven, the horse bounding onwards to the goal.
All of these were manifestly symbolical, and were in no de
gree the objects of reverence or worship.

When, however, the first purity of the Christian Church
was dimmed, and when the decomposition of the Roman
empire and the invasion of the barbarians overcast the civilisation of Europe, the character of art was speedily changed,
and though many of the symbolical representations still con
tinued, there was manifested by the artists a constantly increasing tendency to represent directly the object of their
worship, and by the people to attach a peculiar sanctity to
the image.

Of all the forms of anthropomorphism that are displayed
in Catholic art, there is probably none which a Protestant
deems so repulsive as the portraits of the First Person of the
Trinity, that are now so common. It is, however, a very remarkable fact, which has been established chiefly by the researches of some French archæologists in the present cen-

In the act of attacking a serpent. The passage in the Psalms, about the hart
panting for the waters,' was mixed up with this symbol. In the middle ages,
stags were invested with a kind of prophetic power. See also Ciampini, *De
Sacris Ædificiis* (Romæ), p. 44; and the very curious chapter in Arringhi,
Roma Subterranea, tom. ii. pp. 602–606. The stag was supposed to dread the
thunder so much, that through terror it often brought forth its young prema-
turely; and this was associated with the passage, 'The voice of thy thunder
has made me afraid.'

tury, that these portraits are all comparatively modern, and that the period in which the superstition of Europe was most profound, was precisely that in which they had no existence.[1] In an age when the religious realisations of Christendom were habitually expressed by visible representations—when the nature of a spirit was so inadequately conceived that artists never for a moment shrank from representing purely spiritual beings—and when that instinctive reverence which makes men recoil from certain objects as too solemn and sublime to be treated, was almost absolutely unknown—we do not find the smallest tendency to represent God the Father. Scenes indeed in which He acted were frequently depicted, but the First Person of the Trinity was invariably superseded by the Second. Christ, in the dress and with the features appropriated to Him in the representations of scenes from the New Testament, and often with the monogram underneath his figure, is represented creating man, condemning Adam and Eve to labour, speaking with Noah, arresting the arm of Abraham, or giving the law to Moses.[2] With the exception of a hand sometimes extended from the cloud, and occasionally encircled with a nimbus, we find in this period no traces in art of the Creator. At first we can easily imagine that a purely spiritual conception of the Deity, and also the hatred that was inspired by the type of Jupiter, would have discouraged artists from attempting such a subject; and Gnosticism, which exercised a very great influ-

---

[1] This subject has been briefly noticed by Raoul-Rochette in his *Discours ir l'Art du Christianisme* (1834), p. 7; and by Maury, *Légendes Pieuses ;* but the full examination of it was reserved for M. Didron, in his great work, *Iconographie Chrétienne, Hist. de Dieu* (Paris, 1843), one of the most important contributions ever made to Christian archæology. See, too, Emeric David, *Hist. de la Peinture au Moyen Age*, pp. 19–21.

[2] Didron, pp. 177–182.

ence over Christian art, and which emphatically denied the divinity of the God of the Old Testament, tended in the same direction; but it is very unlikely that these reasons can have had any weight between the sixth and twelfth centuries. For the more those centuries are studied, the more evident it becomes that the universal and irresistible tendency was then to materialise every spiritual conception, to form a palpable image of everything that was reverenced, to reduce all subjects within the domain of the senses. This tendency, unchecked by any sense of grotesqueness or irreverence, was shown with equal force in sculpture, painting, and legends; and all the old landmarks and distinctions that had been made between the orthodox uses of pictures and idolatry had been virtually swept away by the resistless desire to form an image of everything that was worshipped, and to attach to that image something of the sanctity of its object. Yet amid all this no one thought of representing the Supreme Being. In that condition of society men desired a human god, and they consequently concentrated their attention exclusively upon the Second Person of the Trinity or upon the saints, and suffered the great conception of the Father to become practically obsolete. It continued of course in creeds and in theological treatises, but it was a void and sterile abstraction, which had no place among the realisations and no influence on the emotions of mankind. If men turned away from the Second Person of the Trinity, i' was only to bestow their devotions upon saints or martyrs. With the exception, I believe, of a single manuscript of the ninth century,[1] there was no portrait of the Father till the twelfth century; and it was only in the fourteenth century, when the revival of learning had become marked, that these

[1] Raoul-Rochette, *Discours sur les Types de l'Art Chrétien*, p. 71.

portraits became common.[1] From that time to the age of Raphael the steady tendency of art is to give an ever-increasing preëminence to the Father. At first His position in painting and sculpture had been a subordinate one, and He was only represented in the least attractive occupations,[2] and commonly, through a desire to represent the coeternity of the Persons of the Trinity, of the same age as His Son. Gradually, however, after the fourteenth century, we find the Father represented in every painting as older, more venerable, and more prominent, until at last He became the central and commanding figure,[3] exciting the highest degree of reverence, and commonly represented in different countries according to their ideal of greatness. In Italy, Spain, and the ultramontane monasteries of France, He was usually represented as a Pope; in Germany as an Emperor; in England and, for the most part, in France as a King.

In a condition of thought in which the Deity was only realised in the form of man, it was extremely natural that the number of divinities should be multiplied. The chasm between the two natures was entirely unfelt, and something of

---

Didron, pp. 227–230.

[2] See this fact worked out in detail in Didron.

[3] 'On peut donc relativement à Dieu le Père partager le moyen âge en deux périodes. Dans la première, qui est antérieure au XIVᵉ siècle, la figure du Père se confond avec celle du Fils; c'est le Fils qui est tout-puissant et qui fait son Père à son image et ressemblance. Dans la seconde période, après le XIIIᵉ siècle, jusqu'au XVIᵉ, Jésus-Christ perd sa force d'assimilation iconographique et se laisse vaincre par son Père. C'est au tour du Fils à se revêtir des traits du Père, à vieillir et rider comme lui. . . . Enfin, depuis les premiers siècles du Christianisme jusqu'à nos jours nous voyons le Père croître en importance. Son portrait, d'abord interdit par les Gnostiques, se montre timidement ensuite et comme déguisé sous la figure de son Fils. Puis il rejette tout accoutrement étranger et prend une figure spéciale ; puis par Raphaël et enfin par l'Anglais Martin, il gagne une grave et une admirable physionomie qui n'appartient qu'à lui.' (Didron, p. 226.)

the Divine character was naturally reflected upon those who were most eminent in the Church. The most remarkable instance of this polytheistic tendency was displayed in the deification of the Virgin.

A conception of a divine person or manifestation of the female sex had been one of the notions of the old Jewish Cabalists; and in the first century Simon Magus had led about with him a woman named Helena, who, according to the Catholics, was simply his mistress, but whom he proclaimed to be the incarnation of the Divine Thought.[1] This notion, under a great many different forms, was diffused through almost all the sects of the Gnostics. The Supreme Being, whom they very jealously distinguished from and usually opposed to the God of the Jews,[2] they termed 'The Unknown Father,' and they regarded Him as directly inaccessible to human knowledge, but as revealed in part by cer-

[1] See on this subject Franck, *Sur la Kabbale;* Maury, *Croyances et Légendes d'Antiquité* (1863), p. 338; and especially Beausobre, *Hist. du Manichéisme* (1734), tom. i. pp. 35–37. Justyn Martyr, Tertullian, Irenæus, Epiphanius, and several other Fathers, notice the worship of Helena. According to them, Simon proclaimed that the angels in heaven made war on account of her beauty, and that the Evil One had made her prisoner to prevent her return to heaven, from which she had strayed. There is some reason to think that all this was an allegory of the soul.

[2] Most of the Gnostics regarded the God of the Jews or the Demiurge as an imperfect spirit presiding over an imperfect moral system. Many, however, regarded the Jewish religion as the work of the principle of Evil—the god of matter; and the Cainites made everyone who had opposed it the object of reverence, while the Ophites actually worshipped the serpent. We have, perhaps, a partial explanation of the reverence many of the Gnostics had for the serpent in the fact that this animal, which in Christianity represents the principle of Evil, had a very different position in ancient symbolism. It was the general emblem of healing (because it changes its skin), and as such appears in the statues of Æsculapius and Isis, and it was also constantly adopted as a representative animal. Thus in the Mithraic groups, that are so common in later Roman sculpture, the serpent and the dog represent all living creatures. A serpent with a hawk's head was an old Egyptian symbol of a good genius.

tain Æons or emanations, of whom the two principal were Christ, and a female spirit termed the Divine Sophia or En-noia, and sometimes known by the strange name of 'Prou-nice.'[1] According to some sects this Sophia was simply the human soul, which was originally an emanation or child of the Deity, but which had wandered from its parent-source, had become enamoured of and at last imprisoned by matter, and was now struggling, by the assistance of the unfallen Æon Christ, towards its pristine purity. More commonly, however, she was deemed a personification of a Divine attri-bute, an individual Æon, the sister or (according to others) the mother of Christ, and entitled to equal or almost equal reverence.

In this way, long before Catholic Mariolatry had acquir-ed its full proportions, a very large section of the Christian world had been accustomed to concentrate much attention upon a female ideal as one of the two central figures of de-votion. This fact alone would in some degree prepare the way for the subsequent elevation of the Virgin; and it should be added that Gnosticism exercised a very great and special influence over the modes of thought of the orthodox. As its most learned historian has forcibly contended, it should

---

[1] Prounice properly signifies lasciviousness. It seems to have been ap-plied to the Sophia considered in her fallen condition, as imprisoned in matter; but there is an extreme obscurity, which has I think never been cleared up, hanging over the subject. Prounice seems to have been confounded with Beronice, the name which a very early Christian tradition gave to the woman who had been healed of an issue of blood. This woman formed one of the principal types among the Gnostics. According to the Valentinians, the twelve years of her affliction represented the twelve Æons, while the flowing blood was the force of the Sophia passing to the inferior world. See on this subject, Maury, *Croyances et Légendes*, art. *Veronica*; and on the Sophia generally, Matter, *Hist. du Gnosticisme*, tom. i. pp. 275–278. M. Franck says (*La Kabbale*, p. 43) that some of the Gnostics painted the Holy Ghost as a woman, but this I suppose only refers to the Sophia.

not be regarded as a Christian heresy, but rather as an independent system of eclectic philosophy in which Christian
ideas occupied a prominent place. Nearly all heresies have
aroused among the orthodox a spirit of repulsion which has
produced views the extreme opposite of those of the heretic.
Gnosticism, on the other hand, exercised an absorbing and
attracting influence of the strongest kind.   That Neo-Platonic philosophy which so deeply tinctured early theology
passed, for the most part, through a Gnostic medium.   No
sect, too, appears to have estimated more highly or employed more skilfully æsthetic aids.   The sweet songs of Barde-
sanes and Harmonius carried their distinctive doctrines into
the very heart of Syrian orthodoxy, and cast such a spell
over the minds of the people that, in spite of all prohibitions,
they continued to be sung in the Syrian churches till the
Catholic poet St. Ephrem wedded orthodox verses to the
Gnostic metres.[1] The apocryphal gospels, which were for
the most part of Gnostic origin, long continued to furnish
subjects for painters in orthodox churches.[2]   There is even
much reason to believe that the conventional cast of features
ascribed to Christ, which for so many centuries formed the
real object of the worship of Christendom, is derived from the
Gnostic artists.[3]   Besides this, Gnosticism formed the high-

---

[1] Matter, *Hist. du Gnosticisme*, tom. i. pp. 360–362.

[2] Didron, pp. 197, 198. The apocryphal gospel, however, which exercised
most influence over art, was probably that of Nicodemus, which is apparently
of orthodox origin, and was probably written (or at least the second part of
it) against the Apollinarians. We owe to it the pictures of the Descent into
Limbo that are so common in early Byzantine art. The same subject, derived
from the same source, was also prominent in the mediæval sacred plays
(Malone, *History of the English Stage*, p. 19).

[3] For a full discussion of this point, see Raoul-Rochette's *Types de l'Art*,
pp. 9–26, and his *Tableau des Catacombes*, p. 265. The opinion that the type
of Christ is derived from the Gnostics (which Raoul-Rochette says has been

est representation of a process of transformation or unifica-
tion of religious ideas which occupied a very prominent place
among the organising influences of the Church. Christianity
had become the central intellectual power in the world, but
it triumphed not so much by superseding rival faiths as by
absorbing and transforming them. Old systems, old rites,
old images were grafted into the new belief, retaining much
of their ancient character but assuming new names and a new
complexion. Thus in the symbolism of the Gnostics innumerable conceptions culled from the different beliefs of paganism were clustered around the Divine Sophia, and at least
some of them passed through paintings or traditional allegories to the Virgin. The old Egyptian conception of Night,
the mother of day and of all things, with the diadem of stars,
Isis, the sister of Osiris or the Saviour; Latona, the mother of
Apollo; Flora, the bright goddess of returning spring, to
whom was once dedicated the month of May, which is now

embraced by most of the Roman antiquarians) rests chiefly on the following
positions :—1. That in the earliest stage of Christianity all painting and sculpture was looked upon with great aversion in the Church, and that as late as
the time of Constantine portraits of Christ were very rare. 2. That the Gnostics from the beginning cultivated art, and that small images of Christ were
among the most common objects of their reverence. 3. That the Gnostics
were very numerous at Rome. 4. That Gnosticism exercised a great influence
upon the Church, and especially upon her æsthetic development. It may be
added that the Christians carefully abstained from deriving from paganism the
cast of features they ascribed to Christ ; and Theodoret relates (*Hist.*, lib. i.
cap. 15) that a painter having taken Jupiter as a model in a portrait of Christ.
his hand was withered, but was restored miraculously by St. Gennadius, Arch
bishop of Constantinople. At a later period pagan statues were frequently
turned into saints. St. Augustine mentions that in his time there was no
authentic portrait of Christ, and that the type of features was still undeter-
mined, so that we have absolutely no knowledge of His appearance. ' Qua
fuerit ille (Christus) facie nos penitus ignoramus. . . . Nam et ipsius
Dominicæ facies carnis innumerabilium cogitationum diversitate variatur et
fingitur, quæ tamen una erat, quæcumque erat.' (*De Trinitate*, lib. viii. c. 4,
5.) The type, however, was soon after formed.

dedicated to the Virgin; Cybele, the mother of the gods, whose feast was celebrated on what is now Lady-day, were all more or less connected with the new ideal.[1]

But while Gnosticism may be regarded as the pioneer or precursor of Catholic Mariolatry, the direct causes are to be found within the circle of the Church. If the first two or three centuries were essentially the ages of moral appreciation, the fourth and fifth were essentially those of dogmatic definitions, which were especially applied to the nature of the divinity of Christ, and which naturally and indeed necessarily tended to the continued exaltation of one who was soon regarded as, very literally, the Bride of God. During the Nestorian controversy the discussions on the subject assumed an almost physiological character;[2] and the emphasis with which the Church condemned the doctrines of Nestorius, who was supposed to have unduly depreciated the dignity of Mary, impelled the orthodox enthusiasm in the opposite direction. The Council of Ephesus, in A.D. 431, defined the manner in which the Virgin should be represented by artists;

---

[1] On the relation of this to Gnosticism, see Matter, *Hist. du Gnosticisme*, tom. i. pp. 88, 89–98.

[2] The strong desire natural to the middle ages to give a palpable form to the mystery of the Incarnation was shown curiously in the notion of a conception by the ear. In a hymn, ascribed to St. Thomas à Becket, occur the lines—

> ‘Gaude Virgo, mater Christi,
> Quæ per aurem concepisti,
> Gabriele nuntio.’

And in an old glass window, now I believe in one of the museums of Paris, the Holy Ghost is represented hovering over the Virgin in the form of a dove, while a ray of light passes from his beak to her ear, along which ray an infant Christ is descending.—Langlois, *Peinture sur Verre*, p. 157.

[3] St. Augustine notices (*De Trinitate*) that in his time there was no authentic portrait of Mary. The Council of Ephesus wished her to be painted with the Infant Child, and this was the general representation in the early Church. Some of the Byzantine pictures are said to have been influenced by the

and the ever-increasing importance of painting and sculpture
as the organs of religious realisations brought into clearer
and more vivid relief the charms of a female ideal, which acquired an irresistible fascination in the monastic life of celibacy and solitary meditation, and in the strange mixture of
gallantry and devotion that accompanied the Crusades. It
was in this last period that the doctrine of the Immaculate
Conception is said first to have appeared.[1] The lily, as the
symbol of purity, was soon associated with pictures of the
Virgin; and a notion having grown up that women by eating
it became pregnant without the touch of man, a vase wreathed
with lilies became the emblem of her maternity.

The world is governed by its ideals, and seldom or never
has there been one which has exercised a more profound and,
on the whole, a more salutary influence than the mediæval
conception of the Virgin. For the first time woman was
elevated to her rightful position, and the sanctity of weakness was recognised as well as the sanctity of sorrow. No
longer the slave or toy of man, no longer associated only with

favourite Egyptian representations of Isis giving suck to Horus. It has been
observed that in the case of Mary, as in the case of Christ, suffering and deep
melancholy became more and more the prevailing expression as the dark ages
rolled on, which was still further increased by the black tint the mediæval
artists frequently gave her, in allusion to the description in the Song of Solomon. The first notice in writing of the resemblance of Christ to His mother
is, I believe, in Nicephorus.—See Raoul-Rochette, *Types de l'Art Chrétien*,
pp. 30–39; Pascal, *Institutions de l'Art Chrétien.*

[1] Heeren, *Influences des Croisades*, pp. 204, 205. However, St. Augustine
says :—' Excepta itaque Sancta Virgine Maria, de qua, propter honorem Domini,
nullam prorsus cum de peccatis agitur habere volo quæstionem : Unde enim
scimus, quid ei plus gratiæ collatum fuerit ad vincendum omni ex parte peccatum, quæ concipere ac parere meruit eum quem constat nullum habuisse peccatum.' (*De Naturâ et Gratiâ.*) Gibbon notices that the notion acquired consistency among the Mahometans some centuries before it was adopted by the
Christians. St. Bernard rejected it as a novelty. (*Decline and Fall*, ch. l.
note.)

15

ideas of degradation and of sensuality, woman rose, in the person of the Virgin Mother, into a new sphere, and became the object of a reverential homage of which antiquity had had no conception. Love was idealised. The moral charm and beauty of female excellence was for the first time felt. A new type of character was called into being; a new kind of admiration was fostered. Into a harsh and ignorant and benighted age this ideal type infused a conception of gentleness and of purity unknown to the proudest civilisations of the past. In the pages of living tenderness which many a monkish writer has left in honour of his celestial patron; in the millions who, in many lands and in many ages, have sought with no barren desire to mould their characters into her image; in those holy maidens who, for the love of Mary, have separated themselves from all the glories and pleasures of the world, to seek in fastings and vigils and humble charity to render themselves worthy of her benediction; in the new sense of honour, in the chivalrous respect, in the softening of manners, in the refinement of tastes displayed in all the walks of society; in these and in many other ways we detect its influence. All that was best in Europe clustered around it, and it is the origin of many of the purest elements of our civilisation.

But the price, and perhaps the necessary price, of this was the exaltation of the Virgin as an omnipresent deity of infinite power as well as infinite condescension. The legends represented her as performing every kind of prodigy, saving men from the lowest abysses of wretchedness or of vice, and proving at all times the most powerful and the most ready refuge of the afflicted. The painters depicted her invested with the divine aureole, judging man on equal terms with her Son, or even retaining her ascendancy over Him in

Leaven. In the devotions of the people she was addressed in terms identical with those employed to the Almighty.[1] A reverence similar in kind but less in degree was soon bestowed upon the other saints, who speedily assumed the position of the minor deities of paganism, and who, though worshipped, like them, as if ubiquitous, like them had their special spheres of patronage.

While Christendom was thus reviving the polytheism which its intellectual condition required, the tendency to idolatry that always accompanies that condition was no less forcibly displayed. In theory, indeed, images were employed exclusively as aids to worship; but in practice, and with the general assent of the highest ecclesiastical authorities, they very soon became the objects. When men employ visible representations simply for the purpose of giving an increased vividness to their sense of the presence of the person who is addressed, and when the only distinction they make between different representations arises from the degree of fidelity or force with which they assist the imagination, these persons are certainly not committing idolatry. But when they pro-

---

[1] Even at the present day the Psalter of St. Bonaventura—an edition of the Psalms adapted to the worship of the Virgin, chiefly by the substitution of the word *domina* for the word *dominus*—is a popular book of devotion at Rome. In a famous fresco of Orcagna at Pisa the Virgin is represented, with precisely the same dignity as Christ, judging mankind; and everyone who is acquainted with mediæval art has met with similar examples. An old bishop named Gilbert Massius had his own portrait painted between the Virgin giving suck to Christ and a Crucifixion. Underneath were the lines—

> ' Hinc lactor ab ubere,
> Hinc pascor a vulnere,
> Positus in medio.
> Quo me vertam nescio,
> In hoc dulci dubio
> Dulcis est collatio.'

> Pascal, *Art Chrétien*, tom. i. p. 250.

ceed to attach the idea of intrinsic virtue to a particulai
image, when one image is said to work miracles and confei
spiritual benefits that separate it from every other, when it
becomes the object of long pilgrimages, and is supposed by
its mere presence to defend a besieged city or to w u l off
pestilence and famine, the difference between this conception
and idolatry is inappreciable. Everything is done to cast
the devotion of the worshipper upon the image itself, to distinguish it from every other, and to attribute to it an intrinsic efficacy.

In this as in the former case the change was effected by
ι general tendency resulting from the intellectual condition
ɔf society, assisted by the concurrence of special circumstances. At a very early period the persecuted Christians were accustomed to collect the relics of the martyrs, which they regarded with much affection and not
a little reverence, partly, perhaps, from the popular notion that the souls of the dead lingered fondly around
their tombs[1], and partly from the very natural and praise-
worthy feeling which attaches us to the remains of the
good. A similar reverence was speedily transferred to
pictures, which as memorials of the dead were closely con
nected with relics ; and the tendency to the miraculous
that was then so powerful having soon associated some of
them with supernatural occurrences, this was regarded as a

---

[1] Thus the Council of Illiberis in its 34th canon forbade men to light
candles by day in the cemeteries for fear of "disquieting the souls of the
saints." See, too, a curious passage of Vigilantius cited by St. Jerome, Ep.
iii. 13.   To be buried near the tomb of a martyr was one of the most coveted
privileges in the early Church.   See a very remarkable dissertation of Le
Blaut, "Inscriptions Chrétiennes de Gaule," tom. ii., p. 219-229.

Divine attestation of their sanctity. Two of these representations were especially prominent in the early controversies. The first was a portrait which, according to tradition,
Christ had sent to Abgarus, king of Edessa,[1] and which, besides several other miracles, had once destroyed all the be-
sieging engines of a Persian army that had invested Edessa.
Still more famous was a statue of Christ, said to have been
erected in a small town in Phœnicia by the woman who had
been healed of an issue of blood. A new kind of herb had
grown up beneath it, increased till it touched the hem of the
garment of the statue, and then acquired the power of healing all disease. This statue, it was added, had been broken
in pieces by Julian, who placed his own image on the pedes-
tal, from which it was speedily hurled by a thunderbolt.[2]

In the midst of this bias the irruption and, soon after, the
conversion of the barbarians were effected. Vast tribes of
savages, who had always been idolaters, who were perfectly
incapable, from their low state of civilisation, of forming any

---

[1] With a letter, which is still extant, and which Addison, in his work on
Christian Evidences, quoted as genuine. Of course it is now generally admitted to be apocryphal. This portrait was supposed to be miraculously impressed (like that obtained by St. Veronica) on a handkerchief. It was for a
long time at Constantinople, but was brought to Rome probably about A.D.
1198, and deposited in the Church of St. Sylvester in Capite, where it now is.
See Marangoni, *Istoria della Cappella di Sancta Sanctorum di Roma* (Romæ,
1747), pp. 235–239 ; a book which, though ostensibly simply a history of the
Acheropita, or sacred image at the Lateran, contains a fuller account of the
history of the early miraculous pictures of Christ than any other I have met
with.

[2] On these representations, the miracles they wrought, and the great importance they assumed in the Iconoclastic controversies, see Maimbourg
Histoire des Iconoclastes (1686), pp. 44–47 ; and on other early miracles attributed to images, Spanheim, *Historia Imaginum* (1686), pp. 417–420. The first
of these books is Catholic, and the second the Protestant reply. See, too,
Marangoni, *Sancta Sanctorum ;* and Arringhi, *Roma Subterranea*, tom. ii. pp.
452–460.

but anthropomorphic conceptions of the Deity, or of concen
trating their attention steadily on any invisible object, and
who for the most part were converted not by individual persuasion but by the commands of their chiefs, embraced
Christianity in such multitudes that their habits of mind soon
became the dominating habits of the Church. From this
time the tendency to idolatry was irresistible. The old images were worshipped under new names, and one of the most
prominent aspects of the Apostolical teaching was in practice ignored.

All this, however, did not pass without protest. During
the period of the persecution, when the dread of idolatry
was still powerful, everything that tended in that direction
was scrupulously avoided ; and a few years before the first
Council of Nice, a council held at Illiberis in Spain, in a
canon which has been very frequently cited, condemned altogether the introduction of pictures into the churches, ' lest
that which is worshipped should be painted upon the walls.'[1]
The Greeks, among whom the last faint rays of civilisation
still flickered, were in this respect somewhat superior to the
Latins, for they usually discouraged the veneration of images,
though admitting that of pictures.[2] Early in the eighth
century, when image-worship had become general, the sect
of the Iconoclasts arose, whose long struggle against the prevailing evil, though stained with great tyranny and great
cruelty, represents the fierce though unavailing attempts to
resist the anthropomorphism of the age; and when the
second Council of Nice, which the Catholics now regard as

[1] 'Ne quod colitur et adoratur in parietibus depingatur.' The Catholics
maintain that this was a decree elicited by the persecution, and that its object
was to prevent the profanation of Christian images by the pagans.

[2] Probably because there is no reason to believe that pictures had ever been
employed as idols by the ancient Greeks or Romans.

œcumenical, censured this heresy and carried the veneration of images considerably further than had before been authorised, its authority was denied and its decrees contemptuously stigmatised by Charlemagne and the Gallican Church.[1] Two or three illustrious Frenchmen also made isolated efforts in the same direction.[2]

Of these efforts there is one upon which I may delay for a moment, because it is at once extremely remarkable and extremely little known, and also because it brings us in contact with one of the most rationalistic intellects of the middle ages. In describing the persecution that was endured by the Cabalists in the ninth century, I had occasion to observe that they found a distinguished defender in the person of an archbishop of Lyons, named St. Agobard. The very name of this prelate has now sunk into general oblivion,[3] or if it is at all remembered, it is only in connection with the most discreditable act of his life—the part which he took in the deposition of Louis le Débonnaire. Yet I question whether in the whole compass of the middle ages—with, perhaps, the single exception of Scotus Erigena—it would be possible to find another man within the Christian Church who applied himself so zealously, so constantly, and so ably to dispelling the superstitions that surrounded him. To those who have appreciated the character of the ninth century, but few words will be required to show the intellectual eminence of

[1] On the discussions connected with this Council, see Natalis Alexander, *Historia Eccl. Sæcul.* viii.

[2] The most celebrated being Hincmar, Archbishop of Rheims. Baronius inveighed violently against this prelate for terming the sacred images 'dolls,' but Maimbourg contends (introduction to the *Hist. des Iconocl.*) that the expression is not to be found in any of the works of Hincmar.

[3] There is an edition of his works in one volume (Paris, 1605), and another in two volumes (Paris, 1616). I have quoted from the former.

an ecclesiastic who, in that century, devoted one work to displaying the folly of those who attributed hail and thunder to spiritual agencies, a second to in at least some degree attenuating the popular notions concerning epilepsy and other strange diseases, a third to exposing the absurdities of ordeals, and a fourth to denouncing the idolatry of image worship.

At the beginning of this last work Agobard collected a long series of passages from the fathers and early councils on the legitimate use of images. As long as they were employed simply as memorials, they were unobjectionable. But the popular devotion had long since transgressed this limit. Idolatry and anthropomorphism had everywhere revived, and devotion being concentrated on visible representations, all faith in the invisible was declining. Men, with a sacrilegious folly, ventured to apply the epithet holy to certain images,[1] offering to the work of their own hands the honour which should be reserved for the Deity, and attributing sanctity to what was destitute even of life. Nor was it any justification of this practice that the worshippers sometimes disclaimed the belief that a divine sanctity resided in the image itself,[2] and asserted that they reverenced in it only the person who was represented; for if the image was not divine, it should not be venerated. This excuse was only one of the

---

[1] 'Multo autem his deteriora esse quæ humana et carnalis præsumptio fingit etiam stulta consentiunt. In quo genere istæ quoque inveniuntur quas sanctas appellant imagines, non solum sacrilegi ex eo quod divinum cultum operibus manuum suarum exhibent, sed et insipientes sanctitatem eis quæ sine anima sunt imaginibus tribuendo.'—p. 233.

[2] 'Dicit forsitan aliquis non se putare imagini quam adorat aliquid inesse Divinum, sed tantummodo pro honore ejus cujus effigies est, tali eam veneratione donare. Cui facile respondetur, quia si imago quam adorat Deus non est nequaquam veneranda est.'—p. 237.

devices of Satan,[1] who was ever seeking under the pretext of honour to the saints to draw men back to the idols they had left. No image could be entitled to the reverence of those who, as the temples of the Holy Ghost, were superior to every image, who were themselves the true images of the Deity. A picture is helpless and inanimate. It can confer no benefit and inflict no evil. Its only value is as a representation of that which is least in man—of his body, and not his mind. Its only use is as a memorial to keep alive the affection for the dead; if it is regarded as anything more, it becomes an idol, and as such should be destroyed. Very rightly then did Hezekiah grind to powder the brazen serpent in spite of its sacred associations, because it had become an object of worship. Very rightly too did the Council of Illiberis and the Christians of Alexandria[2] forbid the introduction of representations into the churches, for they foresaw that such representations would at last become the objects of worship, and that a change of faith would only be a change of idols; nor could the saints themselves be more duly honoured than by destroying ignominiously their portraits, when those portraits had become the objects of superstitious reverence.[3]

[1] 'Agit hoc nimirum versutus et callidus humani generis inimicus, ut, sub prætextu honoris sanctorum, rursus idola introducat, rursus per diversas effigies adoretur.'—p. 252.

[2] Speaking of the conduct of some Alexandrian Christians, who only admitted the sign of the cross into their churches, he says:—'O quam sincera religio! crucis vexillum ubique pingebatur non aliqua vultus humani similitudo. (Deo scilicet hæc mirabiliter etiam ipsis forsitan nescientibus disponente) si enim sanctorum imagines hi qui dæmonum cultum reliquerant venerari juberentur, puto quod videretur eis non tam idola reliquisse quam simulacra mutasse.' —p. 237.

[3] 'Quia si serpentem æneum quem Deus fieri præcepit, quoniam errans populus tanquam idolum colere cœpit, Ezechias religiosus rex, cum magna pietatis laude contrivit: multo religiosius sanctorum imagines (ipsis quoque

It will I think be admitted that these sentiments are ex
ceedingly remarkable when we consider the age in which
they were expressed, and the position of the person who ex·
pressed them.   No Protestant fresh from the shrines of Lo-
retto or Saragossa ever denounced the idolatry practised
under the shadow of Catholicism with a keener or more
incisive eloquence than did this mediæval saint.   But although
it is extremely interesting to detect the isolated efforts of
illustrious individuals to rise above the general conditions of
their age, such efforts have usually but little result.   Idolatry
was so intimately connected with the modes of thought of
the middle ages, it was so congruous with the prevailing
conception of the government of the universe, and with the
materialising habits that were displayed upon all subjects, that
no process of direct reasoning could overthrow it, and it was
only by a fundamental change in the intellectual condition
of society that it was at last subverted.

It must, however, be acknowledged that there is one example of a great religion, reigning for the most part over
men who had not yet emerged from the twilight of an early
civilisation, which has nevertheless succeeded in restraining
its votaries from idolatry.   This phenomenon, which is the
preëminent glory of Mahometanism, and the most remarkable
evidence of the genius of its founder, appears so much at variance with the general laws of historic development, that it may

---

sanctis faventibus, qui ob sui honorem cum divinæ religionis contemptu eas
adorari more idolorum indignantissime ferunt) omni genere conterendæ et
usque ad pulverem sunt eradendæ; præsertim cum non illas fieri Deus jusserit,
sed humanus sensus excogitaverit.'—p. 244.   'Nec iterum ad sua latibula
fraudulenta recurrat astutia, ut dicat se non imagines sanctorum adorare sed
sanctos; clamat enim Deus, 'Gloriam meam alteri non dabo, nec laudem
meam sculptilibus.'' '—pp. 254, 255.   See too the noble concluding passage on
the exclusive worship of Christ, breathing a spirit of the purest Protestantism.

be well to examine for a moment its cáuses. In the first place, then, it must be observed that the enthusiasm by which Mahometanism conquered the world, was mainly a military enthusiasm. Men were drawn to it at once, and without conditions, by the splendour of the achievements of its disciples, and it declared an absolute war against all the religions it encountered. Its history therefore exhibits nothing of the process of gradual absorption, persuasion, compromise, and assimilation, that was exhibited in the dealings of Christianity with the barbarians. In the next place, one of the great characteristics of the Koran is the extreme care and skill with which it labours to assist men in realising the unseen. Descriptions the most minutely detailed, and at the same time the most vivid, are mingled with powerful appeals to those sensual passions by which the imagination in all countries, but especially in those in which Mahometanism has taken root, is most forcibly influenced. In no other religion that prohibits idols was the strain upon the imagination so slight.[1]

In the last place, the prohibition of idols was extended to every representation of man and animals, no matter how completely unconnected they might be with religion.[2] Ma-

---

[1] Some curious instances of the way in which the early fanaticism of Mahometanism was thus sustained, have been collected by Helvétius, *De l'Esprit*. It is quite true, as Sale contends, that Mahomet did not introduce polygamy, and therefore that the fact of his permitting it could not have been one of the motives urging Asiatics to embrace the new religion; but it is also true that Mahomet and his disciples, more skilfully than any other religionists, blended sensual passions with religion, associated them with future rewards, and converted them into stimulants of devotion.

[2] Some of the early Christians appear to have wished to adopt this course, which would have been the only effectual means of repressing idolatry. In an apocryphal work, called *The Voyages of St. John*, which was circulated in the Church, there was a legend that St. John once found his own portrait in the house of a Christian, that he thought at first it was an idol, and, even

homet perceived very clearly, that in order to prevent his
disciples from worshipping images, it was absolutely necessa
ry to prevent them from making any; and he did this by
commands which were at once so stringent and so precise,
that it was scarcely possible to evade them. In this way
he preserved his religion from idolatry ; but he made it the
deadly enemy of art. How much art has lost by the antagonism it is impossible to say. Certainly the wonderful pro-
ficiency attained by the Spanish Moors in architecture, which
was the only form of art that was open to them, and above
all the ornamentation of the Alhambra, and the Alcazar of
Seville, in which, while the representations of animal life
are carefully excluded, plants and flowers and texts from the
Koran and geometrical figures are woven together in a tra
cery of the most exquisite beauty,[1] seem to imply the possession of æsthetic powers that have never been surpassed.

Mahometanism sacrificed art, but it cannot be said that
Christianity during the middle ages was altogether favourable to it. The very period when representations of Christ or
the saints were regarded as most sacred, was precisely that
in which there was no art in the highest sense of the word,
or at least none applied to the direct objects of worship. The

when told its true character, severely blamed the painter. (Beausobre, *Hist.
du Manichéisme.*) A passage in the invective of Tertullian against Her-
mogenes has been quoted as to the same effect : ' Pingit illicite, nubit assidue,
legem Dei in libidinem defendit, in artem contemnit, bis falsarius et cauteric
et stylo.' Clemens Alexandrinus was of opinion that ladies broke the second
commandment by using looking-glasses, as they thereby made images of themselves.—Barbeyrac, *Morale des Pères.* c. v. § 18.

[1] See on this subject a striking passage from Owen Jones, quoted in Ford's
Spain, vol. i. p. 304. It is remarkable that, while the ornamentation derived
from the vegetable world in the Alhambra is unrivalled in beauty, the lions
which support one of the fountains, and which form, I believe, the solitary instance of a deviation from the command of the Prophet, might rank with the
worst productions of the time of Nicolas of Pisa.

middle ages occasionally, indeed, produced churches of great beauty; mosaic work for their adornment was cultivated with considerable zeal, and in the fifth century, and again after the establishment in the eleventh century of a school of Greek artists at Monte Cassino, with some slight success;[1] similar skill was shown in gold church crnaments,[2] and in the illumination of manuscripts;[3] but the habitual veneration of

[1] According to tradition, the earliest specimen of Christian mosaic work is a portrait of Christ, preserved in the church of St. Praxede of Rome, which St. Peter is said to have worn round his neck, and to have given at Rome to Pudens, his host, the father of St. Praxede. The finest specimens of the mosaics of the fifth and sixth centuries are at Ravenna, especially in the church of St. Vitale, which was built by the Greeks, who were the great masters of this art. Ciampini, who is the chief authority on this subject, thinks (*Vetera Monumenta*, pars i. (Romæ, 1690), p. 84) that the art was wholly forgotten in Rome for the three hundred years preceding the establishment of the Monte Cassino school in 1066; but Marangoni assigns a few wretched mosaics to that period (*Ist. Sanct.* pp. 180–182). A descriptive catalogue of those at Rome has lately been published by Barbet de Jouy, and a singularly interesting examination of their history by M. Vitet (*Études sur l'Histoire de l'Art*, tom. i.). For a general review of the decline of art, see the great history of D'Agincourt.

[2] The art of delicate carving on gold and silver was chiefly preserved in the middle ages by the reverence of relics, for the preservation of which the most beautiful works were designed. Rouen was long famed for its manufacture of church ornaments, but these were plundered, and for the most part destroyed, by the Protestants, when they captured the city in 1562. The luxurious habits of the Italian states were favourable to the goldsmiths, and those of Venice were very celebrated. A large proportion of them are said to have been Jews. Francia, Verocchio, Perugino, Donatello, Brunelleschi, and Ghiberti were all originally goldsmiths. M. Didron has published a manual of this art. The goldsmiths of Limoges had the honour of producing a saint, St. Eloi, who became the patron of the art. Carved ivory diptychs were also very common through the middle ages, and especially after the eighth century.

[3] Much curious information on the history of illumination and miniature painting is given in Cibrario, *Economia Politica del Medio Evo*, vol. ii. pp. 337–346. Peignot says that from the fifth to the tenth century the miniatures in manuscripts exhibited an extremely high perfection, both in drawing and in colouring, and that from the tenth to the fourteenth the drawing detoriated, but revived with the revival of painting (*Essai sur l'Histoire du Parchemin*,

images, pictures, and talismans, was far from giving a general
impulse to art. And this fact, which may at first sight appear perplexing, was in truth perfectly natural. For the
æsthetic sentiment and a devotional feeling are so entirely
different, that it is impossible for both to be at the same
moment predominating over the mind, and very unusual for
both to be concentrated upon the same object. The sensation produced by a picture gallery is not that of religious
reverence, and the favourite idols have in no religion been
those which approve themselves most fully to the taste.[1]
They have rather been pictures that are venerable from their
extreme antiquity, or from the legends attached to them, or
else representations of the most coarsely realistic character.
Painted wooden statues the size of life have usually been the
favourite idols; but these are so opposed to the genius of true
art, that—with the exception of Spain, where religious feeling
has dominated over every other consideration, and where
three sculptors of very great ability, named Juni, Hernandez,
and Montañes, have devoted themselves to their formation—
they have scarcely ever exhibited any high artistic merit,
and never the very highest. The mere fact, therefore, of
pictures or images being destined for worship, is likely to be
rather prejudicial than otherwise to art. Besides this, in an
idolatrous period the popular reverence speedily attaches to

p. 76). Glass painting and miniature painting were both common long before
Cimabue, and probably exercised a great influence over the early artists.

[1] See on this subject, and generally on the influence of mediæval modes of
thought upon art, Raoul-Rochette, *Cours d'Archéologie*, one of the very best
books ever written on art. (It has been translated by Mr. Westropp.) The
history of miracles strikingly confirms the position in the text. As Marangoni says: 'Anzi ella è cosa degna di osservazione che l'Altissimo per ordinario
opera molto più prodigi nelle immagini sagre nelle quali non spicca l' eccel-
lenza dell' arte o alcuna cosa superiore all' umana.'—*Istoria della Capella di
Sancta Sanctorum*, p. 77.

a particular type of countenance, and even to particular ges
tures or dresses; and all innovation, and therefore all improvement, is resisted.

These reasons apply to the art of the middle ages in common with that of all other periods of virtual or avowed idol·
atry. There was, however, another consideration, acting in
the same direction, which was peculiar to Christianity. I
mean the low estimate of physical beauty that characterised
the monastic type of religion. Among the Greeks beauty of
every order ' was the highest object of worship. In art
especially no subject was tolerated in which deformity of any
kind was manifested. Even suffering was habitually idealised. The traces of mental anguish upon the countenance
were exhibited with exquisite skill, but they were never permitted so to contort the features as to disturb the prevailing
beauty of the whole.' The glory of the human body was
the central conception of art, and nakedness was associated

' Even animal beauty. It is one of the most subtle, and, at the same time,
most profoundly just, criticisms of Winckelmann, that it was the custom of
the Greeks to enhance the perfection of their ideal faces by transfusing into
them some of the higher forms of animal beauty. This was especially the case
with Jupiter, the upper part of whose countenance is manifestly taken from
that of a lion, while the hair is almost always so arranged as to increase the
resemblance. There are many busts of Jupiter, which, if all but the forehead
and hair were covered, would be unhesitatingly pronounced to be images of
lions. Something of the bull appears in like manner in Hercules; while in
Pan (though not so much with a view to beauty as to harmony) the human
features always approach as near as human features can to the characteristics
of the brute. As M. Raoul-Rochette has well observed, this is one of the
great distinctive marks of Greek sculpture. The Egyptians often joined the
head of an animal to the body of a man without making any effort to soften
the incongruity; but beauty being the main object of the Greeks, in all their
composite statues—Pan, Centaurs, hermaphrodites—the two natures that are
conjoined are fused and blended into one harmonious whole.

' See the *Laocoön* of Lessing. It is to this that Lessing ascribes the
famous device of Timanthes in his sacrifice of Iphigenia—drawing the veil
over the face of Agamemnon—which Pliny so poetically explains.

rather with dignity than with shame. The gods, it was em
phatically said, were naked.[1] To represent an emperor
naked, was deemed the highest form of flattery, because it
was to represent his apotheosis. The athletic games which
occupied so large a place in ancient life, contributed greatly
to foster the admiration of physical strength, and to furnish
the most admirable models to the sculptors.[2]

It is easy to perceive how favourable such a state of feeling must have been to the development of art, and no less
easy to see how contrary it was to the spirit of a religion
which for many centuries made the suppression of all bodily
passions the central notion of sanctity. In this respect philosophers, heretics, and saints were unanimous. Plotinus,
one of the most eminent of the Neo-Platonic philosophers,
was so ashamed of the possession of a body, that he refused
to have his portrait taken on the ground that it would be to
perpetuate his degradation. Gnosticism and Manicheism,
which in their various modifications obtained a deeper and
more permanent hold in the Church than any other heretical
systems, maintained as their cardinal tenet the essential evil
of matter; and some of the Cathari, who were among the
latest Gnostics, are said to have even starved themselves to
death in their efforts to subdue the propensities of the body.[3]
Of the orthodox saints, some made it their especial boast that
for many years they had never seen their own bodies; others
mutilated themselves in order more completely to restrain their
passions; others laboured with the same object by scourgings
and fastings, and horrible penances. All regarded the body

---

[1] 'Deus nudus est.'—Seneca, *Ep.* xxxi.

[2] Raoul-Rochette, *Cours d'Archéologie*, pp. 269, 270. See also Fortoul,
Études d'Archéologie.

[3] Matter, *Hist. du Gnosticisme*, tom. iii. p. 264.

as an unmingled evil, its passion and its beauty as the most deadly of temptations. Art, while governed by such sentiments, could not possibly arrive at perfection; [1] and the passion for representations of the Crucifixion, or the deaths of the martyrs, or the sufferings of the lost, impelled it still further from the beautiful.

It appears, then, that, in addition to the generally low intellectual condition of the middle ages, the special form of religious feeling that was then dominant, exercised an exceedingly unfavourable influence upon art. This fact becomes very important when we examine the course that was taken by the European mind after the revival of learning.

Idolatry, as I have said, is the natural form of worship in an early stage of civilisation; and a gradual emancipation from material conceptions one of the most invariable results of intellectual progress. It appears therefore natural, that when nations have attained a certain point, they should discard their images. And this is what has usually occurred. Twice, however, in the history of the human mind, a different course has been adopted. Twice the weakening of the anthropomorphic conceptions has been accompanied by an extraordinary progress in the images that were their representatives, and the æsthetic feeling having dominated over the religious feeling, superstition has faded into art.

The period in which the ascetic ideal of ugliness was most supreme in art was between the sixth and twelfth centuries. Many of the Roman mosaics during that period exhibit a hideousness which the inexpertness of the artists was quite insufficient to account for, and which was evidently imitated from the emaciation of extreme asceticism.—See Vitet, *Études sur l'Histoire de l'Art*, tom. i. pp. 268-279. Concerning the art of the middle ages, besides the works that have come down to us, we have a good deal of evidence in a book by a bishop of the thirteenth century, named Durandus, called *Rationale Divinorum Officiorum*. A great deal of curious learning on mediæval art is collected by the Abbé Pascal in his *Institutions de l'Art Chrétien;* but, above all, in the *Iconographie Chrétienne* of Didron.

16

The first of these movements occurred in ancient Greece.
The information we possess concerning the æsthetic history
of that nation is so ample, that we can trace very clearly the
successive phases of its development.[1] Putting aside those
changes that are interesting only in an artistic point of view,
and confining ourselves to those which reflect the changes of
religious realisation, Greek idolatry may be divided into four
distinct stages. The first was a period of fetishism, in which
shapeless stones, which were possibly aërolites, and were, at
all events, said to have fallen from heaven, were worshipped.
In the second, painted wooden idols dressed in real clothes
became common.[2] After this, Dædalus created a higher art,
but one which was, like the Egyptian and Byzantine art, at
the same time strictly religious, and characterised by an intense aversion to innovation. Then came the period in which
increasing intellectual culture, and the prevalence of philosophical speculations, began to tell upon the nation, in which
the religious reverence was displaced, and concentrated rather
on the philosophical conception of the Deity than upon the
idols in the temples, and in which the keen sense of beauty,
evoked by a matured civilisation, gave a new tone and aspect to all parts of religion. The images were not then
broken, but they were gradually regarded simply as the embodiments of the beautiful. They began to exhibit little or no
religious feeling, no spirit of reverence or self-abasement, but

---

[1] See an extremely clever sketch of the movement in Raoul-Rochette,
Cours d'Archéologie ; and Winckelmann, *Hist. of Art.*

[2] According to Winckelmann, wooden statues with marble heads, called
ἀκρόλιθοι, continued as late as the time of Phidias. From the painted wooden
statues was derived the custom of painting those in marble and bronze.
Heyne, who has devoted a very learned essay to Greek sculpture, thinks the
statues of Dædalus were in wood (*Opuscula Academica,* tom. v. p. 339); but
this appears very doubtful. Pausanias says he saw a statue ascribed to Dæda
lus which was of stone.

a sense of harmony and gracefulness, a conception of ideal perfection, which has perhaps never been equalled in other lands. The statue that had once been the object of earnest prayer was viewed with the glance of the artist or the critic. The temple was still full of gods, and those gods had never been so beautiful and so grand ; but they were beautiful only through the skill of the artist, and the devotion that once hallowed them had passed away. All was allegory, poetry, and imagination. Sensual beauty was typified by naked Venus; unconscious loveliness, and untried or natural chastity, by Diana. Minerva, with her downcast eyes and somewhat stern features, represented female modesty and self-control. Ceres, with her flowing robes and her golden sheaf, was the type of the genial summer; or, occasionally with dishevelled hair, and a countenance still troubled with the thought of Proserpine, was the emblem of maternal love. Each cast of beauty, and, after a brief period of unmingled grandeur, even each form of sensual frailty, was transported into the unseen world. Bacchus nurtured by a girl, and with the soft delicate limbs of a woman, was the type of a disgraceful effeminacy. Apollo the god of music, and Adonis the lover of Diana, represented that male beauty softened into something of female loveliness by the sense of music or the first chaste love of youth, which the Christian painters long afterwards represented in St. Sebastian or St. John. Hercules was the chosen type of the dignity of labour. Sometimes he appears in the midst of his toils for man, with every nerve strained, and all the signs of intense exertion upon his countenance. Sometimes he appears as a demigod in the assembly of Olympus, and then his muscles are rounded and subdued, and his colossal frame softened and harmonised as the emblem at once of strength and of repose. In very few instances do we find any conception which can be regarded as purely religious, and even those are of a somewhat Epicurean character. Thus Jupiter, Pluto, and Minos are represented with the same cast of countenance, and the difference is chiefly in their expression. The countenance of Pluto is shadowed by the passions of a demon, the brow of Minos is bent with the inexorable sternness of a judge. Jupiter alone presents an aspect of unclouded calm : no care can darken, and no passion ruffle, the serenity of the king of heaven.[1]

It was in this manner that the Greek mythology passed gradually into the realm of poetry, and that the transition was effected or facilitated by the visible representations that were in the first instance the objects of worship. A somewhat similar change was effected in Christian art at the period of the revival of learning, and as an almost immediate result of the substitution of Italian for Byzantine art.

There are few more striking contrasts than are comprised in the history of the influence of Grecian intellect upon art. At an early period Greece had arrived at the highest point of æsthetic perfection to which the human intellect has yet attained. She bequeathed to us those forms of almost passionate beauty which have been the wonder and the delight of all succeeding ages, and which the sculptors of every land have recognised as the ideal of their efforts. At last, however, the fountain of genius became dry. Not only creative power, but even the very perception and love of the beautiful, seemed to have died out, and for many centuries the Greek Church, the Greek empire, and the Greek artists proved the most formidable obstacles to æsthetic development.[2] It was from

---

[1] See Winckelmann and Ottfried Müller.

[2] This influence is well noticed by M. Rio, in a book called *The Poetry of Christian Art.* An exception, however, should be made in favour of

this quarter that the Iconoclasts issued forth to wage their fierce warfare against Christian sculpture. It was in the Greek Church that was most fostered the tradition of the deformity of Christ, which was as fatal to religious art as it was offensive to religious feeling.[1] It was in Greece too that

Greek architects, to whom Italy owed its first great ecclesiastical structure, the church of St. Vitale at Ravenna (which Charlemagne copied at Aix-la-Chapelle), and at a later period St. Mark's at Venice, and several other beautiful edifices. The exile of the Greek artists during the Iconoclast persecution, and the commercial relations of Venice, Pisa, and Genoa, account for the constant action of Greece on Italy through the middle ages. I have already noticed the skill of the Byzantine artists in mosaic work.

[1] Of which Justin Martyr, Tertullian, and Cyril of Alexandria were the principal advocates. The last declared that Christ had been 'the ugliest of the sons of men.' This theory furnished Celsus with one of his arguments against Christianity. The opposite view was taken by Jerome, Ambrose, Chrysostom, and John Damascene. With a view of supporting the latter opinion, there was forged a singularly beautiful letter, alleged to have been written to the Roman Senate by Lentulus, who was proconsul in Judæa before Herod, and in which the following passage occurs: 'At this period there appeared a man, who is still living—a man endowed with wonderful power—his name is Jesus Christ. Men say that He is a mighty prophet; but his disciples call Him the Son of God. He calls the dead to life, and frees the sick from every form of disease. He is tall of stature, and his aspect is sweet and full of power, so that they who look upon Him may at once love and fear Him. The hair of his head is of the colour of wine; as far as the ears it is straight and without glitter, from the ears to the shoulders it is curled and glossy, and from the shoulders it descends over the back, divided into two parts after the manner of the Nazarenes. His brow is pure and even; his countenance without a spot, but adorned with a gentle glow; his expression bland and open; his nose and mouth are of perfect beauty; his beard is copious, forked, and of the colour of his hair; his eyes are blue and very bright. In reproving and threatening He is terrible; in teaching and exhorting, gentle and loving. The grace and majesty of his appearance are marvellous. No one has ever seen Him laugh, but rather weeping. His carriage is erect; his hands well formed and straight; his arms of passing beauty. Weighty and grave in speech, He is sparing of words. He is the most beautiful of the sons of men.' Nearly all archæologists have inferred from the representations of the fourth century that this description was then in existence. Dean Milman, however, argues from the silence of St. John Damascene, and of the disputants at the Second Council of Nice, that it is of a much later date. See on this whole subject,

arose that essentially vicious, conventional, and unprogressive
style of painting which was universal in Europe for many
centuries, which trammelled even the powerful genius of
Cimabue, and which it was reserved for Giotto and Masaccio
to overthrow. This was the uniform tendency of modern
Greece. It was the extreme opposite of that which had
once been dominant, and it is a most remarkable fact that
it was at last corrected mainly by the masterpieces of Greek
antiquity. It is now very generally admitted that the proxi-
mate cause of that ever-increasing course of progress which
was pursued by Italian art from Cimabue to Raphael, is
chiefly to be found in the renewed study of ancient sculpture
begun by Nicolas of Pisa towards the close of the twelfth century, and afterwards sustained by the discoveries at Rome.

The Church of Rome, with the sagacity that has usually
characterised her, adopted and fostered the first efforts of revived art, and for a time she made it essentially Christian. It
is impossible to look upon the pictures of Giotto and his early
successors without perceiving that a religious feeling pervades and sanctifies them. They exhibit, indeed, a keen sense
of beauty; but this is always subservient to the religious
idea; it is always subdued and chastened and idealised.
Nor does this arise simply from the character of the artists.
Christian art had, indeed, in the angelic friar of Fiesole, one
saint who may be compared with any in the hagiology.
That gentle monk, who was never known to utter a word
of anger or of bitterness, who refused without a pang the
rich mitre of Florence, who had been seen with tears stream-

Emeric David, *Hist. de la Peinture*, pp. 24–26; and Didron, *Iconographie
Chrétienne*, pp. 251–276. I may add, that as late as 1649 a curious book (*De
Formâ Christi*) was published on this subject at Paris by a Jesuit, named
Vavassor, which represents the controversy as still continuing.

ing from his eyes as he painted his crucified Lord, and who never began a picture without consecrating it by a prayer, forms one of the most attractive pictures in the whole range of ecclesiastical biography. The limpid purity of his character was reflected in his works, and he transmitted to his disciple Gozzoli something of his spirit, with (I venture to think) the full measure of his genius.

But in this, as on all other occasions, even the higher forms of genius were ultimately regulated by the law of supply and demand. There was a certain religious conception abroad in the world. That conception required a visible representation, and the painter appeared to supply the want. The revival of learning had broken upon Europe. The study of the classics had given an impulse to every department of intellect, but it had not yet so altered the condition of society as to shake the old belief. The profound ignorance that reigned until the twelfth century had been indeed dispelled. The grossness of taste, and he incapacity for appreciating true beauty, which accompanied that ignorance, had been corrected; but the development of the imagination preceded, as it always does precede, the development of the reason. Men were entranced with the chaste beauty of Greek literature before they were imbued with the spirit of abstraction, of free criticism, and of elevated philosophy, which it breathes. They learned to admire a pure style or a graceful picture before they learned to appreciate a refined creed or an untrammelled philosophy. All through Europe, the first effect of the revival of learning was to produce a general efflorescence of the beautiful. A general discontent with the existing forms of belief was

---

[1] The same thing is related of the Spanish sculptor Hernandez, and of the Spanish painter Juanes.—Ford's *Spain*, vol. ii. p. 271.

not produced till much later. A material, sensuous, and an thropomorphic faith was still adapted to the intellectual condition of the age, and therefore painting was still the special organ of religious emotions. All the painters of that period were strictly religious, that is to say, they invariably subordinated considerations of art to considerations of religion. The form of beauty they depicted was always religious beauty, and they never hesitated to disfigure their works with loathsome or painful images if they could in that manner add to their religious effect.

To these general considerations we should add the important influence of Dante, who may be regarded as the most faithful representative of that brief moment in which the renewed study of the pagan writings served only to ennoble and refine, and not yet to weaken, the conceptions of theology. No other European poet realised so fully the sacred character antiquity attributed to the bard. In the great poems of Greece and Rome, human figures occupied the foreground; and even when supernatural machinery was introduced, it served only to enhance the power or evoke the moral grandeur of mortals. Milton, indeed, soared far beyond the range of earth; but when he wrote, religious conceptions no longer took the form of palpable and material imagery, and even the grandest representations of spiritual beings under human aspects appeared incongruous and unreal. But the poem of Dante was the last apocalypse. It exercised a supreme ascendency over the imagination at a time when religious imagery was not so much the adjunct as the essence of belief, when the natural impulse of every man was to convert intellectual conceptions into palpable forms, and when painting was in the strictest sense the normal expression of faith. Scarcely any other single influence contributed so much, by purifying and feeding the imagination, to give Christian art a grandeur and a religious perfection, and at the same time a sombre and appalling aspect. 'Dipped in the gloom of earthquake and eclipse,' the pencil of the great poet loved to accumulate images of terror and of suffering, which speedily passed into the works of the artists, enthralled and fascinated the imaginations of the people, and completed a transformation that had long been in progress. At first, after the period of the Catacombs, the painters expatiated for the most part upon scenes drawn from the Book of Reve-lation, but usually selected in such a manner as to inspire any sentiment rather than terror. The lamb, which, having been for some centuries the favourite symbol of Christ, was at last condemned by a council in 707,[1] the mystic roll with its seven seals, the New Jerusalem with its jewelled battlements, or Bethlehem transfigured in its image, constantly recurred. But many circumstances, of which the panic produced by the belief that the world must end with the tenth century, and the increased influence of asceticism arising from the permis-sion accorded to the monks of establishing their communities in the cities,[2] were probably the chief, contributed to effect a

[1] Or, according to others, 692. The object of this council (which was held at Constantinople, and is known under the title 'In Trullo') was to repress the love of allegory that was general ; and a very learned historian of art thinks that it first produced pictures of the Crucifixion. (Emeric David, *Hist. de la Peinture*, pp. 59–61.) Its decree was afterwards either withdrawn or neglected, for lambs soon reappeared, though they never regained their former ascend-ency in art. As far as I remember, there is no instance of them in the Cata-combs ; but after Constantine they for nearly three centuries had superseded every other symbol. (Rio, *Art Chrétien*, Introd. p. 49.) Ciampini says that the council which condemned them was a pseudo-council—not sanctioned by the Pope. (*Vetera Monumenta*, pars i. p. 28. See, too, Marangoni, *Istoria della Cappella di Sancta Sanctorum*, p. 159.)

[2] At first they were strictly forbidden to remain in the towns. Even the priest-ridden Theodosius made a law commanding all who had embraced the

profound change The churches in their ornaments, in their
general aspect, and even in their forms,¹ became the images
of death, and painting was tending rapidly in the same
direction, when the *Inferno* of Dante opened a new abyss of
terrors to the imaginations of the artists, and became the
representative, and in a measure the source, of an art that
was at once singularly beautiful, purely religious, and deeply
imbued with terrorism and with asceticism.

These were the characteristics of the first period of revived art, and they harmonised well with the intelletual condition of the day. After a time, however, the renewed energies of the European mind began to produce effects that were
far more important. A spirit of unshackled criticism, a capacity
for refined abstractions, a dislike to materialism in faith and to
asceticism in practice, a disposition to treat with unceremonious
ridicule imposture and ignorance in high places, an impatience
of the countless ceremonies and trivial superstitions that were
universal, and a growing sense of human dignity, were manifested on all sides, and they adumbrated clearly a coming
change. The movement was shown in the whole tone of
literature, and in the repeated and passionate efforts to attain
a more spiritual creed that were made by the precursors of
the Reformation. It was shown at least as forcibly in the
rapid corruption of every organ of the old religion. They
no longer could attract religious fervour; and as their life
was gone, they degenerated and decayed. The monasteries,
once the scenes of the most marvellous displays of ascetic

profession of monks to betake themselves to 'vast solitudes' and 'desert
places.' (*Cod. Theod.* lib. xvi. tit. 3, c. 1.)

¹ That is, by the introduction of the cross, which was the first innovation
on the old basilica architecture, and in many of the churches by a slight in
clination of the extremity from the straight line, it is said, to represent the
verse, 'Jesus *bowed his head* and gave up the ghost.'

piety, became the seats of revelry, of licentiousness, and of avarice. The sacred relics and the miraculous images, that had so long thrilled the hearts of multitudes, were made a source of unholy traffic, or of unblushing imposition. The indulgences, which were intended to assuage the agonies of a despairing conscience, or to lend an additional charm to the devotions of the pious, became a substitute for all real religion. The Papal See itself was stained with the most degrading vice, and the Vatican exhibited the spectacle of a pagan court without the redeeming virtue of pagan sincerity. Wherever the eye was turned, it encountered the signs of disorganisation, of corruption, and of decay. For the long night of mediævalism was now drawing to a close, and the chaos that precedes resurrection was supreme. The spirit of ancient Greece had arisen from the tomb, and the fabric of superstition crumbled and tottered at her touch. The human mind, starting beneath her influence from the dust of ages, cast aside the bonds that had enchained it, and, radiant in the light of recovered liberty, remoulded the structure of its faith. The love of truth, the passion for freedom, the sense of human dignity, which the great thinkers of antiquity had inspired, vivified a torpid and down-trodden people, blended with those sublime moral doctrines and with those conceptions of enlarged benevolence, which are at once the glory and the essence of Christianity, introduced a new era of human development, with new aspirations, habits of thought, and conditions of vitality, and withdrawing religious life from the shattered edifice of the past, created a purer faith, and became the promise of an eternal development.

This was the tendency of the human intellect, and it was faithfully reflected in the history of art. As the old Catholic modes of thought began to fade, the religious idea disappeared from the paintings, and they became purely secular, if not sensual, in their tone. Religion, which was once the mistress, was now the servant, of art. Formerly the painter employed his skill simply in embellishing and enhancing a religious idea. He now employed a religious subject as the pretext for the exhibition of mere worldly beauty. He commonly painted his mistress as the Virgin. He arrayed her in the richest attire, and surrounded her with all the circumstances of splendour. He crowded his pictures with nude figures with countenances of sensual loveliness, with every form and attitude that could act upon the passions, and not unfrequently with images drawn from the pagan mythology. The creation of beauty became the single object of his art. His work was a secular work, to be judged by a secular standard.

There can be no doubt that this secularisation of art was due to the general tone of thought that had been produced in Europe. The artist seeks to represent the conceptions of his time, and his popularity is the proof of his success. In an age in which strong religious belief was general, and in which it turned to painting as to the natural organ of its expression, such a style would have been impossible. The profanity of the painter would have excited universal execration, and all the genius of Titian or Angelo would have been unable to save their works from condemnation. The style became popular, because educated men ceased to look for religion in pictures, or in other words because the habits of thought that made them demand material representations of the objects of their belief had declined.

This was the ultimate cause of the entire movement. There were, however, two minor causes of great importance, which contributed largely to the altered tone of art, while

they at the same time immeasurably increased its perfec
tion—one of them relating especially to colour, and the other
to form.

The first of these causes is to be found in the moral condition of Italian society. The age was that of Bianca di
Capello, and of the Borgias. All Italian literature and all
Italian manners were of the laxest character, and the fact was
neither concealed nor deplored. But that which especially
distinguished Italian immorality is, that, growing up in the
midst of all the forms of loveliness, it assumed from the first
a kind of æsthetic character, united with the most passionate
and yet refined sense of the beautiful, and made art the
special vehicle of its expression. This is one of the peculiar
characteristics of later Italian painting, and it is one of the
chief causes of its artistic perfection. For sensuality has
always been extremely favourable to painting,² the object of

---

¹ German pictures are often indecent, but never sensual. It is all the dif-
ference between Swift and Don Juan. The nude figure as painted by Van der
Werff is ivory—as painted by Titian or Correggio, it is life. Spanish art tried
much to be religious and respectable; and, like the Vergognosa at Pisa, put
her hands before her eyes in the midst of the wickedness that surrounded her.
But I am afraid she sometimes looked through her fingers. This aspect of
Italian art has been most vividly exhibited in the writings of Stendhal (H.
Beyle).

² It is perhaps true, as modern critics say, that the transition of Greek art
from Phidias to Praxiteles was a declension. It is certainly true that that
transition was from the representation of manly strength, and the form of
beauty that is most allied to it, to the representation of beauty of a sensual
cast—from an art of which Minerva was the central figure, to an art of which
Venus was the type—or (as the German critics say) from the ascendency of
the Doric to the ascendency of the Ionic element. But this decadence, if it
really took place, is not, I think, inconsistent with what I have stated in the
text; for sculpture and painting have each their special perfections, and the
success of the artist will in a great degree depend upon his appreciation of the
peculiar genius of the art he pursues. Now sculpture is as far superior to
painting in its capacity for expressing strength and masculine beauty, as painting is superior to sculpture in expressing warmth and passionate beauty. All

the artist being to exhibit to the highest possible degree the beauty and the attractive power of the human body. Twice in the history of art national sensuality has thrown itself into national art, and in each case with the same result. The first occasion was in ancient Greece, at the time when Apelles derived a new inspiration from the voluptuous loveliness of Lais, and the goddess of beauty, glowing with the fresh charms of Phryne or Theodota, kindled a transport of no religious fervour in the Athenian mind. The second occasion was in the Italian art of the sixteenth century.

The rapid progress of a sensual tone in all the schools of Italian art is a fact which is too manifest to be questioned or overlooked; but there is one school which may be regarded especially as its source and representative. This school was that of the Venetian painters, and it reflected very visibly the character of its cradle. Never perhaps was any other city so plainly formed to be the home at once of passion and of art. Sleeping like Venus of old upon her parent wave, Venice, at least in the period of her glory, comprised within herself all the influences that could raise to the highest point the æsthetic sentiment, and all that could lull the moral sentiment to repose. Wherever the eye was turned, it was met by forms of strange and varied and entrancing beauty, while every sound that broke upon the ear was mellowed by the waters that were below. The thousand lights that glittered around the gilded domes of St. Mark, the palaces of

---

the efforts of a Grecian chisel never equalled the voluptuous power of the brush of Titian; and, on the other hand, painting has tried in vain to rival the majesty and the force of sculpture. If there be an exception to this last proposition, it is one which proves the rule, for it is furnished by Michael Angelo, the greatest modern sculptor, in the most sculpture-like frescoes in the world. It should be added, however, that landscape painting is in no sense the creature of sensuality, and Mr. Ruskin has with some force claimed it as a special fruit of Christianity.

matchless architecture resting on their own soft shadows in the wave, the long paths of murmuring water, where the gondola sways to the lover's song, and where dark eyes lustrous with passion gleam from the overhanging balconies, the harmony of blending beauties, and the languid and voluptuous charm that pervades the whole, had all told deeply and fatally on the character of the people. At every period of their history, but never more so than in the great period of Venetian art, they had been distinguished at once for their intense appreciation of beauty and for their universal, unbridled, and undisguised licentiousness.[1] In the midst of such a society it was very natural that a great school of sensual art should arise, and many circumstances conspired in the same direction. Venice was so far removed from the discoveries of the ancient statues, that it was never influenced by what may be termed the learned school of art, which eventually sacrificed all sense of beauty to anatomical studies; at the same time the simultaneous appearance of a constellation of artists of the very highest order, the luxurious habits that provided these artists with abundant patrons, the discovery of oil painting,[2] which attained its highest perfection under the skill of the Venetian colourists, perhaps even the rich merchandise of the East, accustoming the eye to the most gorgeous hues,[3] had all in different ways

[1] On the amazing vice of Venice, and on the violent but unsuccessful efforts of the magistrates to arrest it, see much curious evidence in Sabatier, *Hist. de la Législation sur les Femmes Publiques* (Paris, 1828).

[2] It is generally said to have been invented in the beginning of the fifteenth century by Van Eyck, who died in 1440; but the claim of Van Eyck is not undisputed. It was introduced into Italy about 1452 by a Sicilian painter named Antonello. (Rio, *Art Chrétien*, tom. i. p. 354.)

[3] At an earlier period, oriental robes exercised an influence of a different kind upon art. In the thirteenth century, when they began to pour into France, the ornamentation, and especially the tracery, of the windows of many of the

their favourable influence upon art. The study of the nude figure, which had been the mainspring of Greek art, and which Christianity had so long suppressed, arose again, and a school of painting was formed, which for subtle sensuality of colouring had never been equalled, and, except by Correggio, has scarcely been approached. Titian in this as in other respects was the leader of the school, and he bears to modern much the same relation as Praxiteles bears to ancient art. Both the sculptor and the painter precipitated art into sensuality, both of them destroyed its religious character, both of them raised it to high æsthetic perfection, but in both cases that perfection was followed by a speedy decline.[1] Even in Venice there was one great representative of the early religious school, but his influence was unable to stay the stream. The Virgin of Bellini was soon exchanged for the Virgin of Titian—the ideal of female piety for the ideal of female beauty.

A second influence which contributed to the secularisation, and at the same time to the perfection of art, was the discovery of many of the great works of pagan sculpture.

French cathedrals is said to have been copied accurately from these patterns. See a very curious essay on painted glass by Thèvenot (Paris, 1837). I may add that, at the time of Augustus, the importation of Indian dresses had told powerfully on Roman art, producing the paintings known as arabesque, and (as Vitruvius complains) diverting the artists from the study of the Greek model. In the middle ages both Venice and Florence were famous for their dyers.

[1] Praxiteles is said to have definitively given the character of sensuality to Venus, who had previously floated between several ideals of beauty, and also to have been the especial author of the effeminate type of Apollo. Phryne, who was then the great model of voluptuous beauty—she who, having been condemned to death, was absolved on account of her exceeding loveliness— was his mistress. His contemporary Polycles greatly strengthened the sensual movement by introducing into art the hermaphrodite. See Rio, *Art Chrétien*, Introd. pp. 17–21 ; O. Müller, *Manuel d'Archéologie*, tom. i. pp. 156, 157.

The complete disappearance of these during the preceding centuries may be easily explained by the religious and intellectual changes that had either accompanied or speedily followed the triumph of Christianity. The priests, and especially the monks, being firmly convinced that pagan idols were all tenanted by demons, for some time made it one of their principal objects to break them in pieces, and cupidity proved scarcely less destructive than fanaticism. Among the ancient Greeks, as is well known, marble had never obtained the same ascendency in sculpture as among ourselves. Great numbers of statues were made of bronze, but the masterpieces of the most illustrious artists were of far more valuable materials, usually of ivory or of gold. No features are more wonderful in the history of the Greek states than the immense sums they consented to withdraw from all other objects, to expend upon the cultivation of beauty, and the religious care with which these precious objects were preserved unharmed amid all the vicissitudes of national fortune, amid war, rebellion, and conquest. This preservation was in part due to the intense æsthetic feeling that was so general in antiquity, but in part also to the catholicity of spirit that usually accompanied polytheism, which made men regard with reverence the objects and ceremonies even of worships that were not their own, and which was especially manifested by the Romans, who in all their conquests respected the temples of the vanquished as representing under many forms the aspiration of man to his Creator. Both of these sentiments were blotted out by Christianity. For about 1,500 years the conception that there could be anything deserving of reverence or respect, or even of tolerance, in the religions that were external to the Church, was absolutely unknown in Christendom; and at the same time the

17

ascetic theories I have noticed destroyed all perception of beauty, or at least of that type of beauty which sculpture represented. The bronze statues were converted into coinage, the precious metals were plundered,[1] the marble was mutilated or forgotten. When Christianity arose, the colossal statue of Jupiter Olympus, in gold and ivory, which was deemed the masterpiece of Phidias, and the greatest of all the achievements of art, still existed at Olympia. Our last notice of it is during the reign of Julian. At Rome, the invasion of the barbarians, the absolute decadence of taste that followed their ascendency, and those great conflagrations which more than once reduced vast districts to ruin, completed the destruction of the old traditions, while most of the statues that had been transported to Constantinople, and had survived the fury of the monks, were destroyed by the Iconoclasts, the Crusaders, or the Mahometans.

Towards the close of the twelfth century, as we have already seen, Nicolas of Pisa for the first time broke the slumber of mediæval art by the skill he had derived from the works of antiquity. There was then, however, no ancient model of the highest class known, and the principal subject of his study is said to have been a pagan sarcophagus of third or fourth rate merit, which had been employed for the burial of the mother of the famous Countess Matilda, and which was then in the Cathedral, and is now in the Campo Santo, of Pisa. Giotto, Masaccio, and their contemporaries, all pursued their triumphs without the assistance of any great ancient model. As Flaxman has noticed, Poggio, who wrote at the beginning of the fifteenth century, was only able to enumerate six statues within the walls of Rome. Rienzi and

---

[1] Constantine himself set the example in this respect. See the admiring remarks of Eusebius, *Vita Const.* lib. iii. caps. 5, 6.

Petrarch gave some slight impulse to archæological collections, and during the latter half of the fifteenth century the
exertions of the Medici, and of a long series of popes, sustained by the passionate admiration for antiquity that followed the revival of learning, produced vast works of exca
vation, which were rewarded by the discovery of numerous
statues.[1] Art immediately rose to an unparalleled perfection,
and an unbounded and almost universal enthusiasm was
created. Paul II. indeed, in 1468, directed a fierce persecution against the artists at Rome;[2] but as a general rule his
successors were warm patrons of art, and Julius II. and Leo
X. may even be regarded as the most munificent of their
munificent age. All the artists of Rome and Florence made
the remains of pagan antiquity their models. Michael Angelo
himself proclaimed the Torso Belvedere his true master.[3]
The distinctive type and tone of Christianity was thus almost
banished from art, and replaced by the types of paganism.

Such was the movement which was general in Italian art,
but it did not pass unchallenged, and it was retarded by one
most remarkable reaction. Under the very palace of the
Medici, and in the midst of the noblest collections of pagan
art, a great preacher arose who perceived clearly the dangerous tendency, and who employed the full force of a transcen-

[1] When this impulse had ceased in Italy, it was still in some degree continued by the explorations of the French in Greece, where a French consulate
was formed about 1630. See Vitet, *Études sur l'Histoire de l'Art*, tom. i.
p. 94.
[2] See the description in Platina.
[3] And was accordingly in sculpture (as in painting) singularly unfortunate
in catching the moral expression of Scripture subjects. His Moses—half prize-
fighter, half Jupiter Tonans—is certainly the extreme antithesis to 'the meek-
est man in all the world.' His colossal statue of David after his victory over
Goliath (it would be as rational to make a colossal statue of a Lilliputian)
would be perfect as an Achilles.

dent genius to arrest it. The influence of Savonarola upon painting has been so lately and so fully described by an able living historian of art,[1] that it is not necessary to dwell upon it at length. It is sufficient to say, that during the last few years of the fifteenth century a complete religious revival took place in Tuscany, and that Savonarola, who was much more than a brilliant orator, perceived very clearly that in order to make it permanent it was necessary to ally it with the tendencies of the age. He accordingly, like all successful religious revivalists of ancient and modern times, proceeded to identify religion with liberty and with democracy by his denunciations of the tyranny of the Medici, and by the creation of great lending societies, for the purpose of checking the oppressive usury that had become general. He endeavoured to secure the ascendency of his opinions over the coming generation by guiding the education of the children, and by making them the special objects of his preaching. He attempted above all to purify the very sources of Italian life, by regenerating the sacred music, and by restoring painting to its pristine purity. Week after week he launched from the pulpit the most scathing invectives against the artists who had painted prostitutes in the character of the Virgin, who under the pretext of religious art had pandered to the licentiousness of their age, and who had entirely forgotten their true dignity as the teachers of mankind. As these invectives were not inspired by the fanaticism of the old Iconoclasts, but proceeded from one who possessed to the highest degree the Tuscan perception of the beautiful, they produced an impression that was altogether unparalleled. Almost all the leading painters of Italy were collected at Florence, and almost all, under the influence of Savona

---

[1] Rio—I think the best part of his book.

rola, attempted to revive the religious character of art. The change was immediately exhibited in the painting of Italy, and the impression Savonarola made upon the artists was shown by the conduct of many of them when the great reformer had perished in the flames. Botticelli cast aside his pencil for ever. Baccio della Porta [1] retired broken-hearted into a monastery. Perugino (perhaps the greatest of all the purely religious painters of Catholicism) glided rapidly into scepticism, and on his death-bed refused disdainfully the assistance of a confessor. Raphael, who had derived all the religious sentiment of his early paintings from Perugino, was the first to vindicate the orthodoxy of Savonarola by inserting his portrait among those of the doctors of the Church, in the fresco of the Dispute of the Sacrament.

After the death of Savonarola the secularisation of art was portentously rapid. Even Raphael, who exhibits the tendency less than his contemporaries, never shrank from destroying the religious character of his later works by the introduction of incongruous images. Michael Angelo, that great worshipper of physical force, probably represented the influence to the highest degree. Scarcely any other great painter so completely eliminated the religious sentiment from art, and it was reserved for him to destroy the most fearful of all the conceptions by which the early painters had thrilled the people. By making the Last Judgment a study of naked figures, and by introducing into it Charon and his boat, he most effectually destroyed all sense of its reality, and reduced it to the province of artistic criticism. This fresco may be regarded as the culmination of the movement. There were of course at a later period some great pictures, and even some religious painters, but painting never again

Better known as Fra Bartolommeo.

assumed its old position as the normal and habitual expression of the religious sentiments of the educated. In the first period of mediævalism it had been exclusively religious, and æsthetic considerations were almost forgotten. In the second period the two elements coexisted. In the last period the religious sentiment disappeared, and the conception of beauty reigned alone. Art had then completed its cycle. It never afterwards assumed a prominent or commanding influence over the minds of men.

It is worthy of remark that a transition very similar to that we have traced in painting took place about the same time in architecture. The architect, it is true, does not supply actual objects of worship, and in this respect his art is less closely connected than that of the painter with the history of anthropomorphism; but on the other hand, the period in which men require a visible material object of worship, is also that in which their religious tone and sentiment are most dependent upon imposing sensuous displays. Christianity has created three things which religious poetry has ever recognised as the special types and expressions of its religious sentiment. These are the church bell, the organ, and the Gothic cathedral. The first is said to have been invented by Paulinus, a bishop of Nola in Campania, about the year 400.[1] The second appears to have been first used in the Greek Church, and to have passed into the Western Empire in the seventh or eighth century.[2] The third arose under the

---

[1] Anderson, *Hist. of Commerce*, vol. ii. p. 36. There is a very curious collection of passages from the *Acts of the Saints*, in which bells are alluded to (but none of them apparently earlier than the beginning of the seventh century) in an out-of-the-way quarter. (Suarez, *De Fide*, lib. ii. c. 16.) See, too, Colgan's *Acta Sanctorum Hiberniæ*, tom. i. p. 149.

[2] Anderson, vol. i. p. 30. There had before been known a water organ, called an hydraulicon. There was also a wind instrument which some have

revived sense of beauty of the twelfth century, and preceded
by a little the resurrection of painting. The new pictures
and the new churches were both the occasions of ebullitions
of the most passionate devotion. When Cimabue painted
one of his famous Virgins, the people of Florence gathered
around it as to a religious festival, they transported it with
prayers and thanksgivings to the church, and filled the
streets with hymns of joy, because a higher realisation of a
religious conception had flashed upon them. Just so those
majestic cathedrals that arose almost simultaneously throughout Europe became at once the channel of the enthusiasm of
Christendom; the noblest efforts of self-sacrifice were made
to erect them, and they were universally regarded as the
purest expression of the religious feeling of the age. That
this estimate was correct, that no other buildings the world
has seen are so admirably calculated to produce a sensation
of blended awe and tranquillity, to harmonise or assuage the
qualms of passion, to lull to sleep the rebellious energies of
the intellect, to create around the mind an artificial, un-
worldly, but most impressive atmosphere, to represent a
Church which acts upon the imagination by obscurity and
terrorism, and by images of solemn and entrancing beauty,
will be admitted by all who have any perception of the character, or any knowledge of the history of art. Whenever
these modes of feeling have been very general, Gothic architecture has been the object of rapturous admiration. When-

placed among the antecedents of the organ, but which seems to have been
almost exactly the same as a Scotch bagpipe. I am sorry to say Julian had
the bad taste to praise it in one of his epigrams. (See Burney, *Hist. of Music,*
vol. ii. pp. 65–67.) There is a curious series of papers on the musical instruments in the middle ages, by Coussemaker, in the *Annales Archéologiques*
(edited by Didron), tom. iv. They have since, I believe, been published
separately.

ever these modes of feeling were very rare, Gothic architecture has sunk into neglect and disfavour.[1]

I do not intend to follow at length the vicissitudes of architecture, or to trace the successive phases of its seculari-

---

[1] We have a very striking example of this in both the buildings and the criticisms of the eighteenth century. What (e. g.) should we now say to an imaginative writer who, speaking of York Minster, assured us, as Smollett does, 'that the external appearance of an old cathedral cannot but be displeasing to the eye of every man who has any idea of propriety and proportion;' who could only describe Durham Cathedral as 'a huge gloomy pile;' and who acknowledged that he associated the idea of a church with a spire especially with that of a man impaled (see *Humphrey Clinker*)? Every one, I should think, who was well acquainted with the literature of the eighteenth century, must have been struck with the contempt for Gothic architecture pervading it; but the extent to which this was carried was never fully shown till the publication, a few years ago, of an exceedingly curious book by the Abbé Corblet, called *L'Architecture du Moyen Age jugée par les Écrivains des deux derniers Siècles* (Paris, 1859). The learned antiquarian has shown that, during the last half of the seventeenth century, and during the whole of the eighteenth century, there was scarcely a single writer, no matter what may have been his religious opinions, who did not speak of Gothic architecture not merely without appreciation, but with the most supreme and unqualified contempt. The list includes, among others, Fénelon, Bossuet, Molière, Fleury, Rollin, Montesquieu, La Bruyère, Helvétius, Rousseau, Mengs, and Voltaire. Goethe at one time opposed, but afterwards yielded to, the stream. Milan Cathedral was the special object of ridicule. Gothic architecture was then almost universally ascribed to the Goths of the fifth century, and Bishop Warburton suggested that they had derived the idea from the overarching boughs of their native forests. Some, however (and among others Barry), regarded it as an imperfect imitation of Greek architecture. Many of the criticisms were very curious. Thus, Dupuis thought the zodiacs on the cathedrals were a remnant of the worship of Mithra. Another critic found a connection between the shape of the ogive and the eggs of Isis. A third, named Montluisant, explained all the sculptures on the fronts of Notre Dame de Paris by the science of the philosopher's stone: God the Father, holding an angel in each hand, is the Deity calling into existence the incombustible sulphur and the mercury of life. The flying dragon biting its tail is the philosopher's stone, composed of the fixed and the volatile substances, the former of which devours the latter, &c., &c. (*Œuvres de St. Foix*, tom. iii. pp. 245, 246.) It is to the Catholic revival of the present century that we mainly owe the revival of Gothic architecture

sation. It is sufficient to observe, that about the time when the dense ignorance that had overspread Europe was dispelled, there arose a form of architecture which was exclusively and emphatically Christian, which has been universally admitted to be beyond all others the most accordant with the spirit of mediæval religion, and in which the highest sense of beauty was subordinated to the religious sentiment. At the time when the modern and intellectual chaos that preceded the Reformation was universal, and when painting had been secularised and had passed entirely into the worship of beauty, architecture exhibited a corresponding decadence. The old Gothic style was everywhere discarded, and it was supplanted under the influence of Brunelleschi [1] by a style which some persons may deem more beautiful, but which is universally admitted to be entirely devoid of a religious character. The gorgeous, gay, and beautifully proportioned edifices that then rose to fashion were, in fact, avowedly formed from the model of the great temples of antiquity, and the beauty to which they aspired was purely classic. Cologne Cathedral, the last of the great mediæval works, remained unfinished while the whole energies of Europe were concentrated upon the church of St. Peter at Rome. The design of this great work was confided to Michael Angelo, who had been the chief agent in the secularisation of painting, and the spirit in which he undertook it was clearly expressed in his famous exclamation, that he would suspend the Pantheon in the air.

It is true that the Greek traditions had always lingered in Italy, and that pure Gothic never succeeded in gaining an ascendency there as in other countries. The little church of St. Maria della Spina, at Pisa, which was designed by Nicolas of Pisa, is probably the best specimen of purely Italian origin, for Milan Cathedral is said to be due to German architects; but this fact, while it accounts for Italy having been the great assailant of the Gothic, did not prevent its influence from being cosmopolitan.

Of all the edifices that have been raised by the hand of man, there is none that presents to the historian of the human mind a deeper interest than St. Peter's, and there is certainly none that tells a sadder tale of the frustration of human efforts and the futility of human hopes. It owes its greatest splendour to a worldly and ambitious pontiff,[1] who has not even obtained an epitaph beneath its dome. It was designed to be the eternal monument of the glory and the universality of Catholicism, and it has become the most impressive memorial of its decay. The most sublime associations that could appeal to the intellect or the religious sentiment cluster thickly around it, but an association of which none had dreamed has consecrated it, and will abide with it for ever. The most sacred relics of the Catholic faith are assembled within its walls. The genius of Michael Angelo, Raphael, Bramante, Cellini, Thorwaldsen, and Canova has adorned it. Mosaics of matchless beauty reproduce the greatest triumphs of Christian painting, and mingle their varied hues with those gorgeous marbles that might have absorbed the revenues of a kingdom. Beneath that majestic dome, which stands like the emblem of eternity, and dwarfs the proudest monuments below, rest the remains of those who were long deemed the greatest of the sons of men. There lie those mediæval pontiffs who had borne aloft the lamp of knowledge in an evil and benighted age, who had guided and controlled the march of nations, and had been almost worshipped as the representatives of the Almighty. There too the English traveller pauses amid many more splendid objects at the sculptured slab which bears the names of the last scions of a royal race, that for good or for ill had deeply influenced the destiny of his land. But inexpressi-

---

[1] Julius II.

bly great as are these associations in the eyes of the the010-
gian, the recollection of Luther, and the indulgences, and the
Reformation, will tower above them all; while to the philosophic historian St. Peter's possesses an interest of a still
higher order. For it represents the conclusion of that impulse, growing out of the anthropomorphic habits of an early
civilisation, which had led men for so many centuries to express their religious feelings by sensuous images of grandeur,
of obscurity, and of terrorism. It represents the absorption
of the religious by the æsthetic element, which was the sure
sign that the religious function of architecture had terminated. The age of the cathedrals had passed. The age of
the printing press had begun.

I have dwelt at considerable length upon this aspect cf
the history of art, both because it is, I think, singularly fascinating in itself, and because it reflects with striking fidelity
the religious developments of the time. When the organs
of a belief are entirely changed, it may be assumed that
there is some corresponding change in the modes of thought
of which they are the expression; and it cannot be too often
repeated, that before printing was invented, and while all
conceptions were grossly anthropomorphic, the true course
of ecclesiastical history is to be sought much more in the
works of the artists than of the theologians. It is now admitted by most competent judges, that the true causes of the
Reformation are to be found in the deep change effected in
the intellectual habits of Europe by that revival of learning
which began about the twelfth century in the renewed study
of the Latin classics, and reached its climax after the fall
of Constantinople in the diffusion of the knowledge of
Greek and of the philosophy of Plato by the Greek exiles.
This revival ultimately produced a condition of religious

feeling which found its expression in some countries in Prot
estantism, and in other countries in the prevalence among
the educated classes of a diluted and rationalistic Catholicism
entirely different from the gross and absorbing superstition
of the middle ages.   Which of these two forms was adopted
in any particular country depended upon many special political or social, or even geographical considerations; but,
wherever the intellectual movement was strongly felt, one
or other appeared.   It is surely a remarkable coincidence,
that while the literature of antiquity was thus on a large
scale modifying the mediæval modes of thought, the ancient
sculptures should on a smaller scale have exercised a corresponding influence upon the art that was their expression.
And, although the æsthetic movement was necessarily confined to the upper classes and to the countries in which civilisation was most prominent, it represented faithfully a tendency that in different forms was still more widely displayed.
It represented the gradual destruction of the ascendency which
the Church had once exercised over every department of intellect, the growing difference in realised belief between the
educated and the ignorant, and the gradual disappearance
of anthropomorphic or idolatrous conceptions among the
former.

The aspect, however, of the subject which is peculiarly
significant, is, I think, to be found in the nature of the transition which religious art underwent.   The sense of beauty
gradually encroached upon and absorbed the feeling of reverence.   This is a form of religious decay which is very far
from being confined to the history of art.   The religion of
one age is often the poetry of the next.   Around every living and operative faith there lies a region of allegory and
of imagination into which opinions frequently pass, and in

which they long retain a transfigured and idealised existence after their natural life has died away. They are, as it were, deflected. They no longer tell directly and forcibly upon human actions. They no longer produce terror, inspire hopes, awake passions, or mould the characters of men; yet they still exercise a kind of reflex influence, and form part of the ornamental culture of the age. They are turned into allegories. They are interpreted in a non-natural sense. They are invested with a fanciful, poetic, but most attractive garb. They follow instead of controlling the current of thought, and being transformed by far-fetched and ingenious explanations, they become the embellishments of systems of belief that are wholly irreconcilable with their original tendencies. The gods of heathenism were thus translated from the sphere of religion to the sphere of poetry. The grotesque legends and the harsh doctrines of a superstitious faith are so explained away, that they appear graceful myths foreshadowing and illustrating the conceptions of a brighter day. For a time they flicker upon the horizon with a softly beautiful light that enchants the poet, and lends a charm to the new system with which they are made to blend; but at last this too fades away. Religious ideas die like the sun; their last rays, possessing little heat, are expended in creating beauty.

There can be no question that the steady tendency of the European mind, not merely in the period that elapsed between the revival of learning in the twelfth century and the Reformation, but also in that between the Reformation and our own day, has been to disengage itself more and more from all the conceptions which are connected either with fetishism or with anthropomorphism. The evidence of this meets us on all sides. We find it among the Catholics, in

the steady increase in Catholic countries of a purely rationalistic public opinion, in the vast multiplication of rationalistic
writings, and also in the profound difference in the degree of
reverence attached even by fervent Catholics to images and
talismans, in cities like Paris, which are in the centre of the
intellectual movement of the age, and in cities like Seville
or Naples, which have long been excluded from it. Among
the Protestants the same tendency is displayed with equal
force in the rapid destruction of what is termed the sacra-
mentarian principle. This is manifest in the steady and
almost silent evanescence of that doctrine of consubstantiation which was once asserted with such extreme emphasis as
the distinctive mark of the great Lutheran sect, but which is
now scarcely held, or if held is scarcely insisted on;[1] in the
decadence of the High Church party, which in the seventeenth century comprised the overwhelming majority of the
Anglican clergy, but which in the nineteenth century, notwithstanding a concurrence of favourable circumstances and
the exertions of a leader of extraordinary genius, never included more than a minority;[2] in the constant alteration of

[1] Indeed in Prussia, and some other parts of Germany, the Calvinists and
Lutherans have actually coalesced. The tendency to assimilation appears to
have been strongly felt as early as the middle of the seventeenth century, and
Bishop Bedell exerted himself strongly to promote it. (See some interesting
particulars in his *Life*, by Usher.) On the recent amalgamation of the Lutherans and Calvinists in Germany, and on its relation to rationalism, there are
some remarks worth reading in Amand Saintes' *Hist. de Rationalisme en
Allemagne.*

[2] The principles of parties change so much more than their names, that it
is not easy to get an accurate notion of their strength at different periods.
Shortly after the accession of William III., the Low Church clergy, according
to Macaulay (*History of England*, vol. iii. p. 741), scarcely numbered a tenth
part of the priesthood. On their strength in the present controversy, see some
curious statistics in Conybeare's Essay on *Church Parties*. The failure of
the movement was very candidly confessed by the leader, in his *Anglican
Difficulties.*

the proportion between Anglicans and Dissenters, to the detriment of the former; and in the rapid development of continental Protestantism into rationalism.

The dominating cause of this movement is, as I have said, to be found mainly in that process of education which is effected by the totality of the influences of education, and which produces both a capacity and a disposition to rise above material conceptions, and to sublimate all portions of belief. There is, however, one separate branch of knowledge which has exercised such a deep, and at the same time such a distinct, influence upon it, that it requires a separate notice. I mean the progress of physical science modifying our notions of the government of the universe.

In the early Church the interests of theology were too absorbing to leave any room for purely secular studies. If scientific theories were ever discussed, it was simply with a view to elucidating some theological question, and the controversy was entirely governed by the existing notions of inspiration. On this subject two doctrines prevailed, which did not by any means exclude each other, but were both somewhat different from those that are now professed—one of them being allegorical, the other intensely literal. The first, which had been extremely popular among the Jewish commentators, rested upon the belief, that besides the direct and manifest meaning of a scriptural narrative, which was to be ascertained by the ordinary modes of exegesis, there was an occult meaning, which could be discovered only by the eye of faith, or at all events by human ingenuity guided by the defined doctrines of the Church. Thus, while the historian was apparently relating a very simple narrative, or enforcing a very simple truth, his real and primary object might be to unfold some Christian mystery, of which all the natural objects he mentioned were symbols.

This notion, which in modern times has been systematised and developed with great ingenuity by Swedenborg in his 'Doctrine of Correspondences,' was the origin of many of those extremely far-fetched, and, as they would now appear, absurd interpretations of Scripture that are so numerous in the Fathers, and several of which I have already had occasion to notice. Supposing it to be true, a very important question arose concerning the comparative authority of the historical and the spiritual meanings.

Origen, as is well known, made the principle of allegorical interpretation the basis of a system of freethinking, sometimes of the boldest character. Manichæism having violently assailed the Mosaic cosmogony, he cordially accepted the assault as far as it was directed against the literal interpretation, turned into absolute ridicule, as palpable fables, the stories of the serpent and the trees of life and of knowledge, and contended that they could only be justified as allegories representing spiritual truths.[1] Origen, however, verged far

---

[1] See Beausobre, *Hist. du Manichéisme*, tom. i. pp. 286–288. Barbeyrac, *Morale des Pères*, ch. vii., has collected a number of wonderful extravagances of interpretation into which the love of allegory led Origen. One of the most curious writings of the ancient Church bearing on this subject has been lately printed in the *Spicilegium Solesmense* (curante Dom. J. B. Pitra). It is the *Clavis* of St. Melito, who was bishop of Sardis, it is said, in the beginning of the second century, and consists of a catalogue of many hundreds of birds, beasts, plants, and minerals, that were symbolical of Christian virtues, doctrines, and personages.

A modern High Churchman writes: 'I believe that a geologist deeply impressed with the mystery of baptism—that mystery by which a new creature is formed by means of water and fire—would never have fallen into the absurdities of accounting for the formation of the globe solely by water or solely by fire. He would not have maintained a Vulcanian or a Neptunian theory. He would have suspected that the truth lay in the union of both.'—Sewell, *Christian Morals*, p. 323.

too closely upon heresy to be regared as a representative of the Church; and the prevailing though not very clearly de· fined opinion among the orthodox seems to have been, that the literal and the allegorical interpretations should be both retained.

Perhaps the clearest illustration of this doctrine is to be found in a short treatise of St. Augustine in defence of Gen· esis against the Manichæans, which is very remarkable when we remember that its author was not more distinguished for his great abilities than for the precision and logical charac· ter of his mind. In this work, St. Augustine reviews and answers at length the objections which the Manichæans had brought against each separate portion of the six days' work. Having done this, he proceeds to lay down the principle, that besides the literal meaning, there was a spiritual meaning which was veiled in the form of allegory. Thus the record of the six days' creation contained, not merely a description of the first formation of the material world, but also a pro· phetic sketch of the epochs into which the history of man· kind was to be divided; the sixth day being the Christian dispensation, in which the man and woman, or Christ and the Church, were to appear upon earth.[1] Nor did it fore· shadow less clearly the successive stages of the Christian life. First of all, the light of faith streams upon the mind which is still immersed in the waves of sin; then the firma· ment of discipline divides things carnal from things spiritual; then the regenerated soul is raised above the things of earth, and prepared for the production of virtue; spiritual intelli· gences rise like the planets in their various orders in the

[1] The Church being wedded to Christ, 'bone of his bone, and flesh of his flesh,' that is to say, participating alike of his strength and of his purity (*De Genesi, contra Manichæos*, lib. i. c. 23.)

18

firmament of discipline, good works spring from the waves
of trial as the fish from the sea, the purified mind itself produces its own graces, till, sanctified thought being wedded
to sanctified action, as Eve to Adam, the soul is prepared for
its coming rest.[1] In the same way, when the serpent was
condemned to creep along the earth, this meant that temptation comes commonly by pride and sensuality.[2] When it
was condemned to eat earth, this probably signified the vice
of curiosity, plunging into the unseen. When it is related
that there was a time when no rain fell upon the earth, but
that a mist, rising from the ground, watered its face, this
means that prophets and apostles were once unnecessary, for
every man bore the spring of revelation in his own breast.
The literal narrative was true, and so was the spiritual signification; but if in the first anything was found which could
not be literally interpreted in a manner consonant either with
the doctrines of the Church or with the dignity of the Creator, the passage was to be treated as an enigma, and its true
purport was to be sought in the spiritual meaning.[3] Some
touches of description were inserted solely with a view to
that meaning. Thus, when in the summary of the creation
that is said to have been effected in one day which was really
effected in six, and when the 'green herbs' are specially
singled out among created things, these expressions, which,
taken literally, would be pointless or inaccurate, are intended
merely to direct the mind to particular portions of the allegory.

Together with the method of interpretation laid down in

---

[1] Lib. v. cap. 25. This notion of marriage representing the union of the
two main elements of life, is very beautifully developed by Swedenborg, in a
book on *Conjugal Affection*.

[2] The chest signifying pride, and the stomach sensuality.

[3] Lib. ii. cap. 2,

this and in other works of the early Church, there was another different, though, as I have said, not necessarily antagonistic one, of an intensely literal character.   Theologians
were accustomed to single out any incidental expressions
that might be applied in any way to scientific theories, even
though they were simply the metaphors of poetry or rhetoric,
or the ordinary phrases of common conversation, and to
interpret them as authoritative declarations, superseding all
the deductions of mere worldly science.   The best known
example of this is to be found in those who condemned the
opinions of Galileo, because it had been said that the 'sun
runneth about from one end of heaven to the other,' and
that 'the foundations of the earth are so firmly fixed that
they cannot be moved.'   It may be well, however, to give an
illustration of an earlier date of the extent to which this
mode of interpretation was carried.

Among the very few scientific questions which occupied
a considerable amount of attention in the early Church, one of
the most remarkable was that concerning the existence of the
Antipodes.   The Manichæans had chanced to stumble on the
correct doctrine,[1] and consequently the Fathers opposed it.
Although, however, the leaders of the Church were apparently unanimous in denying the existence of the Antipodes,
it appears that the contrary opinion had spread to a considerable extent among the less noted Christians, and some
fear was entertained lest it should prove a new heresy.

About the year A.D. 535, in the reign of Justinian, there
was living in a monastery of Alexandria an old monk named
Cosmas, to whom the eyes of many were then turned.   He
had been in his youth a merchant, and in that profession had
travelled much, especially in the regions of India and of

---

[1] Beausobre, *Hist. du Manichéisme*, tom. i. p. 246.

Ethiopia. He was also noticed for his keen and inquisitive
mind, and for his scientific attainments, and since he had
embraced a religious life he had devoted himself zealously to
the relations between Scripture and science. At the earnest
request of some of the theologians of his time, he determined, though now somewhat broken in health, and suffering especially, as he tells us, from ' a certain dryness both of
the eyes and of the stomach,' to employ the remainder of
his life in the composition of a great work, which was not
only to refute the ' anile fable ' of the Antipodes, but was to
form a complete system of the universe, based upon the
teaching of Revelation.

   This book is called the ' Topographia Christiana,' or
' Christian Opinion concerning the World.' [1] Independently
of its main interest, as probably the most elaborate work on
the connection between science and the Bible which the early
Church has bequeathed us, it is extremely curious on account
of its many digressions concerning life and manners in the
different nations Cosmas had visited. It opens with a tone
of great confidence. It is ' a Christian topography of the
universe, established by demonstrations from Divine Scripture, concerning which it is not lawful for a Christian to
doubt.' [2] In a similar strain the writer proceeds to censure
with great severity those weak-minded Christians who had
allowed the subtleties of Greek fables, or the deceitful glitter
of mere human science, to lead them astray, forgetting that
Scripture contained intimations of the nature of the universe
of far higher value and authority than any to which un-

----

   [1] This work is published in the Benedictine edition of the Greek Fathers
(Paris, 1706), tom. ii. I have quoted the Benedictine Latin translation. In
his preface, Montfaucon has collected a long chain of passages from the
Fathers denying the existence of the Antipodes.
   [2] Lib. i. prologus 2.

assisted man could attain, and seeking to frame their conceptions simply by the deductions of their reason. Such, Cosmas assures us, is not the course he would pursue. 'To the law and to the testimony' was his appeal, and he doubted not that he could evolve from their pages a system far more correct than any that pagan wisdom could attain.

The system of the universe of which remarks to this effect form the prelude may be briefly stated. According to Cosmas, the world is a flat parallelogram. Its length, which should be measured from east to west, is the double of its breadth, which should be measured from north to south. In the centre is the earth we inhabit, which is surrounded by the ocean, and this again is encircled by another earth, in which men lived before the deluge, and from which Noah was transported in the ark. To the north of the world is a high conical mountain, around which the sun and moon continually revolve. When the sun is hid behind the mountain, it is night; when it is on our side of the mountain, it is day. To the edges of the outer earth the sky is glued. It consists of four high walls rising to a great height and then meeting in a vast concave roof, thus forming an immense edifice of which our world is the floor. This edifice is divided into two stories by the firmament which is placed between the earth and the roof of the sky. A great ocean is inserted in the side of the firmament remote from the earth. This is what is signified by the waters that are above the firmament. The space from these waters to the roof of the sky is allotted to the blest; that from the firmament to our earth to the angels, in their character of ministering spirits.

The reader will probably not regard these opinions as prodigies of scientific wisdom; but the point with which we are especially concerned is the manner they were arrived at.

In order to show this, it will be necessary to give a few sam
ples of the arguments of Cosmas.

In the account of the six days' creation, it will be remembered the whole work is summed up in a single sentence,
'This is the book of the generation of the heaven and the
earth.' These expressions are evidently intended to com-
prise everything that is contained in the heaven and the
earth.   But, as Cosmas contended, if the doctrine of the Antipodes were correct, the sky would surround and consequently contain the earth, and therefore it would only be
said, 'This is the book of the generation of the sky.' [1]   This
very simple argument was capable of great extension, for
there was scarcely any sacred writer who had not employed
the phrase 'the heaven and the earth' to include the whole
creation, and who had not thus implied that one of them did
not include the other.   Abraham, David, Hosea, Isaiah, Zach-
ariah, and many others, were cited.   Even Melchisedec had
thus uttered his testimony against the Antipodes.   If we examine the subject a little further, we are told that the earth
is fixed firmly upon its foundations, from which we may at
least infer that it is not suspended in the air; and we are
told by St. Paul, that all men are made to live upon the 'face
of the earth,' from which it clearly follows that they do not
live upon more faces than one, or upon the back.   With such
a passage before his eyes, a Christian, we are told, should not
'even speak of the Antipodes.'

Such arguments might be considered a conclusive demonstration of the falseness of the Manichæan doctrine.   It re-

---

[1] 'Ait, "Hic est liber generationis cœli et terræ," quasi omnia iis con-
tineantur, et universa quæ in eis sunt cum illis significentur.   Nam si secundum fucatos illos Christianos cœlum tantummodo universa contineat, terram
cum cœlo non nominasset, sed dixisset "Hic est liber generationis cœli."'
(P. 126.)

mained to frame a correct theory to fill its place. The first great point of illumination that meets us in this task, consists in the fact that St. Paul more than once speaks of the earth as a tabernacle. From this comparison some theologians, and Cosmas among the number, inferred that the tabernacle of Moses was an exact image of our world. This being admitted, the paths of science were greatly simplified. The tabernacle was a parallelogram twice as long from east to west as from north to south, and covered over as a room. Two remarkable passages, mistranslated in the Septuagint, in one of which Isaiah is made to compare the heavens to a vault, and in the other of which Job speaks of the sky as glued to the earth, completed the argument,[1] and enabled the writer to state it almost with the authority of an article of faith.[2]

It is easy to perceive how fatal such systems of interpretation must have been to scientific progress. It is indeed true that Cosmas belongs to a period when the intellectual decadence was already begun, that he was himself a writer of no very great abilities, and that some of the more eminent Fathers had treated the subject of the Antipodes with considerable good sense, contending that it was not a matter connected with salvation.[3] But still, from the very beginning, the principles of which this book forms an extreme ex-

[1] These were Isaiah xl. 22, and Job xxxviii. 38. The first was translated 'Qui statuit cœlum sicut fornicem.' The second, 'Cœlum autem in terram inclinavit, effusa est vero sicut terra, calx, conglutinavi autem ipsum quasi lapidem quadrum.'

[2] 'Sic igitur et nos quemadmodum Hesaias figuram primi cœli prima die conditi cum terra facti, cum terra universum complectentis ad fornicis figuram adornati statuimus esse. Ac quemadmodum in Job dictum est cœlum conglutinatum esse terræ, ita quoque nos dicimus. Itemque cum ex Moyse didicerimus terram magis quoad longitudinem extendi, id nos quod fatemur gnari, scilicet Scripturæ divinæ credendum.' (P. 129.)

[3] This very liberal opinion had been expressed by Basil and Ambrose.

ample were floating through the Church. The distinction between theology and science was entirely unfelt. The broad truth which repeated experience has now impressed on almost every unprejudiced student, that it is perfectly idle to quote a passage from the Bible as a refutation of any discovery of scientific men, or to go to the Bible for information on any scientific subject, was altogether undreamed of;[1] and in exact proportion to the increase of European superstition did the doctrine of inspiration dilate, till it crushed every department of the human intellect. Thus, when in the middle of the eighth century an Irish saint, named St. Virgilius, who was one of the very few men who then cultivated profane sciences, ventured in Bavaria to assert the existence of the Antipodes, the whole religious world was thrown into a paroxysm of indignation, St. Boniface heading the attack, and Pope Zachary, at least for a time, encouraging it. At last men sailed for the Antipodes, and they then modified their theological opinions on the subject. But a precisely similar contest recurred when the Copernican system was promulgated. Although the discovery of Coperni-

[1] This doctrine began to dawn upon a few minds during the Copernican controversy. Those who desire to trace its history may read with interest some opinions on the subject that were collected and answered by a contemporary writer on the question between Galileo and the Church (Libertus Fromundus, *Vesta, sive Anti-Aristarchi Vindex*: Antverpiæ, 1634). As I shall have occasion again to quote Fromundus, I may mention that he was a professor and doctor of theology at Louvain; that he was the author of a work on meteorology, in which he combated very forcibly the notion that atmospheric changes were the results of spiritual intervention, which Bodin had lately been defending; and that he was on the whole by no means a superstitious man, except on the subject of comets, of the prophetic character of which he was, I believe, a strenuous advocate. He wrote, in conjunction with a theologian named Fieni, a book about comets, which I have never been fortunate enough to meet with. He was one of the principal defenders of the immobility of the earth, and his works are full of curious information on the theological aspect of the subject. He died in 1653.

cus was at first uncensured, and his book—which was pub
lished in 1543—dedicated to Pope Paul III., as soon as its
views had acquired some weight among the learned, the sus-
picions of the Roman theologians were aroused, and the
opinion of the motion of the earth was authoritatively censured, first of all in the persons of Copernicus and two of his
disciples,[1] and seventeen years later in the condemnation and
imprisonment of Galileo.

It is, indeed, marvellous that science should ever have
revived amid the fearful obstacles theologians cast in her
way. Together with a system of biblical interpretation so
stringent, and at the same time so capricious, that it infallibly came into collision with every discovery that was not in
accordance with the unaided judgments of the senses, and
therefore with the familiar expressions of the Jewish writers,
everything was done to cultivate a habit of thought the di-

[1] The first condemnation was in 1616, and was provoked by the book of a
Carmelite, named Foscarini, in defence of the Copernican view. The cardinals
of the Congregation of the Index, whose function it is to pronounce authoritatively in the name of the Church on the orthodoxy of new books, then issued
a decree, of which the following is the principal part:—'Quia ad notitiam
Sanctæ Congregationis pervenit falsam illam doctrinam Pythagoricam, divinæ-
que Scripturæ omnino adversantem, de mobilitate terræ et immobilitate solis,
quam Nicolaus Copernicus *Revolutionibus orbium cœlestium*, et Didacus Astu-
nica in *Job*, etiam docent, jam divulgari et multis recipi, sicuti videre est ex
quâdam epistolâ impressâ cujusdam P. Carmelitæ, cujus titulus *Lettera del R.
P. Maestro Paolo Foscarini sopra l' Opinione d' i Pythagorici e del Copernico*,
&c., in quâ dictus pater ostendere conatur præfatam doctrinam de immobilitate
solis in centro mundi et mobilitate terræ consonam esse veritati, et non adver-
sari Sacræ Scripturæ: ideo, ne ulterius hujusmodi opinio in perniciem Catholicæ veritatis serpat, censuit dictos hic Copernicum *de Revolut. Orbium* et
Didacum Astunicam in *Job* suspendendos esse donec corrigantur. Librum
vero P. Paulli Foscarini Carmelitæ omnino prohibendum, atque omnes alios
libros pariter idem docentes prohibendos.'—Fromundus, *Anti-Aristarchus, sive
Orbis Terræ immobilis. In quo Decretum S. Congregationis S. R. E. Cardinal.* 1616 *adversus Pythagorico-Copernicanos editum defenditur* (Antverpiæ,
1631), p. 18

rect opposite of the habits of science. The constant exalta·
tion of blind faith, the countless miracles, the childish le·
gends, all produced a condition of besotted ignorance, of
grovelling and trembling credulity, that can scarcely be
paralleled except among the most degraded barbarians.
Innovation of every kind was regarded as a crime ; superior
knowledge excited only terror and suspicion. If it was
shown in speculation, it was called heresy. If it was shown
in the study of nature, it was called magic. The dignity of
the Popedom was unable to save Gerbert from the reputa·
tion of a magician,[1] and the magnificent labours of Roger
Bacon were repaid by fourteen years of imprisonment, and
many others of less severe but unremitting persecution.
Added to all this, the overwhelming importance attached to
theology diverted to it all those intellects which in another
condition of society would have been employed in the investigations of science. When Lord Bacon was drawing his
great chart of the field of knowledge, his attention was

[1] Sylvester II. He was the first Frenchman who sat on the throne of Peter,
the reputed author of Gallican opinions, and it is said the ablest mathematician and mechanician of his time. He died 1003. Among other things, he
invented a kind of clock. He had also a statue, like that of Roger Bacon,
which answered all his questions. According to the popular legend, he was in
communion with the devil, who raised him successively to the sees of Rheims,
Ravenna, and Rome ; and promised that he should never die till he had been
at Jerusalem, which Gerbert construed as a promise of immortality. But, like
that made to Henry IV. of England, it proved to be a cheat, and the Pope felt
the hand of death upon him while officiating in the Chapel of Jerusalem, in
the Basilica of St. Croce. The legend goes on to say that, struck by remorse,
he ordered his body to be cut in pieces, to be placed on a car drawn by oxen,
and to be buried wherever they stopped of themselves, he being unworthy to
rest in the church of God. But, to show that pardon may be extended even
to the most guilty, the oxen stopped at the door of the Lateran. Whenever,
it is said, a pope is about to die, the tomb of Sylvester grows moist, and the
bones of the old magician clatter below. (See Gregorovius, *On the Tombs of the
Popes ,* and the original account in Matthew of Westminster anno 998.)

forcibly drawn to the torpor of the middle ages. That the mind of man should so long have remained tranced and numbed, seemed, at first sight, an objection to his theories, a contradiction to his high estimate of human faculties. But his answer was prompt and decisive. A theological system had lain like an incubus upon Christendom, and to its influence, more than to any other single cause, the universal paralysis is to be ascribed.[1]

At last the revival of learning came, the regeneration of physical science speedily followed it, and it soon effected a series of most important revolutions in our conceptions.

The first of these was to shake the old view of the position of man in the universe. To an uncivilised man, no proposition appears more self-evident than that our world is the great central object of the universe. Around it the sun and moon appear alike to revolve, and the stars seem but inconsiderable lights destined to garnish its firmament. From this conception there naturally followed a crowd of superstitions which occupy a conspicuous place in the belief of every early civilisation. Man being the centre of all things, every startling phenomenon has some bearing upon his acts. The eclipse, the comet, the meteor, and the tempest, are all intended for him. The whole history of the universe centres upon him, and all the dislocations and perturbations it exhibits are connected with his history.[2]

The science which especially corrects these notions is astronomy, but for a considerable period it rather aggravated them, for it was at first inseparably blended with astrology.

---

[1] *Novum Organon.*

[2] Even the sun and stars were supposed to shine with a feebler light since the Fall (St. Isidore, *De Ordine Creaturarum*, cap. v.). On the effects of man's sin on the vegetable world, see St. Augustine, *De Genesi*, lib. i. cap. 13.

It is an extremely ingenious and, at least as far as the period of the revival of learning is concerned, an extremely just observation of M. Comte, that this last study marks the first systematic effort to frame a philosophy of history by reducing the apparently capricious phenomena of human actions within the domain of law.[1] It may, however, I think, be no less justly regarded as one of the last struggles of human egotism against the depressing sense of insignificance which the immensity of the universe must produce. And certainly it would be difficult to imagine any conception more calculated to exalt the dignity of man than one which represents the career of each individual as linked with the march of worlds, the focus towards which the influences of the most sublime of created things continually converge.[2] But, notwithstanding this temporary aberration, there can be no doubt of the eventual tendency of a science which proves that our world is but an infinitesimal fraction in creation, and which, by demonstrating its motion, shows that it is as undistinguished by its position as by its magnitude. The mental importance of such a discovery can hardly be overrated. Those who regard our earth as the centre of the

---

[1] I have already mentioned the bold attempt of Peter of Apono, in the beginning of the fourteenth century, to construct, by the aid of astrology, a philosophy of religions. Cardan, too, cast the horoscope of Christ, and declared that all the fortunes of Christianity were predicted by the stars. Vanini adopted a somewhat similar view. (Durand, *Vie de Vanini*, pp. 93–99.) Pomponazzi attempted to explain the phenomena of magic by the influence of the stars (*Biog. Univ.*, art. *Pomponazzi*); and Bodin, in the very greatest political work of the sixteenth century, having raised the question whether it is possible to discover any principle of order presiding over the development of societies, maintains that such a principle can only be revealed by astrology. (*République*, liv. iv. c. 2.)

[2] As a poet expresses it :—

> 'The warrior's fate is blazoned in the skies ;
> A world is darkened when a hero dies.'

material universe will always attribute to it a similar position in the moral scheme; and when the falsehood of the first position is demonstrated, the second appears incongruous or a difficulty.[1]

It has been reserved for the present century and for a new science to supplement the discovery of Copernicus and Galileo by another which has not yet been fully realised, but is no doubt destined to exercise a commanding influence over all future systems of belief: I mean the discoveries of geology relating to the preadamite history of the globe. To those who regard the indefinite as the highest conception of the infinite, the revelation of eternity is written on the rocks, as the revelation of immensity upon the stars. But to more scientific minds the most important effect of geology has not been that it throws back to an incalculable distance the horizon of creation, nor yet that it has renovated and transformed all the early interpretations of the Mosaic cosmogony; but that it has conclusively disproved what was once the universal belief concerning the origin of death. That this fearful calamity appeared in the universe on account of the transgression of man, that every pang that convulses the frame of any created being, every passion or in-

[1] Whatever may be thought of its justice, there cannot be two opinions about the exquisite beauty of the suggestion by which Dr. Chalmers sought to meet this difficulty—that the parable of the shepherd leaving the ninety-nine sheep to seek that which had gone astray, is but a description of the act of the Deity seeking to reclaim the single world that had revolted against Him, as though it were of more importance than all that remained faithful. It may be added that astronomy itself furnishes a striking illustration of the danger of trusting too implicitly to our notions of the fitness of things. The ancient astronomers unanimously maintained that the motions of the celestial bodies must necessarily be circular and uniform, because they regarded that as the most perfect kind of movement; and the persistence with which this notion was held, till it was overthrown by Kepler, was one of the chief obstacles to astronomical progress.

stinct or necessity that contributes to the infliction of suffering, is but the fruit of the disobedience in Paradise, was long believed with unfaltering assurance, and is even now held by many who cannot be regarded as altogether uneducated. And this general proposition became a great arche type, a centre around which countless congenial beliefs were formed, a first principle or measure of probability guiding the predispositions of men in all their enquiries. If all death and all pain resulted from the sin of Adam, it was natural to give every particular instance of death or pain a special signification; and if these the greatest of terrestrial imperfections were connected with the history of man, it was natural to believe that all minor evils were no less so. But geology has now proved decisively that a profound error lurks in these conclusions. It has proved that countless ages before man trod this earth death raged and revelled among its occupants; that it so entered into the original constitution of things, that the agony and the infirmity it implies were known as at present when the mastodon and the dinotherium were the rulers of the world. To deny this is now impossible: to admit it is to abandon one of the root-doctrines of the past.

A second kind of influence which scientific discoveries have exercised upon belief, has been the gradual substitution of the conception of law for that of supernatural intervention. This substitution I have already had occasion to refer to more than once; but I trust the reader will pardon me for reverting to it for a moment, in order to show with more precision than I have hitherto done the extent and nature of the change. It is the especial characteristic of uncivilised men that their curiosity and, still more, their religious sentiments, are very rarely excited by those phenomena which fall obviously within the range of natural laws, while they are keenly affected by all which appear abnormal. It is indeed true that this expression ' natural law ' has to the uncivilised man only a very vague and faint signification, that he has no conception of the close connection subsisting between different classes of phenomena, and that he frequently attributes each department even of those which are most regular to the action of special presiding spirits ; yet still certain phenomena are recognised as taking place in regular sequences, while others appear capricious, and the latter are associated especially with Divine intervention. Thus comets, meteors, and atmospheric phenomena were connected with religious ideas long after the sun and the stars. Thus, too, games of chance were from a very early period prohibited, not simply on account of the many evils that result from them, but as a species of blasphemy, being an appeal on trivial matters to the adjudication of the Deity.[1] Man being unable to calculate how the die will fall, it was believed that this is determined by a Divine interposition, and accordingly the casting of lots became one of the favourite means of approaching the Deity.[2]

From this habit of associating religious feelings chiefly with the abnormal, two very important consequences ensued, one of them relating to science and the other to theology In the first place, as long as abnormal and capricious phe

[1] See a clear view of the old opinions on this subject in Barbeyrac, *De la Nature du Sort* (Amsterdam, 1714), who sustained an ardent controversy on the subject with a Dutch divine. The first writer, I believe, who clearly and systematically maintained that lots were governed by purely natural laws, was an English Puritan minister named Gataker, in a work *On the Nature and Use of Different Kinds of Lots* (London, 1619)—a well-reasoned and curious book, teeming with quaint learning.

[2] Hence the term 'sortes' was applied to oracles. Hence, too, such words as 'sorteligi,' ' sorcerers.'

nomena are deemed the direct acts of the Deity, all attempts
to explain them by science will be discouraged; for such attempts must appear an irreverent prying into the Divine
acts, and, if successful, they diminish the sources of religious
emotion.[1] In the second place, it is evident that the concep
tion of the Deity in an early period of civilisation must be
essentially different from that in a later period.   The consciousness of the Divine presence in an unscientific age is
identified with the idea of abnormal and capricious action;
in a scientific age with that of regular and unbroken law.
The forms of religious emotions being wholly different, the
conceptions of the Deity around which they centre must be
equally so.   The one conception consists mainly of the ideas
of interference, of miracle, of change, and of caprice; the
other of regularity, of immutability, and of prescience.   The
one conception predisposes most to prayer, the other to reverence and admiration.

The first science that rose to perfection at the period I
am referring to was astronomy, which early attained a great
prominence on account of the revival of astrology that had
been produced in the fourteenth century by the renewed
study of the works of pagan antiquity, and perhaps still
more by the profound influence the Arabian intellect then
exercised on Christendom.   The great work of Copernicus,
the almost simultaneous appearance of Kepler, Galileo, and

---

[1] Thus De Maistre, speaking of the ancients, says:—' Leur physique est à
peu près nulle.   Car non seulement ils n'attachaient aucun prix aux expéri-
ences physiques, mais ils les méprisaient, et même ils attachaient je ne sais
quel légère idée d'impiété; *et ce sentiment confus venait de bien haut.*'
(*Soirées de St. Pétersbourg*, 5me entretien.)   This is the true spirit of superstition.   Speaking of earthquakes, Cosmas says:—' Quod vero terra moveatur id
non a vento fieri dicimus; non enim fabulas comminiscimur ut illi, sed illud
jussu Dei fieri pronuntiamus, *nec curiose rem perquirimus*, ait quippe Scriptura
per Davidem, " Qui respicit terram et facit eam tremere," &c.'—p. 115.

Tycho Brahe, and the invention and rapid improvement of the telescope, soon introduced the conception of natural law into what had long been the special realm of superstition. The Theory of Vortices of Descartes, although it is now known to have no scientific value, had, as has been truly said, a mental value of the very highest order, for it was the first attempt to form a system of the universe by natural law and without the intervention of spiritual agents.[1] Previously the different motions of the heavenly bodies had been for the most part looked upon as isolated, and the popular belief was that they as well as all atmospheric changes were effected by angels.[2] In the Talmud a special angel was assigned to every star and to every element, and similar notions were general throughout the middle ages.[3] The belief in the existence of a multitude of isolated and capricious phenomena naturally suggested the belief in angels to account for them; and on the other hand, the association of angels with phenomena that obtruded themselves constantly on the attention produced a vivid sense of angelic presence, which was shown in countless legends of angelic manifestations. All this passed away before the genius of Descartes and of Newton. The reign of law was recognised as supreme, and the conceptions that grew out of the earlier notion of the celestial system waned and vanished.

For a long time, however, comets continued to be the

[1] This was originally a remark of St. Simon, but it has been adopted and made great use of by M. Comte and some of his disciples. See that very able book, Littré, *Vie de Comte*.

[2] Roccamora, *De Cometis*, p. 17; St. Isidore, *De Ordine Creaturarum*.

[3] Maury, *Légendes Pieuses*, pp. 17–18. Angels were sometimes represented in old Christian painting and sculpture bearing along the stars (and especially the Star of Bethlehem) in their hands. See, e. g., a very curious old bas relief round the choir of Notre Dame at Paris.

refuge of the dying superstition. Their rarity, the eccen
tricity of their course, the difficulty of ascertaining their
nature, and the grandeur and terror of their aspect, had all
contributed to impress men with an extraordinary sense of
their supernatural character. From the earliest ages they
had been regarded as the precursors of calamity, and men
being accustomed to regard them in that light, a vast mass
of evidence was soon accumulated in support of the belief.
It was shown that comets had preceded the death of such
rulers as Cæsar, or Constantine the Great, or Charles V.
Comets were known to have appeared before the invasion of
Greece by Xerxes, before the Peloponnesian war, before the
civil wars of Cæsar and Pompey, before the fall of Jerusalem, before the invasion of Attila, and before a vast number
of the greatest famines and pestilences that have afflicted
mankind.[1] Many hundreds of cases of this kind were collected, and they furnished an amount of evidence which was
quite sufficient to convince even somewhat sceptical minds,
at a time when the supernatural character of comets, harmo-
nising with the prevailing notions of the government of the
universe, appeared antecedently probable. Some theologians
indeed, while fully acknowledging the ominous character of
these apparitions, attempted to explain them in a somewhat
rationalistic manner. According to their view, comets were
masses of noxious vapour exhaled—some said from the
earth, and others from the sky, which by tainting the atmosphere produced pestilence. Kings were indeed especially
liable to succumb beneath this influence, but this was only
because their labours and their luxurious habits rendered

---

[1] The fullest statement of the evidence of the prophetic character of comets
I have met with, is in Raxo, *De Cometis* (1578). The author was a Spanish
physician.

them weaker than other men.[1] Usually, however, comets were simply regarded as supernatural warnings sent to prognosticate calamity. Two or three great men made vain efforts to shake the belief. Thus, during one of the panics occasioned by a great comet, Paracelsus wrote forcibly against the popular notions,[2] which he assailed on theological grounds as forming a species of fatalism, and as being inconsistent with the belief in Providence. In the midst of a similar panic in 1680, Bayle made a similar effort, but, in obedience to the spirit of the age, he adopted not a theological but a philosophical point of view. He displayed with consummate skill the weakness of a process of reasoning which rested on an arbitrary selection of chance coincidences, and he made the subject the text for one of the very best books that have ever been written on the gradual consolidadation of superstitions.[3] But theology and philosophy were alike impotent till science appeared to assist them. Halley predicted the revolution of comets, and they were at once removed to the domain of law, and one of the most ancient of human superstitions was destroyed.

The process which took place in astronomy furnishes but a single though perhaps an extreme example of that which, in the seventeenth century, took place in every field of science. Everywhere the rapid conquests of the new spirit

[1] Roccamora, *De Cometis* (Romæ, 1670), pp. 238, 239.

[2] In a letter to Zwinglius.

[3] And, flying off at a tangent from his main subject, for one of the very best dissertations on the relation between religion and morals. With the greatest possible admiration for the *Critical Dictionary*, which will be always regarded as one of the most stupendous monuments of erudition and of critical acumen ever bequeathed by a single scholar, I cannot but think that the original genius of Bayle shines still more brightly in the *Conrains-les d'Entrer*, in some of the *Pensées diverses sur les Comètes*, and in two or three of his *Nouvelles Lettres*

were substituting the idea of natural law for that of supernatural interference, and persuading men that there must be
a natural solution even where they were unable to discover
it. The writings of Bacon, although their influence has, I
think, been considerably exaggerated, partly through national pride, and partly because men have accepted too
readily the very unfair judgments Bacon expressed of his
contemporaries,[1] probably contributed more than any other
single cause to guide the movement, and have, in England
at least, become almost supreme. Chemistry disengaged
itself from alchemy, as astronomy had done from astrology.
The Academy del Cimento was established in Tuscany in
1657, the Royal Society in London in 1660, and the Academy
of Sciences in Paris in 1666. The many different sciences

---

[1] The age of Bacon was certainly not as benighted and ignorant on scientific matters as he always represented it. On the contrary, when we remember
that it was the age of Copernicus, Galileo, Tycho Brahe, Kepler, and Gilbert,
it would be difficult to name one that was more distinguished. A large portion of the scientific revival in Europe may be justly ascribed to these great
men ; and the only apology that can be offered for the representations of
Bacon is that, notwithstanding his great genius, he was totally unable to grasp
their discoveries. The Copernican system—the greatest discovery of the age—
he rejected to the last. The important discoveries of Gilbert about the magnet
he treated not only with incredulity, but with the most arrogant contempt. In
measuring his influence, we have to remember that it was certainly not dominant outside England till that union between the English and French intellects
that immediately preceded the French Revolution. *Then*, indeed, his philosophy exercised an immense and salutary influence upon the Continent; but
Europe had not been sleeping till then. In Great Britain itself, Bacon produced no perceptible effect upon the great school of literature and science that
grew up beyond the Tweed; and even in England, where he has been almost
omnipotent, two of the very greatest men stood apart from his disciples. The
whole method and mental character of Newton was opposed to that of Bacon,
and, as his biographer, Sir David Brewster, very forcibly contends, there is not
the slightest reason to believe that Newton owed anything to his predecessor ;
while Harvey avowedly owed his great discovery to that doctrine of final causes
which Bacon stigmatised as 'barren, like a virgin consecrated to God that can
bear no fruit.'

that were simultaneously cultivated not merely rescued many distinct departments of nature from superstition, but also by their continual convergence produced the conception of one all-embracing scheme of law, taught men habitually to associate the Divine presence with order rather than with miracle, and accustomed them to contemplate with admiring reverence the evidence of design displayed in the minutest animalcule and in the most shortlived ephemera, and also the evidence of that superintending care which adapts a sphere of happiness for the weakest of created beings.

A very important consequence of this change was that theological systems lost much of their harsh and gloomy character. As long as men drew their notions of the Deity from what they regarded as the abnormal, their attention was chiefly concentrated upon disasters, for these are for the most part exceptional, while the principal sources of happiness are those which are most common. Besides, it is one of the most unamiable characteristics of human nature that it is always more impressed by terror than by gratitude. Accordingly, the devotion of our ancestors was chiefly connected with storms and pestilences and famine and death, which were regarded as penal inflictions, and consequently created an almost maddening terror. All parts of belief assumed a congenial hue, till the miserable condition of man and the frightful future that awaited him became the central ideas of theology. But this, which in an early phase of civilisation was perfectly natural, soon passed away when modern science acquired an ascendency over theological developments; for the attention of men was then directed chiefly to those multitudinous contrivances which are designed for the wellbeing of all created things, while the terrorism once produced by the calamities of life was at least greatly diminished when they were shown to be the result of general laws interwoven with the whole system of the globe, and many of which had been in operation before the creation of man.

Another branch of scientific progress which I may notice on account of its influence upon speculative opinions, is the apid growth of a morphological conception of the universe. According to the great philosophers of the seventeenth century, our world was a vast and complicated mechanism called into existence and elaborated instantaneously in all its parts by the creative fiat of the Deity. In the last century, however, and still more in the present century, the progress of chemistry, the doctrine of the interchange and indestructibility of forces, and the discoveries of geology, have greatly altered this conception. Without entering into such questions as that of the mutability of species, which is still pending, and which the present writer would be altogether incompetent to discuss, it will be admitted that in at least a large proportion of the departments of science, the notion of constant transformation, constant progress under the influence of natural law from simple to elaborate forms, has become dominant. The world itself, there is much reason to believe, was once merely a vapour, which was gradually condensed and consolidated, and its present condition represents the successive evolutions of countless ages. This conception, which exhibits the universe rather as an organism than a mechanism, and regards the complexities and adaptations it displays rather as the results of gradual development from within than of an interference from without, is so novel, and at first sight so startling, that many are now shrinking from it with alarm, under the impression that it destroys the argument from design, and almost amounts to the negation of a Supreme Intelligence. But there can, I think, be little doubt that such fears are, for the most part, unfounded.[1] That matter is governed by mind, that the contrivances and elaborations of the universe are the products of intelligence, are propositions which are quite unshaken, whether we regard these contrivances as the results of a single momentary exercise of will, or of a slow, consistent, and regulated evolution. The proofs of a pervading and developing intelligence, and the proofs of a coördinating and combining intelligence, are both untouched, nor can any conceivable progress of science in this direction destroy them. If the famous suggestion, that all animal and vegetable life results from a single vital germ, and that all the different animals and plants now existent were developed by a natural process of evolution from that germ, were a demonstrated truth, we should still be able to point to the evidences of intelligence displayed in the measured and progressive development, in those exquisite forms so different from what blind chance could produce, and in the manifest adaptation of surrounding circumstances to the living creature, and of the living creature to surrounding circumstances. The argument from design would indeed be changed, it would require to be stated in a new form, but it would be fully as cogent as before. Indeed it is, perhaps, not too much to say, that the more fully this conception of universal evolution is grasped, the more firmly a scientific doctrine of Providence will be established, and the stronger will be the presumption of a future progress.

The effects of this process which physical science is now undergoing are manifested very clearly in the adjacent field of history, in what may be termed the morphological

[1] See the remarks on the consistence of morphological conceptions with the doctrine of final causes in Whewell's *History of Scientific Ideas.*

conception of opinions—that is to say, in the belief that there is a law of orderly and progressive transformation to which our speculative opinions are subject, and the causes of which are to be sought in the general intellectual condition of society. As the main object of this whole book is to illustrate the nature and progress of this conception, it is not necessary to dwell upon it at present, and I advert to it simply for the purpose of showing its connection with the discoveries of science.

It will be remarked, that in this as in most other cases the influence physical sciences have exercised over speculative opinions has not been of the nature of a direct logical proof displacing an old belief, but rather the attracting in fluence of a new analogy. As I have already had occasions to observe, an impartial examination of great transitions of opinions will show that they have been effected not by the force of direct arguments, not by such reasons as those which are alleged by controversialists and recorded in creeds, but by a sense of the incongruity or discordance of the old doctrines with other parts of our knowledge. Each man assimilates the different orders of his ideas. There must always be a certain keeping or congruity or analogy between them. The general measure of probability determines belief, and it is derived from many departments of knowledge. Hence it is that whenever the progress of enquiry introduces a new series of conceptions into physical science, which represents one aspect of the relations of the Deity to man, these conceptions, or at least something like them, are speedily transferred to theology, which represents another.

It must, however, be acknowledged, that there are some influences resulting from physical science which are deeply to be deplored, for they spring neither from logical arguments nor from legitimate analogies, but from misconceptions that are profoundly imbedded in our belief, or from fallacies into which our minds are too easily betrayed. The increased evidence of natural religion furnished by the innumerable marks of creative or coördinating wisdom which science reveals, can hardly be over-estimated,[1] nor can it be reasonably questioned that a world governed in all its parts by the interaction of fixed natural laws implies a higher degree of designing skill than a chaos of fortuitous influences irradiated from time to time by isolated acts of spiritual intervention. Yet still so generally is the idea of Divine action restricted to that of miracle, that every discovery assigning strange phenomena their place in the symmetry of nature has to many minds an irreligious appearance; which is still further strengthened by the fact, that while physical science acquiesces in the study of laws as the limit of its research, even scientific men sometimes forget that the discovery of law is not an adequate solution of the problem of causes. When all the motions of the heavenly bodies have been reduced to the dominion of gravitation, gravitation itself still remains an insoluble problem. Why it is that matter attracts matter, we do not know—we perhaps never shall know. Science can throw much light upon the laws that preside over the development of life; but what life is, and what is its ultimate cause, we are utterly unable to say. The mind of man, which can track the course of the comet and measure the

[1] Laplace, who has done more than any one else to systematise arguments from probability, and who will certainly not be accused of any desire to subordinate science to theology, states the argument for design derived from the motions of the planetary bodies in the following almost bewildering terms: ‘ Des phénomènes aussi extraordinaires ne sont point dûs à des causes irrégulières. En soumettant au calcul leur probabilité, on trouve qu'il y a plus de deux cents mille milliards à parier contre un qu'ils ne sont point l'effet du nasard.’—*Système du Monde*, liv. v, c. 6.

velocity of light, has hitherto proved incapable of explaining
the existence of the minutest insect or the growth of the most
humble plant. In grouping phenomena, in ascertaining their
sequences and their analogies, its achievements have been
marvellous; in discovering ultimate causes it has absolutely
failed. An impenetrable mystery lies at the root of every
existing thing. The first principle, the dynamic force, the
vivifying power, the efficient causes of those successions
which we term natural laws, elude the utmost efforts of our
research. The scalpel of the anatomist and the analysis of
the chemist are here at fault. The microscope, which reveals
the traces of all-pervading, all-ordaining intelligence in the
minutest globule, and displays a world of organised and living
beings in a grain of dust, supplies no solution of the problem.
We know nothing or next to nothing of the relations of mind
to matter, either in our own persons or in the world that is
around us; and to suppose that the progress of natural science
eliminates the conception of a first cause from creation, by
supplying natural explanations, is completely to ignore the
sphere and limits to which it is confined.

It must be acknowledged also, that as the increasing
sense of law appears to many the negation of the reality or
at all events of the continuity of the Divine action, so an in
creased sense of the multiplicity of the effects of matter not
unfrequently leads to a negation of the existence of mind.
The mathematician ridiculed by Berkeley who maintained
that the soul must be extension, and the fiddler who was
convinced that it must be harmony, are scarcely exaggerated
representatives of the tendency manifested by almost every
one who is much addicted to a single study to explain by it
all the phenomena of existence. Nearly every science when
it has first arisen has had to contend with two great obstacles

—with the unreasoning incredulity of those who regard novelty as necessarily a synonyme for falsehood, and with the unrestrained enthusiasm of those who, perceiving vaguely and dimly a new series of yet undefined discoveries opening upon mankind, imagine that they will prove a universal solvent. It is said that when, after long years of obstinate disbelief, the reality of the great discovery of Harvey dawned upon the medical world, the first result was a school of medicine which regarded man simply as an hydraulic machine, and found the principle of every malady in imperfections of circulation.[1] The same history has been continually reproduced. That love of symmetry which makes men impatient to reduce all phenomena to a single cause, has been the parent of some of the noblest discoveries, but it has also, by the imperfect classifications it has produced, been one of the most prolific sources of human error. In the present day, when the study of the laws of matter has assumed an extraordinary development, and when the relations between the mind and the body are chiefly investigated with a primary view to the functions of the latter, it is neither surprising nor alarming that a strong movement towards materialism should be the consequence.

But putting aside these illegitimate consequences, it appears that in addition to the general effects of intellectual development upon theological opinions in enabling men more readily to conceive the invisible, and thus rescuing them from idolatry, and in enabling them to spiritualise and elevate their ideal, and thus emancipating them from anthropomorphism, that particular branch of intellectual progress which is comprised under the name of physical science has exercised a distinct and special influence, which has been

[1] Lemoine, *Le Vitalisme de Stahl*, p. 6.

partly logical, but more generally the assimilating influence of analogy. It has displaced man's early conception of the position of his world in the universe, and of the relation of the catastrophes it exhibits to his history. It has substituted a sense of law for a predisposition to the miraculous, and taught men to associate the Deity with the normal rather than with the abnormal. It has in a great degree divested calamity of its penal character, multiplied to an incalculable extent the evidences of the Divine beneficence, and at the same time fostered a notion of ordered growth which has extended from the world of matter to the world of mind.

These have been its chief effects upon belief. It has also exercised a considerable influence upon the systems of Bibli cal interpretation by which that belief is expressed. The first great impulse to Rationalistic Biblical criticism was probably given by the antagonism that was manifested between the discovery of Galileo and Scripture as it was interpreted by the host of theologians who argued after the fashion of Cosmas. New facts were discovered and therefore a new system of interpretation was required, and men began to apply their critical powers to the sacred writings for the purpose of bringing them into conformity with opinions that had been arrived at independently by the reason. Each new discovery of science that bore upon any Scriptural question, each new order of tendencies evoked by the advance of civilisation, produced a repetition of the same process.

Probably the earliest very elaborate example of this kind of interpretation was furnished by a French Protestant, named La Peyrère, in a book which was published in 1655.[1] The author, who fully admitted though he endeavoured to

[1] *Systema Theologicum ex Præ-Adamitarum Hypothesi*, pars i. The second part never appeared.

restrict the sphere of the miraculous, had been struck by some difficulties connected with the ordinary doctrine of Original Sin, and by some points in which science seemed to clash with the assertions of the Old Testament; and he endeavoured to meet them by altogether isolating the Biblical history from the general current of human affairs. Adam, he maintained, was not the father of the human race, but simply the progenitor of the Jews, and the whole antediluvian history is only that of a single people. Thus the antiquity which the Eastern nations claimed might be admitted, and the principal difficulties attending the Deluge were dissolved. It was altogether a mistake to suppose that death and sickness and suffering were the consequences of the transgression. Adam had by this act simply incurred spiritual penalties, which descended upon the Jews. 'In the day thou eatest thou shalt die' could not have been meant literally, because it was not literally fulfilled; nor could the curse upon the serpent, because the motion of the serpent along the ground is precisely that which its conformation implies. The existence of men who were not of the family of Adam is shadowed obscurely in many passages, but appears decisively in the history of Cain, who feared to wander forth lest men should kill him, and who built a city at a time when, according to the common view, he was almost alone in the world.[1] The mingling of the sons of God and the daughters

---

[1] Some of La Peyrère's arguments on this point are curiously far-fetched. Thus he asks why Abel should have kept sheep if there were no robbers to be feared, and where Cain got the weapon with which he killed his brother. The existence of a race of men not descended from Adam was very strenuously maintained, towards the close of the last century, by an eccentric member of the Irish Parliament named Dobbs, in a very strange book called *A Short View of Prophecy.* It has also been advocated in America, with a view to the defence of Negro Slavery. Mr. Dobbs· thought there was a race resulting from an intrigue of Eve with the Devil.

of men means the intermarriage between the two races. The Deluge is an absolute impossibility if regarded as universal, but not at all surprising if regarded as a partial inundation.

Proceeding to the history of a later period, La Peyrère in the first place denies the Mosaic authorship of the Pentateuch. In defence of this position he urges the account of the death of Moses, and he anticipates several of those minute criticisms which in our own day have acquired so great a prominence. The phrase 'These are the words which Moses spake beyond Jordan,' the notice of the city which is called 'Jair to the present day,' the iron bedstead of Og still shown in Rabbath, the difficulties about the conquest of the Idumeans, and a few other passages, seem to show that the compilation of these books was long posterior to the time of Moses; while certain signs of chronological confusion which they evince render it probable that they are not homogeneous, but are formed by the fusion of several distinct documents. It should be observed, too, that they employ a language of metaphor and of hyperbole which has occasionally given rise to misapprehensions, special instances of providential guidance being interpreted as absolute miracles. Thus, for example, the wool of the Jewish flocks was quite sufficient to furnish materials for clothing in the desert, and the assertion that the clothes of the Jews waxed not old is simply an emphatic expression of that extraordinary providence which preserved them from all want for forty years in the wilderness. At the same time La Peyrère does not deny that the Jewish history is full of miracles, but he maintains very strongly that these were only local, and that the general course of the universe was never disturbed to effect them. The prolongation of the day at the command of Joshua was not produced by any alteration in the course of the earth or sun, but was simply an atmospheric phenomenon such as is sometimes exhibited in the Arctic regions. The darkness at the Crucifixion was also local; the retrogression of the shadow on the sun-dial in the reign of Hezekiah did not result from a disturbance of the order of the heavenly bodies; the light that stood over the cradle of Christ was a meteor, for a star could not possibly mark out with precision a house.

The author of this curious book soon after its publication became a Roman Catholic, and in consequence recanted his opinions, but the school of Biblical interpretation of which he was perhaps the first founder continues actively to the present day. To trace its history in detail does not fall within the plan of the present work. It will be sufficient to say that there are two natural theories by which men have endeavoured to explain the rise of religions, and that each of these theories has in particular ages or countries or conditions of thought exercised a supreme ascendency.[1] The first method, which attributes religions to special and isolated causes, found its principal ancient representative in Euhemerus, who maintained that the pagan gods were originally illustrious kings, deified after death either by the spontaneous reverence of the people or by the cunning of the rulers.[2] The work of Euhemerus, being translated by Ennius, is said to have con tributed largely to that diffusion of scepticism in Rome which preceded the rise of Christianity; and its theory was general· ly adopted by the Fathers, who, however, added that devils had assumed the names of the dead.[3] To this class of criti-

---

[1] See Denis's *Hist. des Idées Morales dans l'Antiquité.*

[2] Locke, in his *Treatise on Government,* adopts very fully the theory of Euhemerus about the origin of the pagan divinities.

The first Christian writer who maintained that the pagan oracles were

cism belong also all attempts to explain miracles by imposture, or by optical delusions, or by the misconception of some
natural phenomenon, or by any other isolated circumstance.
The other method, which is called mythical, and which was
adopted among the ancients by the Pythagoreans, the Neo-
Platonists, and the Gnostics, regards different dogmatic systems as embodying religious sentiments or great moral conceptions that are generally diffused among mankind, or as
giving a palpable and (so to speak) material form to the aspirations of the societies in which they spring. Thus, while
fully admitting that special circumstances have an important
influence over the rise of opinions, the interpreters of this
school seek the true efficient cause in the general intellectual
atmosphere that is prevalent. They do not pretend to explain in detail how different miracles came to be believed,
but they assert that in a certain intellectual condition phenomena which are deemed miraculous will always appear,
and that the general character of those phenomena will be determined by the prevailing predisposition. The first of these
schools of interpretation was general in the seventeenth and
eighteenth centuries, and has been especially favoured by
nations like the ancient Romans, or like the modern English
and French, who are distinguished for a love of precise and
definite conclusions; while the second has been most prominent in the present century, and in Germany.

It must, however, be admitted that the energy displayed
in framing natural explanations of miraculous phenomena
bears no proportion to that which has been exhibited in a

simply impositions, unconnected with dæmons, is said to have been a Dutch
Anabaptist physician named Van Dale; and the same position was afterwards
maintained by Fontenelle, in his *Histoire des Oracles*, which was answered by
a Jesuit named Baltus. (Durand, *Vie de Vanini*, pp. 170–172.)

criticism that is purely disintegrating and destructive. Spinoza, whose profound knowledge not only of the Hebrew language but also of Rabbinical traditions and of Jewish modes of thought and expression made him peculiarly competent for the task, set the example in his 'Tractatus Theologico-Politicus,'[1] and Germany soon after plunged into the bottomless abyss from which she has not emerged. But the fact which must, I think, especially strike the impartial observer, is that these criticisms, in at least the great majority of cases, are carried on with a scarcely disguised purpose of wresting the Bible into conformity with notions that have been independently formed. The two writers who have done most to supply the principles of the movement are Lessing and Kant. The first emphatically asserts that no doctrine should be accepted as part of Scripture which is not in accordance with 'reason,' an expression which in the writings of modern German critics may be not unfairly regarded as equivalent to the general scope and tendency of modern thought.[2] The doctrine of Kant is still more explicit. According to him[3] every dogmatic system, or, as he expresses it, every 'ecclesiastical belief,' should be regarded as the

[1] Spinoza was, as far as I know, the first writer who dwelt much on the possible or probable falsification of some portions of the Old Testament by the insertion of wrong vowel-points, a subject which was a few years since investigated in a work on *Hebrew Interpolations*, by Dr. Wall, of Dublin University. Some of the remarks of Spinoza about the Jewish habit of speaking of the suggestions of their own minds as inspirations are still worth reading, but with these exceptions the value of the *Tractatus Theologico-Politicus* seems to me to be chiefly historical.

[2] See, on Lessing's views, a clear statement in Amand Sainte's *Hist. Critique du Rationalisme en Allemagne*. Strauss, in the Introduction to his *Life of Jesus*, gives a vivid sketch of the progress of German Rationalism; and the manner in which he there treats the subject of miracles illustrates very clearly the wide use made of the term 'reason' in German criticism.

[3] See his *Religion within the Limits of the Reason*.

20

vehicle or envelope of 'pure religion,' or in other words of those modes of feeling which constitute natural religion. The ecclesiastical belief is necessary, because most men are unable to accept a purely moral belief unless it is as it were materialised and embodied by grosser conceptions. But the ecclesiastical belief being entirely subordinate to pure religion, it followed that it should be interpreted simply with a view to the latter—that is to say, all doctrines and all passages of Scripture should be regarded as intended to convey some moral lesson, and no interpretation, however natural, should be accepted as correct which collides with our sense of right.

The statement of this doctrine of Kant may remind the reader that in tracing the laws of the religious development of societies I have hitherto dwelt only on one aspect of the subject. I have examined several important intellectual agencies which have effected intellectual changes, but have as yet altogether omitted the laws of moral development. In endeavouring to supply this omission, we are at first met by a school which admits, indeed, that the true essence of all religion is moral, but at the same time denies that there can be in this respect any principle of progress. Nothing, it is said, is so immutable as morals. The difference between right and wrong was always known, and on this subject our conceptions can never be enlarged. But if by the term moral be included not simply the broad difference between acts which are positively virtuous and those which are positively vicious, but also the prevailing ideal or standard of excellence, it is quite certain that morals exhibit as constant a development as intellect, and it is probable that this development has exercised as important an influence upon society. It is one of the most familiar facts that there are certain virtues that are higher than others, and that many of these belong exclusively to a highly developed civilisation.[1] Thus, that the love of truth is a virtue is a proposition which, stated simply, would have been probably accepted with equal alacrity in any age; but if we examine the extent to which it is realised, we find a profound difference. We find that in an early period, while all the virtues of an uncompromising partisan are cordially recognised, the higher virtue, which binds men through a love of conscientious enquiry to endeavour to pursue an eclectic course when party and sectarian passions rage fiercely around them, is not only entirely unappreciated, but is almost impossible; that it is even now only recognised by a very few who occupy the eminences of thought; and that it must therefore be recognised by the multitude in proportion as they approach the condition of those few. Thus, the pursuit of virtue for its own sake is undoubtedly a higher excellence than the pursuit of virtue for the sake of attaining reward or avoiding punishment; yet the notion of disinterested virtue belongs almost exclusively to the higher ranks of the most civilised ages, and exactly in proportion as we descend the intellectual scale is it necessary to elaborate the system of rewards and punishments.

Humanity again, in theory, appears to be an unchangeable virtue; but if we examine its applications, we find it constantly changing. Bull-baiting, and bear-baiting, and cock-fighting, and countless amusements of a similar kind, were once the favourite pastimes of Europe, were pursued by all classes, even the most refined and the most humane, and were universally regarded as perfectly legitimate.[2] Men of

[1] This has been well noticed by Archbishop Whately—I think in his *Annotations to Bacon.*

[2] For a full view of the extent to which these amusements were carried on

the most distinguished excellence are known to have de
lighted in them. Had anyone challenged them as barbarous,
his sentiments would have been regarded not simply as
absurd but as incomprehensible. There was, no doubt, no
controversy upon the subject.[1] Gradually, however, by the
silent pressure of civilisation, a profound change passed over

and diversified in England, see Strutt's *Sports and Pastimes of the English
People.* Sir Thomas More was accustomed to boast of his skill in throwing
the 'cock stele;' and, to the very last, bull-baiting was defended warmly by
Canning, and with an almost passionate earnestness by Windham.

[1] As Macaulay, with characteristic antithesis, says: 'If the Puritans suppressed bull-baiting, it was not because it gave pain to the bull, but because it
gave pleasure to the spectators.' The long unsuccessful warfare waged by the
Popes against Spanish bull-fighting forms a very curious episode in ecclesiastical history; but its origin is to be found in the number of men who had been
killed. An old theologian mentions that, in the town of Concha, a bull that
had killed seven men became the object of the highest reverence, and the
people were so gratified that a painting representing the achievement was
immediately executed for the public square (Concina, *De Spectaculis,* p. 283).
The writers who denounced Spanish bull-fighting contrasted it specially with
that of Italy, in which the bull was bound by a rope, and which was therefore
innocent (*Ibid.* p. 285).   Bull-fighting was prohibited under pain of excommunication by Pius V., in 1567. In 1575 Gregory XIII. removed the prohibition except as regards ecclesiastics, who were still forbidden to frequent bull-
fights, and as regards festal days, on which they were not to be celebrated.
Some Spanish theologians having agitated much on this subject, Sixtus V., in
1586, confirmed the preceding bull. At last, in 1596, Clement VIII., moved
by the remonstrance of the Spanish king and the discontent of the Spanish
people, removed all prohibitions (in Spain) except those which rested on the
monks, only enjoining caution. At present bull-fights are usually performed
on festal days, and form part of most great religious festivals, especially those
in honour of the Virgin! On this curious subject full details are given in
Thesauro, *De Pœnis Ecclesiasticis* (Romæ, 1640), and in Concina, *De Spectaculis* (Romæ, 1752). Among the Spanish opponents of bull-fighting was the
great Jesuit Mariana. It is curious enough that perhaps the most sanguinary
of all bull-fights was in the Coliseum of Rome, in 1333, when the Roman
nobles descended into the arena and eighteen were killed (Cibrario, *Economia
Politica,* vol. i. pp. 196, 197); but the Pope was then at Avignon. Michelet
has noticed that while bull-fighting was long extremely popular in Rome, the
Romagna, and Spoleto, it never took root in Naples, notwithstanding the long
domination of the Spaniards.

public opinion. It was effected, not by any increase of knowledge, or by any process of definite reasoning, but simply by the gradual elevation of the moral standard. Amusements that were once universal passed from the women to the men, from the upper to the lower classes, from the virtuous to the vicious, till at last the Legislature interposed to suppress them, and a thrill of indignation is felt whenever it is discovered that any of them have been practised. The history of the abolition of torture, the history of punishments, the history of the treatment of the conquered in war, the history of slavery—all present us with examples of practices which in one age were accepted as perfectly right and natural, and which in another age were repudiated as palpably and atrociously inhuman. In each case the change was effected much less by any intellectual process than by a certain quickening of the emotions, and consequently of the moral judgments; and if in any country we find practices at all resembling those which existed in England a century ago, we infer with certainty that that country has not received the full amount of civilisation. The code of honour which first represents and afterwards reacts upon the moral standard of each age is profoundly different. The whole type of virtue in a rude warlike people is distinct from that of a refined and peaceful people, and the character which the latter would admire the former would despise. So true is this, that each successive stratum of civilisation brings with it a distinctive variation of the moral type. In the words of one of the very greatest historians of the nineteenth century, 'If the archæologist can determine the date of a monument by the form of its capital, with much greater certainty can the psychological historian assign to a specific period a moral fact, a predominating passion, or a mode of thought, and can

pronounce it to have been impossible in the ages that pre
ceded or that followed. In the chronology of art the same
forms have sometimes been reproduced, but in the moral life
such a recurrence is impossible: its conceptions are fixed in
their eternal place in the fatality of time. [1]

There is, however, one striking exception to this law in
the occasional appearance of a phenomenon which may be
termed moral genius. There arise from time to time men
who bear to the moral condition of their age much the same
relations as men of genius bear to its intellectual condition.
They anticipate the moral standard of a later age, cast abroad
conceptions of disinterested virtue, of philanthropy, or of
self-denial that seem to have no relation to the spirit of their
time, inculcate duties and suggest motives of action that
appear to most men altogether chimerical. Yet the magnetism of their perfections tells powerfully upon their contemporaries. An enthusiasm is kindled, a group of adherents is
formed, and many are emancipated from the moral condition
of their age. Yet the full effects of such a movement are
but transient. The first enthusiasm dies away, surrounding
circumstances resume their ascendency, the pure faith is
materialised, encrusted with conceptions that are alien to its
nature, dislocated, and distorted, till its first features have
almost disappeared. The moral teaching, being unsuited to
the time, becomes inoperative until its appropriate civilisation
has dawned; or at most it faintly and imperfectly filters
through an accumulation of dogmas, and thus accelerates in
some measure the arrival of the condition it requires.

From the foregoing considerations it is not difficult to
infer the relations of dogmatic systems to moral principles.
In a semi-barbarous period, when the moral faculty or the

sense of right is far too weak to be a guide of conduct, dogmatic systems interpose and supply men with motives of action that are suited to their condition, and are sufficient to sustain among them a rectitude of conduct that would otherwise be unknown. But the formation of a moral philosophy is usually the first step of the decadence of religions. Theology, then ceasing to be the groundwork of morals, sinks into a secondary position, and the main source of its power is destroyed. In the religions of Greece and Rome this separation between the two parts of religious systems was carried so far, that the inculcation of morality at last devolved avowedly and exclusively upon the philosophers, while the priests were wholly occupied with soothsaying and expiations.

In the next place, any historical faith, as it is interpreted by fallible men, will contain some legends or doctrines that are contrary to our sense of right. For our highest conception of the Deity is moral excellence, and consequently men always embody their standard of perfection in their religious doctrines; and as that standard is at first extremely imperfect and confused, the early doctrines will exhibit a corresponding imperfection. These doctrines being stereotyped in received formularies for a time seriously obstruct the moral development of society, but at last the opposition to them becomes so strong that they must give way: they are then either violently subverted or permitted to become gradually obsolete.

There is but one example of a religion which is not naturally weakened by civilisation, and that example is Christianity. In all other cases the decay of dogmatic conceptions is tantamount to a complete annihilation of religion; for although there may be imperishable elements of moral truth mingled with those conceptions, they have nothing

distinctive or peculiar.   The moral truths coalesce with new
systems, the men who uttered them take their place with
many others in the great pantheon of history, and the religion having discharged its functions is spent and withered.
But the great characteristic of Christianity, and the great moral
proof of its divinity, is that it has been the main source of
the moral development of Europe, and that it has discharged
this office not so much by the inculcation of a system of
ethics, however pure, as by the assimilating and attractive
influence of a perfect ideal.   The moral progress of mankind
can never cease to be distinctively and intensely Christian as
long as it consists of a gradual approximation to the character
of the Christian Founder.   There is, indeed, nothing more
wonderful in the history of the human race than the way in
which that ideal has traversed the lapse of ages, acquiring a
new strength and beauty with each advance of civilisation,
and infusing its beneficent influence into every sphere of
thought and action.   At first men sought to grasp by minute
dogmatic definitions the divinity they felt.   The controversies of the Homoousians or Monophysites or Nestorians or
Patripassians, and many others whose very names now
sound strange and remote, then filled the Church.   Then
came the period of visible representations.   The handkerchief of Veronica, the portrait of Edessa, the crucifix of
Nicodemus, the paintings of St. Luke,' the image traced by
an angel's hand which is still venerated at the Lateran, the

As Lami and Lanzi have shown, this legend probably resulted from a
confusion of names; a Florentine monk, named Luca, of the eleventh century,
being, there is much reason to believe, the chief author of the 'portraits by St.
Luke.'   They are not, however, all by the same hand, or of exactly the same
age, though evidently copied from the same type.   Others think they are
Byzantine pictures brought to Italy during the time of the Iconoclasts and of
the Crusades

countless visions narrated by the saints, show the eagerness with which men sought to realise as a palpable and living image their ideal. This age was followed by that of historical evidences, the age of Sebonde and his followers. Yet more and more with advancing years the moral idea stood out from all dogmatic conceptions; its divinity was recognised by its perfection; and it is no exaggeration to say, that at no former period was it so powerful or so universally acknowledged as at present. This is a phenomenon altogether unique in history; and to those who recognise in the highest type of excellence the highest revelation of the Deity, its importance is too manifest to be overlooked.

I trust the reader will pardon the tedious length to which this examination, which I would gladly have abridged, has extended. For the history of rationalism is quite as much a history of moral as of intellectual development, and any conception of it that ignores the former must necessarily be mutilated and false. Nothing, too, can, as I conceive, be more erroneous or superficial than the reasonings of those who maintain that the moral element of Christianity has in it nothing distinctive or peculiar. The method of this school, of which Bolingbroke may be regarded as the type, is to collect from the writings of different heathen writers certain isolated passages embodying precepts that are inculcated by Christianity; and when the collection had become very large, the task was supposed to be accomplished. But the true originality of a system of moral teaching depends not so much upon the elements of which it is composed, as upon the manner in which they are fused into a symmetrical whole, upon the proportionate value that is attached to different qualities, or, to state the same thing by a single word, upon the type of character that is formed. Now it is quite certain that the Christian type differs not only in degree, but in kind, from the Pagan one.

In applying the foregoing principles to the history of Christian transformations, we should naturally expect three distinct classes of change. The first is the gradual evanescence of doctrines that collide with our moral sense. The second is the decline of the influence of those ceremonies, or purely speculative doctrines, which, without being opposed to conscience, are at least wholly beyond its sphere. The third is the substitution of the sense of right for the fear of punishment as the main motive to virtue.

I reserve the consideration of the first of these three changes for the ensuing chapter, in which I shall examine the causes of religious persecution, and shall endeavour to trace the history of a long series of moral anomalies in speculation which prepared the way for that great moral anomaly in practice. The second change is so evident, that it is not necessary to dwell upon it. No candid person who is acquainted with history can fail to perceive the difference between the amount of reverence bestowed in the present day, by the great majority of men, upon mere speculative doctrines or ritualistic observances, and that which was once general. If we examine the Church in the fourth and fifth centuries, we find it almost exclusively occupied with minute questions concerning the manner of the co-existence of the two natures in Christ. If we examine it in the middle ages, we find it absorbed in ritualism and pilgrimages. If we examine it at the Reformation, we find it just emerging beneath the pressure of civilisation from this condition; yet still the main speculative test was the doctrine concerning the Sacrament, which had no relation to morals; and the main practical test on the

Continent, at least, was the eating of meat ȯn Fridays.¹ In the present day, with the great body of laymen at least, such matters appear simply puerile, because they have no relation to morals.

The third change is one which requires more attention, for it involves the history of religious terrorism—a history of the deepest but most painful interest to all who study the intellectual and moral development of Europe.

It would be difficult, and perhaps not altogether desira· ble, to attain in the present day to any realised conception of the doctrine of future punishment as it was taught by the early Fathers, and elaborated and developed by the mediæval priests. That doctrine has now been thrown so much into the background, it has been so modified and softened and explained away, that it scarcely retains a shadow of its an-

¹ In France especially the persecution on this ground was frightful. Thus, Bodin tell us that in 1539 the magistrates of Angers burnt alive those who were proved to have eaten meat on Friday if they remained impenitent, and hung them if they repented. (*Demon. des Sorciers*, p. 216.) In England the subject was regarded in a very peculiar light. Partly because Anglicanism clung closely to the Fathers, and partly because England was a maritime country, fasting was not only encouraged, but strictly enjoined ; and a long series of laws and proclamations were accordingly issued between 1548 and the Restoration enjoining abstinence on Wednesdays and Fridays, and throughout Lent; 'considering that due and godly abstinence is a mean to virtue, and to subdue men's bodies of their souls and spirits; and considering, also, *especially* that fishers, and men using the trade of fishing in the sea, may thereby the rather be set on work.' See a list of these laws in Hallam's *Const. Hist.* vol. i. A homily also enjoins fasting on the same complex ground. There are some very good remarks on the tendency of theologians to condemn more severely error than immorality, and in condemning different errors to dwell most severely on those which are purely speculative, in Bayle, *Pensées Diverses*, cxcix. He says: 'Si un docteur de Sorbonne avoit la hardiesse de chanceler tant soit peu sur le mystère de l'Incarnation, . . . il couroit risque du feu ie la Grève; mais s'il se contentoit d'avancer quelques propositions de morale relâchée, comme le fameux Escobar, on se contenteroit de dire que cela n'est pas bien, et peut-être on verroit la censure de son livre.'

cient repulsiveness. It is sufficient to say, that it was generally maintained that eternal damnation was the lot which
the Almighty had reserved for an immense proportion of his
creatures; and that that damnation consisted not simply of
the privation of certain extraordinary blessings, but also of the
endurance of the most excruciating agonies. Perhaps the most
acute pain the human body can undergo is that of fire; and
this, the early Fathers assure us, is the eternal destiny of the
mass of mankind. The doctrine was stated with the utmost
literalism and precision. In the two first apologies for the
Christian faith it was distinctly asserted. Philosophy, it was
said, had sometimes enabled men to look with contempt upon
torments, as upon a transient evil; but Christianity presented
a prospect before which the stoutest heart must quail, for its
punishments were as eternal as they were excruciating.[1]   Origen, it is true, and his disciple Gregory of Nyssa, in a somewhat hesitating manner, diverged from the prevailing opinion,
and strongly inclined to a figurative interpretation, and to
the belief in the ultimate salvation of all;[2] but they were alone
in their opinion. With these two exceptions, all the Fathers
proclaimed the eternity of torments, and all defined those torments as the action of a literal fire upon a sensitive body.[3]

---

[1] 'Sic et Epicurus omnem cruciatum doloremque depretiat modicum quidem contemptibilem pronuntiando magnum vero non diuturnum. Enimvero
nos qui sub Deo omnium speculatore dispungimur, quique æternam ab eo
pœnam providemus merito soli innocentiæ occurrimus et pro scientiæ plenitu
dine et pro magnitudine cruciatus non diuturni verum sempiterni.' (Tertullian,
Apol., cap. xlv.)

[2] The opinions of this last Father on the subject, which are very little
known, are clearly stated in that learned book, Dallæus, *De Pœnis et Satisfactionibus* (Amsterdam, 1649), lib. iv. c. 7.   For Origen's well-known opinions, see *Ibid.* lib. iv. c. 6.

[3] A long chain of quotations establishing this will be found in Swinden,
On the Fire of Hell (London, 1727); and in Horberry's *Enquiry concerning
Future Punishment* (London, 1744).

When the pagans argued that a body could not remain for ever unconsumed in a material flame, they were answered by the analogies of the salamander, the asbestus, and the volcano; and by appeals to the Divine Omnipotence, which was supposed to be continually exerted to prolong the tortures of the dead.[1]

We may be quite sure that neither in the early Church, nor in any other period, was this doctrine universally realised. There must have been thousands who, believing, or at least professing, that there was no salvation except in the Church, and that to be excluded from salvation meant to be precipitated into an abyss of flames, looked back nevertheless to the memory of a pagan mother, who had passed away, if not with a feeling of vague hope, at least without the poignancy of despair. There must have been thousands who, though they would perhaps have admitted with a Father that the noblest actions of the heathen were but 'splendid vices,' read nevertheless the pages of the great historians of their country with emotions that were very little in conformity with such a theory. Nor, it may be added, were these persons those whose moral perceptions had been least developed by contemplating the gentle and tolerant character of the Christian Founder. Yet still the doctrine was stamped upon the theology of the age, and though it had not yet been introduced into art, it was realised to a

[1] See the long argument based on these grounds in St. Aug. *De Civ. Dei,* lib. xxi. cc. 1–9. Minutius Felix treats the same subject in a somewhat ferocious passage: 'Ipse rex Jupiter per torrentes ripas et atram voraginem jurat religiose: destinatam enim sibi cum suis cultoribus poenam praescius perhorrescit: nec tormentis aut modus ullus aut terminus. Illic sapiens ignis membra urit et reficit: carpit et nutrit sicut ignes fulminum corpora tangunt nec absumunt: sicut ignes Ætnæ et Vesuvii et ardentium ubique terrarum flagrant nec erogantur: ita poenale illud incendium non damnis ardentium pascitur sed inexesa corporum laceratione nutritur.' (*Octavius,* cap. xxxv.)

degree which we at least can never reproduce; for it was taught in the midst of persecution and conflict, and it flashed upon the mind with all the vividness of novelty. Judaism had had nothing like it. It seems now to be generally admitted that the doctrine of a future life, which is often spoken of as a central conception of religion, was not included in the Levitical revelation, or at least was so faintly intimated that the people were unable to perceive it.[1] During the captivity, indeed, the Jews obtained from their masters some notions on the subject, but even these were very vague; and the Sadducees, who rejected the new doctrine as an innovation, were entirely uncondemned. Indeed, it is probable that the chosen people had less clear and correct knowledge of a future world than any other tolerably civilised nation of antiquity. Among the early popular traditions of the pagans, there were, it is true, some faint traces of a doctrine of hell, which are said to have been elaborated by Pythagoras,[2] and especially by Plato, who did more then any other ancient philosopher to develop the notion of expiation;[3] but

---

[1] This fact had been noticed by several early English divines (Barrow and Berkeley among the number); but it was brought into especial relief by Warburton, who, as is well known, in his *Divine Legation*, based a curious argument in favour of the divine origin of the Levitical religion upon the fact that it contained no revelation of a future world. Archbishop Whately, who strongly took up the view of Warburton concerning the fact, has, in one of his *Essays on the Peculiarities of the Christian Religion*, applied it very skilfully to establishing the divine origin, not indeed of Judaism, but of Christianity, because Christianity does contain a revelation of the future world. Both these writers contend that the well-known passage in Job does not refer to the resurrection. The subject has been dwelt on from another point of view by Chubb, Voltaire, Strauss, and several other writers. On the growth of the doctrine among the Jews, see Mackay's *Religious Development of the Greeks and Hebrews*, vol. ii. pp. 286–297.

[2] Denis, *Histoire des Idées Morales dans l'Antiquité*, tom. i. pp. 18, 19.

[3] *Ibid.* pp. 104–106.

these, at the period of the rise of Christianity, had little or
no influence upon the minds of men; nor had they ever pre
sented the same characteristics as the doctrine of the Church.
For among the pagans future torture was supposed to be
reserved exclusively for guilt, and for guilt of the most
extreme and exceptional character. It was such culprits as
Tantalus, or Sisyphus, or Ixion, that were selected as examples, and, excepting in the mysteries,[1] the subject never
seems to have been brought very prominently forward. It
was the distinctive doctrine of the Christian theologians, that
sufferings more excruciating than any the imagination could
conceive were reserved for millions, and might be the lot of
the most benevolent and heroic of mankind. That religious
error was itself the worst of crimes, was before the Reformation the universal teaching of the Christian Church. Can
we wonder that there were some who refused to regard it as
an Evangel?

If we pursue this painful subject into the middle ages, we
find the conception of punishment by literal fire elaborated
with more detail. The doctrine, too, of a purgatory even for
the saved had grown up. Without examining at length the
origin of this last tenet, it may be sufficient to say that it
was a natural continuation of the doctrine of penance; that
the pagan poets had had a somewhat similar conception,
which Virgil introduced into his famous description of the
regions of the dead; that the Manichæans looked forward to
a strange process of purification after death;[2] and that some

[1] On the place representations of Tartarus had in the mysteries, see Ma-
guin, *Origines du Théâtre*, tom. i. pp. 81–84.

[2] The Manichæans are said to have believed that the souls of the dead were
purified in the sun; that they were then borne in the moon to the angels; and
that the phases of the moon were caused by the increase or diminution of the
freight. (Beausobre, *Hist. Critique du Manichéisme*, tom. i. pp. 243, 244.)

of the Fathers appear to have held that at the day of judgment all men must pass through a fire, though apparently
rather for trial than for purification, as the virtuous and
orthodox were to pass unscathed, while bad people and people with erroneous theological opinions were to be burnt.
Besides this, the doctrine perhaps softened a little the terror
ism of eternal punishment, by diminishing the number of
those who were to endure it; though, on the other hand, it
represented extreme suffering as reserved for almost all men
after death.   It may be added, that its financial advantages
are obvious and undeniable.

There was in the tenth century one striking example of a
theologian following in the traces of Origen, and, as far as I
know, alone in the middle ages, maintaining the figurative
interpretation of the fire of hell.   This was John Scotus
Erigena, a very remarkable man, who, as his name imports,[2]
and as his contemporaries inform us, was an Irishman, and
who appears to have led, for the most part, that life of a wandering scholar for which his countrymen have always been
famous.   His keen wit, his great and varied genius, and his
knowledge of Greek, soon gained him an immense reputation.
This last acquirement was then extremely rare, but it had
been kept up in the Irish monasteries some time after it had
disappeared from the other seminaries of Europe.   Scotus

---

[1] Dallæus, *De Pœnis et Satisfactionibus*, lib. iv. c. 9.   Some of the ancients
had a notion about fire being the portal of the unseen world.   Herodotus (lib.
v. c. 92) tells a curious story about Periander, a tyrant of Corinth, who invoked the shade of his wife; but she refused to answer his questions, alleging
that she was too cold; for though dresses had been placed in her tomb, they
were of no use to her, as they had not been burnt.

[2] Scoti was at first the name of the Irish; it was afterwards shared and
finally monopolised by the inhabitants of Scotland.   Erigena means, born in
Erin—the distinctive name of Ireland.   There is an amusing notice of Scotus
Erigena in Matthew of Westminster (An. 880).

threw himself with such ardour into both of the great systems of Greek philosophy, that some have regarded him
principally as the last representative of Neoplatonism, and
others as the founder of Scholasticism.[1] He displayed on all
questions a singular disdain for authority, and a spirit of the
boldest free thought, which, like Origen, with whose works
he was probably much imbued, he defended by a lavish employment of allegories.   Among the doctrines he disbelieved,
and therefore treated as allegorical, was that of the fire of hell.[2]

Scotus, however, was not of his age.   The material conceptions of mediævalism harmonised admirably with the material doctrine; and after the religious terrorism that followed the twelfth century, that doctrine attained its full elabo-
ration.   The agonies of hell seemed then the central fact of
religion, and the perpetual subject of the thoughts of men.
The whole intellect of Europe was employed in illustrating
them.   All literature, all painting, all eloquence, was concentrated upon the same dreadful theme.   By the pen of Dante
and by the pencil of Orcagna, by the pictures that crowded
every church, and the sermons that rang from every pulpit,
the maddening terror was sustained.   The saint was often permitted in visions to behold the agonies of the lost, and to re-
count the spectacle he had witnessed.   He loved to tell how by
the lurid glare of the eternal flames he had seen millions writhing in every form of ghastly suffering, their eyeballs roll-
ing with unspeakable anguish, their limbs gashed and muti-

---

[1] He is regarded in the first light by M. Guizot in his *History of Civilisation;* and in the second by M. St. René Taillandier, in his able and learned
treatise on Scotus.
[2] On the doctrines of Scotus, and especially on that about hell, see Taillandier, *Scot Erigène*, pp. 176-180 ; Ampère, *Hist. Littéraire de la France*,
tom. iii. p. 95 ; Alexandri, *Hist. Eccles.*, tom. vi. pp. 361-363.   According to
this last writer, Scotus admitted literal torments for the devil, but not for man.

lated and quivering with pain, tortured by pangs that seemed ever keener by the recurrence, and shrieking in vain for mercy to an unpitying heaven. Hideous beings of dreadful aspect and of fantastic forms hovered around, mocking them amid their torments, casting them into cauldrons of boiling brimstone, or inventing new tortures more subtle and more refined. Amid all this a sulphur stream was ever seething, feeding and intensifying the waves of fire. There was no respite, no alleviation, no hope. The tortures were ever varied in their character, and they never palled for a moment upon the sense. Sometimes, it was said, the flames while retaining their intensity withheld their light. A shroud of darkness covered the scene, but a ceaseless shriek of anguish attested the agonies that were below.

It is useless to follow the subject into detail. We may reproduce the ghastly imagery that is accumulated in the sermons and in the legends of the age. We may estimate the untiring assiduity with which the Catholic priests sought in the worst acts of human tyranny, and in the dark recesses of their own imaginations, new forms of torture, to ascribe them to the Creator. We can never conceive the intense vividness with which these conceptions were realised, or the madness and the misery they produced. For those were ages of implicit and unfaltering credulity; they were ages when none of the distractions of the present day divided the intellect, and when theology was the single focus upon which the imagination was concentrated. They were ages, too, when the modern tendency to soften or avoid repulsive im-

---

* The details of many of these visions are given in their full force in Swinden; and in Plancy, *Dictionnaire Infernale*, art. *Enfer*. Dean Milman, in his *Hist. of Latin Christianity*, has noticed this passion for detailed pictures of hell (which seems to date from St. Gregory the Great) with his usual force and justice.

ages was altogether unknown, and when, in the general paralysis of the reason, every influence was exerted to stimulate
the imagination.   Wherever the worshipper turned, he was
met by new forms of torture, elaborated with such minute
detail, and enforced with such a vigour and distinctness, that
they must have clung for ever to the mind, and chilled every
natural impulse towards the Creator.   How, indeed, could it
be otherwise ?   Men were told that the Almighty, by the
fiat of his uncontrolled power, had called into being countless millions whom He knew to be destined to eternal, excruciating, unspeakable agony ; that He had placed millions in
such a position that such agony was inevitable; that He had
prepared their place of torment, and had kindled its undying
flame ; and that, prolonging their lives for ever, in order that
they might be for ever wretched, He would make the contemplation of those sufferings an essential element of the
happiness of the redeemed.[1]   No other religious teachers had
ever proclaimed such tenets, and as long as they were realised intensely, the benevolent precepts and the mild and
gentle ideal of the New Testament could not possibly be influential.   The two things were hopelessly incongruous.
The sense of the Divine goodness being destroyed, the whole
fabric of natural religion crumbled in the dust.   From that
time religion was necessarily diverted from the moral to the
dogmatic, and became an artificial thing of relics and ceremonies, of credulity and persecution, of asceticism and terrorism.   It centred entirely upon the priests, who supported it
mainly by intimidation.

I have already, when examining the phenomena of witch

---

[1] St. Thomas Aquinas says, 'Beati in regno cœlesti videbunt pœnas damna
torum, UT BEATITUDO ILLIS MAGIS COMPLACEAT.' (*Summa Suppl.*, quæs⁹. xciv
art. 1.)

craft, noticed the influence of this doctrine upon the imagination, which it has probably done more to disease than almost
all other moral and intellectual agencies combined. I shall
hereafter touch upon its effects upon the intellectual history
of Europe—upon the timidity and disingenuousness of enquiry, the distrust and even hatred of intellectual honesty,
it encouraged. There is, however, a still more painful effect
to be noticed. That the constant contemplation of suffering,
especially when that contemplation is devoid of passion, has
a tendency to blunt the affections, and thus destroy the emotional part of humanity, is one of the most familiar facts of
common observation. The law holds good even in men, like
surgical operators, who contemplate pain solely for the benefit of others. The first repulsion is soon exchanged for indifference, the indifference speedily becomes interest, and the
interest is occasionally heightened to positive enjoyment.
Hence the anecdotes related of surgeons who have derived
the most exquisite pleasure from the operations of their profession, and of persons who, being unable to suppress a morbid delight in the contemplation of suffering, have determined to utilise their defect, and have become the most
unflinching operators in the hospitals. Now it is sufficiently
manifest that upon this emotional part of humanity depends
by far the greater number of kind acts that are done in the
world, and especially the prevailing ideal and standard of
humanity. There are, no doubt, persons who are exceedingly
benevolent through a sense of duty, while their temperament
remains entirely callous. There are even cases in which the
callousness of temperament increases in proportion to the
active benevolence, for it is acquired in contemplating suffering for the purpose of relieving it, and, as Bishop Butler re-
minds us, 'active habits are strengthened, while passive im-

pressions are weakened, by repetition.' But the overwhelming majority are in these matters governed by their emotions. Their standard and their acts depend upon the liveliness of their feelings. If this be so, it is easy to conceive what must have been the result of the contemplations of mediævalism. There is a fresco in the great monastery of Pavia which might be regarded as the emblem of the age. It represents a monk with clasped hands, and an expression of agonising terror upon his countenance, straining over the valley of vision where the sufferings of the lost were displayed, while the inscription above reveals his one harrowing thought, ' Quis sustinebit ne descendam moriens ? '

In such a state of thought, we should naturally expect that the direct and powerful tendency of this doctrine would be to produce a general indifference to human sufferings, or even a bias towards acts of barbarity. Yet this only gives an inadequate conception of its effects. For not only were men constantly expatiating on these ghastly pictures, they were also constantly associating them with gratitude and with joy. They believed that the truth of Christianity implied the eternal torture of a vast proportion of their fellow-creatures, and they believed that it would be a gross impiety to wish that Christianity was untrue. They had collected with such assiduity, and had interpreted with such a revolting literalism, every rhetorical passage in the Bible that could be associated with their doctrine, that they had firmly persuaded themselves that a material and eternal fire formed a central truth of their faith, and that, in the words of an Anglican clergyman, ' the hell described in the Gospel is not with the same particularity to be met with in any other religion that is or hath been in the whole world.' [1] Habitually

[1] Swinden, p. 129.

treating the language of parable as if it was the language of history, they came to regard it as very truly their ideal of happiness, to rest for ever on Abraham's bosom, and to contemplate for ever the torments of their brother in hell. They felt with St. Augustine that 'the end of religion is to become like the object of worship,' and they represented the Deity as confining his affection to a small section of his creatures, and inflicting on all others the most horrible and eternal suffering.

Now it is undoubtedly true, that when doctrines of this kind are intensely realised, they will prove most efficacious in dispelling the apathy on religious subjects which is the common condition of mankind. They will produce great earnestness, great self-sacrifice, great singleness of purpose. Loyola, who had studied with profound sagacity the springs of enthusiasm, assigned in his spiritual exercises an entire day to be spent in meditating upon eternal damnation, and in most great religious revivals the doctrine has occupied a prominent place. It is also undoubtedly true, that in a few splendid instances the effect of this realisation has been to raise up missionary teachers of such heroic and disinterested zeal, that their lives are among the grandest pages in the whole range of biography. But although this may be its effect upon some singularly noble natures, there can be little question that in the vast majority of cases its tendency will be to indurate the character, to diffuse abroad a callousness and insensibility to the suffering of others that will profoundly debase humanity. If you make the detailed and exquisite torments of multitudes the habitual object of the thoughts and imaginations of men, you will necessarily produce in most of them a gradual indifference to human suffering, and in some of them a disposition to regard it with

positive delight. If you further assure men that these sufferings form an integral part of a revelation which they are
bound to regard as a message of good tidings, you will induce them to stifle every feeling of pity, and almost to encourage their insensibility as a virtue. If you end your
teaching by telling them that the Being who is the ideal of
their lives confines His affection to the members of a single
Church, that He will torture for ever all who are not found
within its pale, and that His children will for ever contemplate those tortures in a state of unalloyed felicity, you will
prepare the way for every form of persecution that can be
directed against those who are without. He who most fully
realised these doctrines, would be the most unhappy or the
most unfeeling of mankind. No possible prospect of individual bliss could reconcile a truly humane man, who followed
the impulse of his humanity, to the thought that those who
were external to his faith were destined to eternal fire.   No
truly humane man could avoid wishing, that rather than this
should be the case, he and all others should sleep the sleep of
annihilation.   When the doctrine was intensely realised and
implicitly believed, it must, therefore, have had one or other
of two effects. It must have produced an intensity of compassion that would involve an extreme unhappiness and
would stimulate to extreme heroism, or it must have produced an absolute callousness and a positive inclination to
inflict suffering upon the heretic. It does not require much
knowledge of human nature to perceive that the spirit of
Torquemada must be more common than that of Xavier.

That this was actually the case must be evident to any
one who is not wilfully blind to the history of Christendom.
I have mentioned that writer who in the second century
dilated most emphatically on the doctrine of eternal punish-

ment by fire as a means of intimidation. In another of his works he showed very clearly the influence it exercised upon his own character. He had written a treatise dissuading the Christians of his day from frequenting the public spectacles. He had collected on the subject many arguments, some of them very powerful, and others extremely grotesque; but he perceived that to make his exhortations forcible to the majority of his readers, he must point them to some counter-attraction. He accordingly proceeded—and his style assumed a richer glow and a more impetuous eloquence as he rose to the congenial theme—to tell them that a spectacle was reserved for them, so fascinating and so attractive that the most joyous festivals of earth faded into insignificance by the comparison. That spectacle was the agonies of their fellow-countrymen, as they writhe amid the torments of hell. 'What,' he exclaimed, 'shall be the magnitude of that scene! How shall I wonder! How shall I laugh! How shall I rejoice! How shall I triumph when I behold so many and such illustrious kings, who were said to have mounted into heaven, groaning with Jupiter their god in the lowest darkness of hell! Then shall the soldiers who had persecuted the name of Christ burn in more cruel fire than any they had kindled for the saints. . . . Then shall the tragedians pour forth in their own misfortune more piteous cries than those with which they had made the theatre to resound, while the comedian's powers shall be better seen as he becomes more flexible by the heat. Then shall the driver of the circus stand forth to view all blushing in his flaming chariot, and the gladiators pierced, not by spears, but by darts of fire. . . . Compared with such spectacles, with such subjects of triumph as these, what can prætor or consul, quæstor or pontiff, afford ? And even now faith can bring them near, imagination can depict them as present.'[1]

I have quoted this very painful passage not so much as an instance of the excesses of a morbid disposition embittered by persecution, as because it furnishes a striking illustration of the influence of a certain class of realisations on the affections. For in tracing what may be called the psychological history of Europe, we are constantly met by a great contradiction, which can only be explained by such considerations. By the confession of all parties, the Christian religion was designed to be a religion of philanthropy, and love was represented as the distinctive test or characteristic of its true members. As a matter of fact, it has probably done more to quicken the affections of mankind, to promote pity, to create a pure and merciful ideal, than any

---

[1] 'Quæ tunc spectaculi latitudo ! Quid admirer ! Quid rideam ! ubi gaudeam ! ubi exultem, spectans tot et tantos reges, qui in cœlum recepti nuntiadantur, cum ipso Jove et ipsis suis testibus in imis tenebris congemescentes ! Item præsides persecutores dominici nominis sævioribus quam ipsi flammis sævierunt insultantibus contra Christianos liquescentes ! quos præterea sapientes illos philosophos coram discipulis suis una conflagrationibus erubescentes, quibus nihil ad Deum pertinere suadebant, quibus animas aut nullas aut non in pristina corpora redituras affirmabant ! Etiam poetas non ad Rhadamanti nec ad Minois, sed ad inopinati Christi tribunal palpitantes. Tunc magis tragœdi audiendi magis scilicet vocales in sua propria calamitate. Tunc histriones cognoscendi solutiores multo per ignem. Tunc spectandus auriga in flammea rota totus rubens ; tunc xystici contemplandi non in gymnasiis sed in igne jaculati ; nisi quod ne tunc quidem illos velim visos, ut qui malim ad eos potius conspectum insatiabilem conferre qui in dominum desævierunt. Hic est ille dicam fabri aut quæstuariæ filius, sabbati destructor, Samarites et dæmonium habens. Hic est quem a Juda redemistis, hic est ille arundine et colaphis diverberatus, sputamentis dedecoratus, felle et aceto potatus. Hic est quem clam discentes subripuerunt ut resurrexisse dicatur, vel hortulanus detraxit ne lactucæ suæ frequentia commeantium læderentur. Ut talia spectes, ut talibus exultes quis tibi prætor, aut consul, aut quæstor, aut sacerdos de suâ .iberalitate præstabit ? Et tamen hæc jam quodammodo habemus per fidem spiritu imaginante repræsentata.' (Tertullian, *De Spectac.*, cap xxx.)

other influence that has ever acted on the world. But while the marvellous influence of Christianity in this respect has been acknowledged by all who have mastered the teachings of history, while the religious minds of every land and of every opinion have recognised in its Founder the highest conceivable ideal and embodiment of compassion as of purity, it is a no less incontestable truth that for many centuries the Christian priesthood pursued a policy, at least towards those who differed from their opinions, implying a callousness and absence of the emotional part of humanity which has seldom been paralleled, and perhaps never surpassed. From Julian, who observed that no wild beasts were so ferocious as angry theologians, to Montesquieu, who discussed as a psychological phenomenon the inhumanity of monks, the fact has been constantly recognised. The monks, the Inquisitors, and in general the mediæval clergy, present a type that is singularly well defined, and is in many respects exceedingly noble, but which is continually marked by a total absence of mere natural affection. In zeal, in courage, in perseverance, in self-sacrifice, they towered far above the average of mankind; but they were always as ready to inflict as to endure suffering. These were the men who chanted their Te Deums over the massacre of the Albigenses or of St. Bartholomew, who fanned and stimulated the Crusades and the religious wars, who exulted over the carnage, and strained every nerve to prolong the struggle,—and, when the zeal of the warrior had begun to flag, mourned over the languor of faith, and contemplated the sufferings they had caused with a satisfaction that was as pitiless as it was unselfish. These were the men who were at once the instigators and the agents of that horrible detailed persecution that stained almost every province of Europe with the blood of Jews and heretics, and which exhibits an amount of cold, passionless, studied, and deliberate barbarity unrivalled in the history of mankind.[1]

Now, when a tendency of this kind is habitually exhibited among men who are unquestionably actuated by the strongest sense of duty, it may be assumed that it is connected with some principle they have adopted, or with the moral atmosphere they breathe. It must have an intellectual or logical antecedent, and it must have what may be termed an emotional antecedent. By the first I understand certain principles or trains of reasoning which induce men to believe that it is their duty to persecute. By the second I understand a tendency or disposition of feeling that harmonises with persecution, removes the natural reluctance on the subject, and predisposes men to accept any reasoning of which persecution is the conclusion. The logical antecedents of persecution I shall examine in the next chapter. The most important emotional antecedent is, I believe, to be found in the teaching concerning the future world. It was the natural result of that teaching, that men whose lives present in many respects examples of the noblest virtue, were nevertheless conspicuous for ages as prodigies of barbarity, and proved absolutely indifferent to the sufferings of all who dissented from their doctrines. Nor was it only towards the heretic that this inhumanity was displayed; it was reflected

---

[1] We shall have ample evidence of this in the next chapter. At present it is sufficient to say that the use of the *slow* fire in burning heretics was in many districts habitual. In that curious book, the *Scaligerana* (a record of the conversation of Joseph Scaliger, by an intimate friend who lived in his house), we have a horrible description of one of these executions in Guienne : ' J'avois environ scize ans que je vis brusler un Jacobin qui fermoit la bouche aux Papistes: on le dégrada et on le brusla à petit feu, le liant avec des cordes mouillées par les aisselles près la potence, et là on mettoit le feu dessous tellement qu'il estoit demy consumé avant qu'il fut mort.' (Art. Heretici. See, too, art. Sorciers.) See, too, Cousin's account of the execution of Vanini.

more or less in the whole penal system of the time. We
have a striking example of this in the history of torture. In
ancient Greece, torture was never employed except in cases
of treason. In the best days of ancient Rome, notwithstanding the notorious inhumanity of the people, it was exclusively confined to the slaves. In mediæval Christendom it was
made use of to an extent that was probably unexampled in
any earlier period, and in cases that fell under the cognisance of the clergy it was applied to every class of the community.[1] And what strikes us most in considering the mediæval tortures, is not so much their diabolical barbarity,
which it is indeed impossible to exaggerate, as the extraordinary variety, and what may be termed the artistic skill, they
displayed. They represent a condition of thought in which
men had pondered long and carefully on all the forms of suffering, had compared and combined the different kinds of
torture, till they had become the most consummate masters
of their art, had expended on the subject all the resources of
the utmost ingenuity, and had pursued it with the ardour of
a passion. The system was matured under the mediæval
habit of thought, it was adopted by the inquisitors, and it
received its finishing touches from their ingenuity.[2] In every

---

[1] In cases of heresy and treason, but the first were of course by far the
most common. As one of the old authorities on the subject says: 'In crimine
hæresis omnes illi torquendi sunt qui in crimine læsæ majestatis humanæ torqueri possunt; quia longe gravius est divinum quam temporalem lædere
majestatem, ac proinde nobiles, milites, decuriones, doctores, et omnes qui
quantâlibet prærogativâ præfulgent in crimine hæresis et in crimine læsæ
majestatis humanæ torqueri possunt . . . quo fit quod minores viginti
quinque annis propter suspicionem hæresis et læsæ majestatis torqueri possunt,
minores etiam quatuordecem annis terreri et habenâ vel ferulâ cædi.' (Suarez
de Paz, *Praxis Ecclesiastica et Sæcularis* [1619], p. 158.)

[2] The extraordinary ingenuity of the mediæval tortures, and the extent to
which they were elaborated by the clergy, is well shown in an article on tor-
ure by Villegille, in Lacroix, *Le Moyen Age et la Renaissance* (Paris, 1848).

prison the crucifix and the rack stood side by side, and in almost every country the abolition of torture was at last effected by a movement which the Church opposed, and by men whom she had cursed. In England, it is true, torture had always been illegal, though it had often been employed, especially in ecclesiastical cases;[1] but almost every other country illustrates the position I have stated. In France, probably the first illustrious opponent of torture was Montaigne, the first of the French sceptics; the cause was soon afterwards taken up by Charron and by Bayle; it was then adopted by Voltaire, Montesquieu, and the Encyclopædists; and it finally triumphed when the Church had been shattered by the Revolution.[2] In Spain, tor-

tom. iii. The original works on the subject are very numerous, and possess a great but painful interest. Perhaps the fullest is Marsilius' (a lawyer of Bologna) *Tractatus de Quæstionibus* (1529 and 1537—both editions in black letter). Marsilius boasted that he was the inventor of the torture that consisted of depriving the prisoner of all sleep—a torture which was especially used in the States of the Church: 'In Statu Ecclesiastico hi duo modi magis in usu sunt, ut et tormentum taxillorum, et vigiliæ per somni subtractionem, quem modum invenisse asserit Marsilius.' (*Chartario Praxis Interrogandum Reorum* [Romæ, 1618], p. 198.) Besides these works, there are full accounts of the nature of the tortures in Simancas' *De Catholicis Institutionibus*, Eymericus' *Directorium Inquisitorum*. and many other works to which they refer.

[1] On the extent to which it was employed by the Catholics, under Mary, in the trials of Protestants, see Strutt's *Manners of the English People*, vol. iii. p. 46; and on the extent to which it was employed by Protestants in the trials of Catholic priests, see Hallam, *Const. Hist.* (ed. 1827), vol. i. p. 159; and the evidence collected in Milner's *Letters to a Prebendary.* Bishops Grindal and Coxe suggested the application of torture to the Catholic priests. (Froude, *Hist.*, vol. vii. pp. 418, 419.) See, too, Barrington *On the Statutes*, pp. 80, and 440, 441.

[2] The suppression of one department of torture was effected in France as early as 1780, and was one of the measures of reform conceded to the revolutionary party. All torture, however, was not abolished till the Revolution was actually triumphant, and the abolition was one of the first acts of the democrats. (See Loiseleur, *Sur les Peines.*) Besides the essays of Montaigne,

ture began to fall into disuse under Charles III., on one of
the few occasions when the Government was in direct opposition to the Church.[1] In Italy the great opponent of torture was Beccaria, the friend of Helvetius and of Holbach,
and the avowed exponent of the principles of Rousseau.[2]
Translated by Morellet, commented on by Voltaire and
Diderot, and supported by the whole weight of the French
philosophers, the work of Beccaria flew triumphantly over
Europe, and vastly accelerated the movement that produced
it. Under the influence of that movement, the Empress of
Russia abolished torture in her dominions, and accompanied
the abolition by an edict of toleration. Under the same
influence Frederick of Prussia, whose adherence to the philosophical principles was notorious, took the same step, and
his example was speedily followed by Duke Leopold of Tuscany. Nor is there, upon reflection, anything surprising in
this. The movement that destroyed torture was much less
an intellectual than an emotional movement. It represented

torture was denounced in the *Sagesse* of Charron, in the *Contrains-les Entrer*
of Bayle, and in many parts of the writings of Voltaire (see, e. g., art. Torture,
in *Phil. Dict.*) and his contemporaries.

[1] Buckle's *Hist.*, vol. ii. p. 140, note. Luis Vives, a rather famous Spanish
philosopher, in his Annotations to St. Augustine, had protested against torture
as early as the first half of the sixteenth century. His opinions on this subject were vehemently denounced by a bishop named Simancas, in a very remarkable book called *De Catholicis Institutionibus ad præcavendas et extir-
pandas Hæreses* (1569), to which I shall have occasion hereafter to refer.
Simancas observes that 'Inquisitores Apostolici sæpissime reos torquere so
lent;' he defends the practice with great energy, on the authority of theologians; and he gives a very vivid description of different modes of torture the
Inquisitors employed in their dealings with heretics (pp. 297-309.) See also,
on this horrible subject, Llorente, *Hist. of the Inquisition.* Simanacas notices
that, in other countries, criminals were in his day tortured in public, but in
Spain in secret (p. 305).

[2] On the influence of Beccaria, see Loiseleur, pp. 335-338. Morellet's
translation passed through seven editions in six months.

much less a discovery of the reason than an increased intensity of sympathy. If we asked what positive arguments can be adduced on the subject, it would be difficult to cite any that was not perfectly familiar to all classes at every period of the middle ages.[1] That brave criminals sometimes escaped, and that timid persons sometimes falsely declared themselves guilty; that the guiltless frequently underwent a horrible punishment, and that the moral influence of legal decisions was seriously weakened;[2]—these arguments, and such as these, were as much truisms in the eleventh and twelfth centuries as they are at present. Nor was it by such means that the change was effected. Torture was abolished because in the progress of civilisation the sympathies of men became more expansive, their perceptions of the sufferings of others more acute, their judgments more indulgent, their actions more gentle. To subject even a guilty man to the horrors of the rack seemed atrocious and barbarous, and therefore the rack was destroyed. It was part of the great movement which abolished barbarous amusements, mitigated the asperities and refined the manners of all classes. Now it is quite certain that those who seriously regarded eternal suffering as the just punishment of the fretfulness of a child, could not possibly look upon torture with the same degree and kind of repulsion as their less orthodox neighbours. It is also certain, that a period in which religion,

---

[1] There is, perhaps, one exception to this. Beccaria grounded much of his reasoning on the doctrine of the social compact. I cannot, however, think that this argument had much influence in producing the change.

[2] It is worthy of notice that St. Augustine perceived very clearly the evil of torture, and stated the case against it with his usual force and terseness : ' Cum quæritur utrum sit nocens cruciatur et innocens luit pro incerto scelere certissimas pœnas' (*De Civ. Dei*, lib. xix. cap. 6); but he concluded that it was necessary.

by dwelling incessantly on the legends of the martyrs, or on the agonies of the lost, made the combination of new and horrible forms of suffering the habitual employment of the imagination, was of all others that in which the system of torture was likely to be most atrocious. It may be added, that the very frame of mind that made men assail the practice of torture, made them also assail the mediæval doctrine of future punishment. The two things grew out of the same condition of society. They flourished together, and they declined together.

The truth is, that in every age the penal code will in a great degree vary with the popular estimate of guilt. Philosophers have written much on the purely preventive character of legal punishments; but it requires but little knowledge of history, or even of human nature, to show that a code constructed altogether on such a principle is impossible. It is indeed true, that all acts morality condemns do not fall within the province of the legislator, and that this fact is more fully appreciated as civilisation advances.[1] It is true, too, that in an early stage, the severity of punishment results in a great measure from the prevailing indifference to the infliction of suffering. It is even true that the especial prominence or danger of some crime will cause men to visit it for a time with penalties that seem to bear no proportion to its moral enormity. Yet it is, I think, impossible to examine penal systems without perceiving that they can only be efficient during a long period of time, when they accord substantially with the popular estimate of the enormity of guilt.

---

[1] The tendency of all penal systems constructed under the influence of the clergy to make the legal code coextensive with the moral code, and to make punishments as much as possible of the nature of expiation, is well known. As a modern instance of this, Sweden is perhaps the most remarkable. See the striking book of Mr. Laing, upon its present condition.

Every system, by admitting extenuating circumstances and graduated punishments, implies this, and every judgment that is passed by the public is virtually an appeal to an ideal standard. When a punishment is pronounced excessive, it is meant that it is greater than was deserved. When it is pronounced inadequate, it is meant that it is less than was deserved. Even regarding the law simply as a preventive measure, it is necessary that it should thus reflect the prevailing estimate of guilt, for otherwise it would come into collision with that public opinion which is essential to its operation. Thus, towards the close of the last century, both murder and horse-stealing were punished by death. In the first case, juries readily brought in verdicts, the public sanctioned those verdicts, and the law was efficacious. In the second case, the criminals were almost usually acquitted; and when they were executed, public opinion was shocked and scandalised. The reason of this was, that men looked upon death as a punishment not incommensurate with the guilt of murder, but exceedingly disproportionate to that of theft. In the advance of civilisation, there is a constant tendency to mitigate the severity of penal codes, for men learn to realise more intensely the suffering they are inflicting; and they at the same time become more sensible of the palliations of guilt. When, however, such a doctrine concerning the just reward of crime as I have noticed is believed and realised, it must inevitably have the effect of retarding the progress.

Such, then, were the natural effects of the popular teaching on the subject of future punishment which was universal during the middle ages, and during the sixteenth and the greater part of the seventeenth century. How completely that teaching has passed away must be evident to any one

22

who will take the pains of comparing old theological literature with modern teaching. The hideous pictures of material fire and of endless torture which were once so carefully elaborated and so constantly enforced, have been replaced
by a few vague sentences on the subject of 'perdition,' or by
the general assertion of a future adjustment of the inequalities
of life; and a doctrine which grows out of the moral faculty,
and is an element in every truly moral religion, has been
thus silently substituted for a doctrine which was the greatest of all moral difficulties. The eternity of punishment is,
indeed, still strenuously defended by many; but the nature
of that punishment, which had been one of the most prominent points in every previous discussion on the subject, has
now completely disappeared from controversy. The ablest
theologians once regarded their doctrine as one that might
be defended, but could not possibly be so stated as not at
first sight to shock the feelings. Liebnitz argued that offences against an infinite Being acquired an infinite guilt,
and therefore deserved an infinite punishment. Butler argued that the analogy of nature gave much reason to suspect
that the punishment of crimes may be out of all proportion
with our conceptions of their guilt. Both, by their very de-
fences, implied that the doctrine was a grievous difficulty.
As, however, it is commonly stated at present, the doctrine
is so far from being a difficulty, that any system that was
without it would be manifestly imperfect, and it has accordingly long since taken its place as one of the moral evidences
of Christianity.

This gradual and silent transformation of the popular
conceptions is doubtless chiefly due to the habit of educing
moral and intellectual truths from our own sense of right,
rather than from traditional teaching, which has accompa-

nied the decline of dogmatic theology, and which first became conspicuous in the seventeenth century. Descartes, who was the chief revi\er of moral philosophy, may be regarded as its leading originator; for the method which he applied to metaphysical enquiries was soon applied (consciously or unconsciously) to moral subjects. Men, when seeking for just ideas of right and wrong, began to interrogate their moral sense much more than the books of theologians, and they soon proceeded to make that sense or faculty a supreme arbiter, and to mould all theology into conformity with its dictates. At the same time the great increase of similar influences, and the rapid succession of innovations, made theologians yield with comparative facility to the pressure of their age.

But besides this general rationalistic movement, there was another tendency which exercised, I think, a real though minor influence on the movement, and which is also associated with the name of Descartes. I mean the development of a purely spiritual conception of the soul. The different effects which a spiritual or a material philosophy has exercised on all departments of speculation, form one of the most interesting pages in history. The ancients—at least the most spiritual schools—seem to have generally regarded the essence of the soul as an extremely subtle fluid, or substance quite distinct from the body; and, according to their view, and according to the views that were long afterwards prevalent, this excessive subtlety of essence constituted immateriality. For the soul was supposed to be of a nature totally different from surrounding objects, simple, incapable of disintegration, and emancipated from the conditions of matter. Some of the Platonists verged very closely upon, and perhaps attained, the modern idea of a soul whose essence is purely intellectual; but the general opinion was, I think, that which I have described. The distinct and, as it was called, immaterial nature of the soul was insisted on by the ancients with great emphasis as the chief proof of its immortality. If mind be but a function of matter, if thought be but 'a material product of the brain,' it seems natural that the dissolution of the body should be the annihilation of the individual. There is, indeed, an instinct in man pointing to a future sphere, where the injustices of life shall be rectified, and where the chain of love that death has severed shall be linked anew, which is so closely connected with our moral nature that it would perhaps survive the rudest shocks of a material philosophy; but to minds in which the logical element is most prominent, the psychological argument will always appear the most satisfactory. That there exists in man an indivisible being connected with, but essentially distinct from the body, was the position which Socrates dwelt upon as one of the chief foundations of his hopes in the last hours of his life, and Cicero in the shadow of age; and the whole moral system of the school of Plato was based upon the distinction. Man, in their noble imagery, is the horizon line where the world of spirit and the world of matter touch. It is in his power to rise by the wings of the soul to communion with the gods, or to sink by the gravitation of the body to the level of the brute. It is the destiny of the soul to pass from state to state; all its knowledge is but remembrance, and its future condition must be determined by its present tendency. The soul of that man who aspires only to virtue, and who despises the luxury and the passions of earth, will be emancipated at last from the thraldom of matter, and, invisible and unshackled, will drink in perfect bliss in the full fruition of wisdom. The soul of that man who seeks his chief gratification in the body, will after death be imprisoned in a new body, will be punished by physical suffering, or, visible to the human eye, will appear upon earth in the form of a ghost to scare the survivors amid their pleasure.

Such were the opinions that were held by the school of Plato, the most spiritual of all the philosophers of antiquity. When Christianity appeared in the world, its first tendency was very favourable to these conceptions, for it is the effect of every great moral enthusiasm to raise men above the appetites of the body, to present to the mind a supersensual ideal, and to accentuate strongly the antagonism by which human nature is convulsed. We accordingly find that in its earlier and better days the Church assimilated especially with the philosophy of Plato, while in the middle ages Aristotle was supreme; and we also find that the revival of Platonism accompanied the spiritualising movement that preceded the Reformation. Yet there were two doctrines that produced an opposite tendency. The pagans asserted the immateriality of the soul, because they believed that the body must perish for ever; and some of the Christians, in denying this latter position, were inclined to reject the distinction that was based upon it. But above all, the firm belief in punishment by fire, and the great prominence the doctrine soon obtained, became the foundation of the material view. The Fathers were early divided upon the subject. One section, compris-

---

This theory is developed in the *Phædon*. The Greeks had an extreme fear of the dead, and consequently a strong predisposition to see ghosts.

[2] 'Not one of them (the early Fathers) entertained the same opinion as the majority of Christians do at the present day, that the soul is perfectly simple, and entirely destitute of all body, figure, form, and extension. On the contrary, they all acknowledge it to contain something corporeal, although of a different kind and nature from the bodies of this mortal sphere. But yet they

ing the ablest and the best, maintained that there existed in
man an immaterial soul, but that that soul was invariably
associated with a thin, flexible, but sensitive body, visible to
the eye.   Origen added that the Deity alone could exist as a
pure spirit unallied with matter.[1]   The other school, of which
Tertullian may be regarded as the chief, utterly denied the
existence in man of any incorporeal element, maintained that
the soul was simply a second body, and based this doctrine
chiefly on the conception of future punishment.[2]   Apparitions were at that time regarded as frequent.   Tertullian
mentions a woman who had seen a soul, which she described
as 'a transparent and lucid figure in the perfect form of a
man.'[3]   St. Antony saw the soul of Ammon carried up to
heaven.   The soul of a Libyan hermit named Marc was
borne to heaven in a napkin.   Angels also were not unfre-

---

are divided into two opinions.   For some contend that there are two things in
the soul—spirit, and a very thin and subtle body in which this spirit is clothed.
. . .   Those who follow Plato and the Platonists (i. e. Clement, Origen, and
their disciples), adopt the Platonic doctrine respecting the soul also, and pronounce it to be most simple in itself, but yet always invested with a subtle
body.   But the others, who keep far aloof from Plato, and consider his philosophy to be prejudicial to Christian principles, repudiate this doctrine of his as
well, and maintain that the soul altogether is nothing more than a most subtle
body. . . .   They very frequently assail the Platonists with bitter invectives, for inculcating that the soul is of a nature most simple, and devoid of
all concretion.'—Note by Mosheim to Cudworth's *Intell. System* (Harrison's
ed.), vol. iii. p. 325.   Mr. Hallam says: 'The Fathers, with the exception,
perhaps the single one, of Augustine, had taught the corporeity of the thinking substance.' (*Hist. of Lit.*)

   [1] Cudworth, vol. iii. p. 318.   The same Father based his doctrine of the
soul in a great measure on apparitions. (Ibid. p. 330.)

   [2] 'Corporalitas animæ in ipso evangelio relucebit.   Dolet apud inferos
anima cujusdam, et punitur in flammâ et cruciatur in linguâ et de digito animæ
felicioris implorat solatium roris.'—Tertullian, *De Anima*, cap. vii.

   [3] Ibid. cap. ix.   I should mention that this book was written after Tertullian had become a Montanist, but there is no reason to believe that this had
anything to say to his psychology

quently seen, and were universally believed to have cohabited with the daughters of the antediluvians.

Under the influence of mediæval habits of thought, every spiritual conception was materialised ; and what at an earlier and a later period was generally deemed the language of metaphor, was universally regarded as the language of fact. The realisations of the people were all derived from painting, sculpture, or ceremonies that appealed to the senses, and all subjects were therefore reduced to palpable images.[1] The angel in the Last Judgment was constantly represented weighing the souls in a literal balance, while devils clinging to the scales endeavoured to disturb the equilibrium. Sometimes the soul was portrayed as a sexless child, rising out of the mouth of the corpse.[2] But above all, the doctrine of purgatory arrested and enchained the imagination. Every church was crowded with pictures, representing the souls of those who had just died as literal bodies writhing with horrible contortions in a literal fire. The two doctrines were strictly congruous, and each supported the other. Men who believed in a ' physical soul,' readily believed in a physical punishment. Men who materialised their view of the punishment, materialised their view of the sufferers.

We find, however, some time before the Reformation, evident signs of a desire on the part of a few writers to rise to a purer conception of the soul. The pantheistic writings that flowed from the school of Averroes, reviving the old Stoical notion of a soul of nature, directed attention to the great problem of the connection between the worlds of matter and

[1] See on this subject Maury, *Légendes Pieuses*, pp. 125–127.

[2] Maury, *Légendes Pieuses*, p. 124.   There is an example of this in the Triumph of Death, by Orcagna, at Pisa.   In the Greek churches the souls of the blessed were sometimes represented as little children clasped in the mighty hand of God.   (Didron, *Iconographie*, p. 216.)

of mind. The conception of an all-pervading spirit, which sleeps in the stone, dreams in the animal, and wakes in the man;'[1] the belief that the hidden vital principle which produces the varied forms of organisation, is but the thrill of the Divine essence that is present in them all—this belief, which had occupied so noble a place among the speculations of antiquity, reappeared, and was, perhaps, strengthened by the rapid progress of mysticism, which may be regarded as the Christian form of pantheism. Coalescing at first with some lingering traditions of Gnosticism, mysticism appeared in the thirteenth century in the sect of the Bégards, and especially in the teachings of David de Dianant, Ortlieb, and Amaury de Bène; and in the following century, under the guidance of Eckart, Tauler, Suso, and Ruysbroek, it acquired in Germany an extraordinary popularity, to which the strong religious feeling elicited by the black death, and the reaction that had begun against the excessive aridity of scholasticism, both contributed.[2] The writings ascribed to Dionysius the Areopagite, which have always been the Bible of mysticism, and which had been in part translated by Scotus Erigena, and also some of the works of Scotus himself, rose to sudden favour, and a new tone was given to almost all classes of theological reasoners. As the philosophical aspect of this tone of thought, an order of investigation was produced, which was shown in curious enquiries about how life is first generated in matter. The theory of spontaneous generation, which Lucretius had made the basis of a great portion of his system, and on which the philosophers of the eighteenth century laid so great stress, was strongly asserted,[3] and all

[1] Schelling.

[2] See Schmidt, _Études sur le Mysticisme Allemand du XIVe Siècle_, in the _Mémoires des Sciences Morales et Politiques de l'Institut de France_, tom. ii.

[3] The following passage from Vives is interesting both as giving a concise

the mysteries of generation treated with a confidence that elicits a smile,[1] not unmixed with melancholy when we think how completely these great questions of the nature and origin of life, which may be almost said to form the basis of all real knowledge, have eluded our investigations, and how absolutely the fair promise of the last century has in this respect been unfulfilled. From enquiries about the genesis of the soul, it was natural to proceed to examine its nature. Such enquiries were accordingly earnestly pursued, with the assistance of the pagan writers; and the conclusions arrived at on this point by different schools exercised, as is always the case, a very wide influence upon their theological conceptions. I cannot doubt, that when at last Descartes maintained that thought is the essence of the soul, and that the thinking substance is therefore so wholly and generically different from the body, that none of the forms or properties of matter can afford the faintest image of its nature, he contributed much to that frame of mind which made men naturally turn with contempt from ghosts, visible demons,

---

view of the notions prevailing about spontaneous generation, and on account of the very curious notion in it about mice: 'De viventibus alia generationem habent spontaneum, ut muscæ, culices, formicæ, apes: quæ nec sexum ullum habent. Alia ex commixtione sexuum prodeunt, ut homo, equus, canis, leo. Sunt quæ ambiguam habent procreationem, ut mures; nam eorum alii ex sordibus sine concubitu, alii ex concubitu proveniunt.' (*De Anima*, lib. i.) Van Helmont, as is well known, gave a receipt for producing mice. St. Augustine, after taking great pains to solve different objections to the goodness of Providence, oddly enough selects the existence of mice as an impenetrable one which faith alone can grasp: 'Ego vero fateor me nescire mures et ranæ quare creati sunt, aut muscæ, aut vermiculæ.' (*De Genesi contra Manichæos*, c. xvi.)

[1] Thus, Melanchthon deals, in a tone of the most absolute assurance, with the great question of the cause of the difference of sex: 'Mares nascuntur magis in dextrâ parte matricis, et a semine quod magis a dextro testiculo oritur. Fœmellæ in sinistrâ matricis parte nascuntur.' Melanchthon, *De Anima*, p. 420.

and purgatorial fires.[1] It is true that the Cartesian doctrine was soon in a measure eclipsed, but it at least destroyed for ever the old notion of an inner body.[2]

From the time of Descartes, the doctrine of a material fire may indeed be said to have steadily declined.[3] The sceptics of the seventeenth and eighteenth centuries treated it with great contempt, and in England, at least, the last great controversy on the subject in the Church seems to have taken place during the first half of the eighteenth century. Swinden, Whiston, Horberry, Dodwell, and in America Jonathan Edwards, discussed it from different points of view,[4] and at·

---

[1] The sharp line Descartes tried to draw between the body and the soul explains his doctrine of animals, which has often been grossly misunderstood. Thought, he contended, is the essence of the soul, and all that is not thought (as life and sensibility) is of the body. In denying that brutes had souls, he denied them the power of thought, but left them all besides. This distinction in its full rigidity would now be maintained by very few; and Stahl gave psychology an impulse in quite another direction by his doctrine (which seems to have been that of Aristotle), that the soul includes the vital principle—all that separates living from dead bodies. He thus founded the psychology of animals, and in a great measure fused psychology and medicine. There is a clear statement on this point in Maine de Biran, *Nouveaux Rapports Physiques et Morales.* There is at present a remarkable revival of the doctrine of Stahl in France in the writings of Tissot, Boullier, Charles, and Lemoine.

[2] A doctrine, however, something like that of the old Fathers, but applied to the bodies of the blessed, has been lately advocated in two very ingenious American books—Hitchcock's *Religion of Geology,* and *Lectures on the Seasons.* The author has availed himself of Reichenbach's theories of 'odic light,' &c.

[3] Descartes himself gives us the opinion of his contemporaries on the subject: 'Bien que la commune opinion des théologiens soit que les damnés sont tourmentés par le feu des enfers, néanmoins leur sentiment n'est pas pour cela qu'ils sont deçus par une fausse idée que Dieu leur a imprimée, d'un feu qui les consume, mais plutôt qu'ils sont véritablement tourmentés par le feu; parceque "comme l'esprit d'un homme vivant, bien qu'il ne soit pas corporel, est néanmoins détenu dans le corps, ainsi Dieu par sa toute-puissance peut aisément faire qu'il souffre les atteintes du feu corporel après la mort."' (*Réponses aux Sixième Objections.*)

[4] This was, as far as I know, the last of the great controversies concerning

tested the rapid progress of the scepticism. Towards the close of the century the doctrine had passed away, for though there was no formal recantation or change of dogmas, it was virtually excluded from the popular teaching, though it even now lingers among the least educated Dissenters, and in the Roman Catholic manuals for the poor.

I have dwelt at length upon this very revolting doctrine, because it exercised, I believe, an extremely important influence on the modes of thought and types of character of the past. I have endeavoured to show how its necessary effect was to chill and deaden the sympathies, to predispose men to inflict suffering, and seriously to retard the march of civilisation. It has now virtually passed away, and with it the type of character that it did so much to form. Instead of the old stern Inquisitor, so unflinching in his asceticism, so heroic in his enterprises, so remorseless in his persecution—instead of the men who multiplied and elaborated the most hideous tortures, who wrote long cold treatises on their application, who stimulated and embittered the most ferocious wars, and who watered every land with the blood of the innocent—instead of this ecclesiastical type of character, we meet with an almost feminine sensibility, and an almost morbid indisposition to inflict punishment. The preëminent characteristic of modern Christianity is the boundless philanthropy it displays. Philanthropy is to our age what asceticism was to the middle

the locality of hell—a question which had once excited great attention. The common opinion, which St. Thomas had sanctioned, was that it was in the centre of the earth. Whiston, however, who denied the eternity of punishment, contended that it was the tail of a comet; while Swinden (whose book seems to have made a considerable sensation, and was translated into French) strenuously contended that it was the sun. According to Plancy (*Dict. Infernal*, art. Enfer), some early theologians not only held this, but explained the spots in the sun by the multitude of the souls.

ages, and what polemical discussion was to the sixteenth and seventeenth centuries. The emotional part of humanity, the humanity of impulse, was never so developed, and its development, in Protestantism at least, where the movement has been most strikingly evinced, has always been guided and represented by the clergy. Indeed, this fact is recognised quite as much by their opponents as by their admirers. A certain weak and effeminate sentimentality, both intellectual and moral, is the quality which every satirist of the clergy dwells upon as the most prominent feature of their character. Whether this quality, when duly analysed, is as despicable as is sometimes supposed, may be questioned; at all events, no one would think of ascribing it to the ecclesiastics of the school of Torquemada, of Calvin, or of Knox.

The changes that take place from age to age in the types of character in different professions, though they are often very evident, and though they form one of the most suggestive branches of history, are of course not susceptible of direct logical proof. A writer can only lay the general impressions he has derived from the study of the two periods before the judgments of those whose studies have resembled his own It is more, therefore, as an illustration than as a proof, that I may notice in conclusion the striking contrast which the history of punishments exhibits in the two periods of theological development. We have seen that the popular estimate of the adequacy of the penalties that are affixed to different crimes must in a great measure vary with the popular realisations of guilt. We have seen, too, that the abolition of torture was a movement almost entirely due to the opponents of the Church, and that it was effected much less by any process of reasoning than by the influence of certain modes of feeling which civilisation produced. Soon, how-

ever, we find that the impulse which was communicated by
Voltaire, Beccaria, and the Revolution, passed on to the orthodox, and it was only then it acquired its full intensity.
The doctrine of a literal fire having almost ceased to be a
realised conception, a growing sense of the undue severity
of punishments was everywhere manifested; and in most
countries, but more especially in England, there was no single subject on which more earnestness was shown. The first
step was taken by Howard. Nowhere perhaps in the annals
of philanthropy do we meet a picture of more unsullied and
fruitful beneficence than is presented by the life of that great
dissenter, who, having travelled over more than 40,000 miles
in works of mercy, at last died on a foreign soil a martyr to
his cause. Not only in England, but over the whole of
Europe, his exertions directed public opinion to the condition
of prisons, and effected a revolution the results of which can
never be estimated. Soon after followed the mitigation of
the penal code. In England the severity of that code had
long been unexampled; and as crimes of violence were especially numerous, the number of executions was probably
quite unparalleled in Europe. Indeed, Fortescue, who was
chief justice under Henry VI., notices the fact with curious
complacency, as a plain proof of the superiority of his countrymen. 'More men,' he tells us, 'are hanged in Englonde
in one year than in Fraunce in seven, because the English
have better hartes. The Scotchmenne, likewise, never dare
rob, but only commit larcenies.'[1] In the reign of Henry
VIII. when an attempt was made to convert the greater
part of England into pasture land,[2] and when the suppression

---

[1] Barrington, *On the Statutes* (London, 1769), p. 461.

[2] Sir Thomas More, in his *Utopia* (book i.), gives a frightful description of
the misery and the crimes resulting from the ejectments necessitated by this
change. He speaks of twenty men hung on one gibbet.

of the monasteries had destroyed the main source of charity
and had cast multitudes helplessly upon the world, Holinshed
estimates the executions at the amazing number of 72,000, or
2,000 a year.[1] The poor law of Elizabeth to a certain extent
mitigated the evil, yet at the end of her reign the annual executions were still about 400.[2] In the middle of the eighteenth century, however, though the population had greatly
increased, they had fallen to less than one hundred.[3] A little
before this time Bishop Berkeley, following in the steps that
had been traced by More in his 'Utopia,' and by Cromwell
in one of his speeches, raised his voice in favour of substituting other punishments for death.[4] But all through the reign
of George III. the code was aggravated, and its severity was
carried to such a point, that when Romilly began his career,
the number of capital offences was no less than 230.[5] It was
only at the close of the last and in the beginning of the
present century, that this state of things was changed. The
reform in England, as over the rest of Europe, may be ultimately traced to that Voltairian school of which Beccaria
was the representative, for the impulse created by the
treatise 'On Crimes and Punishments' was universal, and
it was the first great effort to infuse a spirit of philanthropy
into the penal code, making it a main object of legislation to
inflict the smallest possible amount of suffering. Beccaria is
especially identified with that great cause of the abolition of
capital punishment, which is slowly but steadily advancing

---

[1] Barrington, pp. 461, 462.   [2] Ibid.

[3] Barrington says this was the case when he wrote, which was in 1766.

[4] He asks 'whether we may not, as well as other nations, contrive employment for our criminals; and whether servitude, chains, and hard labour for a
term of years, would not be a more discouraging as well as a more adequate
punishment for felons than even death itself.' (*Querist*, No. 54.)

[5] See Romilly's *Life* for many statistics on the subject.

towards its inevitable triumph. In England the philosophical element of the movement was nobly represented by Bentham, who in genius was certainly superior to Beccaria, and whose influence, though perhaps not so great, was also European. But while conceding the fullest merit to these great thinkers, there can be little doubt that the enthusiasm and the support that enabled Romilly, Mackintosh, Wilberforce, and Brougham to carry their long series of reforms through Parliament, was in a very great degree owing to the untiring exertions of the Evangelicals, who, with a benevolence that no disappointment could damp, and with an indulgence towards crime that sometimes amounted even to a fault, cast their whole weight into the cause of philanthropy. The contrast between the position of these religionists in the destruction of the worst features of the ancient codes, and the precisely opposite position of the mediæval clergy, is very remarkable. Sectarians will only see in it the difference between rival churches, but the candid historian will, I think, be able to detect the changed types of character that civilisation has produced; while in the difference that does undoubtedly in this respect exist between Protestantism and Catholicism, he will find one of the results of the very different degrees of intensity with which those religions direct the mind to the debasing and indurating conceptions I have reviewed.

It has been said that the tendency of religious thought in the present day 'is all in one direction—towards the identification of the Bible and conscience.' It is a movement that may be deplored, but can scarcely be overlooked or denied. Generation after generation the power of the moral faculty becomes more absolute, the doctrines that oppose it wane and vanish, and the various elements of theology are absorbed and recast by its influence. The indifference of most men to dogmatic theology is now so marked, and the fear of tampering with formularies that are no longer based on general conviction is with some men so intense, that general revisions of creeds have become extremely rare; but the change of belief is not the less profound. The old words are indeed retained, but they no longer present the old images to the mind, or exercise the old influence upon the life. The modes of thought, and the types of character which those modes produce, are essentially and universally transformed. The whole intellectual atmosphere, the whole tenor of life, the prevailing enthusiasms, the conceptions of the imagination, are all changed. The intellect of man moves onward under the influence of regular laws in a given direction; and the opinions that in any age are realised and operative, are those which harmonise with its intellectual condition. I have endeavoured in the present chapter to exhibit the nature of some of these laws, the direction in which some of these successive modifications are tending. If the prospect of constant change such an enquiry exhibits should appear to some minds to remove all the landmarks of the past, there is one consideration that may serve in a measure to reassure them. That Christianity was designed to produce benevolence, affection, and sympathy, being a fact of universal admission, is indefinitely more certain than that any particular dogma is essential to it; and in the increase of these moral qualities we have therefore the strongest evidence of the triumph of the conceptions of its Founder.

CHAPTER IV.

ON PERSECUTION.

PART I.

THE ANTECEDENTS OF PERSECUTION.

WHEN it is remembered that the Founder of Christianity summed up human duties in the two precepts of love to God and love to man, and illustrated the second precept by a parable representing the sentiment of a common humanity destroying all the animosities of sectarianism, the history of persecution in the Christian Church appears as startling as it is painful. In the eighteenth century, when the minds of men were for the first time very sensible of the contrast, it was commonly explained by imputing interested motives to the clergy, and in all the writings of Voltaire and his school hypocrisy was represented as the usual concomitant of persecution. This notion may now be said to have quite passed away. While it is undoubtedly true that some persecutions, and even some that were very atrocious, have sprung from purely selfish motives, it is almost universally admitted that these are far from furnishing any adequate explanation for the facts. The burnings, the tortures, the imprisonments, the confiscations, the disabilities, the long wars and still longer animosities that for so many centuries marked the conflicts of great theological bodies, are chiefly due to men whose lives were spent in absolute devotion to what they believed to be true, and whose characters have passed unscathed through the most hostile and searching criticism. In their worst acts the persecutors were but the exponents and representatives of the wishes of a large section of the community, and that section was commonly the most earnest and the most unselfish. It has been observed too, since the subject has been investigated with a passionless judgment, that persecution invariably accompanied the realisation of a particular class of doctrines, fluctuated with their fluctuations, and may therefore be fairly presumed to represent their action upon life.

In the last chapter I have, I trust, done something towards the solution of the difficulty. I have shown that the normal effect of a certain class of realisations upon the character would be to produce an absolute indifference to the sufferings of those who were external to the Church, and consequently to remove that reluctance to inflict pain which is one of the chief preservatives of society. I have now to trace the order of ideas which persuaded men that it was their duty to persecute, and to show the process by which those ideas passed away. The task is a painful one, for the doctrines I must refer to are those which are most repugnant to our moral sense, and in an age in which they are not realised or believed the bare statement of them is sufficient to shock the feelings of many: at the same time a clear view of their nature and influence is absolutely essential to an understanding of the past.

There are two moral sentiments which seem universally diffused through the human race, and which may be regarded as the nuclei around which all religious systems are formed.

They are the sense of virtue, leading men to attach the idea of merit to certain actions which they may perform; and the sense of sin, teaching men that their relation to the Deity is not that of claimants but of suppliants. Although in some degree antagonistic, there probably never was a religious mind in which they did not coexist, and they may be traced as prominent elements in the moral development of every age and creed, but at the same time their relative importance is far from being the same. There are certain ages in which the sense of virtue has been the mainspring of religion; there are other ages in which this position is occupied by the sense of sin. This may be partly owing to the differences in the original constitutions of different races, or to those influences of surrounding nature which act so early upon the mind that it is scarcely possible to distinguish them from natural tendencies; but it is certainly in a great measure due to the political and intellectual circumstances that are dominant. When prosperity and victory and dominion have long continued to elate, and when the virtues that contribute most to political greatness, such as fortitude and self-reliance, are cultivated, the sense of human dignity will become the chief moral principle, and every system that opposes it will be distasteful. But when, on the other hand, a religious system emanates from a suffering people, or from a people that is eminently endowed with religious sentiment, its character will be entirely different. It will reflect something of the circumstances that gave it birth; it will be full of pathos, of humility, of emotion; it will lead men to aspire to a lofty ideal, to interrogate their conscience with nervous anxiety, to study with scrupulous care the motives that actuate them, to distrust their own powers, and to throw themselves upon external help.

Now, of all systems the world has ever seen, the philosophies of ancient Greece and Rome appealed most strongly to the sense of virtue, and Christianity to the sense of sin. The ideal of the first was the majesty of self-relying humanity; the ideal of the other was the absorption of the manhood into God. It is impossible to look upon the awful beauty of a Greek statue, or to read a page of Plutarch, without perceiving how completely the idea of excellence was blended with that of pride. It is equally impossible to examine the life of a Christian saint, or the painting of an early Christian artist, without perceiving that the dominant conception was self-abnegation and self-distrust. In the earliest and purest days of the Church this was chiefly manifested in the devotional frame of mind which was habitual, and in the higher and more delicate moral perception that accompanied it. Christianity was then strictly a religion; that is to say, it consisted of modes of emotion and not of intellectual propositions. It was not till about the third century that the moral sentiments which at first constituted it were congealed into an elaborate theology, and were in consequence necessarily perverted. I say necessarily perverted, because a dogma cannot be an adequate or faithful representative of a mode of feeling. Moral sentiments do not possess the logical precision and rigidity which belong to the articles of a creed, and to convert the former into the latter invariably leads to the most fatal consequences. Thus, while the sense of virtue and the sense of sin have always coexisted, though in different degrees, in every religious mind, when expressed in a dogmatic form, under the names of Justification by Faith and Justification by Works, they became directly opposed to one another; and while each doctrine grew in the first instance out of the moral faculty. each was at last developed to consequences from which that faculty indignantly revolts. As the result of one doctrine, men con structed a theory in which the whole scheme of religion was turned into a system of elaborate barter; while that attitude of self-distrust and humility which was produced by the sensitiveness of an awakened conscience was soon trans- formed into a doctrine according to which all the virtues and all the piety of the heathen contained nothing that was pleasing to the Almighty, or that could ward off the sen- tence of eternal damnation.

In considering, however, the attitude which mankind oc- cupied towards the Almighty in the early theology of the Church, we have another important element to examine: I mean the conception of hereditary guilt. To a civilised man, who regards the question abstractedly, no proposition can appear more self-evident than that a man can only be guilty of acts in the performance of which he has himself had some share. The misfortune of one man may fall upon another, but guilt appears to be entirely personal. Yet, on the other hand, there is nothing more certain than that the conceptions both of hereditary guilt and of hereditary merit pervade the belief and the institutions of all nations, and have under the most varied circumstances clung to the mind with a tenacity which is even now but beginning to relax. We find them in every system of early punishment which involved children in the destruction of a guilty parent, in every account of curses transmitted through particular fami- lies or particular nations, in every hereditary aristocracy, and in every legend of an early fall. All these rest upon the idea that there is something in the merit or demerit of one man that may be reflected upon his successors altogether irre- spectively of their own acts. It would perhaps be rash to draw with much confidence any law concerning the relations of this idea to different conditions of society from the history of Christendom, but, as far as we may judge, it seems to be strongest in ages when civilisation is very low, and on the whole to decline, but not by any means steadily and continuously, with the intellectual advance. There seems to be a period in the history of every nation when punishments involving the innocent child with the guilty parent are acquiesced in as perfectly natural, and another period when they are repudiated as manifestly unjust. We find, however, that in a portion of the middle ages when the night of barbarism was in part dispelled, a vast aristocratical system was organised which has probably contributed more than any other single cause to consolidate the doctrine of hereditary merit. For the essence of an aristocracy is to transfer the source of honour from the living to the dead, to make the merits of living men depend not so much upon their own character and actions as upon the actions and position of their ancestors; and as a great aristocracy is never insulated, as its ramifications penetrate into many spheres, and its social influence modifies all the relations of society, the minds of men become insensibly habituated to a standard of judgment from which they would otherwise have recoiled. If in the sphere of religion the rationalistic doctrine of personal merit and demerit should ever completely supersede the theological doctrine of hereditary merit or demerit, the change will, I believe, be mainly effected by the triumph of democratic principles in the sphere of politics.

The origin of this widely diffused habit of judging men by the deeds of their ancestors is one of the most obscure and contested points in philosophy. Some have seen in it a dim and distorted tradition of the Fall; others have attrib ated it to that confusion of misfortune with guilt which is so prominent in ancient beliefs. Partly in consequence of the universal conviction that guilt deserves punishment, and partly from the notion that the events which befall mankind are the results not of general laws but of isolated acts directed to special purposes, men imagined that whenever they saw suffering they might infer guilt. They saw that the effects of an unrighteous war will continue long after those who provoked it have passed away; that the virtue or vice, the wisdom or folly, of the parent will often determine the fortunes of the children; and that each generation has probably more power over the destiny of that which succeeds it than over its own. They saw that there was such a thing as transmitted suffering, and they therefore concluded that there must be such a thing as transmitted guilt. Besides this, patriotism and Church feeling, and every influence that combines men in a corporate existence, makes them live to a certain degree in the past, and identify themselves with the actions of the dead. The patriot feels a pride or shame in the deeds of his forefathers very similar to that which springs from his own. Connected with this, it has been observed that men have a constant tendency, in speaking of the human race, to forget that they are employing the language of metaphor, and to attribute to it a real objective existence distinct from the existence of living men. It may be added too that that retrospective imagination which is so strong in some nations, and which is more or less exhibited in all, leads men to invest the past with all the fascination of poetry, to represent it as a golden age incomparably superior to their own, and to imagine that some great catastrophe must have occurred to obscure it.

These considerations, and such as these, have often been

urged by those who have written on the genesis of the notion of hereditary guilt. Fortunately, however, their examination is unnecessary for my present purpose, which is simply to ascertain the expression of this general conception in dogmatic teaching, and to trace its influence upon practice. The expression is both manifest and emphatic. According to the unanimous belief of the early Church, all who were external to Christianity were doomed to eternal damnation, not only on account of their own transgression, but also on account of the transmitted guilt of Adam; and therefore even the new-born infant was subject to the condemnation until baptism had united it to the Church.

The opinion which was so graphically expressed by the theologian who said 'he doubted not there were infants not a span long crawling about the floor of hell,' is not one of those on which it is pleasing to dilate. It is one, however, which was held with great confidence in the early Church, and if in times of tranquillity it became in a measure unrealised, whenever any heretic ventured to impugn it, it was most unequivocally enforced. At a period which is so early that it is impossible to define it, infant baptism was introduced into the Church; it was adopted by all the heretics, as well as by the orthodox; it was universally said to be for 'the remission of sins;' and the whole body of the Fathers, without exception or hesitation, pronounced that all infants who died unbaptized were excluded from heaven. In the case of unbaptized adults a few exceptions were admitted,'

' Martyrdom, or, as it was termed, the baptism of blood, being the chief. Some, however, relying on the case of the penitent thief, admitted a 'baptism of perfect love,' when a baptism by water could not be obtained. This consisted, of course, of extraordinary exercises of faith. Catechumens also, who died during the preparation for baptism, were thought by some to be saved See Lamet et Fromageau, *Dict. des Cas de Conscience*, tom. i. p. 208.

but the sentence on infants was inexorable.   The learned
English historian of Infant Baptism states that, with the exception of a contemporary of St. Augustine, named Vincen-
tius, who speedily recanted his opinion as heretical, he has
been unable to discover a single instance of an orthodox
member of the Church expressing the opposite opinion before
Hincmar, who was Archbishop of Rheims in the ninth cen
tury.[1]   In the time of this prelate, a bishop who had quar-
relled with his clergy and people ventured to prohibit baptism
in his diocese ; and Hincmar, while severely condemning the
act, expressed a hope that it would not be visited on the
infants who died when the interdict was in force.   With this
exception the unanimity seems to have been unbroken.   Some
of the Greek Fathers, indeed, imagined that there was a special
place assigned to infants, where there was neither suffering
nor enjoyment, while the Latins inferred from the hereditary
guilt that they must descend into a place of torment ; but
both agreed that they could not be saved.   The doctrine was
so firmly rooted in the Church, that even Pelagius, who was
one of the most rationalistic intellects of his age, and who
entirely denied the reality of hereditary guilt, retained infant baptism, acknowledged that it was for the remission of
sins, and did not venture to deny its necessity.   It was on
this point that he was most severely pressed by his opponents, and St. Augustine says that he was driven to the
somewhat desperate resource of maintaining that baptism
was necessary to wash away the guilt of the pettishness of
the child ![2]   Once, when severely pressed as to the conse

---

[1] Wall's *History of Infant Baptism*, vol. ii. p. 211.   St. Thomas Aquinas
afterwards suggested the possibility of the infant being saved who died within
the womb · 'God may have ways of saving it for aught we know.'

[2] Wall vol. i. pp. 282, 283.   It is gratifying to know that St. Augustine,

quences of the doctrine, St. Augustine was compelled to
acknowledge that he was not prepared to assert dogmatically that it would have been better for these children not to
have been born; but at the same time he denied emphatically
that a separate place was assigned them, and in one of his
sermons against the Pelagians he distinctly declared that
they descended into 'everlasting fire.'[1] Origen and many of
the Egyptians explained the doctrine by the theory of pre-
existence.[2] Augustine associated it with that of imputed
righteousness, maintaining that guilt and virtue might be
alike imputed;[3] and this view seems to have been generally
adopted. Among the writings of the Fathers there are few
which long possessed a greater authority than a short treatise
'De Fide,' which is one of the clearest and most forcible extant epitomes of the Patristic faith, and which till the time
of Erasmus was generally ascribed to St. Augustine, though
it is now known to have been written, in the beginning of
the sixth century, by St. Fulgentius.[4] In this treatise we
find the following very distinct statement of the doctrine:—
'Be assured,' writes the saint, 'and doubt not that not only
men who have obtained the use of their reason, but also little
children who have begun to live in their mothers' womb and
have there died, or who, having been just born, have passed
away from the world without the sacrament of holy baptism,
administered in the name of the Father, Son, and Holy
Ghost, must be punished by the eternal torture of undying
fire; for although they have committed no sin by their own

in answering this argument, distinctly declared that the crying of a baby is not
sinful, and therefore does not deserve eternal damnation.

[1] *Ibid.* vol. ii. pp. 192–206,—a full view of St. Augustine's sentiments on
the subject.

[2] Hieronym., *Epist.* lib. ii. ep. 18.   [3] *Epist.* 28.

[4] He was born about A.D. 467. (*Biog. Univ.*)

will, they have nevertheless drawn with thém the condemnation of original sin, by their carnal conception and nativity.'[1] It will be remembered that these saints, while maintaining that infants whose existence was but for a moment descended into eternal fire on account of an apple that was eaten four thousand years before they were born, maintained also that the creation and the death of those infants were the direct, personal, and uncontrolled acts of the Deity.

All through the middle ages we trace the influence of this doctrine in the innumerable superstitious rites which were devised as substitutes for regular baptism. Nothing indeed can be more curious, nothing can be more deeply pathetic, than the record of the many ways by which the terror-stricken mothers attempted to evade the awful sentence of their Church. Sometimes the baptismal water was sprinkled upon the womb; sometimes the stillborn child was baptised, in hopes that the Almighty would antedate the ceremony;

---

[1] 'Firmissime tene, et nullatenus dubites, non solum homines jam ratione utentes, verum etiam parvulos, qui, sive in uteris matrum vivere incipiunt et ibi moriuntur, sive jam de matribus nati sine sacramento sancti baptismatis quod datur in nomine Patris et Filii et Spiritus Sancti de hoc sæculo transeunt, ignis æterni sempiterno supplicio puniendos; quia etsi peccatum propriæ actionis nullum habuerunt, originalis tamen peccati damnationem carnali conceptione et nativitate traxerunt.'—*De Fide*, § 70. So also St. Isidore: 'Pro soli originali reatu luunt in inferno nuper nati infantuli pœnas, si renovati per lavacrum non fuerint.' (*De Sentent.* lib. i. c. 22.) St. Avitus, being of poetical turn of mind, put the doctrine into verse:—

'Omnibus id vero gravius, si fonte lavacri
Divini expertem tenerum mors invida natum
Præcipitat, durâ generatum sorte, gehennæ,
Qui mox ut matris cessarit filius esse
Perditionis erit: tristes tunc edita nolunt
Quæ flammis tantum genuerunt pignora matres.'

Ad Fuscinam Sororem.

For several other testimonies of the later Fathers to the same effect, see Natalis Alexander, *Historia Ecclesiastica* (Paris, 1699), tom. v. pp. 130, 131.

sometimes the mother invoked the Holy Spirit to purify by His immediate power the infant that was to be born; sometimes she received the Host or obtained absolution, and applied them to the benefit of her child. These and many similar practices ' continued all through the middle ages in spite of every effort to extirpate them, and the severest censures were unable to persuade the people that they were entirely ineffectual. For the doctrine of the Church had wrung the mother's heart with an agony that was too poignant even for that submissive age to bear. Weak and superstitious women, who never dreamed of rebelling against the teaching of their clergy, could not acquiesce in the perdition of their offspring, and they vainly attempted to escape from the dilemma by multiplying superstitious practices, or by attribut-

---

' For a very full account of these curious superstitions, see the chapter on 'Baptism' in Thiers' *Superstitions*, and also a striking memoir in the first volume of *Le Moyen Age*, by Lacroix. We can now hardly realise a condition of thought in which the mind was concentrated so strongly upon the unborn fœtus; but we should remember that, besides the doctrine of baptism, there were two subjects much discussed in the early Church which tended to produce an order of realisations to which we are not accustomed. Some of the early writers, and especially the Nestorians, had agitated questions concerning the time when the divinity of Christ was united to the fœtus in the womb, that had filled the Church with curious physiological speculations. Besides this, one of the earliest struggles of the Church was for the suppression of the custom of destroying the offspring in the womb, which was extremely common among the pagans, and which they scarcely regarded a crime. Tertullian (*Apol.* c. 9) and the author of the Epistle ascribed to St. Barnabas appear to have been among the first to denounce this pagan practice. Another illustration of the estimate in which baptism was held is furnished by the notion that bodily distempers followed irregular baptism. I have already referred to the belief that somnambulists had been baptised by a drunken priest; but perhaps the most curious example was in a great epidemic attack of St. Vitus's dance, which appeared in the Netherlands in 1375. The common people then believed that the disease resulted from unchaste priests having baptised the children, and their fury was so great that it was with difficulty that the lives of the ecclesiastics were saved. (Hecker, *Epidemics of the Middle Ages*, pp. 153, 154.)

mg to them a more than orthodox efficacy. But the vigilance
of the theologians was untiring. All the methods by which
these unhappy mothers endeavoured to persuade themselves
that their children might have been saved are preserved in
the decrees of the Councils that anathematised them.

At last the Reformation came. In estimating the character of that great movement, we must carefully distinguish its
immediate objects from its ultimate effects. The impulse of
which it was in part the cause, and in part the consequence,
at last issued in a diffusion of a rationalistic spirit which no
Church, however retrograde or dogmatic, has been able to
exclude. The essence of that spirit is to interpret the articles
of special creeds by the principles of universal religion—by
the wants, the aspirations, and the moral sentiments which
seem inherent in human nature. It leads men, in other
words, to judge what is true and what is good, not by the
teachings of tradition, but by the light of reason and of conscience; and where it has not produced an avowed change of
creed, it has at least produced a change of realisations. Doctrines which shock our sense of right have been allowed gradually to become obsolete, or if they are brought forward they
are stated in language which is so colourless and ambiguous,
and with so many qualifications and exceptions, that their original force is almost lost. This, however, was the ultimate, not
the immediate effect of the Reformation, and most of the Reformers were far from anticipating it. They designed to construct a religious system which should be as essentially dogmatic, distinct, and exclusive as that which they assailed, but
which should represent more faithfully the teachings of the first
four centuries. The Anabaptist movement was accompanied
by so many excesses, and degenerated so constantly into
anarchy. that it can scarcely be regarded as a school of reli-

gious thought; but it had at least the effect of directing the
minds of theologians to the subject of infant baptism. The
Council of Trent enunciated very clearly the doctrine of
Rome. It declared the absolute necessity of baptism for
salvation; it added, to guard against every cavil, that baptism must be by literal water,[1] and it concluded with the
usual formulary of a curse. Among the Protestants two
opposite tendencies were manifest. One of the first objects
of the Reformers was to oppose or restrict the doctrine that
ceremonies possessed an intrinsic merit independently of the
disposition of the worshipper, and it was not difficult to perceive that this doctrine had been favoured by infant baptism
more than by any other single cause. On the other hand,
the Protestant taught even more clearly than the Catholic the doctrine of imputed righteousness, and was therefore more disposed to dwell upon the doctrine of imputed
guilt. The Lutherans, in the Confession of Augsburg, asserted the absolute necessity of baptism quite as emphatically as
the Tridentine theologians,[2] and in one respect many of the
Protestants went beyond the Roman Catholics; for they
taught explicitly that the penalty due to original sin was
'eternal fire,' whereas the Church of Rome had never for-
mally condemned the notion of a third place which the
Greek Fathers had originated, which some of the schoolmen
had revived, and which about the time of the Reformation
was very general among the Catholics.[3] Calvin was in some

---

[1] A great deal of controversy had been excited in the middle ages about a
Jew, who, being converted to Christianity in a desert, where there was no
water, and being as was supposed in a dying state, was baptised with sand.
There were also some cases of women baptising their children with wine. For
full details about these, see Thiers' *Traité des Superstitions.*

[2] Arts. ii. and ix.

[3] Wall. The notion of a limbo had been so widely diffused that Sarpi

respects more favourable to unbaptised infants than the disciples of Luther, for he taught that the children of believers
were undoubtedly saved, that the intention to baptise was
as efficacious as the ceremony, and that, although infant bap-
ism should be retained, the passage in the discourse to Nicodemus which had previously been universally applied to it,
was susceptible of a different interpretation.[1] But these
doctrines arose simply from the reluctance of Calvin and his
followers to admit the extraordinary efficacy of a ceremony,
and not at all from any moral repugnance to the doctrine of
transmitted guilt. No school declared more constantly and
more emphatically the utter depravity of human nature, the
sentence of perdition attaching to the mere possession of
such a nature, and the eternal damnation of the great
majority of infants. A few of the enthusiastic advocates
of the doctrine of reprobation even denied the universal salvation of baptised infants, maintaining that the Almighty

says the Tridentine Fathers at one time hesitated whether they should not
condemn as heretical the Lutheran proposition that unbaptised infants went
into ‘ eternal fire.’ We find Pascal, however, stating the doctrine in a very
repulsive form: ‘ Qu’y a-t-il de plus contraire aux règles de notre misérable
justice que de damner éternellement un enfant incapable de volonté pour un
péché où il paroit avoir eu si peu de part qu’il est commis six mille ans avant
qu’il fut en être ? Certainement rien ne nous heurte plus rudement que cette
doctrine, et cependant sans ce mystère le plus incompréhensible de tous nous
sommes incompréhensibles à nous-mêmes.’ (*Pensées*, cap. iii. § 8.) I have
little doubt, however, that the more revolting aspect of the doctrine was nearly
obsolete in the Church at the time of the Reformation. In the twelfth century, St. Bernard had said : ‘ Nihil ardet in inferno nisi propria voluntas.’
According to Wall, Calvin was the very first theologian who denied that
he passage, ‘ Except a man be born of water and of the spirit,’ &c., applied
to baptism. (Vol. ii. p. 180.) Jeremy Taylor strongly supported Calvin’s view :
‘ The water and the spirit in this place signify the same thing ; and by water is
meant the effect of the spirit cleansing and purifying the soul, as appears in its
parallel place of Christ baptising with the spirit and with fire.’ (*Liberty of
Prophesying*, § 18.)

might have predestinated some of them to destruction. All
of them maintained that the infants who were saved were
saved on account of their connection with Christianity, and
not on account of their own innocence. All of them declared
that the infant came into the world steeped in guilt, and
under the sentence of eternal condemnation. Jonathan Edwards, who was probably the ablest as he was one of the
most unflinching of the defenders of Calvinism, has devoted
to this subject all the resources of his great ingenuity. No
previous writer developed more clearly the arguments which
St. Augustine had derived from the death of infants, and
from the pangs that accompany it; but his chief illustrations
of the relations of the Deity to His creatures are drawn from
those scenes of massacre when the streets of Canaan were
choked with the multitude of the slain, and when the sword
of the Israelite was for ever bathed in the infant's blood.[1]

So far, then, the Reformation seems to have made little
or no change. The doctrine of Catholicism, harsh and repulsive as it appears, does not contrast at all unfavourably
with those of the two great founders of dogmatic and conservative Protestantism. At a period when passions ran
high, and when there was every disposition to deepen the
chasm between Catholicity and the Reformed Churches—
at a period therefore when any tendency to rebel against the
Catholic doctrine of transmitted guilt would have been
clearly manifested, that doctrine was in all essentials fully
accepted. Questions concerning the nature of the sacra-
ments, the forms of Church government, the meaning of
particular passages of Scripture, the due order and subordination of different portions of theological systems, were

[1] See Jonathan Edwards on *Original Sin*—one of the most revolting books
that have ever proceeded from the pen of man.

discussed with the most untiring and acrimonious zeal. All Europe was convulsed with controversy, and the most pas sionate enthusiasm was evoked. But the whole stress and energy of this enthusiasm flowed in a dogmatic channel. It was not the revolt of the reason claiming a supreme authority in the domain of thought; it was not the rebellion of the moral faculty against doctrines that collided with its teaching: or if such elements existed, they were latent and unavowed, and their position in the first ebullitions of Protestantism was entirely subordinate. The germ of Rationalism had indeed been cast abroad, but more than a century was required to develop it. There was no subtlety of interpretation connected with the eucharistic formularies that did not excite incomparably more interest than the broad questions of morality. Conscience was the last tribunal to which men would have referred as the supreme authority of their creed. There was much doubt as to what historical authorities were most valuable, but there was no doubt that the ultimate basis of theology must be historical.

To this statement there were, however, two eminent exceptions. Two theologians, who differed widely in their opinions and in their circumstances, were nevertheless actuated by the same rationalistic spirit, were accustomed to form their notions of truth and goodness by the decisions of their own reason and conscience, and, disregarding all the interpretations of tradition, to mould and adapt their creed to their ideal. These theologians were Socinus and Zuinglius, who may be regarded as the representatives of Rationalism in the first period of Protestantism.

The school of thought which Lælius Socinus contributed to plant at Vicenza, and which his more illustrious nephew, in conjunction with other Italians, spread through the greater
24

part of Europe, was the natural result of a long train of circumstances that had been acting for centuries in Italy. The great wealth of the Italian republics, their commercial relations with men of all nations and of all creeds, the innumerable memorials of paganism that are scattered over the land, and the high æsthetic development that was general, had all in different ways and degrees contributed to produce in Italy a very unusual love of intellectual pursuits and a very unusual facility for cultivating them. Upon the fall of Constantinople, when the Greek scholars were driven into exile, bearing with them the seeds of an intellectual renovation, Italy was more than any other country the centre to which they were attracted. In the Italian princes they found the most munificent and discerning patrons, and in the Italian universities the most congenial asylums. Padua and Bologna were then the great centres of free thought. A series of professors, of whom Pomponatius appears to have been the most eminent, had pursued in these universities speculations as daring as those of the eighteenth century, and had habituated a small but able circle of scholars to examine theological questions with the most fearless scrutiny. They maintained that there were two spheres of thought, the sphere of reason and the sphere of faith, and that these spheres were entirely distinct. As philosophers, and under the guidance of reason, they elaborated theories of the boldest and most unflinching scepticism; as Catholics, and under the impulse of faith, they acquiesced in all the doctrines of their Church.[1]   The fact of their accepting certain doctrines

---

[1] See, on the career of Pomponatius, Matter, *Histoire des Doctrines Morales des trois Derniers Siècles*, tom. i. pp. 51–67. Pomponatius was born at Mantua in 1462, and died in 1524. His principal work is on *The Immortality of the Soul.* He was protected by Leo X. (*Biog. Univ.*) Vanini said that the

as a matter of faith did not at all prevent them from repu-
diating them on the ground of reason; and the complete
separation of the two orders of ideas enabled them to pursue
their intellectual speculations by a method which was purely
secular, and with a courage that was elsewhere unknown.
Even in Catholicism a dualism of this kind could not long
continue, but it was manifestly incompatible with Protestantism, which at least professed to make private judgment
the foundation of belief. Faith considered as an unreasoning
acquiescence disappeared from theology, and the order of
ideas which reason had established remained alone. As a
consequence of all this, the Reformation in Italy was almost
confined to a small group of scholars, who preached its principles to their extreme limits, with an unflinching logic, with
a disregard for both tradition and consequences, and above
all with a secular spirit that was elsewhere unequalled. With
the peculiar tenets connected with the name of Socinus we
are not now concerned, for the question of theological
method is distinct from that of theological doctrines. It is,
however, sufficiently manifest that although Socinus laid a
far greater stress on the authority of Revelation than his followers, the prevailing sentiment which actuated him was a

soul of Averroes had passed into Pomponatius. The seventeenth century furnishes some striking examples of this separation of the philosophical and
theological points of view. Thus Charron, who as a philosopher wrote one of
the most sceptical books of his age, was a priest, and author of a treatise on
Christian Evidences. Pascal too, in whose great mind scepticism and faith
were strangely interwoven, accepted with delight the Pyrrhonism of Montaigne
as representing the ultimate fruits of reason, while firmly grasping Catholicism
by faith. Luther himself had maintained that a proposition may be true in
theology and false in philosophy—an opinion which the Sorbonne condemned:
Sorbona pessime definivit idem esse verum in philosophia et theologia, impie-
que damnavit eos qui contrarium docuerint.' (Amand Saintes, *Hist. du Rationalisme en Allemagne,* p. 29.)

desire to subordinate traditional tenets to the dictates of reason and of conscience, and that his entire system of interpretation was due to this desire. It is also evident that it was this spirit that induced him to discard with unqualified severity the orthodox doctrines of the sinfulness of error and of the transmission of guilt.[1]

It may appear at first sight a strange paradox to represent the career of Zuinglius as in any degree parallel to that of Socinus. Certainly the bold and simple-minded pastor of Zurich, who bore with such an unflinching calm the blaze of popularity and the storms of controversy, and perished at last upon the battle-field, forms in most respects a glaring contrast to the timid Italian who spent his life in passing from court to court and from university to university, shrinking with nervous alarm from all opposition and notoriety, and instilling almost furtively into the minds of a few friends whom his gentle manners had captivated the great principles of religious toleration. Certainly, too, nothing could be further from the mind of Zuinglius than the doctrines which are known as Socinianism, nor did the antecedents of the two Reformers bear any resemblance. Yet there can, I think, be no doubt that the dominant predisposition of Zuinglius also was to interpret all tenets according to the *à priori* conceptions of reason and conscience. Though a man of much more than common ability, he had but slight pretensions to learning, and this, in an age when men are endeavouring to break loose from tradition, has sometimes proved a positive and a most important advantage. The tendency of his mind was early shown in the position he assumed on the eucharistic controversy. There was no single subject in which the leading Reformers wavered so much, none on which they

[1] Neander, *Hist. of Dogmas*, vol. ii. pp. 657, 658.

found so great a difficulty in divesting themselves of their
old belief. The voice of reason was clearly on one side, the
weight of tradition inclined to the other, and the language
of Scripture was susceptible of either interpretation. Luther
never advanced beyond consubstantiation ; Calvin only arrived at his final views after a long series of oscillations ; the
English Reformers can scarcely be said to have ever arrived
at any definite conclusions. Zuinglius alone, from the very
beginning, maintained with perfect confidence the only doctrine which accords with the evidence of the senses, stated it
in language of transparent precision, and clung to it with
unwavering tenacity. The same tendency was shown still
more clearly in his decisions on those points in which tradition clashes with conscience. It is surely a most remarkable fact that in the age of such men as Luther and Calvin,
as Melanchthon and Erasmus, Zuinglius, who in intellectual
power was far inferior to several of his contemporaries,
should almost alone have anticipated the rationalistic doctrine of the seventeenth century concerning the innocence of
error, and the tolerance that should be accorded to it. On
the subject of original sin he separated himself with equal
boldness from the other leaders of the Reformation, maintaining that it was nothing more than a malady or evil tendency,
and that it did not in any degree involve guilt.[1]

---

[1] Neander, *Hist. of Dogmas*, vol. ii pp. 658, 659. Bossuet made a violen
attack upon this notion of Zuinglius, which he regarded with extreme horror
because, as he plaintively observes, supposing it to be true, then ' le péché
originel ne damne personne, pas même les enfants des paiens.' (*Variations
Protestants*, liv. ii. c. 21.) The remarks of Bossuet are especially worthy of
attention on account of the great clearness with which he maintains the uni
versality of the belief in the damnable nature of original sin in all sections of
the Christian Church. He has, however, slightly overstated the doctrine of
Zuinglius. The Reformer distinctly declared original sin to be simply a dis
ease, and not properly a sin. From his language in his *Treatise on Baptism,*

It was thus that two of the leaders of the Reformation
were induced by the rationalistic character of their minds to
abandon the notion of transmitted guilt, and the doctrine
concerning unbaptised infants which was connected with it.
If the current of opinions has since then been flowing in the
same direction, this is entirely due to the increased diffusion
of a rationalistic spirit, and not at all to any active propagandism or to any definite arguments. Men have come
instinctively and almost unconsciously to judge all doctrines
by their intuitive sense of right, and to reject or explain
away or throw into the background those that will not bear
the test, no matter how imposing may be the authority that
uthenticates them.   This method of judgment, which was
once very rare, has now become very general.   Every generation its triumph is more manifest, and entire departments
of theology have receded or brightened beneath its influence.[1]
How great a change has been effected on the doctrine concerning unbaptised children must be manifest to any one
who considers how completely the old doctrine has dis-

---

it was inferred that he asserted the salvation of pagan infants. However, in
1526, he wrote a short treatise *On Original Sin*, in which he said that his former work had been misrepresented ; that he maintained indeed that the word
' sin ' was only applied to our original malady by a figure of speech ; that he
was quite sure that that malady never in itself damned Christian children, but
that he was not equally sure that it never damned pagan children. He inclined, however, strongly to the belief that it did not : ' De Christianorum natis
certi sumus eos peccato originali non damnari, de aliorum non itidem; quam-
vis, ut ingenue fateor, nobis probabilior videtur sententia quam docuimus, non
temere pronunciandum esse de gentilium quoque natis et eis qui opus legis
faciunt ex lege intus digito Dei scripta.' (P. 28.)

[1] Chillingworth treated the subject with his usual admirable good sense :
' This is certain, that God will not deal unjustly with unbaptised infants ; but
how in particular He will deal with them concerns not us, and so we need not
much regard it.' (*Religion of Protestants*, chap. vii.) Jeremy Taylor strongly
rejected both original sin, in the sense of transmitted guilt, and the damnation
of infants that was inferred from it.

appeared from popular teaching, and what a general and intense repugnance is excited by its simple statement. It was once deemed a mere truism; it would now be viewed with horror and indignation: and if we desired any further proof of the extent of this change, we should find it in the position which the Quakers and the Baptists have assumed in Christendom. It is scarcely possible to conceive any sects which in the early Church would have been regarded with more unmingled abhorrence, or would have been deemed more unquestionably outside the pale of salvation. It is no exaggeration to say that the feeling of repugnance with which men now look upon the polygamy of the Mormons presents but a very faint image of that which the Fathers would have manifested towards those who systematically withheld from their children that baptism which was unanimously pronounced to be essential to their salvation. Yet the Quakers and the Baptists have now obtained a place among the most respected sections of the Church, and in the eyes of very many Protestants the peculiarities of the second, at least, are not sufficiently serious to justify any feeling of repulsion or to prevent the most cordial coöperation. For a great change has silently swept over Christendom: without controversy and without disturbance, an old doctrine has passed away from among the realisations of mankind.

But the scope of the doctrine we are considering was not confined to unbaptised children; it extended also to all adults who were external to the Church. If the whole human race existed under a sentence of condemnation which could only be removed by connection with Christianity, and if this sentence was so stringent that even the infant was not exempt from its effects, it was natural that the adult heathen who added his personal transgressions to the guilt of Adam should be doomed at last to perdition. Nor did the Fathers who constructed the early systems of theology at all shrink from the consequence. At a time when the Christian Church formed but an infinitesimal fraction of the community, at a time when almost all the members who composed it were themselves converts from paganism, and reckoned among the pagans those who were bound to them by the closest ties of gratitude and affection, the great majority of the Fathers deliberately taught that the entire pagan world was doomed to that state of punishment which they invariably described as literal and undying fire. In any age and under any circumstances such a doctrine must seem inexpressibly shocking, but it appears most peculiarly so when we consider that the convert who accepted it, and who with a view to his own felicity proclaimed the system of which he believed it to form a part to be a message of good tidings, must have acquiesced in the eternal perdition of the mother who had borne him, of the father upon whose knees he had played, of the friends who were associated with the happy years of childhood and early manhood, of the immense mass of his fellow-countrymen, and of all those heroes and sages who by their lives or precepts had first kindled a moral enthusiasm within his breast. All these were doomed by one sweeping sentence. Nor were they alone in their condemnation. The heretics, no matter how trivial may have been their error, were reserved for the same fearful fate. The Church, according to the favourite image of the Fathers, was a solitary ark floating upon a boundless sea of ruin. Within its pale there was salvation; without it salvation was impossible. 'If any one out of Noah's ark could escape the deluge,' wrote St. Cyprian, 'he who is out of the Church may also escape.' 'Without this house,' said Origen, 'that is without the

Church, no one is saved.' 'No one,' said St. Augustine, 'cometh to salvation and eternal life except he who hath Christ for his head; but no one can have Christ for his head except he that is in His body the Church.'[1] 'Hold most firmly,' added St. Fulgentius, 'and doubt not that not only all pagans, but also all Jews, heretics, and schismatics who depart from this present life outside the Catholic Church, are about to go into eternal fire, prepared for the devil and his angels.'[2] So prominent and so unquestionable was this doctrine deemed, that the Council of Carthage, in the fourth century, made it one of the test-questions put to every bishop before ordination.[3]

This doctrine has had a greater influence than perhaps any other speculative opinion upon the history of mankind. How different it is from the conceptions to which the great teachers of antiquity had arrived must be evident to any one who knows how fondly they cherished the doctrine of the

[1] I take these references from Palmer *On the Church* (vol. i. pp. 11–13, 3d ed.), where there is much evidence on the subject collected. Mr. Palmer contends that the Fathers are unanimous on the subject, but Barbeyrac shows that at least two, and those of the earliest (Justin Martyr and Clemens Alexandrinus), admitted the possible salvation of the pagans (*Morale des Pères*, ch. xi. § 11), and that the first expressly said that Socrates and Heraclitus in the sight of God were Christians. I am afraid, however, there is no doubt that the great majority of the Fathers took the other view. Minucius Felix thought the dæmon of Socrates was a devil. (*Octavius*, ch. xxvi.)

[2] *De Fide*, § 81; and again, still more explicitly: 'Omni enim homini qui Ecclesiæ Catholicæ non tenet unitatem, neque baptismus neque eleemosyna quamlibet copiosa, neque mors pro nomine Christi suscepta proficere poterit ad salutem, quamdiu eo vel hæretica vel schismatica pravitas perseverat quæ ducit ad mortem.' (§ 22.)

[3] Palmer, *On the Church*, vol. i. p. 13. And again the Synod of Zerta in A.D. 412. 'Whosoever is separated from the Catholic Church, however innocently he may think he lives, for this crime alone that he is separated from the unity of Christ will not have life, but the wrath of God remaineth on him.' This statement is said to have been drawn up by St. Augustine. See Hawarden's *Charity and Truth*, pp. 39, 40 (Dublin, 1809).

immortality of the soul, how calmly they contemplated the approach of death,[1] and how hopefully they looked forward to the future. Never can men forget that noble Greek who, struck down by an unrighteous sentence, summoned around him his dearest disciples, and having reasoned with them on the immortality of the soul and the rewards of virtue and the goodness of the gods, took with a gentle smile the cup of death, and passed away thanking the god of healing who had cured him of the disease of life. That 'the just man should take confidence in death,'[2] that he who has earnestly, though no doubt imperfectly, tried to do his duty has nothing to fear beyond the grave, had been the consoling faith of all the best minds of antiquity. That the bold, unshackled, and impartial search for truth was among the noblest and, therefore, among the most innocent employments of mankind, was the belief which inspired all the philosophies of the past. Nor was it merely or mainly in the groves of Athens that this spirit was manifested. It should never be

---

[1] I know nothing in the world sadder than one of the sayings of Luther on this matter. I quote it from that beautiful old translation of *The Table Talk* by Bell: 'It were a light and an easy matter for a Christian to suffer and overcome death if he knew not that it were God's wrath; the same title maketh death bitter to us. But an heathen dieth securely away; he neither seeth nor feeleth that it is God's wrath, but meaneth it is the end of nature and is natural. The epicurean says it is but to endure one evil hour.' A distinguished living antiquarian, comparing the heathen and the mediæval representations of death, observes: 'Dans la société païenne, toute composée du sensualisme et de licence, on se gardait bien de répresenter la mort comme quelque chose de hideux; il ne parait même point que le squelette ait été alors le symbole de l'impitoyable divinité. Mais quand le Christianisme eut conquis le monde, quand une éternité malheureuse dut être la punition des fautes commises ici bas, la mort qui avait semblé si indifférente aux anciens devint une chose dont les conséquences furent si terribles pour le chrétien qu'il fallut les lui rapporter à chaque instant en frappant ses yeux des images funèbres. (Jubinal, *Sur les Danses des Morts*, p. 8.)

[2] Plato.

forgotten that the rationalist has always found the highest expression of his belief in the language of the prophet, who declared that the only service the Almighty required was a life of justice, of mercy, and of humility; of the wise man, who summed up the whole duty of man in the fear of God and the observance of His commandments; of the apostle, who described true religion as consisting of charity and of purity; and of that still greater Teacher, who proclaimed true worship to be altogether spiritual, and who described the final adjudication as the separation of mankind according to their acts and not according to their opinions.

But, however this may be, the doctrine of salvation in the Church alone was unanimously adopted when Christianity passed from its moral to its first dogmatic stage, and on two occasions it conferred an inestimable benefit upon mankind. At a time when Christianity was struggling against the most horrible persecutions, and also against the gross conceptions of an age that could obtain but a very partial idea of its elevated purity, the terrorism of this doctrine became an auxiliary, little in harmony indeed with the spirit of a philanthropic religion, but admirably suited to the time, and powerful enough to nerve the martyr with an unflinching courage, and to drive the doubter speedily into the Church. Again, when the ascendency of the new faith had become manifest, it seemed for a time as if its administrative and organizing function would have been destroyed by the countless sects that divided it. The passion for allegory and the spirit of eclecticism that characterised the Eastern converts, the natural subtlety of the Greek mind, and still more the disputatious philosophy of Aristotle, which the Greek heretics introduced into the Church, and which Nestorianism

planted in the great school of Edessa,[1] had produced so many
and such virulent controversies that the whole ecclesiastical
fabric seemed dislocated, and intellectual anarchy was im-
minent.   The conception of an authoritative Church was not
yet fully formed, though men were keenly sensible of the
importance of dogma.   It is computed that there were about
ninety heresies in three centuries.[2]   Such questions as the
double procession of the Holy Ghost, the proper day for celebrating Easter, the nature of the light upon Mount Tabor, or
the existence in Christ of two independent but perfectly co-
incident wills, were discussed with a ferocity that seems
almost to countenance the suggestion of Butler, that communities, like individuals, may be insane.   But here again
the doctrine of exclusive salvation exercised a decisive
influence.   As long as it was held and realised, the diversities of private judgment must have waged a most unequal
warfare with the unity of authority.   Men could not long
rest amid the conflict of opposing arguments; they could not
endure that measure of doubt which is the necessary accom-
paniment of controversy.   All the fractions of Christianity
soon gravitated to one or two great centres, and a spiritual
despotism was consolidated which alone could control and
temper the turbulent elements of mediæval society, could
impose a moral yoke upon the most ferocious tyrants, could
accomplish the great work of the abolition of slavery in
Europe, and could infuse into Christendom such a measure of

---

[1] It is remarkable that Aristotle, whom the schoolmen placed almost on
level with the Fathers, owes his position entirely to the early heretics; that
the introduction of his philosophy was at first invariably accompanied by an
increase of heresy; and that the Fathers, with scarcely an exception, unequivocally denounced it. See much curious evidence of this in Allemand-Lavi-
gerie, *École Chrétienne d'Édesse.* (Thèse présentée à la Faculté des Lettres
de Paris, 1850.)

[2] Middleton's *Free Enquiry*, Introd. p. 86.

pure and spiritual truth as to prepare men* for the better phase that was to follow it.

All this was done by the doctrine of exclusive salvation. At the Reformation, when the old Church no longer har monised with the intellectual condition of Europe, and when the spirit of revolt was manifested on all subjects and in all countries, the doctrine was for the most part unchallenged; and although it undoubtedly produced an inconceivable amount of mental suffering, it had at least the effect of terminating rapidly the anarchy of transition. The tenacity with which it was retained by the Reformers is of course partly due to the difficulty of extricating the mind from old theological modes of thought; but it was, I think, still more the result of that early tendency to depreciate the nature and the works of man which threw them naturally upon dogmatic systems. There were, indeed, few subjects on which they were so unanimous. 'The doctrine of salvation in the Church,' writes a learned living author, ' was held by all the Lutherans and Reformed, and by the sects which separated from them, as well as by the Romish and other Churches. Luther teaches that remission of sins and sanctification are only obtained in it; and Calvin says, "Beyond the bosom of the Church no remission of sins is to be hoped for, nor any salvation." The Saxon Confession, presented to the Synod of Trent A.D. 1551, the Helvetic Confession, the Belgic, the Scottish, all avow that salvation is only to be had in the Church. The Presbyterian divines assembled at West minster, A.D. 1647, in their "Humble Advice concerning a Confession of Faith" (c. 25), declare that "the visible Church, which is also Catholique and universal under the Gospel (not confined to one nation, as before under the Law), con· sists of all those throughout the world that profess the true religion . . . out of which there is no ordinary possibility of salvation." The Independents admitted the same.'[1] Nor was the position of the Anglican Church at all different. The Athanasian Creed was given an honoured place among her formularies, and the doctrine which that creed distinctly asserts was implied in several of the services of the Church, and was strongly maintained by a long succession of her divines.[2] Among the leading Reformers, Zuinglius, and Zuinglius alone, openly and unequivocally repudiated it. In a Confession of Faith which he wrote just before his death, and which marks an important epoch in the history of the human mind, he described in magnificent language that future 'assembly of all the saintly, the heroic, the faithful, and the virtuous,' when Abel and Enoch, Noah and Abraham, Isaac and Jacob, will mingle with 'Socrates, Aristides, and Antigonus, with Numa and Camillus, Hercules and Theseus, the Scipios and the Catos,' and when every upright and holy man who has ever lived will be present with his God.[3] In our age, when the doctrine of exclusive salvation seldom excites more than a smile, such language appears but natural; but when it was first written it excited on all sides amazement and indignation. Luther on reading it said he despaired of the salvation of Zuinglius. Bossuet quotes the passage as a climax to his charges against the Swiss Reformer, and quotes it as if it required no comment, but was in itself sufficient to hand down its author to the contempt and indignation of posterity.

I shall now proceed to examine the more remote conse-

- Palmer, *On the Church*, vol. i. p. 13.

[2] See a great deal of evidence of this in Palmer.

' This passage is given in full by Bossuet, *Variations Protestantes*, liv. ii. s. 19. The original Confesssion was published by Bullinger in 1536, with a very laudatory preface.

quences of the doctrine of exclusive salvation, in order to trace the connection between its decline and some other remarkable features of rationalistic development. In the first place, it is manifest that the conceptions I have reviewed are so directly opposed to our natural sense of what is right and just, to all the conclusions at which those great teachers arrived who evolved their doctrines from their own moral nature, that they must establish a permanent opposition between dogmatic theology and natural religion. When the peace of the Church has long been undisturbed, and when the minds of men are not directed with very strong interest to dogmatic questions, conscience will act insensibly upon the belief, obscuring or effacing its true character. Men will instinctively endeavour to explain it away, or to dilute its force, or to diminish its prominence. But when the agitation of controversy has brought the doctrine vividly before the mind, and when the enthusiasm of the contest has silenced the revolt of conscience, theology will be developed more and more in the same direction, till the very outlines of natural religion are obliterated. Thus we find that those predestinarian theories which are commonly identified with Calvin, though they seem to have been substantially held by St. Augustine, owe their reception mainly to the previous action of the doctrine of exclusive salvation upon the mind. For the one objection to the metaphysical and other argu-ments the Calvinist can urge, which will always appear con-clusive to the great majority of mankind, is the moral objec-tion. It is this objection, and this alone, which enables men to cut through that entangling maze of arguments concerning freewill, foreknowledge, and predetermination, in which the greatest intellects both of antiquity and of modern days have been hopelessly involved, and which the ablest metaphysicians have pronounced inextricable. Take away the moral argument: persuade men that when ascribing to the Deity justice and mercy they are speaking of qualities generically distinct from those which exist among mankind—qualities which we are altogether unable to conceive, and which may be compatible with acts that men would term grossly unjust and unmerciful: tell them that guilt may be entirely uncon nected with a personal act, that millions of infants may be called into existence for a moment to be precipitated into a place of torment, that vast nations may live and die, and then be raised again to endure a never-ending punishment, because they did not believe in a religion of which they had never heard, or because a crime was committed thousands of years before they were in existence: convince them that all this is part of a transcendentally perfect and righteous moral scheme, and there is no imaginable abyss to which such a doctrine will not lead. You will have blotted out those fundamental notions of right and wrong which the Creator has engraven upon every heart; you will have extinguished the lamp of conscience; you will have taught men to stifle the inner voice as a lying witness, and to esteem it virtuous to disobey it. But even this does not represent the full extent of the evil. The doctrine of exclusive salvation not only destroys the moral objection to that ghastly system of religious fatalism which Augustine and Calvin constructed; it directly leads to it by teaching that the ultimate destiny of the immense majority of mankind is determined entirely irrespectively of their will. Millions die in infancy; millions live and die in heathen lands; millions exist in ranks of society where they have no opportunities for engaging in theological research; millions are so encumbered by the prejudices of education that no mental effort can emancipate

.hem from the chain. We accordingly find that predestina-
rianism was in the first instance little more than a development of the doctrine of exclusive salvation. St. Augustine
illustrated it by the case of a mother who had two infants.
Each of these is but 'a lump of perdition;' neither has ever
performed a moral act. The mother overlies one, and it
perishes unbaptised; the other is baptised, and is saved.

But the doctrine of Augustine and Ambrose never seems
to have been pushed in the early Church to the same ex-
tremes, or to have been stated with the same precision, as it
afterwards was by the Reformers.[1] The mild and sagacious
Erasmus soon perceived in this one of the principal evils of
the Reformation, and he wrote a treatise in defence of free-
will, which elicited from Luther one of the most unequivocal
declarations of fatalism in the whole compass of theology,
and certainly one of the most revolting. 'The human will,'
said Luther, 'is like a beast of burden. If God mounts it, it
wishes and goes as God wills; if Satan mounts it, it wishes
and goes as Satan wills. Nor can it choose the rider it
would prefer, or betake itself to him, but it is the riders who
contend for its possession.'[2] 'This is the acme of faith, to be-

[1] The doctrine of double predestination was, however, maintained in the
ninth century by a monk named Gotteschalk, who was opposed by Hincmar,
Archbishop of Rheims, in the spirit of a theologian, and by Scotus Erigena in
the spirit of a freethinker. For an account of this once-famous controversy
see the learned work of M. St. René Taillandier, *Scot Erigène et la Philosophie
Scholastique* (Strasbourg, 1843), pp. 51–58 ; and for a contemporary view of
the opinions of Gotteschalk, see a letter by Amulo, Archbishop of Lyons (the
immediate successor of Agobard), printed with the works of Agobard (Paris,
1666). According to Amulo, Gotteschalk not only held the doctrines of reprobation and particular redemption, but even declared that the Almighty rejoiced
and exulted over the destruction of those who were predestinated to damnation. Gotteschalk was condemned to be degraded from the priesthood, to be
imprisoned, and to be scourged. (Llorente, *Hist. de l'Inquisition*, tom. i.
p. 20.)
[2] 'Sic humana voluntas in medio posita est ceu jumentum. Si insederit
25

lieve that He is merciful who saves so few and who condemns
so many; that He is just who at His own pleasure has made
us necessarily doomed to damnation; so that, as Erasmus
says, He seems to delight in the tortures of the wretched,
and to be more deserving of hatred than of love. If by any
effort of reason I could conceive how God could be merciful
and just who shows so much anger and iniquity, there
would be no need for faith.'[1] 'God foreknows nothing subject to contingencies, but He foresees, foreordains, and accom-
plishes all things by an unchanging, eternal, and efficacious
will. By this thunderbolt freewill sinks shattered in the dust.'[2]

Such were the opinions of the greatest of the Reformers.
The doctrine of Calvin and his school was equally explicit.
According to them, the Fall, with all its consequences, was
predetermined ages before the Creation, and was the neces-

Deus, vult et vadit quo vult Deus, ut Psalmus dicit : " Factus sum sicut jumentum et ego semper tecum." Si insederit Satan, vult et vadit quo vult Satan.
Nec est in ejus arbitrio ad utrum sessorem currere aut eum quærere, sed ipsi
sessores certant ob ipsum obtinendum et possidendum.' (*De Servo Arbitrio*,
pars i. sec. 24.)

[1] 'Hic est fidei summus gradus, credere illum esse clementem qui tam
paucos salvat tam multos damnat; *credere justum qui sua voluntate nos neces-
sario damnabiles facit*; ut videatur, referente Erasmo, delectari cruciatibus
miserorum, et odio potius quam amore dignus. Si igitur possem ulla ratione
comprehendere quomodo is Deus misericors et justus, qui tantum iram et
iniquitatem ostendit, non esset opus fide.' (Ibid. sec. 23.)

[2] 'Est itaque et hoc imprimis necessarium et salutare Christiano nosse,
quod Deus nihil præscit contingiter, sed quod omnia incommutabilia et æterna,
infallibilique voluntate et prævidet et præponit et facit. Hoc fulmine sternitur
et conteritur penitus liberum arbitrium.' (Sec. 10.) I give these sections
according to Vaughan's translation (1823), for in the original edition (1526)
there are no divisions, and the pages are not numbered. Melanchthon, in the
edition of his *Commonplaces*, expressed extreme predestinarian views, but
omitted them in later editions. Luther, in his old age, said he could not review with perfect satisfaction any of his works except, perhaps, his *Catechism*
and his *De Servo Arbitrio* (Vaughan's *Preface*, p. 57). There is a full notice
of this book in one of Sir W. Hamilton's essays.

sary consequence of that predetermination.* The Almighty, they taught, irrevocably decided the fate of each individual long before He called him into existence, and has predestinated millions to His hatred and to eternal damnation. With that object He gave them being—with that object He withholds from them the assistance that alone can correct the perversity of the nature with which He created them. He will hate them during life, and after death He will cast them into the excruciating torments of undying fire, and will watch their agonies without compassion through the countless ages of eternity.[1]

It is needless to comment upon such teaching as this. That it makes the Deity the direct author of sin,[2] that it subverts all our notions of justice and of mercy, that the simple

---

[1] On Calvin's views, see especially his *De Æterna Dei Prædestinatione*, and his *Institut. Christ.* lib. iii. c. 21–23. But perhaps their clearest and most emphatic statement is in a work of Beza, *De Æterna Dei Prædestinatione, contra Sebastianum Castellionem* (published in the *Opuscula* of Beza, Genevæ, 1658). The pointed objections on the score of moral rectitude of his rationalistic opponent brought the enormities of the Calvinistic doctrine into the fullest relief. There is a curious old translation of this work, under the title of *Beza's Display of Popish Practices, or Patched Pelagianism*, translated by W. Hopkinson (London, 1578). Beza especially insists on the unfairness of accusing Calvinists of asserting that God so hated some men that He predestinated them to destruction; the truth being that God of His free sovereignty predestinated them to destruction, and therefore to His hatred; so that 'God is not moved with the hatred of any that He should drive him to destruction, but He hath hated whom He hath predestinated to destruction.' Another point on which Jonathan Edwards especially has insisted (in his *Freedom of Will*) is that there can be no injustice in punishing *voluntary* transgression, and that the transgressions of the reprobate are voluntary; men having been since Adam created with wills so hopelessly corrupt that without Divine assistance they must *inevitably* be damned, and God having in the majority of cases resolved to withhold that assistance. The fatality, therefore, does not consist in man being compelled to do certain things whether he wishes it or not, but in his being brought into the world with such a nature that his wishes necessarily tend in a given direction.

[2] Calvinists, indeed, often protest against this conclusion; but it is almost

statement of it is inexpressibly shocking and revolting, can scarcely be denied by its warmest supporters. Indeed, when we combine this teaching with the other doctrines I have considered in the present chapter, the whole may be regarded as unequalled in the religious history of mankind. In our age such tenets have retired from the blaze of day; they are found only in the obscure writings of obscure men. Since Jonathan Edwards they have had no exponent of undoubted genius, and no distinguished writer could venture without a serious loss of reputation openly to profess them. Such language as was employed on this subject by men like Luther, Calvin, and Beza, while in the zenith of their popularity, would not now be tolerated for a moment outside a small and uninfluential circle. The rationalistic spirit has so pervaded all our habits of thought, that every doctrine which is repugnant to our moral sense excites an intense and ever-increasing aversion; and as the doctrine of exclusive salvation, which prepared the mind for the doctrine of reprobation, is no longer realised, the latter appears peculiarly revolting.

Another very important subject upon which the doctrine of exclusive salvation has exercised great influence, is the relation between dogmas and morals. The older theologians invariably attributed to dogmas an intrinsic efficacy which was entirely independent of their effect upon life. Thus we

self-evident, and the ablest writer of the school admits it in a sense which is quite sufficiently large for his opponents: 'If by the author of sin is meant the permitter or not hinderer of sin, and at the same time a disposer of the state of events in such a manner for wise, holy, and most excellent ends and purposes that sin, if it be permitted or not hindered, will most certainly and infallibly follow; I say, if this be all that is meant, I do not deny that God is the author of sin.' (Jonathan Edwards, *Freedom of Will*, p. 369.) The predestination of the fall of Adam, whose will was not hopelessly corrupt, has of course its own peculiar difficulties.

nave already had occasion to observe, that in the early
Church no controversies were deemed so important as those
which concerned the connection between the two natures in
Christ, and that at the Reformation the acceptance or rejection of transubstantiation was made the habitual test of orthodoxy.   On the other hand, the politician, in a secular age,
is inclined to value religious systems solely according to
their influence upon the acts of mankind.   He sees that religious controversies have often dislocated the social system,
have presented an insuperable obstacle to the fusion of the
different elements of a nation, have produced long and sanguinary wars, and have diverted a large proportion of intellect and energy from enterprises that are conducive to the
welfare of society.   These he considers the evils of theology,
which are compensated for by the control that it exercises
over the passions of mankind, by the high sense of duty it
diffuses, and by the intensity of the philanthropy it in-
spires.   His object therefore is to encourage a system in
which the moral restraint shall be as great as possible, and
the dogmatic elements shall be few and torpid.   The rationalist occupies a central position between the two.   Like the
early theologian, he denies that the measure of theological
excellence is entirely utilitarian ; like the politician, he denies that dogmas possess an intrinsic efficacy.   He believes
that they are intended to act upon and develop the affective
or emotional side of human nature, that they are the vehicles
by which certain principles are conveyed into the mind
which would otherwise never be received, and that when
they have discharged their functions they must lose their
importance.   In the earlier phases of society men have never
succeeded in forming a purely spiritual and moral conception
of the Deity, an l they therefore make an image which they

worship. By this means the conception of the Deity is falsified and debased, but the moral influence of worship is retained: a great evil is the price of an inestimable benefit.
As, however, men obtain with increasing civilisation a capacity for forming purer and more moral conceptions, idolatry becomes an unmingled evil, and is in consequence at last
abandoned. Just in the same way a purely moral religion,
appealing to a disinterested sense of duty and perception of
excellence, can never be efficacious in an early condition of
society. It is consequently materialised, associated with innumerable ceremonies, with elaborate creeds, with duties
that have no relation to moral sentiments, with an ecclesiastical framework, and with a copious legendary. Through
all this extraneous matter the moral essence filters down to
the people, preparing them for the higher phases of development. Gradually the ceremonies drop away, the number of
doctrines is reduced, the ecclesiastical ideal of life and character is exchanged for the moral ideal; dogmatic conceptions
manifest an increased flexibility, and the religion is at last
transfigured and regenerated, radiant in all its parts with the
pure spirit that had created it.

It is manifest that according to this view there exists a
perpetual antagonism between the dogmatic and the moral
elements of a religious system, and that their relative influence will depend mainly on the degree of civilisation; an
amount of dogmatic pressure which is a great blessing in one
age being a great evil in another. Now one of the most obvious consequences of the doctrine of exclusive salvation is,
that it places the moral in permanent subordination to the
dogmatic side of religion. If there be a Catholic faith 'which
except a man believe he cannot be saved,' it is quite natural
that men should deem it 'before *all* things' necessary to

hold it. If the purest moral life cannot atone for error, while a true religion has many means of effacing guilt, the mind will naturally turn to the doctrinal rather than to the practical side. The extent to which this tendency has been manifested in the Church of Rome is well known. Protestant controversialists have often drawn up long and perfectly authentic lists of celebrated characters who were stained with every crime, and who have nevertheless been among the favourites of the Church, who have clung to her ordinances with full orthodox tenacity, who have assuaged by her absolution every qualm of conscience, and who have at last, by endowing a monastery or undergoing a penance or directing a persecution against heretics, persuaded themselves that they had effaced all the crimes of their lives. In Protestantism this combination of devotion and immorality, which is not to be confounded with hypocrisy, is I think more rare. Lives like that of Benvenuto Cellini, in which the most atrocious crimes alternate with ecstasies of the most rapturous and triumphant piety, are scarcely ever to be met with, yet it would be rash to say that the evil is unknown. The two countries which are most thoroughly pervaded by Protestant theology are probably Scotland and Sweden; and if we measure their morality by the common though somewhat defective test that is furnished by the number of illegitimate births, the first is well known to be considerably below the average morality of European nations, while the second, in this as in general criminality, has been pronounced by a very able and impartial Protestant witness, who has had the fullest means of judging, to be very far below every other Christian nation.

[1] See Laing's *Sweden*, pp. 108–141, where this question is minutely examined. This is a mere question of figures. The following passage from

These are the contradictions that result from the doctrine of exclusive salvation among those who do not belong to a high order of sanctity, and who gladly purchase a licence for the indulgence of their passions by an assiduous cultivation of what they deem the more important side of their faith. A very much more general tendency, and one which has exercised a far more pernicious influence upon the history of mankind, is displayed by those whose zeal is entirely unselfish. Being convinced that no misfortune can be so great as heresy, and that the heretic is doomed to eternal misery, they have habitually supported their creed by imposture and falsehood. That they should do this is quite natural. Whatever may be the foundation of the moral law, it is certain that in the eyes of the immense majority of mankind there are some overwhelming considerations that will justify a breach of its provisions. If some great misfortune were to befall a man who lay on a sickbed, trembling between life and death; if the physician declared that the knowledge

---

another work of the same writer is less susceptible of decisive proof, and is, I am inclined to think, somewhat overstated, but is nevertheless very suggestive: 'The Swiss people present to the political philosopher the unexpected and most remarkable social phenomenon of a people eminently moral in conduct, yet eminently irreligious : at the head of the moral state in Europe, not merely for absence of numerous or great crimes, or of disregard of right, but for ready obedience to law, for honesty, fidelity to their engagements, for fair-dealing, sobriety, industry, orderly conduct, for good government, useful public institutions, general wellbeing, and comfort ; yet at the bottom of the scale for religious feeling, observances, or knowledge, especially in the Protestant cantons, in which prosperity, wellbeing, and morality seem to be, as compared to the Catholic cantons, in an inverse ratio to the influence of religion on the people. . . . It is a very remarkable social state, similar, perhaps, to that of the ancient Romans, in whom morality and social virtue were also sustained without the aid of religious influences.' (Laing's *Notes of a Traveller*, pp. 146, 147.) Dr. Arnold said, I think truly, that the popular notion about the superior prosperity of the Protestant over the Catholic cantons is greatly exaggerated : it exists in some cases and not in others.

of that misfortune would be certain deatĥ to the patient; and if concealment was only possible by a falsehood, there are very few moralists who would condemn that falsehood. If the most ardent denouncer of ' pious frauds ' were to meet an assassin in pursuit of an innocent man, and were able by misdirecting the pursuer to save the fugitive, it may be safely predicted that the lie would be unscrupulously uttered. It is not very easy to justify these things by argument, or to draw a clear line between criminal and innocent falsehood; but that there are circumstances which justify untruth has always been admitted by the common sentiment of mankind, and has been distinctly laid down by the most eminent moralists.[1] When therefore a man believes that those who ∨ adopt an erroneous opinion will be consigned to perdition; when he not only believes this, but realises it as a living and operative truth; and when he perceives that it is possible either by direct falsehood or by the suppression or distortion of truth to strengthen the evidences of his faith, he usually finds the temptation irresistible. But there are two very important distinctions between the hypothetical cases I have mentioned and the pious frauds of theologians. The first are the results of isolated moral judgments, while the latter are systematised and raised to the dignity of a regular doctrine. The first, again, spring from circumstances that are so extremely rare and exceptional that they can scarcely have any perceptible influence upon the general veracity of the person who utters them, while the second induce a habit of continual falsehood. The Fathers laid down as a distinct proposition that pious frauds were justifiable and even

---

[1] Thus, not to quote Roman Catholic authorities, Jeremy Taylor, in the *Ductor Dubitantium*, lib. iii. c. 2, lays down several cases of justifiable falsehood.

laudable;[1] and if they had not laid this down, they would nevertheless have practised them as a necessary consequence of their doctrine of exclusive salvation. Immediately all ecclesiastical literature became tainted with a spirit of the most unblushing mendacity. Heathenism was to be combated, and therefore prophecies of Christ by Orpheus and the Sibyls were forged, lying wonders were multiplied, and ceaseless calumnies poured upon those who, like Julian, opposed the faith. Heretics were to be convinced, and therefore interpolations of old writings or complete forgeries were habitually opposed to the forged Gospels. The veneration of relics and the monastic system were introduced, and therefore innumerable miracles were attributed to the bones of saints or to the prayers of hermits, and were solemnly asserted by the most eminent of the Fathers.[2] The tendency

[1] See on this subject the evidence collected in Middleton's *Free Enquiry ;* the curious panegyric on the habit of telling lies in St. Chrysostom *On the Priesthood ;* the remarks of Coleridge in *The Friend,* and of Maury, *Croyances et Légendes,* p. 268. St. Augustine, however, is in this respect an exception. In his treatise *Contra Mendacium* he strongly denounces the tendency, and especially condemns the Priscillianists, among whom it appears to have been very common, and also certain Catholics who thought it justifiable to pretend to be Priscillianists for the purpose of discovering the secrets of that sect. The most revolting aspect of this subject is the notion that heretics are so intensely criminal as to have no moral rights—a favourite doctrine in Catholic countries where no Protestant or sceptical public opinion exists. Thus the Spanish Bishop Simancas—' Ad pœnam quoque pertinet et hæreticorum odium, quod fides illis data servanda non est. Nam si tyrannis, piratis, et cæteris prædonibus quia corpus occidunt fides servanda non est, longe minus hæreticis pertinacibus qui occidunt animas.' (*De Catholicis Institutionibus,* p. 365.)

[2] Since the last note was written, this subject has been discussed at some length by Dr. Newman, in his *Apologia pro Vita sua.* I do not, however, find anything to alter in what I have stated. Dr. Newman says (Appendix, p. 77): ' The Greek Fathers thought that, when there was a *justa causa,* an untruth need not be a lie. St. Augustine took another view, though with great misgiving, and, whether he is rightly interpreted or not, is the doctor of the great and common view that all untruths are lies, and that there can be *no* just

was not confined to those Eastern nations which had been always almost destitute of the sense of truth; it triumphed wherever the supreme importance of dogmas was held. Generation after generation it became more universal; it continued till the very sense of truth and the very love of truth seemed blotted out from the minds of men.

That this is no exaggerated picture of the condition at which the middle ages arrived, is known to all who have any acquaintance with its literature; for during that gloomy period the only scholars in Europe were priests and monks, who conscientiously believed that no amount of falsehood was reprehensible which conduced to the edification of the people. Not only did they pursue with the grossest calumny every enemy to their faith, not only did they encircle every saint with a halo of palpable fiction, not only did they invent tens of thousands of miracles for the purpose of stimulating devotion—they also very naturally carried into all other subjects the indifference to truth they had acquired in theology. All their writings, and more especially their histories, became tissues of the wildest fables, so grotesque and at the same time so audacious, that they were the wonder of succeeding ages. And the very men who scattered these fictions broadcast over Christendom, taught at the same time that credulity was a virtue and scepticism a crime. As long as the doctrine of exclusive salvation was believed and realised, it was necessary for the peace of mankind that they should be absolutely certain of the truth of what they believed; in order to be so certain, it was necessary to sup-

cause of untruth. . . . Now, as to the just cause, the Greek Fathers make them such as these—self-defence, charity, *zeal for God's honour*, and the like.' It is plain enough that this last would include all of what are commonly termed pious frauds.

press adverse arguments; and in order to effect this object, it was necessary that there should be no critical or sceptical spirit in Europe. A habit of boundless credulity was therefore a natural consequence of the doctrine of exclusive salvation; and not only did this habit necessarily produce a luxuriant crop of falsehood, it was itself the negation of the spirit of truth. For the man who really loves truth cannot possibly subside into a condition of contented credulity. He will pause long before accepting any doubtful assertion, he will carefully balance opposing arguments, he will probe every anecdote with scrupulous care, he will endeavour to divest himself of every prejudice, he will cautiously abstain from attributing to probabilities the authority of certainties. These are the essential characteristics of the spirit of truth, and by their encouragement or suppression we can judge how far a system of doctrine coincides with that spirit.

We have seen that there were three ways in which the indissoluble association of salvation with a particular form of belief produced or promoted the absolute indifference to truth and the boundless credulity that characterised the ages in which theology was supreme. It multiplied to an enormous extent pious frauds, which were perpetrated without scruple because they were supposed to produce inestimable benefits to mankind. It rendered universal that species of falsehood which is termed misrepresentation, and which consists mainly of the suppression of all opposing facts; and it crushed that earnestness of enquiry which is at once the essential characteristic of the love of truth, and the sole bulwark against the encroachments of error. There was, however, yet another way, which, though very closely connected with the foregoing, is sufficiently distinct to claim a separate consideration.

A love of truth, by the very definition of the terms, implies a resolution under all circumstances to approach as nearly as possible to its attainment; or in other words, when demonstration is impossible, to adopt the belief which seems most probable. In this respect there is an important difference between speculative and practical life. He who is seeking for truth is bound always to follow what appears to his mind to be the stress of probabilities; but in action it is sometimes wise to shape our course with a view to the least probable contingency; because we have to consider not merely the comparative probabilities of success afforded by different courses, but also the magnitude of the results that would ensue. Thus, a man is justly regarded as prudent who insures his house against fire, though an absolute and unrequited loss is the most probable consequence of his act; because the loss he would suffer in the more probable contingency is inconsiderable, and the advantage he would derive from the insurance in the less probable contingency is very great. From this consideration Pascal—who with Fermat was the founder of what may be termed the scientific treatment of probabilities—derived a very ingenious argument in defence of his theological opinions, which was afterwards adopted by an English mathematician named Craig.[1] They contended, that when a religious system promises infinite rewards and threatens infinite punishments, it is the part of a wise man to sacrifice the present to embrace it, not merely if he believes the probabilities to preponderate in its favour, but even if he regards its truth as extremely improbable, provided the probabilities against it are not infinite. Now, as long as such an argument is urged simply with a view of

---

[1] In a very curious book called *Theologiæ Christianæ Principia Mathematica.* (Londini, 1699.)

inducing men to adopt a certain course of action, it has no necessary connection with morals, and should be judged upon prudential grounds.¹ But the case becomes widely different when to adopt the least probable course means to acknowledge a Church which demands as the first condition of allegiance an absolute and heartfelt belief in the truth of what it teaches. When this is the case, the argument of Pascal means, and only can mean, that men should by the force of will compel themselves to believe what they do not believe by the force of reason; that they should exert all their efforts, by withdrawing their attention from one side and concentrating it upon the other, and by the employment of the distorting influences of the affections, to disturb the results of their judgment. Nor is this merely the speculation of some isolated mathematicians; it is a principle that is constantly acted on in every society which is governed by the doctrine we are considering.² Mere sophisms or imperfect reasonings have a very small place in the history

* The reader may find a review of it made on those grounds in Laplace, *Théorie des Probabilités.* It is manifest that, if correct, obedience would be due to any impostor who said he dreamed that he was a Divine messenger, provided he put his promises and threatenings sufficiently high.

Thus in the seventeenth century the following was a popular Catholic argument. Protestants admit that Catholics may be saved, but Catholics deny that Protestants can; therefore it is better to become a Catholic. Considering that this argument was designed, by playing on superstitious terrors, and by obscuring the sense of the Divine goodness, to induce men to tamper with their sense of truth, and considering too that its success depended mainly on the timidity, self-distrust, and modesty of the person to whom it was addressed, I may probably be regarded as thoroughly base and demoralising as any that it is even possible for the imagination to conceive. Yet it was no doubt very effective, and was perfectly in harmony with the doctrine we are considering. Selden asked, 'Is their Church better than ours, because it has less charity?' and Bedell, in a passage which Coleridge justly pronounced one of the most beautiful in English prose, compared the two churches in this respect to the rival mothers before Solomon.

of human error; the intervention of the* will has always been the chief cause of delusion. Under the best circumstances we can but imperfectly guard against its influence; but wherever the doctrine of exclusive salvation is held, it is reduced to a system and regarded as a virtue.

Certainly, whatever opinion may be held concerning the general tendencies of the last three centuries, it is impossible to deny the extraordinary diffusion of a truthful spirit, as manifested both in the increased intolerance of what is false and in the increased suspicion of what is doubtful. This has been one of the general results of advancing civilisation to which all intellectual influences have converged, but the improvement may be said to date more especially from the writings of the great secular philosophers of the seventeenth century These philosophers destroyed the old modes of thought, not by the force of direct polemical discussion, but by introducing a method of enquiry and a standard of excellence incompatible with them. They taught men to esteem credulity discreditable, to wage an unsparing war against their prejudices, to distrust the verdicts of the past, and to analyse with cautious scrutiny the foundation of their belief. They taught them, above all, to cultivate that love of truth for its own sake which is perhaps the highest attribute of humanity; which alone can emancipate the mind from the countless influences that enthral it, and guide the steps through the labyrinth of human systems; which shrinks from the sacrifice of no cherished doctrine, and of no ancient tie; and which, recognising in itself the reflex of the Deity, finds in itself its own reward.

The conspicuous place which Bacon, Descartes, and Locke have obtained in the history of the human mind, depends much less on the originality of their doctrines or

their met. ods than on the skill with which they developed
and diffused them.   Long before Descartes, St. Augustine
had anticipated the 'cogito ergo sum;' but that which St.
Augustine had thrown out as a mere truism, or, at best, as a
passing suggestion, Descartes converted into the basis of a
great philosophy.   Half a century before Bacon, Leonardo
da Vinci had discovered the superiority of the inductive
method, and had clearly stated its principles; but even if
Leonardo had published his work, it may be safely asserted
that the magnificent development of Bacon was necessary
to make that method supreme in science.   Each of these
great men attacked with vast ability and marvellous success
some intellectual vice which lay at the very root of the old
habits of thought.   Descartes taught that the beginning of
all knowledge was the rejection of every early prejudice,
and a firm resolution to bring every opinion to the test of
individual judgment.   Locke taught the necessity of map-
ping out the limits of human faculties, and by his doctrine
concerning innate ideas, and above all by his masterly
analysis of Enthusiasm, he gave the deathblow to the opinions of those who would remove a certain class of mental
phenomena altogether from the jurisdiction of the reason.[1]
Bacon, whose gigantic intellect made excursions into every
field, was pre-eminently noted for his classification of the
idola or distorting influences that act on the mind, and for

[1] It has been observed by a very able French critic (M. Littré) that the
increasing tendency, as civilisation advances, to substitute purely psychological
for miraculous solutions is strikingly illustrated by a comparison of *Orestes*
with *Hamlet*.   The subject of both pieces is essentially the same—a murdered
king, a guilty wife, a son distracted between his duty to his dead father and to
his living mother; but while the Greek found it necessary to bring the Furies
upon the scene to account for the mental paroxysms of Orestes, the English-
man deemed the natural play and conflict of the emotions amply sufficient to
account for the sufferings of Hamlet.

his constant injunction to correct theory by confronting it with facts. Descartes also, in addition to the vast intrinsic value of his works, had the immense merit of doing more than any previous writer to divorce philosophy from erudition, and to make it an appeal to the reasoning powers of ordinary men. The schoolmen, though they had carried philosophical definition almost to the highest conceivable point of perfection, had introduced a style of disquisition so pedantic and monotonous, so full of subtle distinctions and endless repetitions, that all but the most patient students were repelled by their works; while their constant appeal to authority, and the fact that they wrote only in Latin, excluded those who were but little learned from the discussion. The great prominence academic prælections obtained about the time of the Reformation contributed, I imagine, largely to introduce a simpler and more popular style. Rather more than sixty years before 'The Method' of Descartes, Ramus, in his 'Dialectics,' had set the example of publishing a philosophical work in French, and Bruno had thrown some of his dreamy speculations into Italian; but neither of these men was sufficiently able to form a new epoch in the history of philosophy, and their ends were not calculated to encourage imitators—the first having been murdered by the Catholics on the night of St. Bartholomew, and the second burnt alive at Rome by the Pope. Descartes more than any one else was the author of what may be called the democratic character of philosophy, and this is not the least of his merits. The influence of Locke and Bacon, again, was especially powerful as a corrective of the old tendency to fiction, on account of a certain unimaginative character that was exhibited by the philosophies of both—a character that was perfectly congenial to the intellect of Locke, but very

26

remarkable in the case of Bacon, among whose great faculties imagination occupied an almost disproportionate prominence. That this feature of the Baconian philosophy is at present exercising a decidedly prejudicial influence on the English intellect, by producing an excessive distaste for the higher generalisations, and for all speculations that do not lead directly to practical results, has been maintained by many Continental writers, and by at least three of the most eminent English ones.[1] It is, indeed, quite true that Bacon never went in this respect so far as some of his disciples. He certainly never made utility the sole object of science, or at least never restricted utility to material advantages. He asserted in the noblest language the superiority of abstract truth to all the fruits of invention,[2] and would never have called those speculations useless which form the intellectual character of an age. Yet, on the other hand, it must be acknowledged that the general tone of his writings, the extraordinary emphasis which he laid upon the value of experiments, and above all upon the bearing of his philosophy on material comforts, represents a tendency which was very naturally developed into the narrowest utilitarianism. Those who regarded natural science simply as the minister to the material comforts of mankind were the disciples of Bacon, in much the same sense as Condillac and his followers were the disciples of Locke: they did not accurately represent the

---

[1] Coleridge, Buckle, and Mill.

[2] 'And yet (to speak the whole truth), just as we are deeply indebted to light because it enables us to enter on our way, to exercise arts, to read, to distinguish one another, and nevertheless the sight of light is itself more excellent and beautiful than the manifold uses of it; so, assuredly, the very contemplation of things as they are, without superstition or imposture, without error or confusion, is in itself more worthy than all the produce of discoveries. (*Novum Organon.*)

doctrines of their master, but they représented the general
tendency of his teaching.

But, whatever may be thought of the influence which the
inductive philosophy now exercises on the English mind,
there can be no doubt that both that philosophy and the
essay of Locke were peculiarly fatal to the mediæval modes
of thought on account of the somewhat plodding character
they displayed. By enlarging the domain of the senses, by
making experience the final test of truth, and by greatly
discouraging the excursions of theorists, they checked the
exuberance of the European imagination, imparted an air of
grotesqueness to the wild fictions that had so long been received, and taught men to apply tests both to their traditions and to their emotions which divested them of much of
their apparent mystery. It was from the writings of Locke
and Bacon that Voltaire and his followers drew the principles that shattered the proudest ecclesiastical fabrics of
Europe, and it is against these philosophers that the ablest
defenders of mediæval theology have exhibited the most
bitter animosity.[1]

---

[1] Thus De Maistre, the great apostle of modern Ultramontanism, assures us
that 'dans l'étude de la philosophie, le mépris de Locke est le commencement
de la sagesse;' and that '*l'Essai sur l'Entendement Humain* est très-certaine-
ment, et soit qu'on le nie ou qu'on en convienne, tout ce que le défaut absolu
de génie et de style peut enfanter de plus assommant.' (*Soirées de St. Pétersbourg*, 6ᵐᵉ Entretien.) Bacon he calmly terms 'un charlatan,' and, speaking
of his greatest works, says: 'Le livre *De la Dignité et de l'Accroissement des
Sciences* est donc un ouvrage parfaitement nul et méprisable. . . . Quant
au *Novum Organon*, il est bien plus condamnable encore, puisque, indépen-
damment des erreurs particulières dont il fourmille, le but général de l'ouvrage
le rend digne d'un Bedlam.' (*Examen de la Philosophie de Bacon.*) In the
same way, though in very different language, the Tractarian party, and especially Dr. Newman (both before and after his conversion), have been ceaselessly carping at the psychology of Locke and the inductive philosophy of
Bacon.

It was thus that the great teachers of the seventeenth century, who were themselves but the highest representatives of the tendencies of their age, disciplined the minds of men for impartial enquiry, and, having broken the spell that so long had bound them, produced a passionate love of truth which has revolutionised all departments of knowledge. It is to the impulse which was then communicated that may be traced the great critical movement which has renovated all history, all science, all theology—which has penetrated into the obscurest recesses, destroying old prejudices, dispelling illusions, rearranging the various parts of our knowledge, and altering the whole scope and character of our sympathies. But all this would have been impossible but for the diffusion of a rationalistic spirit obscuring or destroying the notion of the guilt of error. For, as we have seen, whenever the doctrine of exclusive salvation is generally believed and realised, habits of thought will be formed around it that are diametrically opposed to the spirit of enquiry and absolutely incompatible with human progress. An indifference to truth, a spirit of blind and at the same time wilful credulity, will be encouraged, which will multiply fictions of every kind, will associate enquiry with the ideas of danger and of guilt, will make men esteem that impartiality of judgment and study which is the very soul of truth, an unholy thing, and will so emasculate their faculties as to produce a general torpor on every subject. For the different elements of our knowledge are so closely united that it is impossible to divide them into separate compartments, and to make a spirit of credulity preside over one compartment while a spirit of enquiry is animating the others. In the middle ages theology was supreme, and the spirit of that theology was absolute credulity, and the same spirit was speedily diffused through all forms of thought. In the seventeenth century the preëminence of theology was no longer decisive, and the great secular writers introduced a love of impartiality and of free research which rapidly passed from natural science and metaphysics into theology, and destroyed or weakened all those doctrines which were repugnant to it. It was between the writings of Bacon and Locke that Chillingworth taught, for the first or almost for the first time in England, the absolute innocence of honest error. It was between the writings of Bacon and Locke that that latitudinarian school was formed which was irradiated by the genius of Taylor, Glanvil, and Hales, and which became the very centre and seedplot of religious liberty. It was between the same writings that the writ *De Hæretico comburendo* was expunged from the Statute Book, and the soil of England for the last time stained with the misbeliever's blood !

(2)

END OF THE FIRST VOLUME.

WORKS OF WILLIAM EDWARD HARTPOLE LECKY, M.P.

History of the Rise and Influence of the Spirit of Rationalism in Europe.

2 vols. 8vo. Cloth, $4.00 ; half calf, extra, $8.00.

" Mr. Lecky is one of the most accomplished writers and one of the most ingenious thinkers of the time, and his book deserves the highest commendation we can bestow upon it. We hope to see it take its place among the best literary productions of the age."—*The Edinburgh Review.*

History of European Morals from Augustus to Charlemagne.

2 vols. 12mo. Cloth, $3.00 ; half calf, extra, $7.00.

" It is scarcely possible to overrate the value of Mr. Lecky's able and vigorous book. No book, more full of scholarly learning and popular interest, more graphic in thought, more lucid in exposition, more candid in temper, has been submitted for many years."—*The Spectator.*

History of England in the Eighteenth Century.

8 vols. 8vo. Cloth, $20.00 ; half calf, $36.00. Cabinet Edition. 12 vols. 7 of England and 5 of Ireland. 12mo. Cloth. Per vol., $1.00.

" The materials accumulated in these volumes attest an industry more strenuous and comprehensive than that exhibited by Froude or by Macaulay. But it is his supreme merit that he leaves on the reader's mind a conviction that he not only possesses the acuteness which can discern the truth, but the unflinching purpose of truth-telling."—*New York Sun.*

The American Revolution : 1763–1783.

Chapters and Passages from the Author's History of England in the Eighteenth Century. Arranged, with Notes, by JAMES ALBERT WOODBURN, Professor of History in Indiana University. 12mo. Cloth, $1.25.

" A writer of Lecky's mind, with his rich imagination, his fine ability to appreciate imagination in others, and his disposition to be himself an orator upon the written page, could hardly have found a period in history more harmonious with his literary style."—*New York Evening Post.*

The French Revolution.

Chapters from the Author's History of England in the Eighteenth Century. With Historical Notes by HENRY ELDRIDGE BOURNE, Professor of History in Western Reserve University. 12mo. Cloth, $1.25.

D. APPLETON AND COMPANY, NEW YORK.

Printed in Dunstable, United Kingdom